THE CAMBRIDGE COMPANION
TO EARLY AMERICAN LITERATURE

This *Companion* covers American literary history from European colonization to the early republic. It provides a succinct introduction to the major themes and concepts in the field of early American literature, including New World migration, Indigenous encounters, religious and secular histories, and the emergence of American literary genres. This book guides readers through important conceptual and theoretical issues, while also grounding these issues in close readings of key literary texts from early America.

Bryce Traister is a Canada-based academic who reads and writes mainly about early American literature, religion, and culture. He has published one monograph, *Female Piety and the Invention of American Puritanism* (2016), and edited a collection of essays, *American Literature and the New Puritan Studies* (2017).

A complete list of books in the series is at the back of this book.

T0370947

THE CAMBRIDGE
COMPANION TO
EARLY AMERICAN
LITERATURE

EDITED BY
BRYCE TRAISTER
University of British Columbia, Okanagan

CAMBRIDGE
UNIVERSITY PRESS

University Printing House, Cambridge CB2 8BS, United Kingdom

One Liberty Plaza, 20th Floor, New York, NY 10006, USA

477 Williamstown Road, Port Melbourne, VIC 3207, Australia

314–321, 3rd Floor, Plot 3, Splendor Forum, Jasola District Centre,
New Delhi – 110025, India

103 Penang Road, #05–06/07, Visioncrest Commercial, Singapore 238467

Cambridge University Press is part of the University of Cambridge.

It furthers the University's mission by disseminating knowledge in the pursuit of
education, learning, and research at the highest international levels of excellence.

www.cambridge.org
Information on this title: www.cambridge.org/9781108840040
DOI: 10.1017/9781108878623

First published 2021

A catalogue record for this publication is available from the British Library.

Library of Congress Cataloging-in-Publication Data
NAMES: Traister, Bryce, editor.
TITLE: The Cambridge companion to early American literature / edited by Bryce Traister.
DESCRIPTION: Cambridge ; New York, NY : Cambridge University Press, 2021. | Series:
Cambridge companions to literature | Includes bibliographical references and index.
IDENTIFIERS: LCCN 2021027042 (print) | LCCN 2021027043 (ebook) | ISBN
9781108840040 (hardback) | ISBN 9781108793490 (paperback) | ISBN 9781108878623
(ebook)
SUBJECTS: LCSH: American literature – Colonial period, ca. 1600–1775 – History and
criticism. | American literature – Revolutionary period, 1775–1783 – History and criti-
cism. | American literature – 1783–1850 – History and criticism. | BISAC: LITERARY
CRITICISM / American / General
CLASSIFICATION: LCC PS185 .C36 2021 (print) | LCC PS185 (ebook) | DDC 810.9/001–dc23
LC record available at https://lccn.loc.gov/2021027042
LC ebook record available at https://lccn.loc.gov/2021027043

ISBN 978-1-108-84004-0 Hardback
ISBN 978-1-108-79349-0 Paperback

CONTENTS

FIGURES

CONTRIBUTORS

ALLISON BIGELOW is the Tom Scully Discovery Chair and Associate Professor in the Department of Spanish, Italian, and Portuguese and affiliate faculty in Latin American Studies and Women, Gender, and Sexuality at the University of Virginia, located on the lands of the Monacan Indian Nation. She is the author of *Mining Language: Racial Thinking, Indigenous Knowledge, and Colonial Metallurgy in the Early Modern Iberian World* (2020).

MICHELLE BURNHAM is Professor of English and Director of the Center for the Arts and Humanities at Santa Clara University. Her most recent book is *Transoceanic America: Risk, Writing, and Revolution in the Global Pacific* (2019). She is the editor of the Re-Editions series at Lever Press, which publishes quality critical digital editions of recovered literary and cultural texts from archives, special collections, and the dustbins of history.

MATT COHEN is Professor of English and Affiliate Faculty in Native American Studies at the University of Nebraska–Lincoln. He is the author of *The Networked Wilderness: Communicating in Early New England* (2010) and, with Jeffrey Glover, edited *Colonial Mediascapes: Sensory Worlds of the Early Americas* (2014).

KATHLEEN DONEGAN is Associate Professor of English and the Daniel E. Koshland Distinguished Chair in Writing at the University of California, Berkeley. Her first book, *Seasons of Misery: Catastrophe and Colonial Settlement in Early America* (2014), won an honorable mention in the 2014 Early American Book Prize. She is currently working on a manuscript entitled *The Spectral Plantation: The Other Worlds of Slavery*.

PAUL DOWNES teaches in the Department of English at the University of Toronto where he specializes in eighteenth- and nineteenth-century American literature and in the relationship between literature and political philosophy. He is the author of *Democracy, Revolution and Monarchism in Early American Literature* (2002) and *Hobbes, Sovereignty and Early American Literature* (2015). His current research addresses questions of sovereignty and ecology in works by Herman Melville.

MOLLY FARRELL is Associate Professor of English at Ohio State University. She researches early American literature, the history of science, early modern affects, and feminism. Her first book, *Counting Bodies: Population in Colonial American Writing* (2016; paperback, 2019), argued that colonial writing naturalized the idea that states could count people like any other commodity.

JONATHAN BEECHER FIELD was born in New England and educated in the Midwest. He is the author of *Errands into the Metropolis* (2009) and *Town Hall Meetings and the Death of Deliberation* (2019). Among other venues, his writing has appeared in *The Awl, Boston Review, Decider, Early American Literature*, and *Vice*.

RAMESH MALLIPEDDI is Associate Professor of English at the University of British Columbia, Vancouver. He is the author of the book *Spectacular Suffering: Witnessing Slavery in the Eighteenth-Century British Atlantic* (2016). His work has appeared in *The Eighteenth Century: Theory and Interpretation* (2014), *English Literary History* (2014), and the edited collection *Emergent Nation: Early Modern British Literature in Transition* (2019). He is the editor of *Eighteenth-Century Studies*, the flagship journal of the American Society for Eighteenth-Century Studies (ASECS).

AMY M. E. MORRIS is Associate Professor of American Literature at the University of Cambridge and a fellow of Newnham College, Cambridge. She has published on a variety of early and not so early American topics, including Puritan responses to mastodon teeth, Shakespeare's *Cymbeline* in revolutionary America, and images of homelessness in twentieth-century literature.

DANA NELSON holds the Gertrude Conaway Vanderbilt chair in English and American studies at Vanderbilt University. She has published numerous books on the historical and literary cultures of the American political imagination, including, most recently, *Commons Democracy: Reading the Politics of Participation in the Early United States* (2016).

MARION RUST is Professor of English at the University of Kentucky and the editor of *Early American Literature*. Recent essays include work on gendered and raced self-inscription in scholarly discourse, the novel in early America, and postmenopausal sexuality in early American print culture.

SANDRA SLATER is Associate Professor of History and Director of the Carolina Lowcountry and Atlantic World Program at the College of Charleston in South Carolina. Slater, a proud Appalachian coal miner's daughter, received her doctorate in the field of Colonial America and the Early Modern Atlantic World from the University of Kentucky in 2009. Publications include a variety of articles in scholarly journals, including *Church History* and the *Journal of Early American History*. Slater is finishing a book manuscript, *"Pompe and Pride of Man": Pride and Humility in Early New England*.

CASSANDER SMITH is Associate Professor of English and Associate Dean of Academic Affairs for the Honors College at the University of Alabama. Her recent publications include *The Earliest African American Literatures* (2021), cowritten with Zachary Hutchins. She has served as the president of the Early Caribbean Society.

LAURA M. STEVENS is Chapman Professor of English at the University of Tulsa. She is the author of *The Poor Indians: British Missionaries, Native Americans, and Colonial Sensibility* (2004) and the forthcoming *Friday's Tribe: Eighteenth-Century English Missionary Fantasies* and was editor of *Tulsa Studies in Women's Literature* from 2005 to 2016.

BRYCE TRAISTER is Professor of English and Dean of the Faculty of Creative and Critical Studies at the University of British Columbia's Okanagan campus. He is the author of *Female Piety and the Invention of American Puritanism* (2016) and editor of *American Literature and the New Puritan Studies* (2017).

CAROLINE WIGGINTON is Associate Professor and Chair of English at the University of Mississippi. Her work has appeared in such journals as *Early American Literature, William and Mary Quarterly, American Literature,* and *Native American and Indigenous Studies.* Her next book, *Indigenuity: Native Craftwork and the Art of American Literatures,* is forthcoming.

BRYCE TRAISTER

Introduction
Narratives of Early America Old and New

For many years, the period covered by "early American literature" ran from about 1620 to 1800, or, on one end, from the launch of the Mayflower Pilgrims from the western shores of Cornwall to, on the other, the presidential election of Thomas Jefferson and the end of the Federalist period. In the last twenty years or so, and for reasons many of the chapters in this collection discuss, scholars have widened the temporal and geographic scope of the area and have, as a consequence, both broadened the field's archive and changed the literary historical perspective a reader today might have on it. No longer exclusively focused on the mostly male-authored texts and experiences of English settlement in New England and Virginia, scholars now consider writing by Spanish, French, and Portuguese settlers; previously ignored writing and communication by both women and Indigenous persons; and writing by both enslaved and formerly enslaved peoples not just in the colonial southern United States but across the Caribbean, the Atlantic ocean, and the Gulf of Mexico. This last area of research, it should be noted, was one of the primary locations of the late seventeenth- and eighteenth-century Atlantic trade in enslaved human beings, one of the key economic engines of imperial colonialism in what are now deemed the continents of North and South America.

Early American literature, as the saying goes, ain't what it used to be. Perhaps one way to measure the distance between former and current concepts of the field would be a brief return to the first *Cambridge Companion to Early American Literature*, written in 2002 by the late Emory Elliott. It's a terrific book in every way, definitive of the Cambridge Companion genre's commitment to presenting literary history to a range of readerships in readable prose and accessible, sharply framed concepts. The 2002 installment is also a monograph, a solo-authored effort, and one which, in fairness, reflected the scholarship not just of the day but of its author as well. It offers a view of the field through a solitary, albeit widely read and deeply respected voice – I will suggest that such a version of a *Cambridge Companion to Early*

American Literature could only with great conceptual difficulty be written today. This is not faultfinding; rather, it speaks only to the idea that a single author could effectively capture the range and diversity of early American literature as it manifested itself at the turn of the twenty-first century. The field's blossoming has made that idea strange.[1]

"Early American literature" no longer means the literature of colonial New England, and it does not necessarily even speak English. In 1997, Gordon Sayre published *Les Sauvages Americains*, a study of English and, significantly, French colonial encounters with Indigenous peoples in New England, Quebec, and what used to be called "Upper Canada." To be sure, Sayre was not the first to study colonial history in a francophone cultural and historical setting, but it was one of the first such studies written from within a contemporary early American scholarly context with the specific aim of confronting that context's exclusionary and monolinguistic traditions. The book was, in retrospect, something of a game changer, and we now have a much more robust set of studies, conferences, conversations, and curricular developments that together assume a multilingual scholarly perspective and sweep. French, Spanish, Portuguese, Japanese, Chinese, African, and Native-Indigenous language(s) are now broadly considered to be part of the linguistic universe and historical record of the early Americas.[2]

As a consequence of the geographic and linguistic diversification of the colonial archive, the old temporal boundaries have become more fluid as well. They now extend earlier, into the sixteenth and even fifteenth centuries, with Columbus and the Spanish missionary landings in what is now the southern United States emerging as contributing voices of this diversified archive of early American coloniality (as an example, see Allison Bigelow's chapter in this volume). On the other end of this expanding timeline, we now read later into the nineteenth century, as scholars reconceptualize the persistence of colonialism into the War of 1812 and beyond, even to the election of Andrew Jackson in 1828 as signaling the United States' transformation from colonial to imperial nation. Marion Rust's chapter in this volume, for example, offers insights into how to read early American novels, ur-novels, and novel-like prose texts produced up to 1827. While some might observe that such broadening entails a blurring of focus and others might judge it to be anachronistic, the generally expansive trajectory of early American literary and cultural studies has made a huge impact on how we teach and think about the nation's complicated historical pasts.[3]

And this is altogether a good thing, most would agree, not least because the diversification of the field's constituent parts, voices, and histories has led to one of the most intellectually exciting periods of professional study in the area. The robust culture of early American literary and cultural studies has also aligned with and, to some extent, driven the conversations of the broader community of American studies scholarship.[4] Take any one of the important conversations in American studies of the last twenty years, be it race-slavery and its continuing aftermath; Indigenous encounter, removal, or genocide; national identity and America's exceptional "special status" as a nation; aesthetic development and cultural sovereignty; the transformation of the "commons" as space to "the public sphere" of democracy; women's rights; questions of citizenship and "belonging"; the persistence (or decline, as one will) of religious influence in American political culture – all of these persistent preoccupations of nineteenth-, twentieth-, and twenty-first-century American literary study are absolutely central to the contemporary conversations of early American literary and cultural studies. Indeed, all of these large-scale conceptual issues find their historical antecedent or origin in the colonial period and its study today. The chapters contained in this *Cambridge Companion to Early American Literature* reflect, comment on, and extend the set of deepened conversations between the earlier and later fields of Americanist scholarship and thought.

That said, the idea that colonial literature and culture gave rise to, led into, and served as an "origin" for the US nation (and its study) that followed is itself a problematical claim. Early American literature was for many years understood to be the immature precursor to a more fulsomely realized and grown-up version of American literature in the nineteenth century: the seed, if you will, of the great bloom that was the American renaissance.[5] Early colonial scholarship scanned the colonial archive – and, here it should be said, a primarily English and Atlantic seaboard–located historical archive – for signs of "pre-American" or "proto-American" concepts, language use, and stylistic features. The more interesting poems of Anne Bradstreet, in this older approach, are those in which specifically American themes or preoccupations emerge; Charles Brockden Brown's novels are worthwhile subjects for literary criticism insofar as they anticipate or give rise to the southern gothic haunts of Poe or the religious searchings of a Hawthorne. Viewed in the specific context of American literary history, the colonial period and its meager and mongrel literary archive mattered less as a worthwhile object of study in its own right than as a kind of rough-hewn "source" for the literature that would really matter.

Most infamously, the religious intensities and ambitions of the Puritans have long been viewed as leading into and securing a narrative of national origin, special status, and ultimate destiny that Americans tell even to this day.[6] The "New England Mind," as Perry Miller identified this historical and religious construct, perforce grounded national identity as a legacy of the seventeenth-century settlement period. This legacy persisted as both intellectual history and political self-fashioning over the course of the latter half of the twentieth century, as scholars refined, criticized, and qualified Miller's articulation of a dominant Protestant mode of "being American" and politicians positioned themselves in various ways as the true inheritors (or even critics) of the New England way.[7] Although long criticized on any number of fronts, Miller's thesis was the engine that drove the first fifty years of academic American literary criticism, no doubt fueled by the emergent ideologies of the post–World War II political settlement, not least of which was the "Cold War" between the Protestant United States and the Godless Soviet Union. The point here is that, whether or not one fully subscribes to the "New England Mind" as a defining and still dominant understanding of what matters about the colonial period or its impact on American national identity, it is still understood by many to be the case with which one still feels compelled to argue or engage.

A few decades into the twenty-first century, one would be hard-pressed into find many professional readers of the field who would support this limited view of the colonial period's legacy today.[8] Instead, we have an essay like Jonathan Beecher Field's chapter in this volume, which takes a critical view of how "Puritanism" emerges in popular culture today. It is still worth asking, how different is yesterday's "origins story" from the ones we are telling today? We – following the lead of nineteenth-century authors – used to tell the story of "American cultural independence" from England; today, we talk about "Anglo-American transnational culture." We used to tell the story of the "rise of democracy" and the tensions between popular and elected sovereignty; today, we talk about "the commons" and the emergence of a tensile "popular voice" as antidotes to the infection of oligarchy and hereditary privilege (see Dana Nelson's chapter in this volume). However, in both sets of these critical narratives, the colonial still leads to the national, and as a disciplinary frame, "early America" still derives at least some of its internal coherence and authority from its ability to explain the implicitly more important and relevant national story of the United States. In the broader view, one might still be inclined to say, early American literature remains derivative, pre-formational, marginal to the metropole, inchoate, incubatory, arcane, always leading to some more developed version of itself – in a word, *colonial*. Early American literature has always, to put the matter differently, been about something other than itself.

Our modern conception of the colonial period could be said to mirror this awkward logic. The early period tells us something important, for example, about a national religious origin story we claim as "ours," at least in part, by forsaking it. The Salem witch episode of 1692, possibly the most mined of the all the colonial ores, indicates much that was regrettable about the nation's religious incubation, when it isn't being recast in contemporary popular media culture or invoked as a metaphor to claim unjust political or institutional persecution.[9] So when we claim the "witch hunt" as a legacy of "our" past, is that a good thing? Or do we invoke such a past only to insist that the "superstitious" religious beliefs and murderous gullibility that animated the Salem witchcraft trials was some sort of process error – something fundamentally different and separate from the "American Puritanism" we might otherwise want to claim as one of the nation's foundational narratives. It is curious at times to hear today's politicians claiming the nation's religious heritage to justify their views on everything from reproductive rights to the so-called war on Christmas while at the same time decrying the terrible injustice of "witch hunts," a legacy of the same "religious heritage" the same politician is trying to enforce as today's expression of American Christmas. (The New England Puritans, it is worth noting here, also despised the folk traditions of Christmas and actually banned its celebration from 1659 to 1681. Let us provisionally suppose that those most ready to claim the witch's victim status tend not to be outstanding students of colonial history.)

We read early American literature to learn what it was like to become (but not necessarily to *be*) American; to learn how or why we became something other than religious, or royalist, or slaveholding, or comfortable with eroticism, and so forth. Or why we didn't, as the contributions from Ramesh Mallipeddi on the Atlantic traffic in enslaved persons, Paul Downes on how early Black petitions for freedom sponsored a new language of human rights, or Sandra Slater on the cultural politics of sexuality all indicate. Early American literature may be foundational to American origins, but it is neither definitive nor exhaustive. It opens vistas into the still moving picture of settler–Indigenous relationships and recalls the trauma, both inflicted and endured, by settler and Indigenous cultures. It charts pathways from the early to the postmodern American novel; from religious to sentimental feeling; from colonial conceptions of "liberty" to contemporary defenses of its curtailment; from the story of early modern women to the gendered story of national citizenship; from assertions of colonial to national and human sovereignty. We are still, in all of these accounts, talking about stories of continuity from the early to the late, even as we strive not to recapitulate and reinforce the older nationalist models of the colonial origins stories.[10] Put another way, early American literature today invokes multiple narratives of American identities rather than perforce insisting that one colonial past gave rise to one national present. Early American literature is nothing if not an incubator for the intellectual and political pluralism many Americans want to privilege as the colonial period's best and most important gift to the nation.

So where the successful expansion and diversification of early American literature have contributed to an increasingly influential role in American literary and cultural studies more broadly, it hasn't really solved or explained away some of the field's most abiding challenges in terms of conceptual coherence, or even, more simply, its appeal to new readers. This isn't to say that, generally speaking, Americans ignore or don't care about its colonial past. They do, even if many don't remember it particularly well or invoke it for the wrong reasons. Early American literature belongs to the nation's colonial history, its mostly pre-national past, and its relevance to contemporary life in the United States has long been invoked by recalling episodes and events reckoned to be important touchstones in the nation's founding. The Pilgrims and the Puritans; the frontier "Indian wars"; Salem witchcraft; the "Great Awakening"; the revolutionary troubles and resolution; the Declaration of Independence; the Constitution. This is something of a restatement of the "derivation" problem – that "true" American literature derives from its rustic colonial origins. These widely assumed touchpoints of the colonial inheritance – sources of an American "unusable past" as it has been called – are not in any direct way about *literature* at all.[11] Political history, religious history, imperial history, intellectual history, national history – but where are the famous touchpoints involving poems, novels, and plays written during the US colonial period? Where is the *good* literature that everybody knows and loves?

The short answer is that there isn't any really – at least none that truly extends its reach beyond academic settings into the popular – and this has bedeviled the study of early American literature from its earliest professional beginnings.[12] That is, there is no single or even collective literary effort produced in the period that approaches the notoriety or "obviousness" of the more easily recalled ("The Boston Tea Party") historical record of the nation. The *Journal of Sarah Kemble Knight*, a fascinating and virtually unique travel narrative written by a colonial Englishwomen at the beginning of the eighteenth century, is mostly of interest to a handful of academic readers, teachers, and their captive students. The same could be said of Phillis Wheatley's *Poem's on Various Subjects* (1773) or John Marrant's *Narrative of the Lord's Wonderful Dealings*, written in 1785. The first collection of poetry known to be published by an enslaved woman in the colonial United States; an extraordinary autobiography of a free Black who went on to perform missionary work among the Cherokee – noteworthy, convention-breaking, aesthetically rich they all may be, but none comes close to breaking through into popular awareness on the order of "the Declaration of Independence." Colonial American literature is interesting for "inside academic" reasons, for historical reasons, one might reasonably say. Yet there's not a lot of casual knowledge about Mary Rowlandson (Patty Hearst's foremother) or Michael Wigglesworth (the notorious Puritan masturbator) out there, and not a lot of clearly understood or deeply researched *literary* reasons to turn to these religious and aesthetic pioneers beyond the demands of an undergraduate course syllabus or the pleasures of specialist intellectual enthusiasm. As with the colonial period more broadly, the study of early American literature seems dependent on other factors.

One such factor is history, or, more specifically, its manufacture, or historiography. As has long been remarked, the study of early American literature is deeply historical, even more historical, it seems somehow, than even committed "historicist" study of literary outputs in later periods. The generative and complicated relationship between historiography and literary studies has long been remarked, but it probably goes deeper than methodological skepticism or academic-style gatekeeping. For some, what makes a colonial literary text "interesting" is less its literariness than its history-worthy significance. The case of America's first deliberately published Black poet, Phillis Wheatley, is particularly instructive in respect of this point. Over the years – and, in fairness, many years ago – some commentators have remarked that we read her work today less for its literary significance than for the remarkable fact of its existence at all. Of course, today we read her poems for other, equally if not more important reasons – as an indication of an enslaved person's resistance to the terms of her captivity; as an alternate account of African American authorship; as part of a Black "counterpublic"; or as the voice of a specifically African-inflected voice of Protestant evangelical culture, to name a few. Another accomplished colonial poet, the seventeenth-century congregational minister Edward Taylor, receives attention as much for the quality of his writing as for his having written so many poems at all, for the way he wrote many of those poems (as part of his preparation of formal sermons), for the way he kept his poetic activity a secret – in short, for all of the nonpoetic, which is to say, nonliterary or "para-literary" reasons. As such, both Taylor and Wheatley indicate the "para-American" status of early American literature more generally.

For neither of these writers were, strictly speaking, "American" at all; some would even suggest that the entire field of early American literature is a critical chimera that either has little persuasive evidence to support it or is convened around unexamined assumptions about what makes a literature "national."[13] Edward Taylor was a seventeenth-century English settler and ordained minister of the Puritan gospel; Wheatley was an African woman, an involuntary settler, stolen from her home and forced into the conditions of human slavery. The older – we tend to call it "classic" now – version of early American literary study found, in these and other authors, "the beginning" of an American story it was at the time convenient or necessary to tell. The tension between Taylor's visible ministry and his private contemplative poetry gave us purchase on what would become a tension between public and private American selves that defined a "uniquely American" conception of individualism. Wheatley's performance offered a glimpse of America's fantasy of Black American uplift and the personal opportunities afforded by white civilization to the "barbarous" other. Yet none of these ideas were operative at the time Taylor and Wheatley were writing in very different historical circumstances, and the "proto-American" narratives we have appended to their writing have no more historical validity than the idea that the seventeenth-century religious dissident Anne Hutchinson was an intersectional feminist who anticipated the twenty-first-century's #MeToo movement. We claim these historical figures and their writing – and for good reason, from certain modern political perspectives – as and for the people and texts we need them to be today, but in doing so we rehearse another version of the derivation argument about the early period: that early American literature is of interest, worth talking about, considering carefully again, for reasons having little to do with what the literature *really* is or was at the time. We read the field as much to better understand what early American literature was in its time as for what reading it teaches us about our American world today.

This, however, is why the study of colonial literature is, perhaps, all the more necessary today: it obdurately reminds us of a truth that applies not merely to the academic study of literature writ large but to the fate of reading and interpretation in the contemporary. That is, we are always – we have never not been – reading within our moment, always thinking about the historical past through the lens of the interpretive present, always looking to create fresh narratives and perspectives about the past that might better help to understand and to act for the present. We used to think this "presentist" perspective was a curse, even a fundamental interpretive and scholarly error (and, to be fair, some still do, although they tend to reside in history departments).

How else do we make sense of the ongoing fascination with someone like Anne Hutchinson? Hutchinson has been an object of historical reflection, more or less, from the time she began holding prayer meetings in her kitchen to discuss the weekly sermons in the mid-1630s. John Winthrop wrote *The Short Story* about her in 1647 – it was anything but short – and we have been writing about her ever since. Edward Johnson, another colonial historian and contemporary of Hutchinson, recorded her theology as political and biological miscarriage and concupiscence. Cotton Mather called her a hydra in about 1702, around about the time he was again taking heat for his role in the Salem trials. Yet she has also been claimed as a hero, a heroine for some: an early voice in America's search for toleration and free speech. The mid-nineteenth-century's Nathaniel Hawthorne told yet another series of stories about her, ambivalently recalling and fictionalizing her involuntary leadership and inimitable moral integrity in one of the most famous novels ever written by an American. Over the course of 200 or more years, professional, amateur, and schoolhouse historians and scholars have all "had a go" at Hutchinson, each providing slightly different and often competing versions of this most unlikely "American Jezebel." She is both "America" and its undoing; the revolutionary voice of the nation and the impediment to the nation's unfolding; a proto-feminist heroine for later American women like Angelica Grimke and Susan B. Anthony, and a radical insurgent whose gender identity is completely irrelevant to why she is (or is not) important to us today.[14] All of these "Anne Hutchinsons" offer us something valuable not just about the nation's historical past but about its contemporary moment as well – that is, to recall the earlier phrase, the fact that earlier American culture is always about something other than itself need not be understood as some sort of liability or shortcoming of the field. It is rather a reminder that, as our present-day needs and preoccupations evolve and shift, so too will the conclusions we derive from our encounter with the past.

In the twenty-first century, "the Americas" as sites of settlement and conquest have emerged as the location where scholars and readers have most significantly intervened in this idea of America's "usable past" and have therefore as a consequence broadly shifted the terms of scholarship across multiple areas and time periods of study. These shifts have coincided with public and political conversations, in North America particularly, about the continuing challenges of Indigenous and settler peoples and the belief, for many, that a greater accountability for the infliction of trauma and violence on Indigenous peoples must precede any reasonable hope for a lasting reconciliation. Here is where national (and nationalist) histories and divergence separate the United States, Canada, and Mexico from each other, to be sure, but the renewed consideration of indigeneity becomes, at the same time, a basis for reconceiving the entirety of North American settlement history from a perspective that places the Indigenous–settler encounter at the center, rather than the periphery, of contemporary historiography and literary scholarship. The idea of "settlement" has emerged as a more complicated conceptual frame for broadly reimagining early American colonial experiences, or "coloniality" as it is sometimes called. The idea of "settlement" puts the concepts of place, location, and geography at the forefront of the conversation – that questions of how, when, what, and who cannot be asked independently of "where." Part III of this volume groups a cluster of chapters that pivot on the concept of place and location.

This ongoing expansion and revision to the field, in terms of both its historical span and its constitutive voices, has produced radically new and robust work on the settlement period and the new nation that followed it. Two of the chapters in this volume, "How to Read Things That Weren't Written Down in Early America," by Matt Cohen, and "Indigenous Colonial America," by Caroline Wigginton, conceptualize both the problems and the opportunities of working closely with Indigenous cultural heritage and memory. Both chapters articulate ways to approach the complex archive of the Native peoples of the Western hemisphere. They also, just as importantly, invite us to think about how the Indigenous historical and representational record complicates and enriches scholarship about settler colonial writing.

Indeed, nearly every chapter in this Cambridge Companion acknowledges or investigates the ways in which Indigenous encounter inflected the emergence of the colonial period's settler civilization. For example, in her chapter, "How to Read Gender in Early America," Laura M. Stevens presents a fascinating approach to John Marrant's well-known *A Narrative of the Lord's Wonderful Dealings with John Marrant* that reads the encounter between Indigenous people and Western spirituality as one inflected by the politics of gender in the colonial setting. This work, undertaken by both self-identified Indigenous and settler scholars, has transformed the field, not just in terms of peer-reviewed published scholarship like that contained in this volume but, just as (if not more) importantly, in terms of what and how we teach early American literature in the undergraduate classroom; who we recruit into graduate programs and later into the faculty ranks; and how we include Indigenous perspectives at our conferences, colloquia, and the like. We've come a long way, that is to say, from the triumphalist account of the Pilgrims and the "first Thanksgiving," or the egregiously saccharine story of Pocahontas and the Virginians. This better reckoning of the past holds promise for the contemporary.

How This Book Works

This book departs from the "encyclopedia" tradition of essay anthologies in several ways. Part I invites new and seasoned readers into a series of reflective chapters that offer pathways for reading unfamiliar texts and contexts. Matt Cohen (Chapter 1) considers the challenge of reading "texts" that weren't recorded as language. The chapters in this section take the invitational gesture to the curious seriously and propose strategies for reading different texts and textual traditions. Molly Farrell (Chapter 2) offers an approach to a new conception of reading the natural world less as simple empirical reality than as always framed through a cultural lens. Amy M. E. Morris's chapter (Chapter 3) offers a primer on colonial poetry that provides readers with a series of interpretive questions with which to frame and deepen their experience of early American poetry. Laura M. Stevens (Chapter 4) considers how gender informs, complicates, and extends the significance of a range of early American textualities. Marion Rust (Chapter 5) takes us off the well-beaten tracks of Charles Brockden Brown and Susanna Rowson to introduce us to some of the novels that early Americans actually read and why they appealed to so many. Finally, in the last chapter of this section, Dana Nelson (Chapter 6) reintroduces us to the messy, complicated, and shifting landscapes of democratic theory and practice in the early national period.

Part II offers a series of readings, "applications" if you will, of contemporary early American scholarly practice. Kathleen Donegan (Chapter 7) develops an account of disaster in a time of "creating." Jonathan Beecher Field (Chapter 8) considers the role and practice of cultural memory in contemporary popular and political cultures. In a pair of chapters about the problem of human enslavement in the "New World," Paul Downes (Chapter 9) and Ramesh Mallipeddi (Chapter 10) present accounts of Black resistance against the terms and the experience of their enslavement. This section ends with the historian Sandra Slater's discussion (Chapter 11) of the cultural and political meanings of eroticism and sexual identity in a variety of settler encounter zones.

Part III locates early American literature in a variety of specific spatial and geographic settings. Cassander Smith (Chapter 15) charts the cultural and historical archipelago of "the Caribbean," easily one of the most important "new" locations of scholarship in the colonial period, and one whose constituent authors, texts, and peoples have long been claimed (divided) on behalf of competing and divergent imperial and national entities. Two such entities, the Spanish and Portuguese colonial holdings we call "Latin America," receive careful treatment in Allison Bigelow's chapter (Chapter 13), and Michelle Burnham (Chapter 14) makes a pathbreaking contribution to the colonial period by locating our attention on the emergence of "the Pacific" as a meaningful regional configuration of settlement.

Notes

1. Emory Elliott, *The Cambridge Companion to Early American Literature* (Cambridge: Cambridge University Press, 2003).
2. For a discussion of Spanish contributions here, see Kirsten Silva Gruesz and Rodrigo Lazo, "The Spanish Americas: Introduction," *Early American Literature*

53 (2018): 641–664 and Rolena Adorno, "A Latin Americanist Looks at Early American Literature," *Early American Literature* 50, no. 1 (2015): 41–61.

3. Or even what many outside of the United States understand "early American literature" to be. In Canadian academics, at least, "early American literature" means American literature before the twentieth century. For a recent discussion of periodization in the field, see Sandra M. Gustafson, "What's in a Date? Temporalities of Early American Literature," *PMLA: Publications of the Modern Language Association of America* 128, no. 4 (2013): 961–967.

4. As an example of the kind of scholarship that represents the expansion of the field's historical remit and its diversified archive, see Anna Brickhouse, *The Unsettlement of America: Translation, Interpretation, and the Story of Don Luis de Velasco, 1560–1945* (New York: Oxford University Press, 2015).

5. This view of early American literature, long disavowed if not altogether abandoned, was central to the early American Studies movement of the 1950s, which sought to develop and export a coherent and unbroken narrative of American literary development beginning in the colonial period and progressing into the national period and beyond, or, in the words of Philip Gura, a "prologue to the literature of the United States in the nineteenth-century." See Gura, "The Study of Colonial American Literature, 1966–1978: A Vade Mecum," *William and Mary Quarterly* 45, no. 2 (1988): 308.

6. For a now classic study in this vein, see Alan Heimert, *Religion and the American Mind: From the Great Awakening to the Revolution* (Cambridge, MA: Harvard University Press, 1966).

7. The scholarship on Miller and the intellectual framework of the New England Mind is extensive. Important book-length engagements include Sacvan Bercovitch, *The Puritan Origins of the American Self* (New Haven, CT: Yale University Press, 1975) and Bercovitch, *The American Jeremiad* (Madison: University of Wisconsin Press, 1977); Ann Douglas, *The Feminization of American Culture* (New York: Farrar, Straus and Giroux, 1977).

8. That said, it is also fair to say that early American literature and its study continue to serve as convenient straw-arguments for critics wanting to make grand statements about their continuing – usually nationalistic and malignant influence – on American studies more broadly. For some discussion of these tendencies, see Ralph Bauer, "Early American Literature and American Literary History at the 'Hemispheric Turn'," *American Literary History* 22 (2010): 250–262.

9. Witches have been a frequent presence in popular culture throughout the twentieth and twenty-first centuries, and the "witch-hunt" has been a familiar political slogan for just as long. One might be tempted to blame Arthur Miller and his 1953 play *The Crucible* for both of these phenomena. Of course, Miller's play was about the fallout of an actual search for nonexistent witches in Salem, Massachusetts, whereas the "witch-hunt" defense is, as often as not, a defensive phrase invoked by people who are probably trying to hide something.

10. For examples of each of these arguments from an arguably "new" early American studies perspective, see, respectively, Matt Cohen, *The Networked Wilderness: Communicating in Early new England* (Minneapolis: University of Minnesota Press, 2009); Kathleen Donegan, *Seasons of Misery: Catastrophe and Colonial Settlement in Early America* (Philadelphia: University of Pennsylvania

Press, 2016); Monique Allewaert, *Ariel's Ecology: Plantations, Personhood, and Colonialism in the American Tropics* (Minneapolis: University of Minnesota Press, 2013); Abram Van Engen, *Sympathetic Puritans: Calvinist Fellow Feeling in Early New England* (New York: Oxford University Press, 2015); Nancy Ruttenburg, *Democratic Personality: Popular Voice and the Trials of American Authorship* (Stanford: Stanford University Press, 1998); Elizabeth Dillon, *The Gender of Freedom: Fictions of Liberalism and the Literary Public Sphere* (Stanford: Stanford University Press, 2005); Paul Downes, *Hobbes, Sovereignty, and Early American Literature* (New York: Cambridge University Press, 2015).

11. In American studies, the term derives from Russell Reising, *The Unusable Past: Theory and the Study of American Literature* (New York: Methuen, 1987).

12. A 2016 special issue of *Early American Literature* proposed a return to aesthetics, or a turn, at least, toward questions of form, judgment, and beauty long ignored or abandoned by early American scholarship. See especially Edward Cahill and Edward Larkin, "Aesthetics, Feeling and Form in Early American Literary Studies," *Early American Literature* 51, no. 2 (2016): 235–254.

13. The still influential book on this point remains William Spengemann, *A New World of Words: Redefining Early American Literature* (New Haven, CT: Yale University Press, 1994).

14. I discuss these differing version of Hutchinson at greater length in *Female Piety and the Invention of American Puritanism* (Columbus: Ohio State University Press, 2016).

PART I

How to Read (in) Early America

I

MATT COHEN

How to Read Things
That Weren't Written Down in Early
America

Most communications are not written down. This is as true now, in a supposedly information-saturated age, as it was in early colonial America. The point stands even if we understand the Western notion of "writing," with a generously broad interpretation, as including all forms of inscribed human communication. Some of what was transmitted among people of the past, consequently, we have to leave to the void or to the imagination – the uncountable facial expressions; the furtive gestures; a thousand accents; the qualities of colors; the taste of a 1628 Madeira; the movements of an Inca *khipucamayoc* at work. For others, we have well-elaborated historical frameworks and methods of recovery. In the fields of art history and architecture, historical performance in music and dance, theater history, material culture studies, and ethnobotany, for example, ways to read much of the uninscribed have been maintained and extended. There are also other domains in which the unwritten of the past has been vectored into the present, including Indigenous communities across the Americas, the church, women's communities, annual festivals from New Orleans to Rio de Janeiro, and scholarly institutions, with their many rituals and forms.[1]

This chapter focuses more on the "how" than the "things" of its title. The past few decades have seen the emergence of both new ways of "reading" and an interrogation of the act of "reading" itself. The former has drawn on everything from new technologies to archaeological discoveries and interdisciplinary collaborations. The latter has offered a mixed message. On one hand, skepticism about the centrality of the written text to the humanities has widened the definition of "reading" such that movies, pottery, landscape, computer interfaces, clothing styles, and more are things to be "read." At the same time, strict definitions of what exactly we mean by "writing" have eroded, as alphabetic forms of writing take their place in scholarly analysis across a whole range of inscriptive practices, including bookbinding, scrapbook-making, sewing, graffiti, and more. On the other hand, the degree to which authoritative, academy-based "reading" tends to serve the interests of the university (or of what some call the "settler community") far more than the interests of the colonized communities whose media are being "read" has resulted in calls for new approaches to, even new purposes for, reading itself. Those new approaches sometimes involve restricting who can "read" some colonial-era Indigenous media, privileging access by traditional knowledge communities over open access. It can also mean collaborative forms of curation of non-textual objects and practices. In certain cases, it can even mean thinking beyond human communication itself, a demand that we listen to what larger forces are telling us.[2]

Yet because there is no "how" to read without "things," I will focus these methodological and ethical discussions in three media domains: Indigenous media of the colonial era; human relations to and movement in landscape; and the environment as an agent of change. To support a movement into this kind of historical analysis, I suggest a shift from "writing" or "text" as the focus of attention and, following the media theorist John Durham Peters, center on acts of communication instead. In the case of the first two areas of inquiry, Indigenous media and the landscape, the acts of communication largely involve humans trying to communicate with each other. In the second domain, which involves the question of what the environment might be "saying" either to or through humans, the traditional sense of human agency's centrality to communication is less important. It may be that here the concept of "communication" will fail to express the forms of relation in question and something more cosmological, such as spirit, is entailed. Still, as Benjamin Franklin might say, a speckled ax can still cut wood.

It is true that, in many cases in the study of the past, reading texts that were written down is the starting point for understanding things that weren't. Yet if we think about media in a way that is concomitantly broad with the understanding of communication as the pivotal goal of a message, we can entertain properties of "media" that might help us better appreciate the functioning of colonialism and its historiography. Consider two recent redefinitions of the notion of the medium, by Jussi Parikka and John Durham Peters. In explaining why it is productive to think of insects and animals as "media," Parikka writes:

> Media are a contraction of forces of the world into specific resonating milieus ... An animal has to find a common tune with its environment, and a technology has to work through rhythmic relations with other force fields such as politics and economics ... In other words, there is a whole cosmology of media technologies that spans much more of time than the human historical

approach suggests. In this sense, insects and animals provide an interesting case of how to widen the possibilities to think media and technological culture.[3]

Here a medium is a relatively coherent field (or "milieu") defined by its internal affordances and external relations. It is not just that we are asked to think about what an insect might consider to be a medium. We are also asked to understand the degree to which entities we have considered animate in one way might in fact be animate in other ways as well, or the degree to which the distinction between animate and inanimate limits the agility of our imaginative perception.

Peters extends this suggestion, with different philosophical grounds, to the classical mediums of air, water, fire, and earth. "What if we took not two human beings trying to share thoughts as our model of communication," Peters asks, "but a population evolving in intelligent interaction with its environment?" In Peters's vision, the conception of communication as message-sending must be wrenched away – even Marshall McLuhan's famous formulation of the medium as the message needs to be unleashed into the messageless yet meaningful world of natural forces and the evolution of their forms.[4] In short, when we think about communication just in terms of messages being encoded and then decoded, we make two mistakes. First, we miss much of the point of communicating for senders and what is actually being understood by receivers; and second, by insisting that only humans can be senders and receivers, we make it hard to tell sometimes where meaningful communication is happening at all. In an era in which the sustainability of earthly life appears to hinge on vast communication systems and their seemingly uncontrollable deployment by human communities, using media as an organizing feature of literary or historical study is before all else a claim for scholarly relevance. Yet, as such, the field tends to want to hold "history" and "literature" in place as things, evolving to be sure but structurally formal givens. Looking at media as meaning-bearing but not message-bearing, however, calls the very means by which one tells a story – *history* as a medium – into question.

How Do You "Read" a Hole in the Ground in Early America?

It depends on who made it, perhaps. If it was made by Europeans trying to trap wolves, you might understand it one way: a means to preserve cattle, fundamental to the English way of life; an expression of the Christian conviction that animals were created to serve man; a message to Indigenous people about the way English settlers understood the control of space. If it was made by Wampanoag people alongside an important land route, other kinds of reading are required, because Wampanoags were known to use holes in the ground to record human events.

The Pilgrim negotiator Edward Winslow, one of the more sympathetic and attentive English observers of Indigenous ways, published a description of such holes and how to "read" them:

> Instead of Records and Chronicles, they take this course, where any remarkable act is done, in memory of it, either in the place, or by some path-way near adjoining, they make a round hole in the ground about a foot deep, and as much over, which when others passing by behold, they enquire the cause and occasion of the same, which being once known, they are careful to acquaint all men, as occasion serveth therewith. And lest such holes should be filled, or grown up by any accident, as men pass by they will oft renew the same: By which means many things of great Antiquity are fresh in memory. So that as a man travelleth, if he can understand his guide, his journey will be the less tedious, by reason of the many historical Discourses will be related unto him.[5]

Rather than claim a relation – inferior, universal, or otherwise – to Western practices, Winslow's description breaks down the archiving of "historical discourses" into components: a material inscription, a method of transmission, a conservation strategy. Memory and social practice are regarded as key, just as in the interpretation of any kind of inscription, since the holes cannot interpret themselves.

The choice of location, "in the place" or nearby, is also significant, as the interaction with archival information proceeds within the richly informative space of the event recorded. Information access is mostly, but not completely, open: a passerby can request the information, which triggers a "careful" reproduction of the information from the archive, but with the minor, significant qualification that the telling is "as occasion serveth therewith" and only if you can understand your guide. The final protocol, of rounding out the hole after telling the story to keep it distinctive, blends pragmatism, a lesson about the decay that nature brings on all attempts at remembering, and a symbolic representation of the social nature of information – of the participatory potential of memorial institutions. Almost everyone is a historian here; in the logic of this preservation system, to hear or to tell the "many historical discourses" of the Algonquian forests is to take some responsibility for perpetuating them.

How to read a hole may also depend on how it was made. One of the earliest means by which the Pilgrims survived in the northeastern winter in which they landed was to dig up Native grain storage holes. These holes first made for the sacred purpose of preserving one group of kin were dug out again, in theft, to preserve another. The English also dug up a burial site:

a hole made with the sacred purpose of honoring the dead, excavated and subjected to another kind of theft:

> [W]e found, first, a mat, and under that was a fair bow, and there another mat, and under that a board about three quarters long, finely carved and painted, with three tines, or broaches, on the top, like a crown. Also between the mats we found bowls, trays, dishes, and such like trinkets . . . We brought sundry of the prettiest things away with us, and covered the corpse up again.[6]

The Indigenous messages to the invisible world encoded here were misread or ignored, trinkets and crowns drawn from the colonial European vocabulary for dealing with non-Christian nations. "The planks the Algonquians left uncovered at grave sites were grave markers or grave houses and were put there so that spirits could orient themselves to their altered state of being," Betty Booth Donohue points out; "Fledgling spirits could see the planks, recognize their 'new homes,' and have a reference point for their travels." Each of the objects and images in the burial site – the bowls, the red ocher, the knife, the "old iron things" – was rich with meaning and with messages not intended only for human audiences.

One could list the formal factors that usually matter in a reading of non-textual communications in the early colonial era. These would be relevant when one is trying to understand the meaning made in any cultural contexts, from the exchange of wampum to English settler uses of magic such as burying poppets in house walls and to Amerindian symbolic patterns appearing across textiles, ceramics, and counting systems. With respect to the circumstances of the communication, there are at least these things to consider: the time of year; the geographic location; the state of colonial relations; intentions of a ritual occasion; the clan, family, rank, gender, and age of the meaning creator or creators; and the clan, family, rank, gender, and age of they for whom the utterance, act, or object is designed to have meaning. With respect to the communication itself: the symbolic designs, spatial placement or orientation, choice or source of materials or language, use of repetition or pattern, melody, decibel level, color, smell, texture, heft, dimensions, and fabrication process. There are more, and each of the first group of factors can profoundly qualify the meanings of choices from the second group. "Symbols are integral to corresponding rituals," the Mohegan tribal historian Melissa Jayne Fawcett writes.[7] The Englishmen who dug up that burial site in 1620 found two bodies – one a man, the other probably his male child, buried with white wampum strings and a tiny bow – but if they noticed it, they did not record which direction the bodies were facing. Was it to the southwest, where after their spirit journey they would be welcomed at Cautantowwit's house, embraced by both the ancient people and those, like them, recently passed as a result of the plagues that preceded the Pilgrims' arrival?[8]

Scholarship in Mesoamerican and Andean contexts has similarly pointed to the need to understand Indigenous American signifying practices as functioning across media – cosmological patterns can be found on pottery, clothing, and accounting devices; vocabulary terms referring to inscription practices appear in both spiritual and governmental contexts. The practices associated with the creation of media in these cases seem to define them, in tune with McLuhan's claim that each medium has a sort of "grammar, an underlying language-like set of protocols." "Semiotic functions" in Indigenous systems, writes Galen Brokaw, "are distributed across a number of different media, most, if not all, of which also employ to one degree or another multiple types of semiotic conventions."[9] In many cases, this approach helps us understand European non-written forms as well.

This scholarship powerfully demonstrates another important "how" lesson from the study of non-textual forms in the colonial past: that these forms have not been replaced, or in many cases even eroded, by the spread of alphabetic literacy, writing, and print. The "cord keepers" of Peru's Huarochirí region, still using khipus as part of civic rituals today, the Krewes of Mardi Gras, and the Indigenous people of New England maintain not just the memory of the use of non-textual forms but versions of those forms themselves, often because they are crucial to making sovereignty claims – these forms simultaneously recall the past and make history in the present. Indeed, as our media world increasingly elaborates non-textual forms with the spread of smartphones and other modes of portable computing, the meaning-making fabric of aural, visual, architectural, and motion-based communication forms is returning to analytical centrality even for the bookish. So, to read things not written down in the past often means finding their genealogical ties to the unstable media of the present.

This is true of the genealogy of studying Indigenous media as well. As the acts of recording the two 1620s vignettes suggest, the study of American Native media forms has a history as long as colonization itself. Lately, it has grown and deepened, and its practitioners have refocused colonial studies around questions of Native sovereignty, politics, and kinship. Yet this was not always the case. "The aural and written evidence that colonizers, and more distant scholars benefiting from empire, found in language," Sean Harvey reminds us, "also impelled attempts to define how Native people thought, almost always in a way that highlighted ostensible differences between Native and Euro-American psychologies." Theorizations based on Native American oral and visual cultures played key roles, Harvey shows, in the development of Western philosophies of language; and as Brian

Hochman demonstrates, the very innovations in recording media that brought us modern audiovisual technologies were forged in part through the effort to "preserve" evidence of the supposedly "vanishing Indian."[10] In this way, the study of Native American non-written communication has been a pivotal site for generating damaging judgments to rationalize Indigenous removal and forced assimilation. Every mode, channel, or medium of communication is itself a factor in history, and the same is true for every act of studying them or writing about them. Every book or article about media under colonialism has at least two kinds of meanings: one about its subject matter that is historical and one about cultural politics in the present. The first step in how to read things not written down, then, is to question your motivation for doing so.

How Do You Read a Mountain Range or a Tree?

The fertile river valley of the Connecticut, with its surrounding mountain ranges, profoundly shapes the meanings of Indigenous communication in the region. The landscape is storied, each conjunction of streams and each mountain peak tied to a history both human and other-than-human. Yet it is also the natural phases created by the shape of the land and water here, and the temperature changes of the air, that matter in reading the exchanges between Natives and settlers that have happened in this area for centuries since the start of colonization. The annual arrival of fish and birds prompted Native movements in this space and spawned stories about those fish and birds. For Mohegans, shad-fishing season had arrived when the dogwood trees began to blossom, and corn-planting time just after they began to leaf out.[11] Hunting successfully in the corrugated landscape of the region, so dependent on temperature, color, smell, and sound, required knowledge that was shared by many means.

An ethics of mutual dependence was developed among the human cultures in this area long before the arrival of Europeans, and it determined the course of settler politics and cultural creolization. As Lisa Brooks explains, the Native concept of the "common pot," or the combination of plant and animal life, earthly shelter, and social networks that sustain life, appears in a range of colonial interactions and increasingly as struggles over the control of land burgeoned. That conception is profoundly tied to the land itself:

> In the Abenaki language, the word for "dish" is *wlôgan*. This word has a direct linguistic relationship to the word for the river intervales where Abenaki families flourished: *wôlhanak*. These "hollowed-out" places were not empty spaces to be filled but deeply situated social and ecological environments. There

is a certain poetic resonance between these words and the phrase that invokes "thanks to all our relations," *wlidôgawôgan*. In the coincidental formation of letters, "all our relations" can be contained within the "dish." The land, *aki*, is a self-sustaining vessel, but it requires participation from all its interwoven inhabitants.[12]

The shape of the landscape, the shape of the medium of sustenance, and the shape of human relations are all related by the metaphor of the common pot, in a way that makes the landscape a reminder of the forms of human commitment required to live within it.

Settlers relied upon similar reminders from the land. The case of Pennsylvania's "Treaty Elm" is instructive. Believed to be the site of a historic seventeenth-century agreement between the Lenape people and William Penn that established a long-standing peace, the tree became a touchstone for both Natives and settlers, an emblem of a treaty that represented "the best of the colonial past at a time of increasing estrangement from that past," in Andrew Newman's words, "a tradition to be cherished, even as cultural and demographic changes threatened to rupture the chain of memory."[13] The tree – together with the objects made from it after its destruction in a storm and other elms planted to commemorate it – provoked paeans like this one:

> Long may *it* be preserved as a memento of the past, and long may *the trees*, so planted, endure to link one generation with another, – to stand like *living monuments* speaking forth their solemn and soothing lessons, as from fathers to sons and the sons of sons.[14]

This appreciation of the cultural power of trees comes not from a Native leader but from John Watson, a popular historian of colonial Pennsylvania. As Newman observes, the Treaty Elm, like Plymouth Rock, could in part function as an imagined permanent emblem of the virtues of colonization precisely because of the absence of written records respecting them. As a consequence, the hagiography of the Treaty Elm produced a paradoxical situation. "In the absence of 'positive proof,' at least so long as the conclusions they supported were desirable, the Native Americans' traditions were more authoritative than those of the Euro-Americans," Newman observes, because "they had not alienated their capacity for memory by coming to depend on writing."[15] Whether one regards the Treaty Elm as a self-serving settler colonial civic myth or a more complex mediating agent between the colonizer and the colonized, it functions as a transmissive element of the land – even in its material absence.

Landscape is a terrain and thus a medium of human and human–divine communication. It is also, these examples show, a site of political and spiritual contest. "Native peoples' connection to land," Maureen Konkle writes, "is not just cultural" but "political – about governments, boundaries, authority over people and territory."[16] Fundamental to how Brooks reads contests over authority in early America is an attentiveness to Indigenous linguistic concepts and their link to landscape. Equally crucial is the use of settler records about property, together with treaties, deeds, and court cases related to the land. Yet the work of Brooks, Newman, and other scholars in this area points to a more basic decoding tactic: talking with cultural heritage keepers in whatever community it is you are studying – whether it is an Indigenous tribe or a religious group or a settler family. The means of interpreting non-written media of the past, and in particular, relations with the land, are often maintained in oral tradition and are generated and sustained socially. Interpretation is itself part of the "common pot"; meanings, like other forms of sustenance, call for careful curation and exchange.

N. Scott Momaday's novel *House Made of Dawn* both evidences the persistence of this interweaving of messaging with landscape and acts as a transmitter of its hermeneutics from an Indigenous past that precedes the settler. The novel's protagonist Abel, on a path to spiritual and physical healing, joins the ancient foot race of the dead at Walatowa, triggered by the sunrise over a particular spot in the mountain range. His grandfather has told him, of this earthly "house of the sun," that "They must know it as they knew the shape of their hands, always and by heart ... They must know the long journey of the sun on the black mesa, how it rode in the seasons and the years, and they must live according to the sun appearing, for only then could they reckon where they were, where all things were, in time" – when to plant corn, when to harvest, when to celebrate each part of the community.

> And then the deep hanging rim ran with fire and the sudden cold flare of the dawn struck upon the arc, and the runners sprang away .... He could see the canyon and the mountains and the sky. He could see the rain and the river and the fields beyond. He could see the dark hills at dawn. He was running, and under his breath he began to sing. There was no sound, and he had no voice; he had only the words of a song. And he went running on the rise of the song. *House made of pollen, house made of dawn. Qtsedaba.*[17]

Reading beyond Human Agency

Momaday's novel bears witness not just to histories of cultural and psychic dispossession and the media used to survive them but to the rise of economic inequalities and industrial-social malaise that have been the outcome of the development for which that dispossession was designed. That global economic disparity, paired with an increasing awareness of the disastrous ecological situation human activity has created in the fossil fuel era, has spurred a widespread interest among scholars in other-than-human forms of agency. What are the planet, the atmosphere, the seas, the insects (builders of that house of pollen), even the planets, trying to tell us about the place of the human in the cosmos? What ethics, what forms of care, what ways of telling stories, do these forces, so paradoxically vast yet fragile, communicate to us in their transformations? Since the surge of environmentalism in the 1960s and 1970s, Indigenous intellectuals have been politely reminding scholars of the ancient cognition respecting these matters in Native communities across America and the world. However, philosophizing about the forms of nonhuman agency and the interdependence of the human with them has a long history in non-American cultures, and not just in the East: Lucretius' *primordia*, Hippocrates' airs, waters, and places, and Balaam's ass seeing the angel all helped make possible something like Michael Pollan's vision of a plant-governed Earth in *The Botany of Desire*.[18]

The study of colonial America has a strong tradition of such approaches, because almost everything in the early colonial environment spoke in some way to America's Natives and its newcomers. Indigenous conceptions of the common pot and European notions of divine messaging through wonders induced a sensitivity that overrode media-specific communicative forms and demoted human power in different but equally complex ways. Still, in most cases, historiographical ways of "reading" environmental communication have been oriented toward telling a story about how change in the human world came about. Settler colonists across the Americas reworked the landscape, reducing old-growth forests, digging mines, redirecting rivers, overhunting and overfishing, and draining swamps. These activities altered the potential economies of vast areas and undermined Indigenous lifeways with devastating consequences. Animal husbandry on a vast scale – and in many cases in North America, the leveraging of roaming animals' destruction of Native plantings – changed disease and nutrition cultures, altered traditional land occupancy patterns, and has, over the long term, altered the very chemistry of the atmosphere.[19] The regime of American slavery involved a sociocultural and legal dehumanization of people of African and Indigenous American origins whose effects wrought epochal changes in Europe and Africa and transformed human societies across the Western hemisphere. Climate was imagined by Europeans to be so integral to human cultures that, for centuries, the question of whether the settlement of America would be a boon or a disaster for European bodies was debated – and with the entrenchment of a fossil fuel economy that debate continues under a broader and more ominous dispensation. Gillen D'Arcy

Wood darkly reminds us, in his study of the 1815 explosion of the Indonesian volcano Mount Tambora, of the devastating global effects of a sharp climate transformation that lasted a mere few years: widespread starvation; the acceleration of the Chinese opium trade; a decade of depression following the collapse of the US economy in the Panic of 1819.[20]

Other scholars "reading" colonial environments have taken a different approach, telling their stories from the perspectives of, for example, animals from otters to wolves.[21] Generically a mix of the object (or animal)-narrating it-narratives of the eighteenth century and new narratological approaches to anthropology, such accounts mix an experience of speculative-empathic wrenching away from the human lens with, inevitably, a reflection on the state of human perceptiveness and values. Just as intriguing are approaches to reading the nonhuman that consider the generative potential of setting aside human subjectivity, that great product or marker of modernity, for many scholars, and the nominal engine of the liberal economic era. In a provocative reconceptualization of non-European colonial subjects as what she calls "parahuman," Monique Allewaert claims that the conditions of colonization might be understood as having radically re-constituted the bodies and minds of both colonizers and those they oppressed. Africans had no choice but to "become deeply familiar with the properties of nonhuman animal and plant life" in order to survive in the disease- and heat-ridden, unfamiliar ecology of the colonial Americas.[22] Prominently, the fetish objects used in botanical-cosmological religions like Obeah or Vodou, "far from being wordless or mute, could be conceived as dense interiorities or constellations of force that could store, process, and actualize information and that were also crucial to the production of the collectivities ... through which personhood was articulated."[23] Both interfaces with other bodies and powers and parts of the self, the knotted packets, medicines, and stones of the *nkisi Nkubulu* wove together beings human and other-than-human in an adaptive, collective resistance to colonial denials of individual personhood. In turn, these adaptations, no less than the mosquitoes, parasites, swamps, and sun of the American environment, transformed Europeans' bodies – and their minds, as the shaky dependence upon an ontological differentiation from the colonized and enslaved took hold. Those Africans who embraced the merge with the natural and supernatural worlds "did not simply resist Anglo-European colonialism," Allewaert concludes, "but also undercut its central assumptions about the organization of human and nonhuman forms."[24]

How one approaches reading the environment as an agent in early America matters not merely because of the high stakes of climate change on one hand or the always present risk of political and cultural dehumanization on the other. Just as in the case of the study of Indigenous or African diaspora media forms, or the consideration of sovereignty and agency in landscape analysis, the study of environmental signaling itself inscribes cultures, creates communities, even as it proceeds in a way that sometimes seems to transcend them by looking beyond human concerns. "Perhaps the big project of the nonhuman turn," Jane Bennett speculates, "is to find new techniques, in speech and art and mood, to disclose the participation of nonhumans in 'our' world."[25] In contemplating that formulation, we might, as a caution cast our minds back to the efforts of Indigenous and enslaved people to make their voices heard and their feelings felt during the colonial era – to disclose their participation in 'their' world. It may be that the big project has more to do with understanding how our world, even when we put the phrase in scare quotes, is a persistent colonial fiction, and the degree to which old techniques of speech, art, and mood might still hold liberatory – or healthily self-disciplinary – potential for us in an age in which care of ourselves and care of the planet increasingly seem to merge.

So now: how to read a hole in the ground, or a mountain range, or a tree? The French philosopher Michel Serres wonders if our insistence on meaning itself might stand in the way of a rich engagement both with reading and with the planet. Triggered by a contemplation of the ancient Roman rite of the *mundus cerialis* – in which three times a year a pit at the heart of Rome was opened with the declaration *"mundus patet"* and offerings made to the gods of the earth – he declares:

> The meaning of the living and the non-meaning of things converge in the muteness of the world; this meaning and non-meaning plunge there and come out, the ultimate eddy. *Mundus patet*: through a fissure, through an opening, a fault, a cleft come noises, calls as small as these apertures. I'm listening, attentive, I'm translating, I'm advancing in the scaled-down meaning and science. *Mundus patet*: should the world open greatly, it will launch me into its silence. The totality remains silent.[26]

"He was running and there was no reason to run but the running itself and the land and the dawn appearing," Momaday's narrator says. Serres encourages us to "think like the mountain; to live like the earth on fire, the fire that warms with love and consumes with hate: to think like the elements of a science ... being born in its totality."[27] Serres, like generations of Indigenous thinkers, asks that we orient our decoding of the world to the recognition of the struggle between love and hate at the root of every communication, that we think in terms less of knowledge than of wisdom. The mountains may mean particular things to particular people, the holes in the earth the same. Yet the mountains are also the ancient preservers and cleansers of water; transformers of weather patterns; the refuge for dispossessed people from Araucanian warriors to the maroons of Moore Town to Wampanoag and Nipmuc families fleeing King Philip's War. The beavers of the American northeast changed the course of water and human history; the insects, armadillos, and coyotes spreading across the continent into places new to them and disappearing from others will do the same. Whether that history will be written remains to be seen, as the oceans and mountains draw closer together. The final step in how to read things not written down, then, is, sometimes: don't.

Notes

1. The *khipucamayoc* was an interpreter of the khipu, a record-keeping device made of colored and knotted strings. See Frank Salomon, *The Cord Keepers: Khipus and Cultural Life in a Peruvian Village* (Durham, NC: Duke University Press, 2004) and the concept of *grafismo* in Salomon and Mercedes Niño-Murcia, *The Lettered Mountain: A Peruvian Village's Way with Writing* (Durham, NC: Duke University Press, 2014); Walter Mignolo and Elizabeth Hill Boone, eds., *Writing without Words: Alternative Literacies in Mesoamerica and the Andes* (Durham, NC: Duke University Press, 1994); Keith Basso's notion of "The Ethnography of Writing," in R. Bauman and J. Sherzer, eds., *Explorations in the Ethnography of Speaking* (New York: Cambridge University Press, 1974), 425–432; Joseph Roach, *Cities of the Dead: Circum-Atlantic Performance* (New York: Columbia University Press, 1996); Richard Rath, *How Early America Sounded* (Ithaca, NY: Cornell University Press, 2003); Matt Cohen and Jeffrey Glover, eds., *Colonial Mediascapes: Sensory Worlds of the Early Americas* (Lincoln: University of Nebraska Press, 2014); and the introduction and essays in Alyssa Mt. Pleasant, Caroline Wigginton, and Kelly Wisecup, "*Forum*: Materials and Methods in Native American and Indigenous Studies: Completing the Turn," *William and Mary Quarterly* 75, no. 2 (2018) and *Early American Literature* 53, no. 2 (2018).
2. For work centered on the ways Native American people took up European forms of reading and writing as a means of sustaining or defending themselves or their communities, see among others Lisa Brooks, *The Common Pot: The Recovery of Native Space in the Northeast* (Minneapolis: University of Minnesota Press, 2008) and *Our Beloved Kin: A New History of King Philip's War* (New Haven, CT: Yale University Press, 2018); Christopher Teuton, *Deep Waters: The Textual Continuum in American Indian Literature* (Lincoln: University of Nebraska Press, 2010); Hilary Wyss, *Writing Indians: Literacy, Christianity, and Native Community in Early America* (Amherst: University of Massachusetts Press, 2000); Drew Lopenzina, *Red Ink: Native Americans Picking Up the Pen in the Colonial Period* (Albany, NY: SUNY Press, 2012); and Phillip H. Round, *Removable Type: Histories of the Book in Indian Country, 1663–1880* (Chapel Hill: University of North Carolina Press, 2010).
3. Jussi Parikka, *Insect Media: An Archaeology of Animals and Technology* (Minneapolis: University of Minnesota Press, 2010), xiv.
4. John Durham Peters, *The Marvelous Clouds: Toward a Philosophy of Elemental Media* (Chicago: University of Chicago Press, 2015), 4.

5. Edward Winslow, *Good News from New England by Edward Winslow: A Scholarly Edition*, ed. Kelly Wisecup (Amherst: University of Massachusetts Press, 2014), 111.

6. *Mourt's Relation: A Journal of the Pilgrims at Plymouth*, ed. Dwight Heath (Bedford, MA: Applewood Books, 1963), 27–28.

7. Melissa Jayne Fawcett, *Medicine Trail: The Life and Lessons of Gladys Tantaquidgeon* (Tucson: University of Arizona Press, 2000), 120.

8. For more on burial sites in this region, see Patricia Rubertone, *Grave Undertakings: An Archaeology of Roger Williams and the Narragansett Indians* (Washington, DC: Smithsonian Institution, 2001). For ways of understanding Native symbolic practices relevant to this account, see among others Kathleen J. Bragdon, *Native People of Southern New England, 1500–1650* (Norman: University of Oklahoma Press, 1995); Neal Salisbury, *Manitou and Providence: Indians, Europeans, and the Making of New England, 1500–1643* (New York: Oxford University Press, 1984); Gladys Tantaquidgeon, *Folk Medicine of the Delaware and Related Algonkian Indians* (Harrisburg: Pennsylvania Historical and Museum Commission, 1972); and Fawcett, *Medicine Trail*. On transmedia analyses of basketry and pictographs, see Stephanie Fitzgerald, "The Cultural Work of a Mohegan Painted Basket," in Kristina Bross and Hilary E. Wyss, eds., *Early Native Literacies in New England: A Documentary and Critical Anthology* (Amherst: University of Massachusetts Press, 2008), 51–56; and in the same volume, Heidi Bohaker, "Reading Expressions of Identity on a 1725 Peace and Friendship Treaty," 201–212.

9. McLuhan summarized in Peters, *Marvelous Clouds*, 15; Galen Brokaw, "Indigenous American Polygraphy and the Dialogic Model of Media," *Ethnohistory* 57, no. 1 (2010): 120. See also Martin Leinhard, *La voz y su huella: Escritura y conflicto étnico-social en América Latina, 1492–1988* (Havana City: Casa de las Américas, 1991).

10. Sean P. Harvey, *Native Tongues: Colonialism and Race from Encounter to the Reservation* (Cambridge, MA: Harvard University Press, 2015), 221; Brian Hochman, *Savage Preservation: The Ethnographic Origins of Modern Media Technology* (Minneapolis: University of Minnesota Press, 2014).

11. See Fawcett, *Medicine Trail*, 16, 42.

12. Brooks, *The Common Pot*, 5.

13. Andrew Newman, *On Records: Delaware Indians, Colonists, and the Media of History and Memory* (Lincoln: University of Nebraska Press, 2012), 96.

14. John F. Watson, *Annals of Philadelphia and Pennsylvania*, 3 vols. (Philadelphia: E.S. Stuart, 1891), 1:142 (emphases in original). See the discussions of Watson and of Lenape records of the treaty in Newman, *On Records*, 104–132.

15. Newman, *On Records*, 120.

16. Maureen Konkle, *Writing Indian Nations: Native Intellectuals and the Politics of Historiography* (Chapel Hill: University of North Carolina Press, 2004), 2–3; see also Jean O'Brien, *Dispossession by Degrees: Indian Land and Identity in Natick, Massachusetts, 1650–1790* (New York: Cambridge University Press, 1997); and Christine M. DeLucia, *Memory Lands: King Philip's War and the Place of Violence in the Northeast* (New Haven, CT: Yale University Press, 2018).

17. N. Scott Momaday, *House Made of Dawn* (New York: Harper Perennial, 1977), 177, 191.
18. See the essays in Richard Grusin, ed., *The Nonhuman Turn* (Minneapolis: University of Minnesota Press, 2015), including especially Jane Bennett, "Systems and Things: On Vital Materialism and Object-Oriented Philosophy," 223–239; and Michael Pollan, *The Botany of Desire: A Plant's-Eye View of the World* (New York: Random House, 2001).
19. William Cronon, *Changes in the Land: Indians, Colonists, and the Ecology of New England* (New York: Hill and Wang, 1983); Virginia DeJohn Anderson, *Creatures of Empire: How Domestic Animals Transformed Early America* (New York: Oxford University Press, 2004); see also many colonial histories of natural and man-made commodities, among them Judith Carney and Richard Nicholas Rosomoff, *In the Shadow of Slavery: Africa's Botanical Legacy in the Atlantic World* (Berkeley: University of California Press, 2011); and Molly Warsh, *American Baroque: Pearls and the Nature of Empire, 1492–1700* (Chapel Hill: University of North Carolina Press, 2018).
20. Joyce Chaplin, *Subject Matter: Technology, the Body, and Science on the Anglo-American Frontier, 1500–1676* (Cambridge, MA: Harvard University Press, 2003); Gillen D'Arcy Wood, *Tambora: The Eruption That Changed the World* (Princeton: Princeton University Press, 2015).
21. Jon T. Coleman, *Vicious: Wolves and Men in America* (New Haven, CT: Yale University Press, 2004); James T. Clifford, *Routes: Travel and Translation in the Late Twentieth Century* (Cambridge, MA: Harvard University Press, 1997), 299–348.
22. Monique Allewaert, *Ariel's Ecology: Plantations, Personhood, and Colonialism in the American Tropics* (Minneapolis: University of Minnesota Press, 2013), 7. Allewaert's insights into African diaspora fetishes resonate with and extend the work of Grey Gundaker, *Signs of Diaspora, Diaspora of Signs: Literacies, Creolization, and Vernacular Practice in African America* (New York: Oxford University Press, 1998).
23. Allewaert, *Ariel's Ecology*, 118–119.
24. Ibid., 7.
25. Jane Bennett, "Systems and Things: A Response to Graham Harman and Timothy Morton," *New Literary History* 43, no. 2 (2012): 225–233, 225.
26. Michel Serres, *Biogea*, trans. Randolph Burks (Minneapolis, MN: Univocal, 2012), 198.
27. Ibid., 79.

2

MOLLY FARRELL

How to Read the Natural World

The last time I taught an early American literary history survey, a student came with an idea for a research project. She was interested in atmospheric science and wanted to investigate how early American texts like Cabeza de Vaca's 1542 narrative of captivity *La Relación* register encounters with distinctive hemispheric weather patterns. How do European writers narrate early experiences with hurricanes, for example?

As literary critics, we are generally oriented toward issues of representation rather than empirical reality; or in other words, our scholarship tends to privilege a focus on how stories or images work over any reality that may have existed prior to those depictions. Though by no means the only or best disciplinary skill set for this work, it is an orientation that prepares us well for work in what has come to be known as science studies. Science studies encompasses a variety of forms of critical inquiry into how labor, practices, and knowledge deemed scientific operate within and among individuals, cultures, and societies across time. Work in science studies provocatively asserts that, for example, there is no phenomena of "hurricane" that can exist outside of how that category of storm has been constructed through language, culture, and knowledge systems that exert power in the world. As with everything related to reading the natural world in early American literature, it's utterly inseparable from colonialism and genocidal exploitation. The word itself originates from the Taino "hurakán," or "god of the storm," which circulated in fifteenth-century Spanish as "huracán" before it appeared in English as "hurricane." Today, it denotes a storm with "a wind of force 12 on the Beaufort scale," which even those who know little or nothing about either the Beaufort scale or Taino beliefs can recognize means something decidedly different from its linguistic origins, and which is different too from the "sea-change" that William Shakespeare wrote about in *The Tempest*, a play inspired by the 1609 shipwreck of the *Sea Venture* off Bermuda in a fierce Atlantic storm.[1]

Science studies as an approach requires us to recognize that the tools we use to read the natural world are culturally and historically specific. We can investigate questions about how the pre-Columbian Tainos who encountered a hurakán may have experienced something not only phenomenologically but also *ontologically* different than the 2017 Hurricane Maria – by this I mean their worldview had a distinctive conceptualization of what a storm *is*. Yet when we do this historical work, science studies also requires us to recognize the ways that an atmospheric scientist in Maryland who analyzes wind speed measurements cannot be said to be encountering, through her instruments, the same force of nature that a resident of Puerto Rico or Dominica survived.

Confronting the instability of the sense of "storminess" in the face of storms across time, space, and culture can lead to the kind of anxious dilemma that science studies scholar Bruno Latour recalls facing in *Pandora's Hope*, "Do you believe in reality?"[2] Latour's answer is, unsurprisingly, yes and no. By zeroing in on the verb "believe" in that question, reading the natural world from a science studies perspective requires us to recognize that empirical practices did not, as hoped, relieve us of nonuniversal practices of belief, faith, and trust in hierarchical structures of knowledge and power.

Applying this perspective to early American literature points to the multiplicity of ways that early modern colonialism in the Americas, with all of its violence and exploitation, was a knowledge-producing machine. By that I mean that many of the empirical practices, forms of measurement and categorization, and lines drawn between expertise and folk knowledge that we typically recognize as constituting scientific work were forged either directly in colonial environments or indirectly with and through the knowledge, skills, labor, and resources extracted from enslaved Africans and Indigenous peoples by enslavers and colonial settlers. Contemporary science contains within it a heavy load of forgetting, from the "hurakán" in hurricane to the virological contribution Onesimus, an enslaved African, made to virology by teaching colonial Bostonians about smallpox inoculation; and from the relationship, via the cultivation of medicinal herbs, of enslaved Afro-Caribbean practitioners of Obeah to the founding of the British Museum in London.[3]

Just as goods and people circulated around the Atlantic in the service of imperial wealth, so too did natural "curiosities," or specimens of New World plant and animal life, to be collected and studied by European scientific authorities.[4] The social and political dynamics of these exchanges between colonial and European naturalists are complex and shifting, but they all take place within the context of settler colonialism. Settler colonialism is "a structure rather than an event," characterized by violent dispossession by one invading group over others.[5] Settler colonial societies perpetuate oppression and genocide of Indigenous peoples and develop their own distinctive claims of sovereignty on the same land. This system is distinct from – though it may overlap with – other forms of colonialism, such as extraction colonialism as practiced by enslavers on Caribbean sugar plantations, and neocolonialism, the indirect perpetuation of colonial power dynamics within ostensibly independent nation-states.[6] The idea of *terra nullis*, or the legal justification for colonialism claiming that colonial powers have a right to claim empty or neglected lands, makes it essential for colonial settlers to seek or invent a direct encounter with a natural world that is somehow separate from any encounter with people. The fiction of the direct encounter with unpeopled nature is therefore central to the project of settler colonialism and equally central to the history of science. In this way, seeking the "real," the "pure," or the "natural" in the natural world is itself a settler colonial gesture. It both replicates the attitudes of early colonial naturalists and perpetuates the dispossession of the environment from its historical human relationships.

Given these dimensions, the question remains why we seek knowledge of the colonial natural world in the first place. Why would you want to, for example, identify the modern medical definition of "molar pregnancy" for the "monstrous" birth that excommunicated Anne Hutchinson had after she was convicted of heresy in the 1637–1638 antinomian controversy?[7] Why would you want to determine the contemporary diagnosis of disease from which so many Native Americans suffered and died in the wake of English court mathematician Thomas Harriot's visit to Roanoke, as though (according to Harriot's report of local rumors) the English had shot "invisible bullets"?[8] We do, after all, actually need to know whether Atlantic storms 500 years ago were stronger or not than the storms of today so that we can better understand our contemporary climate crisis. When studying, for example, representations of the yellow fever epidemics in early America, we can go beyond the application of contemporary medical knowledge about the disease as a virus transmitted by mosquitoes and understand how the interpretation of it, instead, as an "effluvia of a pestilential nature," as novelist Charles Brockden Brown describes it in 1799 in *Arthur Mervyn*, related to a particular worldview inflected with colonialism, racism, and economics.[9] This kind of work requires drawing on interdisciplinary collaboration at the same time that it highlights the particular contributions made possible by rigorous critiques of representation. Within science studies more broadly, early American literary scholars investigate the complexity of particular representations of natural phenomena and trace their circulation within or against powerful narratives that organized culture.

Yet when working with the early American archive, literary scholars recognize these efforts as acts of translation from one historically and culturally determined system of knowledge-making to another, rather than a reclamation or unearthing of immutable truth. This casts contemporary scientific understandings of natural phenomena as historically and culturally determined, recognizing the settler colonial work scientific expertise can continue to do in the present and contributing to the project of imagining alternative uses for it. The difference between an approach to reading nature in early American literary texts that is modeled on acts of translation rather than processes of decoding can be subtle, but it's a shift that ultimately opens up rather than closes down the present for simultaneous scrutiny as we interrogate the violent structures of the past.[10]

Reading the natural world in early American literature can assist decolonization work in the present by attending to all of the complex, appropriative, genocidal, pious, impassioned, violent, imaginative, philosophical, and conflicting ways that people understood environmental and bodily phenomena at a time when the frames that constrict our systems of scientific knowledge were being formed. By interrogating and highlighting these frames, we have a better chance at repositioning them to see our contemporary world in less familiar ways.

Peopling Natural History

Reading early American literature often means contending with anachronism or exploring the circulation of ideas before they took on modern forms of nomenclature. How do we understand science before science? The terms colonial Americans would have used for early practices of understanding the natural world would be "natural philosophy," a term dating from the fourteenth century and defined as "the study of natural bodies and the phenomena connected with them," or "natural history," a later term that circulated transatlantically in particularly influential ways in the eighteenth century, denoting "a work dealing with the properties of natural objects, plants, or animals."[11] Discerning the differences between these terms matters less than attending to the way they both integrate the study of nature into the broad scholarly enterprises of philosophical inquiry and historical writing. Reports about the natural world from this period thus can illuminate wide-ranging aspects of the worldview that produced them.

Similarly to how the study of nature was inextricable with other forms of inquiry, early modern Europeans understood their own bodies to be bound up with the properties of their environments. Colonial settlers were influenced by early Galenic theories that understood bodily health through the balance of four humors (blood, yellow bile, black bile, and phlegm) that were inseparable from the "passions" or emotional states, and whose balance could be altered or corrected with changes in climate. This was a conception of self – whether constituted by affects, racial characteristics, or sexuality – that was fundamentally shaped by the surrounding environment and therefore had the potentially to be fundamentally altered through migration.[12] The stakes for understanding the natural world in colonial writing were high, since tracking what American climates and ecologies would do to colonial bodies could potentially touch all aspects of culture.

One of the more interesting projects of early American literary studies has been to denaturalize what colonial European writers had constructed as "natural," and by that I mean to learn from and contribute to Indigenous studies and African American studies in order to better understand the constructedness and historicity of the social environmental worlds that early modern European writers misconstrued for their own idiosyncratic ends. Colonialism helped shape ideas about what it means for worlds to be "natural." John Milton drew upon depictions of the Americas when depicting Eden in his epic poem *Paradise Lost*, and Thomas Hobbes had holdings in colonial Virginia when he was conceiving of notions of natural law.[13] John Locke, another theorist of natural law and natural rights, also had dealings in the English colonies, helping to write a draft of the Constitution of the Carolinas. This connection between politics and ideas about nature helped shape the founding of the United States with Thomas Jefferson, whose only writing published in book form in his lifetime, *Notes on the State of Virginia*, was a work of natural history. Jefferson's *Notes* was written in response to Georges-Louis Leclerc, Comte de Buffon's *Natural History*, which proposed classification schemes for species and promoted a climate-based theory of race and species difference, among other topics. Jefferson drew on his own observations, speculations, and archival research to argue against Buffon's claims that, for example, animal species in North America were smaller than those in Europe. Jefferson was keenly interested in fossils, discussing at length large mammoth remains and what they meant for the possibilities of animal life in the hemisphere.

Moving between entries on topics as diverse as plans for republican education, the prospects for enslavement, and the Virginian geologic landscape, Jefferson's *Notes* exemplifies the high political stakes for empirical interpretation of the natural world.[14] Though at first glance the book may appear to contain relatively uninteresting lists and charts chronicling in meticulous detail the names of Virginian birds or the evidence for rethinking an obscure transatlantic quibble, *Notes* shows Jefferson turning to natural history to determine the future vitality of a newly independent republic.

Demonstrating that Virginian animal species are ample, and that diverse bird species remain unrecorded, was, in Jefferson's view, an essential part of promoting the nation.

Perhaps nowhere was surveillance of the natural environment so bound up with speculation about political futures than in the burgeoning science of colonial population. Then, as now, population discourse was inextricable from debates about climate, resources, inequality, race, and questions about a society's chances for growth or decline. Jefferson's *Notes* is no exception, turning to population data to uphold racist systems of settler colonialism and plantation slavery. Though he himself had mixed-race children with Sally Hemmings, a woman he enslaved, Jefferson describes African American physical characteristics in a way that supports racial hierarchies and warnings that attempting equality in a multiracial society can only end in "extermination of one or the other race."[15] Serving the colonial legal doctrine of *terra nullis*, Jefferson takes time to describe North American Indigenous people's use of birth control measures and abortion (favoring small families) and to compile lists of census data of various tribes compiled by white settlers. Jefferson adopts the posture of empiricism to portray Indigenous people as capable of producing large populations but neglecting to do so, thus refuting any speculation that the climate was less than hospitable to human growth while at the same time bolstering legal arguments for genocidal conquest.

Long before Jefferson's *Notes*, Benjamin Franklin had been researching and speculating about colonial population and its relation to the North American environment. In a 1751 pamphlet, *Observations Concerning the Increase of Mankind*, Franklin argued that the "vacant," plentiful, and healthy natural environment of the English North American colonies provided the purest example of the maximum potential growth of human population, "doubled every 20 Years."[16] By the end of the century, in the 1798 *Essay on the Principle of Population*, Thomas Malthus drew on the data Franklin (by then deceased) had compiled from the colonies to support his own influential arguments about the dire consequences of unrestricted population growth on finite resources anywhere. In this way, a particular observation about a historically distinctive place and time came to play a key role in the development of a scientific principle about the relations between humans and environmental resources.

The reason for this dehistoricization of colonial data goes back to the beginnings of European characterizations of the New World as an Edenic space in which all restrictions – or inclinations – are removed that could potentially inhibit maximum growth. As Milton showed, writers often imagined colonial environments as standing in for this mythical space of perfect fertility. Henry Neville's politically philosophical novella, *Isle of*

Pines, had helped circulate this association in the seventeenth century by telling the story of a small group of shipwreck survivors who populate an entire island with the descendants of a single family. Alongside the development over the course of the eighteenth century of empirical methods of observation, classification, recording, and sharing findings with international scholars, this continued association of the colonial landscape as a kind of pure blank slate for measuring the physical potential of European settler population growth persisted.

The first European known to have attempted to calculate the maximum potential human population of the globe in relation to available land and resources was the sixteenth-century court mathematician Thomas Harriot, who traveled to the first ill-fated English colonial settlement at Roanoke and worked with Croatan leader Manteo and Wanchese from Roanoke to craft an orthography of the Algonquian language. This history shows how developments in technologies of calculation and speculation about the existential relation between humans and our environments developed from and were facilitated by settler colonialism.

Depictions of the natural world in early American literature are often also bound up directly with colonial promotional material. John Smith, who helped establish the first permanent English North American colony at Jamestown, Virginia, wrote in "A Description of New England" that "Here nature and liberty affords us that freely, which in England we want, or it costeth us dearly."[17] Returning to these early moments and placing them in a broader contemporary dialogue offers a much more varied and complex portrayal of the environments that early English settlers encountered. The perceived availability of land that led to Smith establishing Jamestown in that particular location was likely a deliberate choice of the powerful Indigenous Powhatan Confederacy to avoid long-term habitation of a swampland inhospitable to human health or cultivation. Far from the favorable land Smith promoted, Jamestown inflicted chilling mortality rates on all who ventured there, resulting in violently repressed revolts and cannibalism of the English dead by their starving companions. It can be hard to pin down the nature of the natural world that teemed outside Jamestown's walls when we read these early modern accounts, since colonial promoters and settler inhabitants portrayed it variously as an enticing realm of possibility and a gaping mouth of death.

Race and Caribbean Curiosity

The influential natural histories published, like Jefferson's *Notes*, in the first decades of the new US republic, continue to focus on the environment as essential to understanding the social, political, and economic distinctiveness of eastern North America. However, by that time works like William Bartram's *Travels* and J. Hector St. John de Crèvecoeur's *Letters to an American Farmer* do so in narratives that evince as much influence from the genre of novel as from that of natural history. These narrative forms grew up together, and the earliest Caribbean natural histories show that this came about because documents of plant and animal life had been from the start inextricable from documents of the system of enslavement and developing ideas about race.[18]

English travelers publishing expensively detailed works about natural curiosities on Caribbean slave plantations played a pivotal role in the development of natural history in general, not merely in the colonies. In 1657, Richard Ligon published his *True and Exact History of the Island of Barbados*, a work that combines natural history, a handbook for prospective sugar planters, a travel narrative, and an art book. Mid-seventeenth-century plantation owner-enslavers reaped large profits of sugar cultivation from the knowledge, skills, and labor of a combination of enslaved Africans, English indentured servants, and Indigenous people. Not until the end of the century did enslaved Africans make up the majority of people living and working on the island. Barbados was a socially and environmentally volatile place: planters quickly exhausted the soil and inflicted brutal conditions on unfree laborers, who themselves responded by orchestrating major revolts throughout the century. While attempting to narrate this social life and draw up prospective plantation budgets promising huge rates of return, Ligon spent long hours looking at plants. For Ligon, documenting plant life was inextricable from attempting to come to terms with the extraordinary social engineering required to extract the high profits resulting from early Caribbean sugar slavery, as well as with descriptions of aesthetic beauty and erotic desire. As Ligon describes when he documents his calculations of the potential size of a Royal Palmetto, "I believe there is not a more Royall or Magnificent tree growing on the earth, for beauty and largeness, not to be paralell'd," he writes, "but how to set her out in her true shape and colour, without a Pencill, would aske a better Pen then mine; yet I will deliver her dimensions as neer truth as I can, and for her beauty much will arise out of that."[19] Feminizing awe of a tree's beautiful magnificence coincides with epistemological practices like, as Ligon goes on to describe, attempting to calculate the height of a tree by comparing measurements of the diameter of individual specimens: "[A]mongst those that I have seen growing, which I have guest to be two hundred foot high, the bodies of which I measured, and found to be but sixteen inches diameter."[20]

This naturalist posture seamlessly fosters the development of early con-
ceptualizations of race. Ligon's *History* is probably best known not for its
pivotal influence on later developments in the history of science but for its
story of the tragic story of the Indigenous woman Inkle and her fickle English
lover Yarico, which was retold by James Addison and Richard Steele in *The
Spectator* and from there circulated widely and in various forms throughout
the eighteenth century and beyond. Ligon depicts the enslaved African and
Indigenous people that he encounters as exotic subjects for study alongside
the palmetto or pineapple, observing their measurements and comparing his
findings with established European ideas of human proportion from the
artist and aesthetic theorist Albrecht Dürer: "I have been very strict, in
observing the shapes of these people; and for the men, they are very well
timber'd, that is, broad between the shoulders, full breasted, well filleted, and
clean leg'd."[21] For Ligon, promotion of sugar slavery, crafting early modern
racial imaginaries, spinning stories of romantic tragedy, and documenting
nature were inseparable activities.

Works of Caribbean natural history like Ligon's played a crucial role in the
creation of scientific institutions and archives, particularly through the work
of Sir Hans Sloane. Building on Ligon's *History of Barbados*, which reached
publication just after the 1655 English accession of Jamaica, sparking interest in Caribbean investment, Sloane published his *A Voyage to the Islands
Madera, Barbados, Nieves, S Christophers and Jamaica* in 1707. Sloane's
extensive multivolume *Voyage to ... Jamaica* not only was an influential
work of natural history but also helped shape the practice of natural history
itself. Sloane was trained as a medical doctor and catalogued medical practices, as well as the many types of flora used in them, that he encountered
among the Indigenous and enslaved peoples in the Caribbean. He continued
collecting natural specimens long after returning from his travels there,
eventually opening his ever-expanding home to visitors interested in learning
about the different species he had encountered. After playing a prominent
role at the Royal Society throughout its early years, he become president
when Sir Isaac Newton stepped down, thereby helping shape transatlantic
dialogues about what we call today scientific investigation. Upon his death,
he bequeathed his by then enormous collection of natural history to the
British people, on the condition that it be housed in a museum open to all.
This collection thus founded the British Museum, which remains today one
of the most visited sites in London and houses such antiquities of world
historical importance as the Rosetta Stone and the Elgin Marbles, exhibits
that, like Sloane's own original collection of Caribbean flora, bear witness to
British imperial plunder even as they offer insight into their particular
historical moment.

Like Ligon, Sloane was keenly interested in cataloging his encounters with the people whose labor drove the British colonial presence in the Caribbean. His *Voyage to … Jamaica* described how enslaved Africans used various plants in their medical practices but also detailed in encyclopedic fashion the narratives of their lives that they shared with him. Nicole Aljoe has called these "embedded slave narratives" and developed a method of reading them next to one another, disembedded from their original contexts, as a way to allow enslaved African voices to speak through the archive, despite being interpreted and transcribed through Sloane's authorial voice.[22] In this way, we can return to a work of natural history like Ligon's or Sloane's, as well as later early English Caribbean natural histories and medical texts like those by Edward Long, Bryan Edwards, or James Thomson, and see enslaved Africans and Indigenous people as herbalists, medical practitioners, and producers of scientific knowledge. At the same time, we can place that scientific work in the context of what we know about their life stories, their culture, and their role in the Atlantic economy – just as we can similarly place men like Sloane, whose contributions to the development of scientific work cannot be divorced from their participation in slavery and colonial exploitation.

Conflict and Belief

From the founding of modern American literary criticism, Puritan studies was synonymous with early American studies. With their high literacy rates, founding of colleges, and archival preservation, settler colonial Puritans in New England left a body of writing that was readily available to critics interested in examining the origins of American exceptionalism. Today, Puritan studies is as transatlantic as it is Atlantic colonial, and as suffused with studies of secularism and religious practice as it is with science. It also constitutes one key node among many in the network of early American literary studies that critics must see in connection to studies of the Caribbean, early modern Europe, Indigenous nations, and (increasingly) the Pacific Rim. One of the problems with centering the Puritans in early American literature is that it fostered a binary approach to the natural world, one which pitted humans against an environment that needed to be catalogued, harnessed, and conquered. Perry Miller's titular formulation of a unifying seventeenth-century Puritan worldview as an "errand into the wilderness" exemplifies this approach by focusing on the trope of the divine errand taking place within an adversarial colonial environment as it appears across poetry, sermons, and captivity narratives.[23] Yet Miller focuses on shared articulations of the "errand," at the expense of depictions of "wilderness," which can be considerably more varying. What is this wilderness, and to whom?

What some settlers would have depicted as an uncharted wilderness was actually, as Matt Cohen has argued, a complex media network with carefully mapped paths, tree markings, and other communication signals constructed of found materials.[24] Between and across languages and nations, North American Indigenous people mapped, wrote, and read on and through their surroundings. Similarly, modern technologies such as Light Detection and Ranging (LiDAR) combined with Global Positioning Satellite (GPS) data have enabled us to see the ways that Indigenous mound-building societies, such as those that constructed the Serpent Mound in what is today Ohio or the regionally dominant metropolis Cahokia outside what is today St. Louis, used architectural engineering as a form of writing.[25] By reconceiving of mound-building as writing, we can see how these ancient societies communicate information about astronomy, philosophy, and the relationship between science and storytelling, even though, today, scholars still don't know what they called themselves. New technologies also can help tell different stories about known histories, like that of King Philip's War in New England in 1675–1676, as Lisa Brooks and Christine M. DeLucia have shown.[26] Working within a settler colonial archive after centuries of oppression of Indigenous languages and knowledge systems, Native scholars study the precise locations and sizes of hills and rivers to place oral, material, and written histories in dialogue with the geographic traces in which events took place. In this way, the physical geography of the natural world becomes a valuable archive in and of itself, one translated with and through contemporary digital technologies.

Methodologies developed in Indigenous studies are so essential to reading the environment in early American literature especially because of the ways that, as early Puritan studies scholars taught us, New England settler colonial writers used practices of biblical typology to understand natural phenomena they encountered within a closed hermeneutic system. Typological reading practices are ones that seek to locate and interpret repetitions of original biblical types, and so the world was filled with signs from God that rigorous study of the Bible could explain. Indigenous people, enslaved Africans, and New England Puritans alike interpreted natural phenomena through their own distinctive belief systems about supernatural forces. Reading bodies and the environment like texts, Puritan writers like Mary Rowlandson, held for ransom during King Philip's War, attempted to draw meaning from their experiences by observing instantiations of biblical precedents like the story of Job. Equally intriguing are moments when encounters with colonial environments stubbornly refuse to fit into Puritan writers' established ways of understanding the world, as when Mary Rowlandson surprises herself by finding food by which she would have previously been disgusted has become "savory to my taste" or when sworn enemies she elsewhere describes as "devils" become those who "many times refreshed … my feeble carcass."[27] At these moments, Rowlandson simultaneously reevaluates her relationship to her captors, to her food, and to her own body as a "carcass."[28]

Far from being uniform or static, settler colonial Puritans' theologically saturated conception of nature in New England is fascinatingly complex and infused with burgeoning epistemological methods. Scientific and theological inquiry went hand in hand in a variety of shifting ways.[29] We can understand how the Puritans gazed at comets, anomalous bodies, and other wonders with a sense that they were witnessing imminent struggles between divine and malevolent forces without distancing ourselves too much from this worldview, and seeing instead how they navigated the coexistence of religious and scientific debates in ways that we can continue to learn from today.[30] In short, Puritan writing offers a fruitful site for understanding secularism less as a linear process than as a constellation of shifts and reframings of the place of religion as a source of knowledge about nature.

Cotton Mather's scientific career offers a window into the sometimes uneasy coexistence of theological and epistemological discourses. Born in Massachusetts into a family of powerful ministers, Mather wrote *The Wonders of the Invisible World*, a history of the murderous 1692 witchcraft trials in Salem shortly after they had ended. Mather's commitment to identifying and eradicating Satanic forces went hand in hand with his enthusiasm for corresponding with the Royal Society in London, of which he became a member in 1713 after sending them his letters about American curiosities. The Royal Society had been founded the year the English monarchy was restored in 1660 as a place to discuss scientific matters very much apart from the religious wars that had consumed England since the Protestant Reformation.[31] It quickly became a place of metropolitan authorization of knowledge where travelers like Sloane could present their colonial extractions. Mather's inclusion there was more complicated given his colonial education and Puritanical writing style.

Increasingly, science studies in early American literature focuses not solely on relationships between metropole and colony, Royal Society and American naturalists, but instead, or more centrally, on dynamics within and between colonial spheres. Understanding Mather's role in the 1722 smallpox inoculation controversy – for which he ultimately contributed memorably to the Royal Society – shows how fruitful this local focus can be. The controversy over Mather's efforts to inoculate people in the wake of the 1722 smallpox epidemic demonstrates the complexity involved when beliefs about natural phenomena begin to shift.[32] Smallpox was endemic in England, meaning that outbreaks were more or less continuous, and therefore a large proportion of adults had acquired immunity. Anglo-American settler colonists, however, encountered not only an unfamiliar environment of climate, flora, and fauna but also a new epidemiological environment. Lacking the density of London or the ease of travel throughout England, smallpox outbreaks tended to be intense and infrequent. The virus would spread quickly and burn itself out over the course of a season, leaving behind a high death toll and a community of immunized survivors. Over the course of a generation without another widespread epidemic of smallpox, however, large numbers of people would again be vulnerable to another outbreak. This is what happened in 1722, after the last smallpox epidemic had raged in 1702.

As I mentioned at the beginning of the chapter, Onesimus, an African man enslaved by Cotton Mather, shared his history of inoculation and his observations of how he had seen it practiced.[33] When Mather cited Onesimus's medical knowledge in his attempts through print to encourage inoculation, he was likely driven by both a desire to protect New England settlers' health and his, by then, long-standing interest in documenting and sharing transatlantic scientific knowledge. An intense war between printers ensued in Boston as a result of Mather's enthusiasm for spreading the knowledge he had taken from Onesimus. James Franklin, the elder brother of Benjamin, was at one point put in jail for printing intense objections to Mather's inoculation campaign. The sides in the 1722 smallpox inoculation print controversy offer a window into the potential complications involved in confronting and popularizing new ways of thinking about nature, the body, and scientific practice. First, it shows with striking clarity the deep indebtedness of the health of settler colonial societies to the appropriation of not solely the economic labor and skills of kidnapped, trafficked, and unfree people like Onesimus but just as crucially their distinctive scientific and medical knowledge. This was no scientific dialogue or exchange like the ones that Mather practiced by sharing papers among his fellow Royal Society members but rather an act of theft. Understanding this simultaneously places enslaved people at the forefront of the history of virology and modern medicine and makes that theft an origin point as well – requiring us to similarly attend to issues of equity, access, racial disparities, labor, and economic justice when we consider advances in public health, medicine, or science in the present.

The print controversy around smallpox inoculation also crystalizes the historically idiosyncratic alignments of theocracy and epistemology working in settler colonial New England. Although Mather was advocating for the adoption of what we now see as a crucial precursor to the safer and more reliable practice of vaccination (using not the smallpox virus but cowpox, which produces the antibodies required for smallpox immunity without being infectious in humans) developed by Edward Jenner in 1796, his critics arguing *against* inoculation were the ones advocating for epistemological methods we would now recognize as scientific. From his position of political and religious power and his determination of its theological appropriateness, Mather attempted to enforce the adoption of inoculation and used his control over the Boston *News-Letter*, the print newspaper, to do it. Yet objections raised in Franklin's comparatively new and decidedly less authorized paper pointed to problems in *how* inoculation was being practiced and to a lack of sufficient data available with regard to its efficacy. Because patients were being infected with a live virus and were therefore contagious until they developed immunity, they needed to be quarantined for a short period after inoculation or else risk spreading the virus to others. Also, even though practitioners like Onesimus had reported that inoculation tended to result in a less severe case of smallpox than one that would be contracted without it, no one in Boston had actually taken the time to compile anything like statistics on this. There were also multiple inoculation practitioners operating with different methods, so it was hard for Bostonians to discern which were safer without any kind of reliable scrutiny. In short, the critiques of adopting a new public health practice and an advanced understanding of the relationship between humans and viruses were actually the voices in the debate arguing for the kinds of methodologies of testing, recording, and comparing outcomes that define modern scientific practice.

Adding another layer of complexity were questions that persisted about the theological implications of meddling in healing practices. Were there not clear biblical precedents for pestilence being a sign from God about the spiritual health of a community? Was not the practice derived from Africans like Onesimus, and thereby itself potentially heretical? Does it not spite God's beneficence to deliberately cut open a healthy body and make it sick? Are not our souls more important than attempting artificially to lengthen our lives here on earth? As James Franklin's imprisonment and the trouble with his newspaper, the *New England Courant*, show, the ability of colonial readers to contemplate and adopt new scientific knowledge depended crucially on the safety and reliability of access to sustained public debate, especially in print. This shows how essential media technologies are to the development of that knowledge; far from being a vehicle, they fuel it, shape it, and make it possible. Any time we attempt to read the natural world in early American literature, we are always already wrestling with the power dynamics and technologies of communication. Thankfully, discourse analysis, book history, generic conventions, and scrutiny of representation are precisely the skill sets that literary critics have to offer this inherently interdisciplinary work, whether we identify it as science studies, health humanities, environmental humanities, or a theoretical framework that the student interested in early modern hurricane reports will soon adopt or invent.

Notes

1. See Monique Allewaert, *Ariel's Ecology: Plantations, Personhood, and Colonialism in the American Tropics* (Minneapolis: University of Minnesota Press, 2013).
2. See Bruno Latour, *Pandora's Hope: Essays on the Reality of Science Studies* (Cambridge, MA: Harvard University Press, 1999).
3. See Ralph Bauer, *The Cultural Geography of Colonial American Literatures: Empire, Travel, Modernity* (Cambridge: Cambridge University Press, 2003); Kelly Wisecup, "Science and the Atlantic World in Early American Literary Studies," *Literature Compass* 9, no. 2 (2012): 129–139; and Britt Rusert, "Plantation Ecologies: The Experimental Plantation in and against James Grainger's *The Sugar-Cane*," *Early American Studies* 13, no. 2 (2015): 341–373.
4. See Susan Scott Parrish, *American Curiosity: Cultures of Natural History in the Colonial British Atlantic World* (Chapel Hill: University of North Carolina Press, 2006).
5. Wolfe, Patrick, "Settler Colonialism and the Elimination of the Native," *Journal of Genocide Research* 8, no. 4(2006): 390.
6. See D. Clayton, "Colonialism," in D. Gregory, ed., *The Dictionary of Human Geography* (Oxford: Blackwell Publishers, 2009); and David Kazanjian, "Colonial," in Bruce Burgett and Glenn Hendler, eds., *Keywords for American Cultural Studies* (New York: New York University Press, 2014).
7. See Jonathan Beecher Field, "Our Antinomians, Ourselves: Or, Anne Hutchinson's Monstrous Birth & The Pathologies of Obstetrics," *Commonplace* 11, no. 2 (2001), http://commonplace.online/article/antinomians-anne-hutchinsons-monstrous-birth-pathologies-obstetrics/.
8. Thomas Harriot, *A Briefe and True Report of the New Found Land of Virginia* (Frankfurt, 1590), 29.
9. Charles Brockden Brown, *Arthur Mervyn, or Memories of the Year 1793*, ed. Philip Barnard and Stephen Shapiro (Indianapolis: Hackett, 2008), 127. See Cristobal Silva, *Miraculous Plagues: An Epidemiology of New England Narrative* (New York: Oxford University Press, 2011); Sari Altschuler, *The Medical Imagination: Literature and Health in the Early United States* (Philadelphia: University of Pennsylvania Press, 2018); and Kyla Schuller, *The Biopolitics of Feeling: Race, Sex, and Science in the Nineteenth Century* (Durham, NC: Duke University Press, 2018).
10. See Anna Brickhouse, *The Unsettlement of America: Translation, Interpretation and the Story of Don Luis de Velasco, 1560–1945* (New York: Oxford University Press, 2015).
11. "natural philosophy, n.," *OED Online* (Oxford University Press), www.oed.com/view/Entry/235692.

12. See Greta LaFleur, *The Natural History of Sexuality in Early America* (Baltimore: Johns Hopkins University Press, 2018).

13. See David Armitage, "Three Concepts of Atlantic History," in David Armitage and Michael J. Braddick, eds., *The British Atlantic World, 1500–1800* (Basingstoke: Palgrave Macmillan, 2002).

14. See Timothy Sweet, *American Georgics: Economy and Environment in American Literature, 1580–1864* (Philadelphia: University of Pennsylvania Press, 2002).

15. Thomas Jefferson, *Notes on the State of Virginia*, ed. Frank Shuffelton (New York: Penguin, [1785] 1999), 145.

16. Benjamin Franklin, "Observations Concerning the Increase of Mankind," in *Franklin: Writings*, ed. J. A. Leo Lemay (New York: Library of America, 1987), 370, 369.

17. John Smith, "A Description of New England," in Robert S. Levine, Michael A. Elliot, Sandra Gustafson, Amy Hungerford, and Mary Loeffelholz, eds., *Norton Anthology of American Literature*, 9th ed. (New York: Norton, 2017), 124.

18. See Christopher P. Iannini, *Fatal Revolutions: Natural History, West Indian Slavery, and the Routes of American Literature* (Chapel Hill: University of North Carolina Press, 2012).

19. Richard Ligon, *A True and Exact History of the Island of Barbados* (London: Humphrey Moseley, 1657), 75.

20. Ibid., 77.

21. Ibid., 51. See Jennifer L. Morgan, *Laboring Women: Reproduction and Gender in New World Slavery* (Philadelphia: University of Pennsylvania Press, 2004).

22. See Nicole N. Aljoe, *Creole Testimonies: Slave Narratives from the British West Indies, 1709–1838* (New York: Palgrave Macmillan, 2012).

23. See Perry Miller, *Errand into the Wilderness*(Cambridge, MA: Harvard University Press, 1956).

24. Matt Cohen, *The Networked Wilderness: Communicating in Early New England* (Minneapolis: University of Minnesota Press, 2009).

25. See Chadwick Allen, "Serpentine Figures, Sinuous Relations: Thematic Geometry in Allison Hedge Coke's Blood Run," *American Literature* 82, no. 4 (2010): 807–834.

26. See Lisa Brooks, *Our Beloved Kin: A New History of King Philip's War* (New Haven, CT: Yale University Press, 2018); and Christine M. DeLucia, *Memory Lands: King Philip's War and the Place of Violence in the Northeast* (New Haven, CT: Yale University Press, 2018).

27. Mary Rowlandson, *The Sovereignty and Goodness of God* (New York: Bedford/ St. Martins, 1997), 78.

28. See Jordan Alexander Stein, "Mary Rowlandson's Hunger and the Historiography of Sexuality," *American Literature* 81, no. 3 (2009): 469–495.

29. See Sarah Rivett, *The Science of the Soul in Colonial New England* (Chapel Hill: University of North Carolina Press, 2011).

30. See David D. Hall, *Worlds of Wonder, Days of Judgment: Popular Religious Belief in Early New England* (New York: Knopf, 1989).

31. See Mary Poovey, *A History of the Modern Fact: Problems of Knowledge in the Sciences of Wealth and Society* (Chicago: University of Chicago Press, 1998).
32. This discussion of the controversy is drawn largely from Carla Mulford, "Pox and 'Hell-Fire': Boston's Smallpox Controversy, the New Science, and Early Modern Liberalism," in Mark L. Kamrath and Sharon M. Harris, eds., *Periodical Literature in Eighteenth-Century America* (Knoxville: University of Tennessee Press, 2005); and Silva, *Miraculous Plagues*.
33. See Kelly Wisecup, *Medical Encounters: Knowledge and Identity in Early American Literatures* (Amherst: University of Massachusetts Press, 2013).

3

AMY M. E. MORRIS

How to Read Early American Poetry

Reading a poem for the first time is a bit like meeting a new person: we look and listen for a minute to form an initial impression and then we make a quick decision about whether or not to pursue the acquaintance any further. The problem with this approach for many early American poems is that their style can be so out of fashion and their point of view so far removed from our own that we may be inclined to turn away before we really get to know them. The purpose of this chapter is to equip a reader new to early American verse with a set of critical questions and interpretive tools in order to get the conversation over those initial hurdles. Through a series of examples, we will explore several different genres, in a variety of regional and temporal contexts. The assumption underlying this chapter is that the more unfamiliar a poem appears, the greater is its potential for revelation: if a poem's appeal or design is not self-evident, then studying it will open up new insights.

Writing Context, Purpose, and Genre

Many of us encounter our first early American poetry in an anthology. Although anthologies and modern editions can be excellent and can supply informative notes, they inevitably transplant poems into an alien context. A number of poets, including Anne Bradstreet, Philip Freneau, Phillis Wheatley, and John Trumbull, had book-length collections of their verse published, but many early American poems were circulated in other formats and sometimes not at all. Edward Taylor kept his poetry in manuscript, preserved in a handbound volume; Annis Boudinot Stockton shared hers with family and friends; and Phillis Wheatley's first print publications were broadside funeral elegies. During the Revolution, a lot of political verse appeared in newsprint, and throughout the period, songs and hymns were composed to be sung. Theatrical prologues, though sometimes printed, were performed onstage. The variety of contexts in which poems were written and

49

read is obscured by the homogeneous format of a modern edition or anthology. So, a good way to start thinking about any early American poem is to envision the situation for which it was originally written. What kind of reader did it envisage? What sort of "cultural work" did it do?[1]

Allied to the question of a poem's purpose is that of its genre or mode. For early American writers in English, poetry encompassed different kinds of verses that suited different purposes: an elegy differed from an epigram and an eclogue, a rhapsody was usually not a parody, and a devotional poem was not quite the same thing as a hymn. Within and across these different classes of poetry, verse form could imply further connections: a lyric poem in tetrameter quatrains might sound hymnlike without being a hymn, heroic couplets might help convey grandeur, a lolloping rhythm could help make a parody sound daft. Since the connotations of verse forms, genres, and modes are suggestive, however, rather than prescriptive, a critical analysis should consider how a poem adapts such "family traits" to its own purposes. In addition, a poet's choice of genre was guided by the literary fashion of the time, so it is helpful to be aware of developments in poetic taste that occurred between the early seventeenth century and the end of the eighteenth. An acrostic poem, or a "metaphysical"-style religious lyric, would have seemed baroque and old-fashioned to an urbane eighteenth-century reader, for instance, who would have esteemed more highly a neoclassical ode, or a poem with a pastoral setting, or georgic verse concerned with the effort to cultivate nature.

Since the colonial book market was dominated by British imports, colonial literary fashions roughly followed those of the metropolis. Transatlantic influences intersected, however, with regional cultures and American politics in the colonies. Much of the English poetry that survives from seventeenth-century America, for instance, is devotional, didactic, or narrative, largely because so much of it came from New England. Unlike Virginia, the New England colonies were founded with the goal of setting up an exemplary Protestant society, and this resulted in poetry that taught or defended Puritanism (or, like Thomas Morton's and Roger Williams's, attacked it). Eighteenth-century American poetry, on the other hand, was written in a variety of genres. Skill at writing in different modes, including off-the-cuff versification, became a demonstration of polished civility. Yet exchanging verses also served as a means for educated people, especially women, to maintain social ties across the geographic separations that were frequently experienced in the sparsely settled colonies. While hymns and devotional verses were still written, and not only in New England, much eighteenth-century poetry was concerned with social life. Even the most common of poetic modes, the funeral elegy, came to express not only religious belief but also the neoclassical aesthetics of smoothness, decorum, and rationality. The development of a sage, often anonymous, voice in public verse reflected the refined sociability of club and coterie culture that Anglo-America shared with Western Europe.[2] In America, however, this poetic voice and style contributed to the fraternalistic discourse that fostered resistance, republicanism, and eventually revolution. During the years of crisis, colonial poems espoused political ends: opposing views were skewered with satire and parody, while conventional verse forms and familiar genres were deployed to present political views as wise and measured.

There are traits that recur in early American poems, such as a sense of providential mission, envisioning the land in Edenic terms, and a suspicion of luxury or self-indulgence that applies to poetry. There is an intriguing convergence, for example, between Cotton Mather's Puritanical caution to seminarians to "Beware of a *Boundless* and *Sickly* Appetite, for the Reading of the *Poems*, which now the *Rickety* Nation swarms withal" and Richard Lewis's secular observation about the demands of colonial life that "'*To raise the Genius*', WE no Time can spare, / A *bare Subsistence* claims our utmost Care."[3] Yet both comments also confirm the presence of opposite forces: Mather's of a widespread fondness for poetry in New England (which earlier in the passage he had seemed to share) and Lewis's of his own efforts to cultivate art by publishing his poetic translation and dedicating it to the governor of Maryland. Such complexities risk getting lost if the priority is to create a narrative about typical traits or the continuity of American poetry up to modern times.[4]

As the term suggests, "early American poetry" is a back-formation, a literary category that developed from the pursuit of the origins of US literature. Retrospective reading has its place in poetic tradition: Adrienne Rich saw a feminist forebear in Anne Bradstreet, and Robert Hass appreciated Edward Taylor as an "early instance of the solitariness, self-sufficiency, and peculiarity of the American imagination."[5] By throwing wobbly bridges over the gulf of time, modern poets open up prior work to a new generation and convey its magnetic pull. However, studying American poetry of the seventeenth and eighteenth centuries primarily as a primitive phase of US literature has a distorting effect. It involves, for instance, the selection and interpretation of texts and traits on the basis of current preoccupations. It also downplays lateral connections between colonial-era writers and the literatures and cultures of other nations, as well as edits out the voices of those whose communities and languages were submerged by the formation of the modern United States. With the recent turn toward transnational and global perspectives in literary studies, the diversity that characterized early American culture now appears less like prequel to be summarized and more like a fascinating mess to unpick. Much recent scholarship, therefore, considers early American poetry in its own right and remains open to its multiplicity.

Early American poetry in English was a fragmentary, diasporic literature. It coexisted with Indigenous oral literature and settler poetry in other languages. Anglophone settler colonialism in North America involved the simultaneous subordination of Indigenous voices and the assertion of a dominant culture whose center was overseas. Elite culture therefore remained Anglocentric in spirit long beyond the Revolution and failed to make reciprocal connections with Indigenous culture. That said, recent research shows that colonists absorbed more Indigenous poetics than they realized.[6] Ethnic and racial dynamics are fascinating though painful to pursue in early American writing. Poetry was fully implicated in colonialism: the genres of pastoral and georgic contributed to the myth of the land as an agricultural idyll, devoid of prior inhabitants. Poetry's elegiac mode (as in Freneau's "The Dying Indian") helped naturalize the political processes by which Indigenous people were removed. Yet certain nonwhite authors, including Samson Occom and Phillis Wheatley, mastered the genres of the English-speaking elite. They created hybrid, layered voices that half-expressed, half-hid their marginalized perspectives.

In outlining the genres, purposes, and contexts of early American poetry, I have traveled some way from the question I began with: What sort of cultural work did a given poem do? Let us take a look at how this question might organize an interpretation. We will consider a range of examples, including didactic religious verse, a gift poem, private and public funeral elegies, and some parodic newsprint verse. This sampling is far from representative, but it will illustrate different kinds of analysis, as we assemble a toolkit of approaches.

Poetry in People's Hands

There is a long tradition of popular poetry in early America. The first full-length book printed in English was a new metrical psalter that claimed to be "faithfully translated from the Hebrew" and was printed in Cambridge, Massachusetts, in 1640 for use as a songbook in the churches of the Bay Colony. Its preface contains the defense that "Gods altar needs not our pollishings." The reference is to Jehovah's command in Exodus 20 (immediately preceding the Ten Commandments) that a rough-hewn altar be built for his worship. It defended the psalter's ungainly verse that resulted largely from translators' efforts to tuck the King James Bible's prose into tetrameter and trimeter quatrains:

> The statutes of the Lord,
>   are right, & glad the heart:
> The Lords commandement is pure,
>   Light doth to eyes impart.[7]

The verse style communicated its own devotional message: that disciplined obedience to God's rules, complemented with the heartwork of singing, was better than literary elegance. That this attitude did not satisfy everyone is clear from the fact that the psalter was rewritten in 1651, partly to improve its poetry.[8] Yet the potential conflict between spiritual and worldly goals expressed in the 1640 preface is instructive not only for what it implies about Puritan poetry but as a reminder about the potential limitations of literary criticism. If we focus on the "pollishings," we may discover much about a poem and yet miss its main point. For popular poetry especially, criticism needs to take into account a text's social role and purpose, in addition to its literary qualities, to create a fuller picture of its contribution.

Take, for example, the work of Michael Wigglesworth, author of two popular works of poetry: *The Day of Doom* (1662), a narrative poem about the Last Judgment; and *Meat Out of the Eater* (1670), a book of consolatory verse named for Samson's riddle about finding honey inside a lion in Judges 14. Wigglesworth's verse is often overlooked in favor of the poems of fellow Puritans Anne Bradstreet and Edward Taylor, which are richer in evocativeness and design and offer more to analyze through techniques of close reading. Yet turns in recent scholarship toward the material text, and toward the historical reconstruction of the reading experience, have opened up new approaches to popular and didactic verse. Figure 3.1 presents a page spread from the 1670 edition of *Meat Out of the Eater*.

Notice the layout with stanza numbers and section dividers but no ornament. The serious, organized format of the pages matches Wigglesworth's writing style. Stanza 8 of the preceding poem instructs the reader about what to expect: "Come, poor distressed Souls," and "Learn how you may with Spiritual Arms / Temptations force repress." It clarifies how they should interpret the dialogue: "Hear what the Flesh suggests / For your discouragement: / Learn what the Spirit may reply / Soul-sinkings to prevent." "Song II" proceeds in straightforward questions and answers, given in a logical, plain style. As the page header reminds us, we are reading a section subtitled "Light in Darkness," one of a list of Christian paradoxes that structures the book. The page layout conveys the idea that, although Puritan belief centers on divine mystery, an individual's spiritual problems can be anticipated, parsed, and tackled in a logical, organized way.

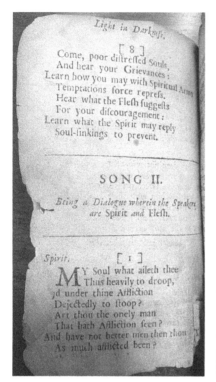
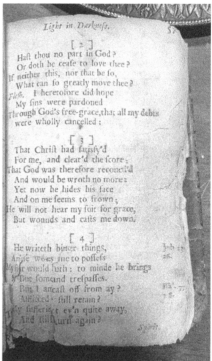

Figure 3.1 Michael Wigglesworth, *Meat out of the Eater: or, Meditations concerning the necessity, end, and usefulness of afflictions unto Gods children* (Cambridge, MA, 1670), 56–57. Courtesy of the John Carter Brown Library.

With its small size and use of quatrains organized into octets, Wigglesworth's book establishes aural and visual connections to the 1651 New England Psalter. The 6686 syllable verse form of "Song II" (sometimes called "short meter") was borrowed from the metrical psalter. Thematically and metrically, the overlap was such that Wigglesworth even incorporated twenty lines from Psalms 49 and 130 in "Song IX" of "Light in Darkness." Through this textual affinity, Wigglesworth authorized his use of lyric subjectivity and religious affect. Moreover, the link with congregational singing underscored the poems' message that, although spiritual problems could feel isolating, they were experiences that belonged more broadly to the life of the faith community.

The colonial print context of Wigglesworth's poetry book gives further clues about his priorities and expectations. In the seventeenth century, the colonial press was in its infancy. Most English books sold and read in America were imported.[9] Books like Wigglesworth's that were published locally had to be tolerant of the relatively inferior print quality and tended to have no designs upon the transatlantic market. During the eighteenth century, print culture in the urban centers began to flourish and contributed to the formation of a colonial public sphere; but in the first century of settlement, printing was rough and ready and served practical local purposes, such as producing laws, almanacs, and proclamations. By publishing a pocket-sized book, in plain but serviceable local print, Wigglesworth was making his poems available as a resource for New England colonists, extending his reach as a local Puritan pastor but not aiming to participate in transatlantic poetic culture.

Judging by the mode of address, Wigglesworth's desired reader was a dejected, struggling believer, and the poetry's task was spiritual coaching. Like much early American verse, this is poetry that does not present itself as an art object but as something functional, in this case a training tool. By supplying words of doubt – "now [God] hides his face / And on me seems to frown;" – the "song" normalizes such thoughts as a common aspect of religious experience and then guides the reader through a mental rescripting process. So did this poetry do its job? There is evidence in the marks made on the books by readers' hands. Although the book was published in five editions between 1670 and 1717, extant copies are rare and Figure 3.1 suggests why. The pages are worn away where they were held open – the book was breaking down from use. Many copies contain inscriptions. One indicates that a husband and wife read the book together, others show that the book was passed between friends and relatives and some express approbation: "Moses Stickney Hath Read this Book and highly he astemeth it."[10] Such marks convey the success of Wigglesworth's poetry in its own time and enable the critic to envisage the rituals of devotional reading that Matthew Brown has characterized as "eye piety" and "hand piety."[11] With its organized layout, *Meat Out of the Eater* made itself available for "pilgrim reading" (front to back) or "bee-reading" (dipping), as the reader could find the sections that spoke most to his or her situation. Sometimes what is strange about a popular-style early American poem is its utter straightforwardness. Wigglesworth's didactic, sing-song verse is verbally unadventurous and aesthetically far removed from what counts as "good" in modern poetry. Approaching such verse through the lens of its purpose and the response of its early readers can vividly restore a sense of its lost power.

Tracing the reception and use of a poem is a complex task, but editions and anthologies supply useful facts, such as whether a poem was preserved in manuscript, circulated, or published and, if so, where. Was the format small and cheap, like Wigglesworth's? Or more lavish, like Trumbull's *M'Fingal* (New York, 1795), Anglo-America's first illustrated poetry book?[12] Such information is suggestive of the envisaged destination of the book – not just the imagined reader but the imagined bookshelf, table, or pocket to which such a book would belong. Thanks to institutional access to online digitized collections (*Early English Books Online* and *Eighteenth-Century Collections Online*), it is possible for many of us to view the page format of early American texts. While bearing in mind that a single digitized copy might not be representative, we can observe the book's condition – does it show signs of avid use or of careful preservation? The ideal companion to supplement online resources is Stoddard and Whitesell's bibliographic catalogue of early American poetry, a mine of information about published poetry (including pamphlets) that records physical characteristics, print statistics, and marginalia.[13]

Poetry in Time

Although the term "early American literature" could imply a perspective that is angled prophetically toward the modern era, poems from this period often had quite a local sense of time. Occasional poetry was the dominant verse genre throughout the colonial period. Now that these events are long past, what critical angles can help us engage with the verse they inspired? Analysis of a poem's cultural work, using its material text, publication history, and reception remains a useful approach. Additionally, one can examine the ways in which the poem moved between the particular and the general. What kinds of extrapolations and interpretations, and what kinds of verse forms and images, were used to produce the commemorative text? Finally, consider occasionality itself: Might the poem have something to say about the significance of the particular?[14]

In some occasional verse, the commemorated events are private or subjective such as Edward Taylor's manuscript poem about observing "a Wasp Chil[le]d with Cold." Using poetry, Taylor turned an ephemeral experience into a divine appointment, as the wasp's recovering its strength in the warmth of the sun becomes an allegory of the soul's dependence on God.[15] A similar back-and-forth movement between experiential particulars and a doctrinal framework occurs in Anne Bradstreet's verses on the burning of her house, which lament her loss but also redirect her thoughts: "The world no longer let me Love / My hope, and Treasure lyes Above."[16] Years later, Richard Lewis wrote "A Journey from Patapsco to Annapolis," beginning with a georgic account of Maryland's fertile landscape and ending in religious meditation.[17] In such poems, poetry helps transform an experience in time into a text with resounding, shareable meaning.

While some poets focused on the relationship between the earthly and the divine, many, especially in the eighteenth century, celebrated horizontal affiliations. Take, for instance, the lines that Annis Boudinot Stockton composed in about 1793 to send with a gift to a child:

> Enclos'd My Dears the promised glass
> Which will reflect your lov'ly face
> And when you'r good, will show most fair
> But if you'r naughty come not there[.][18]

The poem opens with its epistolary purpose ("Enclos'd . . ."), and the ensuing verses giftwrap the mirror in associations. The mirror is to cultivate the child's love of virtue through teaching her to admire her face when she is good. By magic, it will enable the speaker, when she visits, to check the child's progress and reward her:

> And when I come the little glass
> Will shew me all things as they pass
> And I will tell the fairy queen
> Who dances on the newshorn green
> And oft by moon light may be seen
> That she may bring you nuts and flowers
> And every good thing shall be yours.

The sing-song tetrameter and fairy imagery show the author's understanding of the world of the nursery. Although odes to George Washington might seem more determinedly "early American" in theme, Stockton's poem illustrates the role poetry could play in everyday social exchanges. The poem is as trivial as a home-made greetings card, and as precious.

In charge of their homes but excluded from professions and public political roles, upper-class eighteenth-century women like Stockton were less able than their male relatives to maintain their social ties by frequent travel. Epistolary exchange kept their intellectual and friendship networks alive. A gift in itself, Boudinot's poem celebrates relationship: it offers and, through its transmission, fulfills an affectionate promise and, by addressing the child, offers friendship to the mother by joining in her nurturing efforts. As an item that transmits an image across space, a mirror is an apt token of remembrance, and the charmlike poem functions as a talisman of affection. We know, however, that this poem was not so particularized that it couldn't be recycled. Like many of Stockton's poems, it enacted friendship by circulating beyond the bounds of its original context. Besides Stockton's manuscript copy, there is another in the notebook of her friend, Elizabeth Graeme Fergusson, and it addresses a "Betsy" not a "Nancy." Collected like this, the poem has become a memento of Stockton's skill, as Fergusson's appended note in praise of her poetry confirms. A well-known poet in her circle, Stockton wrote in many genres, including pastoral, satire, and impromptus. Writing poetry was a performance of wit and polish that could mark a social occasion in real time and then circulate socially on the poet's behalf.

Stockton expected her poems to be read aloud, copied, sent on, and sometimes published (anonymously) by a male relative. Neither fully private nor fully public, this mode of circulation has been called "relational publication."[19] Although many of the participants in eighteenth-century epistolary coteries were women, other literary coteries existed for men, such as the Tuesday Club of Annapolis. These clubs for the male colonial elite produced different kinds of verse, including satires and virtuoso silliness, but still with an emphasis on the social function. In approaching coterie verse, then, consider how it embodies friendship or enacts membership within a privileged, semi-exclusive circle of readers. Although this kind of verse was semi-private, its urbane civility contributed to the patriotic fraternalism found in newsprint and broadside verse.

Death in Poetry

Verse responded to a wide variety of public events, including the arrival of a new governor, the enforcement of the Stamp Act, theatrical performances, and college commencements. If, however, occasional verse was the commonest kind of verse in early America, the predominant subgenre was the funeral elegy. Coming as we do after Romanticism and Modernism, we tend to expect poetry to be original and unorthodox, to defamiliarize what we know and return it to us in a strikingly new way. For early Anglo-Americans, though, poetry was often relied upon for the opposite reason: because it reiterated conventional wisdom. As the verbal incarnation of tradition, poetry offered continuity after disruptive events like death or the violence of warfare. The earliest extant poem by an African American, Lucy Terry's "Bars Fight," for instance, is a litany of settlers killed in a Native American raid in 1746.[20] Nathaniel Morton's *New-Englands Memoriall* (Cambridge, MA, 1669), the earliest published history of the colony, is peppered with funeral elegies for migrant-generation ministers. Like other occasional poems, funeral elegies could accommodate various features, including allegory and political persuasion, but eulogy and consolation were keynotes. Some elegies commemorated public figures, others lives lived in private, including women and children.

Private elegies provide an opportunity to explore the ways in which poetry functioned to console an intimate loss. For many writers, the consolation was religious, but the poetic techniques used to shape the link between bereavement and theology differ. To illustrate contrasting approaches, one can compare Anne Bradstreet's elegy on her infant grandchild Simon Bradstreet with minister John Wilson's elegy on Abigail Tompson, the wife of a colleague. Bradstreet's elegies on her grandchildren (together with Edward Taylor's "Upon Wedlock and the Death of Children") are among the most moving pieces of verse that have come down to us from early America. The topic elicits sympathy, but the power of these texts lies in their use of poetic technique to create tension. Here is Bradstreet's elegy:

> No sooner come, but gone, and fal'n asleep,
> Acquaintance short, yet parting caus'd us weep,
> Three flours, two scarcely blown, the last i'th' bud,
> Cropt by th' Almighties hand; yet is he good,
> With dreadful awe before him let's be mute,
> Such was his will, but why, let's not dispute,
> With humble hearts and mouths put in the dust,
> Let's say he's merciful, as well as just,
> He will return, and make up all our losses,
> And smile again, after our bitter crosses.
> Go pretty babe, go rest with Sisters twain
> Among the blest in endless joyes remain.[21]

More than any other early seventeenth-century American writer, Bradstreet was steeped in the culture of courtly English poetry. She wrote elegant stylized elegies on Philip Sidney and Edmund Spenser that were published in her book, *The Tenth Muse, Lately Sprung Up in America*, which her brother-in-law had printed on a visit to London in 1650. Although the manuscripts from Bradstreet's later years contain no more courtly verse, poems like "As weary pilgrim" and "Upon the burning of our house," as well as the elegies on her grandchildren continue to show skilled manipulation of imagery and verse form. Even her plain style poetry is highly susceptible to close reading and explication.

Bradstreet's elegy on her grandson is written in neat, end-stopped pentameter couplets, but its syntax has been designed to emphasize disruption. She generates a feeling of effortful containment by repeatedly fracturing lines into opposing parts: "No sooner come, but gone"; "Acquantaince short, yet ..."; "Such was his will, but why ..."; "smile again, after our bitter crosses." Juxtaposing contrasting phrases and perspectives builds the pain of brokenness into the poem. Diction adds to the effect, with ambiguously double-pointed words and phrases: "let's say he's merciful" – does "let's" imply doubt, a feeling of obligation, or a positive, heartfelt urging? "Yet is he good" – is this a buried question? Does "yet" signify opposition between "cropping" the child's life and being "good" or does it affirm God's continuing goodness? The intensity of this poem is produced by techniques that exploit and contain verbal polysemy within the concentrated form of a brief lyric. Although the elegy resolves through a series of logical turns into a hopeful vision of heavenly bliss, the twisted complexity of the path acknowledges the pain en route. To some critics, this poem conveys rebelliousness. To others, Bradstreet's poetic acknowledgment of the struggle to keep faith makes her resolution more convincing. What do you think?

Where Bradstreet and Taylor wrote sophisticated elegies that make a New Critical approach fulfilling, some of their New England colleagues did not. Yet, in such cases, techniques of close reading can be adapted and combined with contextual study to examine what happens when a pedestrian style is put to the task of consolation. John Wilson's elegy on Abigail Tompson, written to announce her death to her husband who was away in Virginia, begins with an anagram on her name: "i am gon to all bliss." Anagrams were common in Puritan funeral elegies and foregrounded the idea that religious truth was hidden in plain sight. Ventriloquizing the voice of the deceased woman, Wilson began: "The blessed news i send to the[e] is this: / That i am goon from the[e] unto all bliss." Announcing that "to a better bridegroom i am gon," the speaker recounts her death: "It was a blessed, a thrice blessed, snow / Which to the meeting i then waded through / .... There never was more happie way i trodd, / That brought me home so soone unto my god / Instead of Braintry Church[.]"[22] Wilson decided that the surest consolation was to blot out the pain of bereavement with a dramatized sermon. To the inevitable question, where is my wife?, he answered in ministerial falsetto: it's OK, I'm in heaven. This pedestrian poetry offered the consolation of banning doubt and marching the bereaved and his wife with a kind but firm hand straight from the literal into the spiritual realm.

By the time Phillis Wheatley was writing, in the mid-eighteenth century, the style of the elegy had changed to fit neoclassical preferences. Wheatley's elegy on George Whitefield, published as a broadside in 1770, is a good example of public commemorative verse. As a broadside it functioned as both news and souvenir: the words "POEM" and "GEORGE WHITEFIELD," together with a woodcut of a dead man and a black border, proclaimed its message. In the smaller print, we find Phillis Wheatley's name, along with her age, owner, and the information that she was "but 9 Years in this Country from Africa."[23] Many public elegies were published anonymously, but in Wheatley's case, her slave status was part of the verse's novelty and perhaps overrode genteel conventions that deterred women from appearing in print.

The text illustrates the poetic techniques used in public elegies to forge a community. It begins by greeting Whitefield in heaven, "HAIL happy Saint," and lamenting the "Unhappy we" who are left behind. Like most public elegies in this period, it reiterates received ideas, fulfills the accepted conventions of the genre, and sounds reminiscent of admired English poets. "Pope in technique and Gray in theme" is one description of Wheatley's typical style.[24] Her elegy illustrates how a poem about a public leader functioned not only to eulogize that figure but also to enable a non-famous person to speak. The loss of Whitefield's eloquence – "We hear no more the music of thy tongue," – becomes a platform for Wheatley's, and she, like many public elegists, seizes the chance to exert political influence. Wheatley gives Whitefield a patriotic meaning, even though he was not a local hero but a British preacher who died on a visit to New England. In Wheatley's hands, as Karen Weyler has shown, this difficulty becomes an advantage as it enables her to describe Whitefield's "charity and love / Towards *America*" and thereby creates a unified, proto-national community:

> When his AMERICANS were burden'd sore,
> When streets were crimson'd with their guiltless gore!
> Unrival'd friendship in his breast now strove [...]

Although the image doubtless refers to the Boston Massacre of March 1770, it is generic enough to encompass any violence between colonists and British officials. Wheatley's elegy was printed in Boston, Newport, New York, and Philadelphia and anthologized. Of the dozen or so elegies on Whitefield that were published in America, it was the most popular, possibly because of its appeal to a national community. The second section transitions from restating Whitefield's message that everyone should receive God's Son ("Take HIM ye starving souls"), through community building ("Take HIM, 'my dear AMERICANS'"), to racial politics:

> Take HIM ye *Africans* he longs for you;
> Impartial SAVIOUR, is his title due;
> If you will chuse to walk in grace's road,
> You shall be sons, and kings, and priests to GOD.

In this poem and others, Wheatley's authoritative religious voice enables her to buck the social hierarchy and challenge prevailing ideas about race. The very conventionality of the New England funeral elegy – which Benjamin Franklin had mocked by publishing a "recipe" for one – provided a perfect poetic opportunity to show that the codes of white middle-class culture could be learned. Wheatley's correspondent, the Mohegan minister Samson Occom, did something similar in his hymns and lyrics. Once learned, as this elegy shows, the code could be used to express a genteel defiance.

Allusion and Parody

Poetic form is based on inherited conventions, including genre, meter, imagery, and style, and the way a poem imitates or adapts previous models becomes part of its meaning. Early American poetry in English often looked back (or across) to British literature and the European classical tradition, so it benefits from being read in a comparative and transatlantic perspective. The first published poem written in English in America was a courtly paraphrase of Ovid's *Metamorphoses*, which George Sandys finished while in Virginia.[25] Years later, poets like Anne Bradstreet and Edward Taylor were still migrants, albeit permanent ones. For these poets, England was their former home, their political metropole, and the heart of their culture. Taylor incorporated into his poetry a number of references to his American context, including rattlesnakes and Native American accounts of a giant.[26] His literary heritage, however, was the British devotional tradition, especially the work of George Herbert. For later writers, like Wheatley and Stockton, British literature remained a major linguistic and cultural inheritance, albeit one that was passed down or foisted upon them. During the revolutionary period, pro-independence writers like Philip Freneau and Mercy Otis Warren came to view Britain as a cultural frenemy. Whereas Edward Taylor's borrowings from Herbert conveyed affinity, during the revolutionary and early national period allusions to British tradition often turned hostile and satirical.

The conservative tendency in early American poetry, from Anne Bradstreet's admiration of Elizabethans to revolutionary-era writers' imitations of Samuel Butler and Alexander Pope, has been interpreted as "frontier consciousness," a nostalgic clinging to the old and familiar in the face of the unknown, or as a provincial lagging behind metropolitan fashions.[27] Yet one can also read transatlantic allusions as strategically adaptive. Although Edward Taylor's "Preparatory Meditations" (written 1693–1725) look back to the English Anglican tradition by invoking George Herbert's *The Temple* (London, 1633), they also express their distinctiveness through contrast. The "Prologue" to Taylor's "Preparatory Meditations" appropriates the phrase "A crumb of dust" from Herbert's "The Temper (I)" and turns that poem's theme of the disparity between God and man into a prayer for inspiration (with some characteristically awkward imagery): "Inspire this Crumb of Dust till it display / Thy Glory through't[.]"[28] All of Taylor's

Meditations repeat the verse form of "The Church Porch," the opening poem of *The Temple*: pentameter sestets that rhyme ababcc. They thereby ally with Herbert's design to prepare the soul to enter into God's presence; but whereas Herbert's poem exhorts outward forms of good behavior, Taylor's poems enact intense self-examination; whereas Herbert varied his verse forms and objects of meditation (including altar, church windows, and floor), Taylor repeated the same verse form and rehearsed the process of initiation in every Meditation, as if to strip his poetic "church" down to a single narrow door. Finally, whereas Herbert used an open perspicuous style, Taylor used an idiosyncratic colloquial idiom. New England Puritans who read and admired Herbert for his piety did not share his ritualism, and thus we find Taylor dialoguing with Herbert to differentiate his theology in his poetic style.

Such affiliative uses of transatlantic allusion continued through the eighteenth century, as Anglo-American writers adapted genres and tropes to their colonial American circumstances. During the pressures of the political crises, however, especially after the Stamp Act of 1765, the cultural connection became more problematic. Poetic techniques of satire and parody came into their own as a means of expressing the fracture and doubleness inherent in colonial resistance to British authority; and American writers felt a renewed connection with British writers of the 1720s, including Pope, Swift, and Gay, who had opposed Walpole's government.[29] So did Loyalists: "The word of Congress, like a round of beef, / To hungry Satire gives a sure relief;" wrote one imitator of Pope.[30] John Trumbull's bestselling four-canto poem *M'Fingal* (1775–1782), a mock-epic that caricatured a foolish Tory, looked back further, to Samuel Butler's *Hudibras* (1663–1678), from which it borrowed its comical tetrameter couplets. Although a few writers, including Trumbull and Freneau, created careers for themselves as patriot poets, most political poetry of the period was anonymous and circulated in newsprint.

One such poem appeared in the *Georgia Gazette* (March 1, 1769) and was reprinted in the *South Carolina Gazette* and the *Massachusetts Spy*.[31] A twenty-eight-line parody of Hamlet's soliloquy, it deployed close allusion to undermine British authority:

> Be taxt, or not be taxt, that is the question;
> Whether 'tis nobler in our minds to suffer
> The sleights and cunning of deceitful statesmen,
> Or to petition against illegal taxes,
> And by opposing end them. ——

Such a full-blown Shakespearean parody was rare, but the complete rewriting of a famous piece of English verse aptly illustrates the twist that revolutionary poetics gave to the relationship between early American poetry and

British tradition. First, the poem assumes that Hamlet's speech will be immediately recognizable to colonial newspaper readers and Whigs. It illustrates how the resistance movement valued anglophone cultural literacy and genteel taste. The parody retains the rhythm of the original and some of the sounds: "slings and arrows" becomes "slights and cunning"; "outragious fortune" is metrically matched by "deceitful statesmen" and keeps the "t" alliteration. [32]

Yet the closeness of the parody to Establishment poetry makes the opposition of the rebel message all the more explosive. Where Hamlet was wistfully considering suicide: "'tis a consummation / Devoutly to be wish'd. To die— to sleep—" the parody warns colonists against lethargy, against being "fast asleep" while their liberties are being stripped: "'Tis a determination directly to be crush'd." Rewriting Hamlet's blank verse so that it addressed the tax burden was a way of talking back to British authority on imperial letterhead. The poetic parody functioned as a correction, an updating of the soliloquy to a stronger purpose, stiffening masculine resolve, and transforming blank verse pondering into oratory that "crushed" opposition. Adapting a fictional dilemma from a play into an engagement with a real-life political drama being reported in newsprint turned belletristic verse into a useful device. "An age employ'd in pointing steel / Can no poetic raptures feel;" lamented Freneau in 1788, though he had participated in the vogue for political invective.[33] Poetry in the revolutionary period was expected to enlist.

Like Wheatley's elegy on Whitefield, the parodic poem works to create a plural constituency, a "we" to replace Hamlet's lonely "I," and aims to guide a community of anglophone admirers of a British author into political action. Wheatley's elegy was attributed, but, like much political verse, the Shakespeare parody was anonymous. Anonymous poetry contributed to the development of an arena of discourse (or "public sphere") that facilitated political discussion and presented it, in print, as ostensibly detached from parochial interests and individual personalities.[34] In the atmosphere of revolutionary fraternalism, anonymity could enhance a poem's moral authority; or, if the views expressed were provocative, it could protect the author. Anonymity also played down the importance of art, implying that the author was not concerned with fame, only with making a point. Yet the implicit exclusivity of the political and poetic constituency is clear from the print context of the *Georgia Gazette* version: a few lines below the parody's protest against "the pangs of slavery" as among the "whips and scorns of time" there are advertised for sale: "THREE NEGROE MEN, TWO NEGROE WOMEN, ONE LIKELY BOY, and FOUR CHILDREN."

There are, of course, many possible ways to read early American poetry; and being open to a variety of approaches, depending on the context and style of the poem, will ensure a good fit. Understanding a poems as an "act of connection" keeps evaluation broad enough to allow exploration of what a given poem did, or was supposed to do, for its author and its earliest readers.[35] Analysis of Bradstreet's and Taylor's poems demonstrates that formalist close reading can be a fruitful critical approach for some early American poems, especially for those whose authors were familiar with and sought to engage in dialogue with their transatlantic poetic inheritance. Other more social, material, and contextual approaches work well for poems that were not written with that kind of ambition and for poems that were designed to serve practical, relational, or political ends.

Notes

1. Jane Tompkins, *Sensational Designs: The Cultural Work of American Fiction, 1790–1860* (New York: Oxford University Press, 1985).
2. On club literature, see David Shields, *Civil Tongues and Polite Letters in British America* (Chapel Hill: University of North Carolina Press, 1997). On women's coteries, see Susan Stabile, *Memory's Daughters: The Material Culture of Remembrance in Eighteenth-Century America* (Ithaca, NY: Cornell University Press, 2003).
3. Cotton Mather, *Manuductio Ministerium* (Boston, 1726), 42; Richard Lewis, "To His Excellency," in Edward Holdsworth, *The Mouse-trap*, trans. Richard Lewis (Annapolis, 1728), vii. See also Richard Ruland, *The Native Muse: Theories of American Literature*, vol. 1 (New York: Dutton, 1976), 18–22, 29.
4. The tension is evident, for instance, in Richard Gray's excellent survey, *A History of American Poetry* (Hoboken, NJ: Wiley, 2015).
5. Adrienne Rich, "Anne Bradstreet and Her Poetry," in *The Works of Anne Bradstreet*, ed. Jeannine Hensley (Cambridge MA: Harvard University Press, 1967), ix–xxi; Robert Hass, "Edward Taylor: What Was He Up To?," *The American Poetry Review* 31, no. 2 (2002): 43–44.
6. Betty Booth Donohue, "Remembering Muskrat," in Alfred Bendixen and Stephen Burt, eds., *The Cambridge History of American Poetry* (Cambridge: Cambridge University Press, 2014), 15–42.
7. Psalm 19, reprinted in David Shields, ed., *American Poetry: The Seventeenth and Eighteenth Centuries* (New York: Literary Classics of the United States, 2007), 23. Poem texts for this chapter have been sourced where possible from this collection.
8. On the Bay Psalm Book, see my *Popular Measures: Poetry and Church Order in Seventeenth-Century Massachusetts* (Newark: University of Delaware Press, 2005), chapter 2.
9. On colonial print culture, see Hugh Amory and David D. Hall, *A History of the Book in America, Vol. 1: The Colonial Book in the Atlantic World* (Cambridge: Cambridge University Press, 2007).

10. Roger Stoddard and David Whitesell, *A Bibliographical Description of Books and Pamphlets of American Verse Printed from 1610 through 1820* (University Park: Pennsylvania State University Press, 2012), 138, 154; and Adrian Chastain Weimer, "From Human Suffering to Divine Friendship: *Meat out of the Eater* and Devotional Reading in Early New England," *Early American Literature* 51, no. 1 (2016): 3–39 (4–6). My discussion of Wigglesworth is indebted to Weimer.

11. Matthew P. Brown, *The Pilgrim and the Bee: Reading Rituals and Book Culture in Early New England* (Philadelphia: University of Pennsylvania Press, 2007), 71, 91–106.

12. Stoddard and Whitesell, *Bibliographical Description of Books*, 53.

13. Ibid.

14. On particularity, see Caroline Wigginton, *In the Neighborhood: Women's Publication in Early America* (Amherst: University of Massachusetts Press, 2016), 6–7.

15. Shields, *American Poetry*, 196–197.

16. Ibid., 62.

17. Ibid., 386–396.

18. Annis Boudinot Stockton, "To a little Miss with a toy lookingglass," in *Only for the Eye of a Friend: The Poems of Annis Boudinot Stockton*, ed. Carla Mulford (Charlottesville: University of Virginia Press, 1995), 172–173, 226 n. 316.

19. Wigginton, *Neighborhood*, 6–7.

20. Shields, *American Poetry*, 570, 872.

21. Ibid., 57.

22. Ibid., 9–11.

23. Phyllis Wheatley, *An Elegiac Poem, on the Death of ... George Whitefield* (Boston: 1770). A digital reproduction is available at the Library Company of Philadelphia website: https://digital.librarycompany.org/islandora/object/digitool%3A37980. My reading of the elegy is based on this text and is indebted to Karen A. Weyler, *Empowering Words: Outsiders and Authorship in Early America* (London: University of Georgia Press, 2013), 36–55. A shorter revised version of the elegy is in Shields, *American Poetry*, 777–778.

24. Rowan Ricardo Phillips, *When Blackness Rhymes with Blackness* (Dallas, TX: Dalkey Archive, 2010), 15.

25. *Ovid's Metamorphosis Englished* (London, 1626).

26. See Meditation 2.161B (1723), Edward Taylor, *Edward Taylor's "Gods Determinations" and "Preparatory Meditations": A Critical Edition*, ed. Daniel Patterson (Kent, OH: Kent State University Press, 2003), 505–506; and Amy M. E. Morris, "Geomythology on the Colonial Frontier: Edward Taylor, Cotton Mather and the Claverack Giant," *William and Mary Quarterly* 70, no. 4 (2013): 701–724.

27. Albert J. Von Frank, *The Sacred Game: Provincialism and Frontier Consciousness in American Literature, 1630–1860* (Cambridge: Cambridge University Press, 1985).

28. Taylor, *"Gods Determinations" and "Preparatory Meditations,"* 123, lines 21–22.

29. Colin Wells, *Poetry Wars: Verse and Politics in the American Revolution and Early Republic* (Philadelphia: University of Pennsylvania Press, 2017), 53.

30. Jonathan Odell, "The Word of Congress," *Royal Gazette,* September 18, 1779: 2; Shields, *American Poetry*, 604.

31. *Georgia Gazette* (March 1, 1769), 3; Jason Shaffer, *Performing Patriotism: National Identity in the Colonial and Revolutionary American Theater* (Philadelphia: University of Pennsylvania Press, 2007), 94.

32. *Hamlet* 3.2, in William Shakespeare, *The Works of Shakespeare*, Vol. 6, ed. Thomas Hanmer (London, 1743–1744), 370.

33. Philip Freneau, "An Author's Soliloquy," in *Miscellaneous Works* (Philadelphia, 1788), 171.

34. Michael Warner, *Letters of the Republic* (Cambridge, MA: Harvard University Press, 1990), 108.

35. Weyler, *Empowering Words*, 38.

4

LAURA M. STEVENS

How to Read Gender in Early America

In 1785, a free Black man named John Marrant acquired some fame in the British Atlantic world, especially among evangelical Christians, when *A Narrative of the Lord's Wonderful Dealings with John Marrant* was published in London. Marrant, who had been wounded while pressed into service for the British navy during the American Revolution, and who was on his way to Nova Scotia from London as a recently ordained minister, had an amazing story to tell about his adolescence in South Carolina. In this story, Marrant experienced a transformative conversion during a revival meeting in Charleston, and because his family would not accept his new beliefs, the fourteen-year-old ran away from home. A Cherokee hunter found him wandering in the Carolina backwoods, half-starved and delirious. He allowed the adolescent to join him on a deer hunt, and he brought him several weeks later to a Cherokee town. There, Marrant was seized, imprisoned, and threatened with deadly torture. For several days in his imprisonment, he prayed out loud, sang hymns, held on to his bible, and prayed more.

Eventually and wondrously, Marrant was saved. The instrument of his salvation was the "eldest daughter" of the Cherokee "king." Entering the chamber where Marrant had been brought before the king to have his fate decided, she stood next to the prisoner, took the bible out of his hand, kissed it, and "seemed much delighted with it." After the king interviewed Marrant about his beliefs, the daughter opened the bible, kissed it once more, and "said, with much sorrow, the book would not speak to her." Then, while Marrant prayed, she along with several other people cried out, even as the king grew angry and condemned him to death. As Marrant was dragged away to his "dungeon," she fell ill and over the following days seemed near to death. Other Cherokees pled with the king that, if Marrant were killed, the king's own daughter would die. A second audience took place and, miraculously, "the king himself was awakened ... the king's house became God's house ... and the poor condemned prisoner had perfect liberty, and was

68

treated like a prince." Having accomplished the spiritual awakening of the entire town, Marrant lived among the Cherokees, eventually returning to Charleston two years after his departure.[1]

We do not know if Marrant actually wandered into Cherokee territory, let alone whether he brought about a transformation in that community's spiritual beliefs. All we have is his uncorroborated account, which, regardless of its facticity, stands as a valuable artifact of an African American man's authorship and worldview. Scholars of early America have devoted much energy and much ink to analyzing this story, which offers important if puzzling clues to the role of race and religion both in the southern colonies of the early 1770s and the transatlantic British world of the 1780s. Less often noticed, but at least as fascinating, is the role that gender plays in this story. Gender is not at the text's center, yet it is always there, framing other words and shaping readers' assumptions along with Marrant's hopes, fears, and ideas.

When the title page of the *Narrative* declared that Marrant was "Now going to Preach the GOSPEL in Nova-Scotia," it was operating within a widely (but not unanimously) accepted Christian outlook going back to St. Paul's epistles about the role that gender played in granting some humans and not others the authority to preach. That is, the text was not challenging prevailing assumptions about the alignment of ministerial authority with maleness in the way that other Christian sects, such as Quakers and early Methodists following John and Charles Wesley, had done.[2] When Marrant described the leader of the Cherokee town as a "king," he was drawing upon notions of political authority rooted in European traditions that also took for granted a patriarchal framework, presuming men to be in authority over family and polity alike. When he described the woman who kissed his bible as the king's daughter, he also evoked feelings and expectations connected with a literary type that had acquired some prominence in Europeans' accounts of America: the Indian princess, who welcomes, nourishes, and even rescues the foreign men who have arrived from afar.

In his account of being saved from execution by Pocahontas, John Smith had done much to invent the Indian princess as a figure of accommodating femininity, who complemented the dashing European explorer even as she was juxtaposed with the savage, hard-hearted tyranny of her father Powhatan.[3] This type had resurfaced in eighteenth-century texts, including the Inkle and Yarico story, in which a kind and beautiful woman, sometimes Native American and sometimes African, saved a shipwrecked European man only to be sold by him later into slavery, and *The Female American* (1767), a historical novel that opens in the Jamestown colony and rehearses some parts of the Pocahontas narrative.[4]

The idea that Marrant "trades up" his racial status by repurposing the types and tales of European colonization has become central to the study of this text.[5] It is also clear that this elevation occurred through an emphasis on prevailing European understandings of gender roles and gender hierarchies. One implied assertion of the *Narrative* is that Marrant should be accepted and understood by the text's predominantly white, English readership as an ordained Christian minister, with the status and authority that accompanies that position, in spite of his race. One crucial underpinning of that assertion is Marrant's identity as male and his self-presentation as conventionally masculine within late eighteenth-century white British norms. The story of Marrant among Cherokees, including his interplay with the Cherokee king's daughter, does much to consolidate that claim.

Just as the term "king" was an imposition of European concepts and words on an Indigenous people – the Cherokee people have never had kings – so also was Marrant's notion that the power the "king's daughter" possessed to save him from execution inhered in her status as a daughter to this male authority. Cherokee society was and is matrilineal, with names and family affiliation following from children's mothers rather than fathers, and eighteenth-century Cherokee towns were organized so that men and women each oversaw distinct aspects of governance.[6] As James Adair, who lived among the Cherokees and other peoples of the American southeast for some three decades in the eighteenth century, noted, "pun-ishment (of captives) is always left to the women," so that women decided whether captives would be adopted into the town, enslaved, or executed.[7] If anything like the scene Marrant relates actually happened, it is probable that he misunderstood what was going on and who possessed authority over his fate. The "king's daughter" was not pleading with her father to show mercy to Marrant because she was swayed by his prayer or motiv-ated by God; rather, she was exercising her customary influence as a Beloved Woman in her town and arguing – perhaps in part because of his literacy, hence her expressions of affection for the book – that it was better for the community to adopt this captive than enslave or kill him. Layering his own assumptions about gender roles in this culture likely meant misunderstanding what had happened to him and why. The inverse also is true: Marrant's story illustrates how understanding early America in all its complexity requires accounting for the intricacies of gender, espe-cially as they were understood and performed in intersection with other identity categories such as race.[8] Indeed, Marrant's negotiation of his racial identity in this publication succeeds in part through his performance and interpretation of gender.

Locating and Defining Gender

To use the term "gender" in relation to early America is to indulge in anachronism. Our contemporary understanding of this word, which has its origins in the Middle French *gendre*, to designate male versus female qualities, was just coming into use in the first century of colonization of the lands Europeans named America. Well into the seventeenth century, this word, which has some connection with the modern word "genre," could indicate any type or group with similar characteristics, as when Shakespeare's Iago, thinking of the body as a garden, recommended: "supply it with one gender of herbs or distract it with many"; or when the eighteenth-century novelist Robert Bage had a character proclaim: "I . . . am . . . of the patriotic gender."[9] Twentieth-century developments in psychology, sociology, and anthropology led to what is still a widespread distinction in both scholarly and everyday parlance between "sex," which indicates biological maleness or femaleness through chromosomes or through bodily characteristics such as genitalia, and "gender," which includes the culturally determined behaviors and appearances associated with each sex. Neither category is as fixed as this definitional distinction would suggest: it is much more commonly understood now that a person's visible sex characteristics may not be the same as the sex indicated by their chromosomes; gender is even more dynamic, fluid, and contested, not only differing between cultures but undergoing constant negotiation within them. In 1987, Candace West and Don H. Zimmerman forwarded this more dynamic model in their influential article, "Doing Gender," when they asserted that gender never "is," in any static way, but rather is always being done as "a recurring accomplishment." Gender "is a situated doing, carried out in the virtual or real presence of others who are presumed to be oriented to its production." It is located in, and comes out of, every here and now, as individuals bring their own culturally shaped assumptions and expressions to their interactions with each other.[10]

Although she did not use the word "gender," Judith Sargent Murray, a writer and early feminist philosopher of New England, voiced similar principles in her essay "On the Equality of the Sexes." First published in *The Massachusetts Magazine* just a few years after the ratification of the US constitution, this essay focused on a specific type of sexual equality: the equality of mental ability, or at least of mental potential, between men and women. In the poetic verses that open her essay, Murray conceded that some humans are smarter than others, and some humans show a greater willingness to learn. She was adamant, however, that the smarter and more curious are not always male. This only appeared to be the case because what she called "the lordly sex . . . Rob us of the power t'improve, / And then declare we only trifles love."[11] In other words, men prevent girls from strengthening their minds by denying them proper educations. They then blame the superficiality and frivolity that poorly educated women exhibit on women's essential inferiority.

In order to make her case, Murray relied on observations of very young humans: "Will it be said that the judgment of a male of two years old, is more sage than that of a female's of the same age? I believe the reverse is generally observed to be true." Here, Murray took on the role of an experimental scientist studying the data of human behavior and pinning down the variable producing divergent data. That variable, she concluded, was environmental, not natural, involving the different types of upbringing and learning available to boys versus girls. Although two-year-old boys and girls are basically equal in their intelligence, adults treat them quite differently: "How is one exalted and the other depressed, by the contrary modes of education which are adopted!" The distinctions between the apparent mental equality of infants and the inequality of adults positioned her to conclude of women: "Grant that their minds are by nature equal, yet who shall wonder at the apparent superiority, if indeed custom becomes second nature." The key not only to asserting women's equality with men but to producing that equality in everyday life was to show that natural sex differences were only physical, while mental differences were the result of "custom." She did not use this word, but Sargent was distinguishing between a physical or natural area of sex and a cultural one of gender.

What English speakers today call gender is always, and has always been, a moving target. The constantly negotiated, ever-shifting qualities of gender pertained even more so to early America, for the most important and constant element of these lands in this era (roughly from 1492 to the early nineteenth century) was the collision of the peoples of two hemispheres who had had almost no contact with each other over the preceding millennia. It also is not as though the peoples within each hemisphere were similar to each other. To the contrary, the continent of Africa; the subcontinent of Europe; and the two continents, isthmus, and nearby archipelagos of the Americas each contained what the authors of *The Atlantic World* describe as "patterns of heterogeneity," brought about as "humans adapted to their environments in distinct and clever ways over the millennia, yielding a kaleidoscope of cultural differences."[12] When Europeans began to arrive in the Americas, and when they later transported enslaved Africans to the Americas, the new arrivals to and longtime residents of these continents possessed their own ideas about what men and women were like and what roles they should fill. Those ideas often clashed with each other; the results ranged from surprise and admiration to violence and contempt.

To consider gender in early America, then, is to contemplate a fractal structure that is equally complex when looked at up close and from afar. Most episodes of intercultural contact in these lands found expression through gender, and often gender constituted what we might call a hot spot of contact, triggering intense emotional responses and confusions. It is not just that gender was at the center of so many interactions among the Americas' new and old peoples but also that intercultural contact made gender visible to the participants in and observers of these interactions as something that *could* be different. In a sense, then, America, with its unprecedented jostling of various and varying peoples, was part of what made human beings aware of a distinction between qualities of male and female that seemed to be stable across place and time and those that were emerging as changeable, even arbitrary. It is no doubt an exaggeration to say that early America gave us gender as we now understand this term, but it is certainly true that the Americas in these centuries provided observant human beings with a serendipitous laboratory of human behavior that, barring perhaps some port cities on the Indian Ocean or Mediterranean Sea, was unprecedented in its complexity and variety.

Gender, Print, and Power: The Example of Amerigo Vespucci

The navigator Amerigo Vespucci, who claimed to have made four voyages to the land that Europeans took to naming after him, provides a vivid example of how contact between the peoples living on either side of the Atlantic could reveal startling differences in what might seem to be natural features of women versus men. Vespucci's own assumptions about gender were on display even before he described the people he had encountered in any detail, being visible in the words "we saw infinite hordes of them on the beach; and they had with them their wives and children."[13] "Them" and "they" here would seem to indicate human beings in general, but the clause "they had with them their wives and children" reveals that "they" means men. Vespucci lived in a world where human beings were assumed first to be male. The people he encountered challenged key aspects of his male-centered and male-dominated view of the world. He could not get over the athleticism and strength of the women he saw on the coastline his ship reached, noting, "a woman recks nothing of running a league or two, as we frequently saw," and marveling that "one woman bears on her back a burden such as no man will carry, thirty or forty leagues." These particular features occasioned admiration, even envy, so that he conceded of both men's and women's physical prowess, "in this they have a very great advantage over us Christians." Other qualities, though, left him disgusted, scandalized, and (obviously, if tacitly) aroused. The absence of women's modesty or shame about their bodies was especially fascinating to him. He was appalled that the people of this land, "both men and women," were "shameless ... in making water." He went on at length about their sexual promiscuity, especially because "in this the woman has as much liberty as the man." He emphasized the women's apparent willingness to abort their own children, claiming that they would do so when they were angry with their husbands or lovers. His sense of the differences between European women and the women of this land ranged well beyond the category of what we today would consider gender, to include the body itself. Most dramatically, he claimed, "They are very fertile women, and their pregnancies avoid no toil."[14] Whether the women's apparent health, fertility, and resiliency were the result of inborn features, their environment, or their methods of childbirth was a question Vespucci did not ask, but such questions emerged from these and other encounters between Europeans, Africans, and the peoples of the Americas.

If the content of Vespucci's letter illustrates how profoundly moments of intercultural encounter reveal the power of culture to shape understandings of male and female, the existence of the letter in more than one version and language reminds us that many of these episodes of human interaction, with their colliding and thus constantly negotiated understandings of gender, did not just press upon the awareness of those experiencing those events, as was true of most of the preceding episodes of gender-negotiation or gender-conflict that fill and shape global human history. What made early America different, along with other sites of intensive intercultural contact starting in the fifteenth century, was the arrival of the technology of moveable type in Western Europe. China had possessed this technology for a while, but in Europe it combined with other factors, including rising literacy rates, an increased demand for material to read, improved access to paper, and enhanced systems of transporting printed material between cities and towns, to create a setting in which descriptions of distant lands could be transmitted fairly quickly to many readers across Europe and then later to other continents. If America was a laboratory of human interaction, those episodes of interaction now had an audience much larger and more widely distributed across the world than just the participants in those encounters. Gender, along with so many other aspects of encounter, could become a *subject* of discussion and analysis. Comparisons could be made between different episodes in different places and times. Those comparisons could yield contemplation, speculation, even analysis.

The letter also shows us that scenes of encounter did not constitute an even playing field. Gender constituted a code, the deciphering of which could yield peace or violence, redistributing wealth and power accordingly. Vespucci could not understand why a scene of friendliness with a particular coastal community suddenly erupted in violence, but expectations of women and men clearly were at the center of this confusion. The coastal men "brought with them 16 of their girls," sending four canoes among the boats, to the astonishment of the Europeans, but when a group of older "women, utter[ed] very loud outcries and t[ore] their hair," the Europeans reached for their weapons, while the girls "dove into the sea, and those in the canoes made away from us, and began with their bows to shoot arrows at us." In the ensuing violence, as many as twenty Indigenous people died, several Europeans were wounded, and the Europeans took five captives.[15] Vespucci interpreted this episode as one of "treachery," but was it? Is it more likely that this community was sending out sixteen young women as bait for an ambush, or that the community was dispatching these women in a ritual of diplomacy? Finding the Indigenous reality through the lens of a European colonizer's description is a challenge, but what we now know of women's centrality to diplomacy for many peoples of the Americas suggests that the Europeans on this expedition misread this scene because of their particular expectations of women.

Misreading and Controlling Gender across Cultural Divides

Juliana Barr has shown how the Spanish struggled to gain power and even survive in a part of America thousands of miles away from the coast Vespucci had visited, the Texas borderlands, in part because they were so incompetent at reading Indigenous codes of gender. "This was a world dominated by Indian nations and to enter that world meant that Europeans had to abide by the kinship categories that ordered it and gave it meaning."[16] She tells the story of the ill-fated missions of San Francisco de los Tejas and Santísmo Nombre de María, which between 1691 and 1693 brought eighteen Spaniards – "four missionaries, three lay brothers, eight soldiers, two young boys, and one servant" – to staff two missions near a cluster of Caddo villages within the Hasinai confederacy. A mere three years later, the Caddos chased the Spaniards off the land and banished them from the region. What had brought about such a disaster? The causes are rooted in clashing understandings of gender.[17]

The matrilineal clans among which the missions were located could not understand why the Spaniards had not brought their wives, who along with children would have "been capable of meeting the socioeconomic obligations of membership within Caddo communities." These obligations included performing ceremonial roles to reciprocally honor Caddo women and children and overseeing regular exchanges of food. Coming from a world that linked women's honor to passivity and sexual modesty, the Spaniards were unprepared to grasp that the Hasinai defined women's honor through their "active contributions to food production and distribution" or to understand the political magnitude of having women present who could welcome guests by serving them food. The Europeans also misconstrued the elaborate body painting and tattoos with which women adorned their body from the waist up, with new lines and decorations added as women married and moved through other stages of life. "They saw only a display of flesh endowed with sexual meaning," and they misconstrued the Hasinais' ceremonies of touch as indicative of "promiscuity." Even as the Caddos' good will was gradually fraying, more than one episode of rape by Spanish soldiers provoked their fury, especially because the rapes went unpunished by the Spanish leadership. It was because of their repeated insults and outrages to the honor of Hasinai women that the Spanish lost whatever presence they had in this region.[18]

If the ability to read gender codes enabled diplomacy, trade, even conquest, it is also true that which beliefs about gender came across as "correct" ultimately depended upon who had more power to foist those assumptions on others. Within the long history of America's colonization, this power tilted toward the Europeans who had invaded this land. The exerting of power, of course, included the straightforward force of bodies and weaponry as well as the vast, multilayered structures of domination seen in the Atlantic slave trade or the *encomienda* systems of Spanish colonialism. It also included the ability to shape culture itself by controlling the story, shaping the words and images through which humans describe to each other what the world is like.

When the Puritans of the New England colonies publicized their efforts to bring the Native peoples of that region to the belief and practice of their particular form of Christianity, they also depicted an imposition of their own gender codes on these peoples. In 1647, Thomas Shepard, minister of Cambridge, Massachusetts, described his own enforcement of English gender norms while preaching to a community of Indigenous converts. When a few women in the congregation asked questions, he responded by advising those women not to speak in public: "because we knew how unfit it was for women so much as to aske questions publiquely immediately by themselves; wee did therefore desire them to propound any questions they would bee resolved about by first acquainting either their Husbands, or the Interpreter privately therewith."[19] The tract that published Shepard's account also printed a list of "Conclusions and Orders made and agreed upon by divers Sachims and other principall men amongst the Indians at Concord," with fines included for breaking those rules. The list showed a concerted attempt to alter not just religious beliefs but also the ways in which the Wampanoag,

Nonantum, Neponset, Nipmuck, Pawtucket, and other Indigenous peoples of this region understood and performed gender. The language of the orders erased women from diplomacy, discipline, or decision-making, noting, for example, that "[N]o *Indian* [*sic*] hereafter shall have any more but one wife" and that "The old Ceremony of the Maide walking alone and living apart so many days [be fined] 20 s[hillings]."[20] Such decrees show us how profoundly and thoroughly this particular form of settler colonialism altered the lives and identities of America's Native peoples, taking their lands and over-powering their governments but also enforcing the most intimate aspects of identity and life, ranging from the treatment of women during their men-strual cycles (most likely the reason why a "Maide" would live apart) to the shape and duration of the sexual and emotional commitments individual men and women had to each other.[21] Gender thus became an expression of colonizing power.

Gender also became an instrument for enforcing race-based chattel slav-ery, with ongoing legacies in destructive stereotypes of African American maleness, femaleness, and sexuality. Among the countless indignities, viola-tions, and horrors of enslavement was the forcing of new expectations and performances of gender. The historian Jennifer L. Morgan has explained, "Gender functioned as a set of power relationships through which early slaveowning settlers and those they enslaved defined, understood, and adjusted to the confines of racial slavery." Even as they were forced to adapt to these new roles, enslaved women and men carried with them some of the expectations of gender with which they were raised in a wide array of communities, but with some concentration in the Gold Coast, Bight of Benin, Bight of Biafra, Senegambia, and West-Central Africa. "By all accounts," Morgan notes, "captured women on slave ships came from communities in which they shouldered important responsibilities," especially "producing agricultural exports essential to regional economies."[22] Historians are still studying the degree to which those who survived the Middle Passage were able to create family structures with attendant gender roles that matched the settings of their birth.[23]

Certainly new divisions between and expectations of men and women occurred from the first moments of enslavement, as slavers categorized their captives by sex in order to control and then sell them. Even as many enslaved men had to adapt to new roles, for example, performing the agri-cultural labor many would have thought of primarily as women's work, some had opportunities to work in occupations designated by whites as male and considered "skilled," with relative status and freedom of move-ment. Women had fewer opportunities for skilled labor, and the skilled roles available to them, such as housekeeper, rarely entailed much freedom of movement, in fact making them more vulnerable to sexual violation because of their proximity. Of enslaved Africans' gender roles, Kirsten Wood also notes, "gender is constituted not solely through contrasts between men and women, but also through contrasts *among* men and *among* women. Thus, as long as some women, like slave owning women or enslaved housekeepers, did not perform fieldwork alongside men, enslaved women who did had a distinct gender in relationship to other women."[24] Gender thus impinged upon the identities and daily lives of the enslaved in many ways.

No discussion of gender in relation to chattel slavery can overlook the ways in which owners deployed expectations of sex and gender specifically to consolidate and gain pleasure from their power over the humans they owned, through manipulation, humiliation, and control. These ways included the forced matching of men and women for breeding purposes, interference in disputes between enslaved men and women over their gender roles and responsibilities to each other, and rape of the enslaved by their owners and overseers. The diary of Thomas Thistlewood, an overseer and then planta-tion owner of mid-eighteenth-century Jamaica, offers an unusually candid portrait of the entitlement he expressed regularly to the bodies of the women he owned. As Trevor Burnard notes, "White men molested slave women in part because they could do so without fear of social consequence and in part because they constantly needed to show slaves the extent of their dominance."[25] Just as Europe's "long tradition of identifying Others through the monstrous physiognomy or sexual behavior of women" facili-tated white owners' assumptions of racial superiority and feelings of entitle-ment to Black bodies, the terrible history of race-based chattel slavery intensified and propagated still-extant racist ideologies of African bodies and sexualities.[26]

Performing Gender across Cultural Divides

If the ability of colonists and slaveowners to exert power over others found expression through the imposition of gender norms, it is also true that occasionally individuals found new lives in these scenes of encounter and conquest, in part by adopting foreign performances of gender. To say that these individuals "chose" these lives and ways of doing gender requires ignoring the multiple coercions, both subtle and obvious, that defined their existence. Yet it is also the case that many of these individuals did make decisions to stay with, even embrace, a culture not of their birth, a culture with quite different notions about what men and women should be like.

The first individual was Catherine Tekakwitha, born in 1656 to a Mohawk father and an Algonquin mother who had been captured by the

Mohawks and adopted into their nation. Named Tekakwitha by her people in the village of Gandouagué, on the Mohawk River, she met the Jesuit missionary Jacques de Lamberville when she was eighteen, told him she wished to be Christian, and a year later was baptized Catherine or Kateri. Six months after that, she moved to the Jesuit mission of Kahnawake on the St. Lawrence River. Until her death at the age of twenty-four, she devoted herself to a pious life filled with rituals of intense penance and self-mortification, and, unusually for a Haudenosaunee woman, she took a vow of chastity.

The second individual is Eunice Williams, or Marguerite Kanenstenhawi, who in 1704, at the age of seven, was captured in the French and multi-tribal raid on Deerfield, Massachusetts, and brought to Kahnawake where she was adopted into the Roman Catholic Mohawk community a generation after Tekakwitha's death. Although she had been born into an elite ministerial family of Puritan New England, and although that family tried many times to ransom her or (later) invite her to return to Massachusetts, Kanenstenhawi stayed with the Kahnawake community. She did visit her siblings in Massachusetts more than once, but she lived out her life as a Mohawk woman, marrying a Mohawk man when she was sixteen and raising three children with him.[27]

It is by no means clear that the received history of both women is accurate, for neither Catherine Tekakwitha nor Marguerite Kanenstenhawi left behind writings of their own, and most of what is known about both women comes from colonial sources with their own biases. The extant accounts of Tekakwitha in particular, by the Jesuits Claude Chauchetière and Pierre Cholenec, are shaped by the genre of hagiography.[28] These accounts, however, make clear that both women were understood by many as remarkable – and for some readers, scandalous – because they adopted foreign ways of being female. Tekakwitha refused her family's wish that she marry and have children, as Mohawk women were supposed to, choosing instead a path of chastity that was entirely legible within European Catholic traditions but aberrant for her own people; Kanenstenhawi, in a sense, committed to the path of Mohawk womanhood that Tekakwitha had refused, including sexual activity and motherhood. The stories of two women who elected to embrace cultures that had invaded theirs illustrate how at least a few individuals found new lives that entailed a transformation in how they did gender.

Gender is always contingent, unstable, and constantly under negotiation by those who perform it and witness its performance. No one is ever not performing or witnessing gender, for it is omnipresent in interactions among humans. Within the scope of human history, early America presents an unusually complex and dynamic setting for the study of gender, with its jostling of individuals and groups hailing from at least three major geo-graphic settings. The history and texts of this capacious setting and era foreground the existence of gender as a production of culture, showing us, through the drama of colliding expectations, that gender is a thing – a human-made thing – demanding our attention. These diverse texts and events reveal that the ability to flourish in scenes of intercultural contact often depended on individuals' skill at interpreting, and sometimes adapting to, the gender codes of the other culture. Conversely, the enforcement of gender norms often became an expression of one people's power over another, marking some of the most poignant and terrible moments of colonization and enslavement.

Notes

1. *A Narrative of the Lord's Wonderful Dealings with John Marrant, a Black, Now Going to Preach the Gospel in Nova-Scotia*, ed. William Aldridge, 4th ed. (London, 1785), 23–25. Eighteenth-Century Collections Online. Scholars generally regard the fourth edition as the authorized one, which is advertised as "Enlarged by Mr. Marrant" and "Printed for the Author," and which includes some anti-slavery commentary not present in the earlier editions.
2. The group that trained Marrant for ministry and ordained him was a Methodist group known as the "Huntingdon Connexion" for its patronage by Selena, Countess of Huntingdon. Unlike some Methodists of the two preceding decades who were more closely connected with the Wesley brothers, the Huntingdon Connexion, which was founded by George Whitefield, took a Calvinist view of sin, redemption, and predestination. It also did not oppose race-based chattel slavery. On Marrant's relation to the Connexion, see Cedric May, "John Marrant and the Narrative Construction of an Early Black Methodist Evangelical," *African American Review* 38, no. 4 (2000): 555.
3. The story of Smith's salvation by Pocahontas first appeared in John Smith, *The Generall Historie of Virginia, New-England, and the Summer Isles* (London, 1624), book 3, 448–449. Online edition in "Documenting the American South," https://docsouth.unc.edu/southlit/smith/smith.html. On this stereotype, see Nancy Marie Mithlo, *"Our Indian Princess": Subverting the Stereotype* (Santa Fe: School for Advanced Research Press, 2009).
4. Frank Felsenstein, ed., *English Trader, Indian Maid: Representing Gender, Race, and Slavery in the New World: An Inkle and Yarico Reader* (Baltimore: Johns Hopkins University Press, 2000); [Unca Eliza Winkfield, pseud.], *The Female American, or, the Adventures of Unca Eliza Winkfield*, ed. Michelle Burnham and James Freitas (Peterborough, ON: Broadview, 2014).
5. Tiya Miles first described Marrant as trading up. "'His Kingdom for a Kiss': Indians and Intimacy in the Narrative of John Marrant," in Ann Stoler, ed., *Haunted by Empire: Geographies of Intimacy in North American History* (Durham, NC: Duke University Press, 2006), 178.

6. On Cherokee women, see, for example, Theda Purdue, *Cherokee Women: Gender and Culture Change, 1700–1835*, 2nd ed. (Lincoln, NE: Bison Books, 1999).

7. James Adair, *The History of the American Indians; Particularly Those Nations Adjoining to the Mississippi, East and West Florida, Georgia, South and North Carolina, and Virginia* (London, 1775), 390, 389. Eighteenth-Century Collections Online.

8. Intersectionality is a now-classic element of feminist theory, first advanced by Kimberlé Crenshaw and Patricia Hill Collins. Crenshaw, "Mapping the Margins: Intersectionality, Identity Politics, and Violence against Women of Color," *Stanford Law Review* 43, no. 6 (1991): 1241–1299; Collins, *Black Feminist Thought, Knowledge, Consciousness, and the Politics of Empowerment*, rev. ed. (New York: Routledge, 2000). My account of gender in this chapter owes much to Greta LaFleur's call for "centering scholarship that theorizes eighteenth-century gender as a structure of relation or architecture of power, and thus as an intersectional or contingent formation." LaFleur, "Sex and 'Unsex': Histories of Gender Trouble in Eighteenth-Century North America," *Early American Studies* 12, no. 3 (2014): 471.

9. William Shakespeare, *Othello*, 1.3; Robert Bage, *Barham Downs* (Tamworth, 1784), 1.274. Eighteenth-Century Collections Online. Both quotations appear in the *Oxford English Dictionary Online*, for the word "gender."

10. Candace West and Don H. Zimmerman, "Doing Gender," *Gender and Society* 1, no. 2 (June 1987): 126. Other central texts shaping the current prevailing usage of these terms include John Money, Joan G. Hampson, and John L. Hampson, "Imprinting and the Establishment of Gender Roles," *AMA Archives of Neurology and Psychiatry* 77, no. 3 (March 1957): 333–336; Gayle Rubin, "The Traffic in Women: Notes on the 'Political Economy' of Sex," in Rayna Reiter, ed., *Towards an Anthropology of Women* (New York: Monthly Review Press, 1975); Joan Scott, "Gender: A Useful Category of Historical Analysis," *American Historical Review* 91, no. 5 (December 1986): 1053–1075.

11. Judith Sargent Murray, "On the Equality of the Sexes," *The Massachusetts Magazine*, March to April 1790. Sharon M. Harris, ed., *Selected Writings of Judith Sargent Murray* (Oxford: Oxford University Press, 1995), published online by the National Humanities Seminar: http://nationalhumanitiescenter .org/pds/livingrev/equality/text5/sargent.pdf.

12. Douglas R. Egerton, Alison Games, Jane G. Landers, Kris Lane, and Donald R. Wright, *The Atlantic World: A History, 1400–1888* (Wheeling, IL: Harland Davidson, 2007), 18.

13. Amerigo Vespucci, *The Soderini Letter in Translation*, trans. George Tyler, in *Vespucci Reprints, Texts and Studies*, Vol. 4 (Princeton: Princeton University Press, 1916), 5. Available online at the Internet Library: https://falklandstimeline .files.wordpress.com/2018/06/amerigo-vespucci-letter-to-piero-soderini-1504-george-tyler-northup.pdf. Vespucci's letter circulated in a few different forms and languages in the early fifteenth century. This translation collates and combines elements of the three extant versions: The Florentine Print (Italian), The Magliabechiana Manuscript (Italian), and the Hylacalomylus Version (Latin). The

introduction to this translation also includes a detailed description of the extant versions and their relation to each other.

14. Vespucci, *The Soderini Letter*, 6–8.

15. Vespucci, *The Soderini Letter*, 13.

16. Juliana Barr, *Peace Came in the Form of a Woman: Indians and Spaniards in the Texas Borderlands* (Chapel Hill: University of North Carolina Press, 2007), 13–14.

17. Barr, *Peace*, 59–60.

18. Ibid., 61–67.

19. Thomas Shepard, *The Cleare Sun-shine of the Gospel, Breaking Forth upon the Indians in New-England* (London, 1648), 41. Early English Books Online; discussed in Kristina Bross, *Dry Bones and Indian Sermons: Praying Indians in Colonial America* (Ithaca, NY: Cornell University Press, 2004), 107–108.

20. Shepard, *Cleare Sun-shine*, 4–5.

21. On Native versus colonial gender roles in New England, see Lisa Brooks, *Our Beloved Kin: A New History of King Philip's War* (New Haven, CT: Yale University Press, 2018), 32–34, 42–43, and passim.

22. Jennifer L. Morgan, *Laboring Women: Reproduction and Gender in New World Slavery* (Philadelphia: University of Pennsylvania Press, 2004), 7, 62.

23. See Trevor Burnard, *Mastery, Tyranny, and Desire: Thomas Thistlewood and His Slaves in the Anglo-Jamaican World* (Chapel Hill: University of North Carolina Press, 2004), 298 n. 9, for a summary of debates over the degree of agency enslaved Africans had in forming family structures. Pages 187–190 provide a detailed survey of the various kinds of households enslaved people formed on Thistlewood's plantation.

24. Kirsten E. Wood, "Gender and Slavery," in Robert L. Paquette and Mark M. Smith, eds., *The Oxford Handbook of Slavery in the Americas* (Oxford: Oxford University Press, 2010), 515–516.

25. Burnard, *Mastery, Tyranny*, 160.

26. Morgan, *Laboring Women*, 16.

27. On the links between these two figures, see Andrew Newman, "Fulfilling the Name: Catherine Tekakwitha and Marguerite Kanenstenhawi (Eunice Williams)," *Legacy: A Journal of American Women Writers* 28, no. 2 (2011): 232–256.

28. Claude Chauchetière and Pierre Cholenec, *La Vie de la B. Catherine Tegakoüita dite à présent la Saincte Sauvagesse* (Manate: Presse Cramoisy de Jean-Marie Shea, 1887); Pierre Cholenec, "Appendix: La Vie de Catherine Tegakouita Première Vierge Irokoise," in *The Life of Catherine Tekakwitha*, ed. William Lonc, S. J. (Ontario: William Lonc, 2002), 1–67.

5

MARION RUST

How to Read an Early American Novel

My life is, and has been, uniformly irregular.

Stephen Burroughs, *Memoirs of the Notorious Stephen Burroughs* (359)

Can novels change the world, or must they merely inscribe, and thereby fortify, its injustices? Today the question seems easy to answer: no one who reads Toni Morrison's *A Mercy: A Novel*, set on a New York farm in the midst of the seventeenth-century slave trade, can doubt its inspirational resonance. Not so regarding the book-length fictions surrounding an "American" revolution that defined happiness as property, property as private, and certain persons as eligible to be owned, either outright or indirectly through marriage, divestment of lands, and other legal and extra-legal measures. Were early American novels just one more object in that edifice? Questioned in their time for their potential to corrupt by introducing the very actions they warned against, today these oddities of world literature remain caught between a critique wherein social determination is inescapable and another that insists on the power of imaginative narrative to change lives. Whether one looks at novels through the critical lenses of new aesthetics, book history, affect theory, environmental humanities, critical slavery studies, Native American and Indigenous studies, network theory, the spatial turn, world-systems, gender studies, network theory, or any combination of the above, tensions run high in early Americanist literary scholarship between a realist conviction that worlds create books and an equally resolute commitment to the possibility that books – especially fictions – create worlds.

Perhaps, then, it is time to take advice from an unlikely source: the above-quoted Stephen Burroughs, an early American author whose "own chief distinction was hypocrisy," in the words of poet Robert Frost.[1] This is not to suggest skepticism as the only appropriate attitude to an early American novel (more in what follows on how I get away with calling this self-professed memoir a novel). Yet Burroughs's understanding of life as "uniform irregularity" may offer the best chance at coming to terms with his 1811 chronicle of chaos, as well as the hundreds (yes hundreds) of other imaginative labors from the period before most people think an American novel had yet been written. Rather than exhaust themselves trying to "explain away the contradictory positions occupied by many of its central texts," I would suggest that readers interested in early America suspend expectations for coherence, while remaining attuned to what other forms of pleasure and meaning (of "entertainment" and "instruction," to use the familiar terms of eighteenth-century British letters) emerge in its absence.[2] With that freedom should also come permission to put narrow definitions of the novel aside in order to include not only contradictory textualities but voices previously undetected in the cacophony. This chapter thus hopes to honor variation and incommensurability in both literary texts and the scholarship that provides their current scaffolding. To create a place for those early American authors, meanwhile, who have not until recently been recognized in literary studies because their textual creations do not meet normative standards for book-length imaginative prose narrative, will be its sustaining goal.

What Counts?

I begin this chapter about how to read an early American novel with a passage from an early American autobiography – an unreliable one, to be sure, but an autobiography nonetheless, according to the standard definition of the genre as a first-person account of a life said to be written by that person. Stephen Burroughs was a late eighteenth-century, financially insecure, white male roamer with a gift for counterfeit. His account was hardly a "self-consciously fictional text," to use one influential definition of the novel.[3] In fact, its eponymous protagonist incessantly declares his sincerity, if not his veracity. This book nevertheless features prominently on a "favorite early American novels" list I compiled through an informal recent survey of specialists in the field. Does this memoir qualify as a novel because the author, even when proclaiming his often improbable innocence, narrates occasion after occasion in which he is found by his peers to be "counterfeiting" – which is to say creating – not only dollars but alias identities, bogus personal histories, fabricated professional degrees, and other counterfactual representations? Or is it that readers simply don't care whether what he wrote really happened, given the book's extraordinary entertainment value? The ease with which scholars novelize Burroughs's memoir suggests a slide from the above "self-consciously fictional" definition of the novel – one based on what the *writer* had in mind – to something more like "impossible to put down" – a definition based on what *readers* wanted that more closely approximates the criteria Burroughs's compatriots and others today would set for the genre many turn to when work is done (unless, of course, reading novels is your job).

For anyone who doubts the correlation between reading novels – even early American novels – and expecting to enjoy oneself, one need only turn to the widespread critique of the genre's enticing depravity that accompanied early Americans' ever-increasing taste for these sweet treats. According to many an early national self-proclaimed expert – journalist, teacher, minister, headmaster, doctor, and even the occasional self-exculpating author herself – novels could kill. They fed especially on the young and even more especially on young white women. Throwing over the darning needle for the pocket-sized volume, well-meaning but impressionable readers might find themselves prioritizing depiction (exciting misadventures) over proclamation (warnings not to try said misadventures). By this definition of the novel, tales full of salacious incident – such as what Greta LaFleur describes as the "short, cheaply printed pamphlets" from around 1815 depicting the vicissitudes of Boston's "Negro Hill" – would in many ways be more novelistic than a book once considered the first American novel, William Hill Brown's 1789 *The Power of Sympathy*, a treatise known better for its defense of the merits of the genre than for possessing any such merits.[4] Many other similarly self-appointed novels from the next few decades – such as 1810's *Rosa; or, American Genius and Education*, with its propertied white widow continuously issuing salutary edicts to her half-Incan foundling daughter – talked a lot about what good books they were compared to the many embedded narratives at which they scoffed. Judging by sales numbers alone, however, these paragons of virtue might not actually have been what "novel"-readers were after. By contrast, *The Adventures of Lucy Brewer* and related "Negro Hill" pamphlet protagonists held an appeal not entirely unlike that of Burroughs himself: promising white teenagers who escaped from small-town Massachusetts into compelling, unorthodox urban subcultures.[5]

Yet the license extended to Burroughs's *Memoirs* in welcoming his bad-boy antics into the novelistic mix is not something every early American narrative has been able to claim. Here are a few items that didn't show up on my aforementioned survey of favorite early American novels, despite the fact that they are at least as hard to put down as any of the above too-short or too-true-to-be novels in the conventional sense. Mohegan Samson Occom's 1769 "A Short Narrative of My Life" conveys the rage of an aggrieved party with all the finesse of the finest revenge plot, putting the slur of the "poor Indian" to devastatingly ironic ends. About sixty years later, Pequot William Apess's

"An Indian's Looking-Glass for the White Man" uses the trope of black ink on a white page to represent black marks on the "white" skin of the preponderance of his readers. By the time he is done building this mirror image, those who look into it expecting to solidify racial difference as a category for legitimating power find themselves terrifyingly transformed. Thus does the equation between "blackness" and sin redound, again with bitter irony, to destroy white readers' complacency.

One might also consider "Theresa: A Haytien Tale," a four-part serialized fiction in the *Freedom's Journal* for 1827 that depicts the Haitian Revolution of the 1790s from the perspective of a female rebel. Who says an early American novel has to say anything particular about the United States, or that wartime adventurers must be men? As a final example of a transfixing nonfictional prose narrative, one might consider the "Letter of Instruction from Oanhekoe, Sachem of the Mohegan Indians in New England, 14 July 1703," which bears pictorial representations common among northeastern Indigenous signatories, with the exception that one of the birds is wearing a crown. This letter is no early American novel – but to read one well, I would suggest, it's worth taking a look at that crowned bird.

Unlike Burroughs's peripatetic misadventures, there is nothing much funny in these works. They don't grip the reader for the same reasons that Burroughs does. They are, though, similarly difficult mirrors to turn away from. What all these documents have in common is that, without any claim to fictionality, their consummate impact results from invention. Yet none of these works has ever been called a novel. Novels, it is said, are book-length fictions, not jeremiads against genocidal treachery or political letters meant for Queen Anne. The result is that a discussion of the genre in an early American context cannot but exclude vast ranges of human experience that would be more accessible were one merely to uncheck the "novel" filter.

There is good reason to be wary of attributing the aesthetic imprimatur of the novel to printed prose works by the variously disenfranchised peoples of what many now call early America. Facts matter when trying to access the experience, imaginative and otherwise, of those facing significant obstacles to writing their own story or having it written correctly. Among the most important Americanist scholarly achievements of the last half-century are some that prove books long considered novels to be factual narratives as well. When two novels by antebellum Black women – one enslaved in the south (*Incidents in the Life of a Slave Girl*, by Harriet Jacobs), the other in servitude in the north (*Our Nig*, by Harriet Wilson) – were separately found to consist exclusively or primarily of biographical truths, these discoveries verified both the historical accuracy of the atrocities these literary artists depicted and the depth of psychic ingenuity and resilience displayed under conditions of enforced servitude.[6]

It remains the case, however, that factuality is disproportionately valorized in narratives by those whose attributed race, ethnicity, gender expression, or other perceived identity marker has been used to differentiate their work from the majority of published material in the early Americas. Think only of the recent firestorm over whether Olaudah Equiano, author of the widely studied 1789 *Interesting Narrative of the Life of Olaudah Equiano, or Gustavus Vassa, The African*, was actually born in West Africa, where he said he was, and truly experienced the Middle Passage firsthand, which he said he did. Equiano called his work a *Narrative* – not, like published versions of the Benjamin Franklin self-narrative against which Equiano's work is so often read, an *Autobiography*.[7] Yet, in the furor that resulted regarding the political stakes of even choosing to undertake an investigation into Equiano's birthplace, few seemed to question that any infidelities of the narrative to the author's biographical experience would, if they were true, lessen its merits. Indeed, the publisher's blurb for the book that introduced this possibility, Vincent Carretta's *Equiano, the African: Biography of a Self-Made Man*, suggested that Equiano "may have lied about his origins," equating potential authorial license with a morally fraught act.[8]

And yet, whether Equiano was speaking from personal experience or making use of existing narratives in order to provide a broad readership something it could put to effective abolitionist use, the *Interesting Narrative* remains equally brilliant, in its absurdist juxtaposition of Igbo captives attempting to leap off ships into the ocean with flying fish flopping onto the deck to suffocate. Whether the author was born in West Africa or South Carolina, and exactly why he wrote the former if the latter is true, bears relevance to how the work signifies but not to its textual power or the author's integrity. Why not take this narrative, then, like Burroughs's, for what it is – an extraordinarily effective rhetorical feat that will engross and transform readers past and present – rather than kindly call the former a "novel" for its lapses while questioning the latter's very deservedness to hold the central place it does in the Americanist canon on the basis of a contested birthplace and transatlantic kidnapping? Instead, it would seem that, while Equiano's narrative has been critiqued for the reliability of his claims to personal experience, Burroughs is celebrated for precisely this unreliability. What impact, then, does an emphasis on veracity or its lack have on how the early Americanist canon figures race and particularly Black personhood and artistry?

Vexed Relationships

I begin with this question because it is one example of a broader query that bedevils and animates early American novel studies: How do aesthetic and political concerns intersect in early American fiction, and to what end? In rough terms, the major parties are skeptics with a keen eye for hypocrisy and visionaries who see reading as a potentially transformative experience. Both aim to disrupt narrowly conceived notions of the novel – but for very different reasons. Let me start with what I will call the realists. For critics such as Philip Barnard, Mark Kamrath, and Stephen Shapiro, coauthors of "Charles Brockden Brown and the Novel in the 1790s," novels at their best allow us "to speculate on the causes of historical events." As a "narrative laboratory" that allows us to "test ... hypothetical situations," these scholars argue, early American fiction matters most for what it can teach us about what lies outside it.[9] By this account, Equiano's unexpectedly "hypothetical" representation of his childhood could indeed qualify his work for study in the lab – but primarily in order to deliver a more detailed and accurate sense of what might motivate such slippage, rather than for any narrative richness this ambiguity might provide on its own terms. It is with this pursuit in mind that Shapiro and his colleagues want to allow more things to be novels than might have been implied by Shapiro's earlier definition of the novel as a "self-consciously fictional text."[10] In contrast with that definition, here they consider "the novel-form as conjectural history and thus as an engagement with socially focused writing that extends well beyond the limits of the novel as conventionally understood."[11] Rather than give up on the novel, Shapiro and his colleagues choose, as I am suggesting in this chapter, to "extend" its "limits" beyond what "convention" has yet allowed; but it remains, nonetheless, "conjectural history."

There are those who would take this emphasis on the primacy of historical context even farther, suggesting not only that early American novels matter most for how they recorded the material circumstances under which they were produced but also that they had little ability to influence those circumstances in return. If, as Ned Watts claims, "empire is constructed through the control of language, narrative, and textual authority," then to exercise "textual authority" is de facto to lose subaltern status rather than challenge the circumstances that create it.[12] Joe Shapiro (no relation to Stephen) makes a similarly strong case for the limited capacities of early American fiction to do more than fortify existing social hierarchies, aiming to "highlight the ways in which foundational early U.S. novelists in fact invest in, endorse, and ratify structures of economic inequality" so as to "naturalize class inequality among whites."[13]

Among the accomplishments of those who would disabuse readers of the comforting fantasy that novelistic imaginaries make for a more egalitarian populace, critics who prioritize historical occurrence also finally seem to be successfully dissuading us from assuming that there was anything like a national imaginary. Countering a long tradition of reading early American novels as allegories for the perils of a narrowly conceived (in both geographic and ideological terms) postrevolutionary self-determination, these critics argue that early American novelists couldn't be wasting their time on creating an origin story for an independent United States, because there was no single entity represented by that term. Global commercial cross-currents, settler colonialist incursions against and inter-actions with Indigenous populations, the obscene fact of an economy prem-ised on enslavement espousing a rhetoric of liberty: nothing could make less sense than mistaking antiquarian nostalgia or patriotic themes for a collective ideological coup by which the many became one.

As it turns out, however, it is not only the materialists who think getting rid of national allegory is important. So, too, do two other groups with distinct but complementary notions of what counts as historical context. One important assemblage consists of those who wish to argue for an emphasis on locality (e.g. "neighborhoods," a common phrase in early America used to refer to a smaller geographic region comprised of diverse peoples, as Caroline Wigginton has described it) and specific life stages such as child-hood (Nazera Wright, Patricia Crain, Anna Mae Duane, to name a few) as a means of attending to individuals and communities often left off the canonical literary page.[14] In this spirit, many critics question the literary nationalism that early American studies once took for granted.

Lastly, there are those who critique an emphasis on nationhood not for being too grand but rather too narrow. Stephen Shapiro, for instance, lodges the following critique: "The early American novel had little concern for allegorizing the nation-state or enunciating patriotic themes ... [It] arose as a local response to a global reconfiguration in the Atlantic political economy in the wake of the French Revolution, brought about as a result of the long confrontation between Great Britain and France for imperial control of global resources."[15] Other critics considering how the early United States featured within a global context grant more agency to the new nation – for instance, the recent assertion that, during the late eighteenth century, "the colonies in British North America asserted their sovereignty and seized control from Britain of the circulation of resources, people, goods, and information through their segments of the North Atlantic trade routes."[16] Those familiar with the plethora of literature that grew up around what was then known as the "Algerine crisis" (e.g. Royall Tyler's *The Algerine*

Captive, Susanna Rowson's *Slaves in Algiers*, or Peter Markoe's *The Algerine Spy in Pennsylvania*) might hesitate at the force of the word "seized," given that trade routes throughout the 1790s remained contested enough for some American ships to be, in literal fact, seized by the North African states.[17] Yet regardless of how strong a role British America played on the global stage, almost all would agree with Tennenhouse and Armstrong that none of "the novels born of this paradox [could] imagine anything like a single bounded community to which members of a national readership might belong."[18]

In sum, if there is one thing that current theorists of the early American novel have in common, it is a communal exasperation with the default tendency to read early American literary dynamics as stand-ins for national self-definitions with which neither author, character nor reader may have had much familiarity or concern. This consensus brings a number of socially focused critics from a variety of ideological and intellectual perspectives into accord; and it may even present an olive branch of sorts to more aesthetically inclined critics. The self-professed formalist Ed Cahill, for instance, begins his case for paying attention to the literariness of early American novels with a slight aimed at those who would wrap everything up in a national-identity bow, claiming that "American writers of the Revolution and the early republic were not too busy with nation building or too ambivalent about the imagination to theorize its powers. Indeed, ideas about pleasure, fancy, association, taste, genius, beauty, and sublimity permeated literary culture."[19]

Cahill's claim also, however, embodies what can only be described as a rift between two groups whose explicit common causes may consist only of the above-described anti-nationalism and this chapter's overall attentiveness to expanding what counts as a novel. Of late, the call for deepening and, indeed, correcting understandings of how to read early American literature often derives from a powerful counterclaim against historicism: one memorably summarized as a "disenchantment with disenchantment."[20] Sometimes referred to as the "aesthetic turn," this school of thought aims to supersede what it considers to be a tired emphasis on historical context to give early American literature a chance to rest on its own merits. Early American literary studies' "vexed relationship to aesthetics," as Cahill and Edward Larkin point out in a special issue of *Early American Literature* titled "Aesthetics, Feeling and Form in Early American Literary Studies," derives in large part from a long-term implicit embarrassment over what founding practitioners in the field assumed to be their primary materials' insuperable lack of innate literary richness."[21] No need to be ashamed, goes this counternarrative: just because early American novels are far from seamless, doesn't mean their scratches and bumps lack value.

An embrace of the literariness of scratches and bumps by definition means an expansion of what counts in any discussion of the novel. Like recent historicist analyses, this kind of reading frees us to find new – but decidedly different – forms of worth in a greater variety of texts. For Ezra Tawil, understanding the preface to the most popular American seduction novel of the 1790s, Susanna Rowson's *Charlotte Temple*, requires reading it as a recasting of the *Bay Psalm Book*, a metrical psalter that was the first book printed in British North America.[22] For Abram Van Engen, in order to progress beyond admittedly worthy sociopolitical understandings of the second most popular seduction novel, Hannah Foster's *The Coquette*, it helps to see it as an extension of Jonathan Edwards's philosophical meditations on freedom in a religious context.[23] Scholarly analysis of same-sex sexuality, such as Caleb Crain's study of the *"a fortiori* sexual" relationship between young adults James Gibson and John Fishbourne Mifflin as expressed in diaries and letters from the 1780s, has been crucial as both a site of archival recovery and a prompt to include such documents in any concept of the literary.[24]

Recent scholarly analysis has also introduced a new, or newly reconceived, kind of reading, one that attends to "play" and even "an emergent autonomy of art," to quote Philipp Schweighauser, in prose narratives that historicist literary scholars have tended to functionalize out of much of their experiential richness. In "render[ing] literature diminutive before a more substantial explanatory context," as Christopher Castiglia describes it, readers can lose track of the following qualities listed by Cindy Weinstein and Christopher Looby:

> the play of imagination, the exploration of fantasy, the recognition and description of literary form, the materiality of literary inscription and publication, the pleasure of the text, sensuous experience in general, the appreciation of beauty, the adjudication and expression of taste, the broad domain of feeling or affect, or some particular combination of several of these elements.[25]

In sum, it would seem that both historicist and aestheticist schools want the same thing – a more capacious definition of, and consistent approach to, the novel – but for different reasons. In what follows, I will explore the consequences of this tension for understanding early American novels. Whether one insists upon historical relevance or stretches for a more text-centered mode of appreciation has a significant impact on how one reads – to say nothing of the broadly conceived novelistic canon that coalesces at these intersecting currents.

Object Lives

Early American novels have been called many things, including nonexistent. Catherine Gallagher notes that "fictionality seems to have been but faintly understood in the infant United States at the end of the eighteenth century."[26] Much recent criticism, however, implicitly replies to this negation by suggesting that unrecognizability is not the same as nonexistence. Hence the most recurrent phrase of late used to describe the early American novel is some version of "strange objects." Schweighauser's early American novels "are *strangely* hybrid *objects* characterized by great tensions," part of the larger field of "*strange objects* and hybrid texts" by which Jennifer Brady characterizes the long nineteenth century.[27] One might think that an emphasis on objects would equate with a rather deterministic view of the world and literature's place in it: a healthy skepticism regarding the text's ability to abstract itself from the arbitrary concatenations of matter that litter its surroundings. While it is true that some studies see no place for the novel beyond an Althusserian functionality, in general, this supposition would be incorrect, as it is precisely those who appreciate the relevance of the term "object" that also recognize its complex and even oxymoronic significance. In other words, discussions of these "strange objects" tend to emphasize fluidity, transmutability, even transformation over the stasis generally accorded objects.

The recent proliferation of this phrase in a variety of disconnected sites fascinates me because, without even meaning to, it joins historicist and aesthetic approaches to the novel under one great if leaky roof. "Objects" are things; they are the stuff of circumstance, the matter of history. "Strange," however, implies unpredictability – if something is strange, it doesn't behave as expected. A "strange object" isn't much good for making patterns (that is, until a pattern renders it no longer strange). It's hard to categorize. It's hard to historicize. At the same time, it's still an "object." It hasn't escaped the material world altogether. "Strange objects" are like the hauntings, the "embodied cognition," that proliferate throughout scholar Michelle Sizemore's postrevolutionary world and, increasingly, that of other critics. Like what Siân Silyn Roberts terms the "[o]bjects that act like subjects" in Washington Irving's "Sleepy Hollow," they are both alive and inert.[28] A strange object, then, is its own kind of subject: it possesses a life of its own.

With strange objects in mind, I think we can return one last time to the debate I have been sketching to come up with an explanation that is not an explaining away of either the materialist or the new aestheticist approach to early American novels. For it becomes apparent that the most profound recent studies of the early American novel insist upon the political dimensions of aesthetic practice and vice versa, such that neither overwrites the other. Cahill summarizes this pursuit: "effective formalism, far from turning us away from history, brings us back to its richest particularities." Benjamin Reiss provides an instantiation, arguing that "[N]ovels were thus not simply *a kind of cargo that circulated* through the Atlantic world and penetrated American interiors, but also *tools for representing* new ways of life in the spaces and places their authors encountered (or imagined encountering)." In her study of the early American gothic, Roberts offers another, noting that it is exactly the "idiosyncratic" and "fantastic" that, precisely on the basis of their having been considered poor matter for constructing a productive citizenry in Britain, make for new forms of sociohistorical affiliation in its former colonies. Thus, in a wonderful synthesis of Looby and Weinstein's "play of imagination" with counterclaims for the primacy of "historical event," she argues: "the American gothic tradition validates precisely those idiosyncratic, fantastic notions of the individual that the British tradition goes out of its way to render phobic and transforms them into the basis of political membership." Finally, Elizabeth Dillon's triumphant definition of the "aesthetic" as "the formation of communities of sense" stands as the single most confident iteration of this perspective. For her, there simply is no aesthetics apart from its communal instantiations. Shifting the emphasis, as I attempted at the outset of this chapter, from *what* is read to the *act* of reading (or writing, or seeing, or touching, or listening, or not listening) allows Dillon a new term, "aesthesis," which in an early Atlantic world context represents a "generative and creative force ... in the shadow of imperial violence."[29]

There are those who would consider critical gestures toward reconciling the tensions between an approach to literature grounded in aesthetics and one grounded in historical circumstance wishful thinking. The noted poet and theorist Charles Altieri, for instance, protests that foregrounding aesthetic considerations in the study of history and politics can only be successful if critics "build predicates for social use into the definition of aesthetic from the start." This devalues the importance of the aesthetic altogether, he suggests, because it forecloses upon "conditions of aesthetic experience in which a variety of properties function together to establish the kind of event that has traditionally been proclaimed as somehow denying referential functions because the state of attention becomes valuable in itself."[30] For me, however – and I hope for you after reading this chapter – the quixotic nature of the quest to experience profound "state[s] of attention" without losing referentiality altogether is worth the necessary inadequacy of the outcome, because it allows for a richer reading (which is to say living) experience.

Running away, getting lost, strapping oneself into the state fair Gravitron ride: these things thrill as well as discomfort only because subjects know that their vertigo speaks to the possibility of balance regained. Participants may have lost their points of reference, but these points still exist, or at least they did. As surroundings begin to lose their familiarity, this encounter with the strange motivates readers to appreciate the significance along with the impermanence of what they once found ordinary. The strangest object of all may be that one-time seeming repository of generic stasis, the novel itself: centerpiece of English department syllabi, bookstore bestseller shelves, and the American literary canon in all its exclusivity. If I were to summarize how to read an early American novel in one sentence, it would be: Read anything you want from the period before you thought there was literature in America, and read it however you want, as long as you remember that you are engaged in deadly serious play.

Notes

1. Robert Frost, "Preface," in Stephen Burroughs, *Memoirs of the Notorious Stephen Burroughs, of New Hampshire* (Whitefish, MT: Kessinger Publishing, 2010), 6.
2. Jared Gardner, "The Literary Museum and the Unsettling of the Early American Novel," *ELH* 67, no. 3 (2000): 745.
3. Stephen Shapiro, *The Culture and Commerce of the Early American Novel* (University Park: Pennsylvania State University Press, 2008), 780.
4. Greta LaFleur, *The Natural History of Sexuality in Early America* (Baltimore: Johns Hopkins University Press, 2018), 165. William Hill Brown, *The Power of Sympathy* (Digireads.com, 2011).
5. *Rosa; or, American Genius and Education*, ed. Duncan Faherty and Ed White, as part of the "Just Teach One" project, for *Commonplace: The Journal of Early American Life* (fall 2017): http://jto.common-place.org/just-teach-one-homepage /rosa-1810/. On *The Adventures of Lucy Brewer* and other "Female Marine" texts that engage with "Negro Hill," see LaFleur, *Natural History of Sexuality*, 165–166.
6. Harriet Jacobs, *Incidents in the Life of a Slave Girl, Written by Herself*, ed. Jean Fagan Yellin (Cambridge, MA: Harvard University Press, 2009); Harriet Wilson, *Our Nig: or, Sketches from the Life of a Free Black*, ed. P. Gabrielle Foreman (New York: Addison Wesley, 2009).
7. Olaudah Equiano, *The Interesting Narrative and other Writings*, ed. Vincent Carretta (New York: Penguin 2003); *Benjamin Franklin's Autobiography*, ed. Joyce E. Chaplin (New York: Norton Critical Editions, 2012).
8. See "Equiano, the African: Biography of a Self-Made Man, By Vincent Carretta," Penguin Random House, www.penguinrandomhouse.com/books/298843/ equiano-the-african-by-vincent-carretta/. For counterarguments to Carretta's thesis, see, for example, Paul E. Lovejoy, "Autobiography and Memory: Gustavus Vassa, Alias Olaudah Equiano, the African" *Slavery and Abolition* 27, no. 3 (2006):

317–347; and Lovejoy, "Issues of Motivation: Vassa/Equiano and Carretta's Critique of the Evidence," *Slavery and Abolition* 28, no. 1 (2007): 121–125.

9. Philip Barnard, Mark Kamrath, and Stephen Shapiro, "Charles Brockden Brown and the Novel in the 1790s," in Theresa Gaul, ed., *Blackwell Companion to American Literature, Vol. 1: Beginnings to 1820* (London: Wiley-Blackwell, 2020), 456.

10. Shapiro, *780.*

11. Ibid., 446.

12. Edward Watts, "Settler Postcolonialism As a Reading Strategy," *Early American Literature* 45, no. 2 (2010): 450. For a foundational text on the paradox of subalternity, see Gayatri Spivak, "Can the Subaltern Speak?," in *Marxism and the Interpretation of Culture*, ed. Cary Nelson (Urbana Champaign: University of Illinois, 1988), 271–316, 308, whose last paragraph begins, "The subaltern cannot speak" – because to speak is to render oneself no longer subaltern.

13. Joe Shapiro, *The Illiberal Imagination: Class and the Rise of the U.S. Novel* (Charlottesville: University of Virginia Press, 2017), 4.

14. Caroline Wigginton, *In the Neighborhood: Women's Publication in Early America* (Amherst: University of Massachusetts Press, 2016); Nazera Sadiq Wright, *Black Girlhood in the Nineteenth Century* (Urbana: University of Illinois Press, 2016); Patricia Crain, *Reading Children: Literacy, Property, and the Dilemmas of Childhood in Nineteenth-Century America* (Philadelphia: University of Pennsylvania Press, 2016). Anna Mae Duane, *Suffering Childhood in Early America: Violence, Race, and the Making of the Child Victim* (Cambridge: Cambridge University Press, 2010).

15. Stephen Shapiro, *The Culture and Commerce of the Early American Novel* (University Park: Pennsylvania State University Press, 2008), 4.

16. Nancy Armstrong and Leonard Tennenhouse, *Novels in the Time of Democratic Writing: The American Example* (Philadelphia: University of Pennsylvania Press, 2018), 2.

17. Royall Tyler, *The Algerine Captive: or, the Life and Adventures of Doctor Updike Underhill*, ed. Caleb Crain (New York: Modern Library Classics, 2002); Susanna Rowson, *Slaves in Algiers; or, A struggle for freedom: a play, interspersed with songs, in three acts*, ed. Jennifer Margulis and Karen Poremski (Acton, MA: Copley Publishing Group, 2001); Peter Markoe, *The Algerine Spy in Pennsylvania* (Yardley, PA: Westholme Publishing, 2008).

18. Armstrong and Tennenhouse, *Novels in the Time of Democratic Writing*, 2.

19. Ed Cahill, *Liberty of the Imagination: Aesthetic Theory, Literary Form, and Politics in the Early United States* (Philadelphia: University of Pennsylvania Press, 2012), 2.

20. Nancy Bentley, "Conjunctions: Jacques Rancière and African American Twoness," in Cindy Weinstein and Christopher Looby, eds., *American Literature's Aesthetic Dimensions* (New York: Columbia University Press, 2012).

21. Ed Cahill and Edward Larkin, "Aesthetics, Feeling, and Form in Early American Literary Studies," introduction to the Special Issue of *Early American Literature* 51, no. 2 (2016): 235.

22. Susanna Rowson, *Charlotte Temple: A Norton Critical Edition*, ed. Marion Rust (New York: W.W. Norton & Co, 2010); Richard Mather et al., *The Bay Psalm Book* (Carlisle, MA: Applewood Books, 2011); Ezra Tawil, "Seduction, Sentiment, and the Transatlantic Plain Style," *Early American Literature* 51, no. 2 (2016): 277–278.

23. Hannah Foster, *The Coquette* (Oxford: Oxford University Press, 1987); Abram Van Engen, "Eliza's Disposition: Freedom, Pleasure, and Sentimental Fiction," *Early American Literature* 51, no. 2 (2016): 297–331.

24. Caleb Crain, "Leander, Lorenzo, and Castalio: An Early American Romance," in Thomas A. Foster, ed., *Long Before Stonewall: Histories of Same-Sex Sexuality in Early America* (New York: New York University Press, 2007), 243.

25. Philipp Schweighauser, *Beautiful Deceptions: European Aesthetics, the Early American Novel, and Illusionist Art* (Charlottesville: University of Virginia Press, 2016), 20, 17; Christopher Castiglia, "Revolution Is a Fiction: The Way We Read (Early American Literature) Now," *Early American Literature* 51, no. 2 (2016): 401; Cindy Weinstein and Christopher Looby, "Introduction," in Weinstein and Looby, *American Literature's Aesthetic Dimensions*, 4.

26. Catherine Gallagher, "The Rise of Fictionality," in Franco Moretti, ed., *The Novel, Vol. 1: History, Geography, and Culture* (Princeton: Princeton University Press, 2006), 345.

27. Schweighauser, *Beautiful Deceptions*, 16. Jennifer Brady, in Jennifer Brady and Erin Pearson, "Teaching the Weird Nineteenth Century," Call for Papers for 2020 C19 Conference in Coral Gables, Florida. L-C19-AMERICANISTS @LISTS.PSU.EDU; emphases added.

28. Michelle Sizemore, *American Enchantment: Rituals of the People in the Post-Revolutionary World* (Oxford: Oxford University Press, 2017); Siân Silyn Roberts, *Gothic Subjects: The Transformation of Individualism in American Fiction, 1790–1861* (Philadelphia: University of Pennsylvania Press, 2014), 15.

29. Cahill, *Liberty*, 10; Benjamin Reiss, "Introduction: Inventing the American Novel," in Leonard Cassutto, Clare Virginia Eby, and Benjamin Reiss, eds., *The Cambridge History of the American Novel* (Cambridge: Cambridge University Press, 2011), 18 (emphases added); Roberts, *Gothic Subjects*, 15; Elizabeth Dillon, "Atlantic Aesthesis: Books and *Sensus Communis* in the New World," *Early American Literature* 51, no. 2 (2016): 367–395 (367–368).

30. Charles Altieri, "Afterword: Are Aesthetic Models the Best Way to Talk about the Artfulness of Literary Texts?," in Weinstein and Looby, *American Literature's Aesthetic Dimensions*, 393–394.

6

DANA D. NELSON

How to Read Democracy in the Early United States

Americans know the story of democracy. We learn it in middle and high school or in citizenship classes. We learn, for instance, that the "correct" answer to the question "What is the United States' form of government?" is not "democracy" but rather "*a Republic.*" In those civics classes, America's young citizens learn about the Framers' skepticism about direct democracy, a caution that grew from their careful study of world history. Aiming to ensure political stability for a people unaccustomed to self-governing, the Founding Fathers crafted a government that would deter political tyranny whether from a single source or a group. The Revolution enacted the Framers' repudiation of monarchy, while their fear of the mobs and bullying majorities made them cautious about democracy. Unmediated participation led to the possibility of what they termed "democratic excess": to political unpredictability and even lawlessness, and worse, to undercutting of the political and economic liberties of minorities. To guard against both forms of tyranny, they crafted a republican machine: a constitutional government with branches that would check and balance each other, that would derive its authority and powers from the sovereign citizens, filtered through and refined by their elected representatives. That republican form of government has allowed for the safe growth of democracy in the United States, as citizens, within structures of representative democracy, have grown up and into their project of self-government. As the nation grew, it expanded citizenship. Americans and indeed people all over the world casually refer to the US system of government as "democracy" but it is in fact the seat-belting representative republican framework provided by the Framers that has ensured the safe and stable democratization of our country over time.[1]

The story we learn as schoolchildren encourages us to see early citizens of the United States in the same capacity: eager youth, schooled by the sage Framers for their new democratic citizenship. We think of the nation in its "infancy," full of ordinary folk ignorant of the workings of complex political systems and maturing over time and through practice into the full adulthood of citizenship, just as the United States over time matured into its status as the "world's leading democracy." This well-rehearsed story of American democracy encourages citizens to imagine American democracy as a bequest from the Framers. In it, democratic power is "having a vote" – that once-every-four-years moment of popular sovereignty when citizens mark ballots, elect representatives, and turn the work of self-governing over to them. Finally, it teaches citizens to understand political self-government as emanating from the political elite – the Framers or subsequent political leadership – and not from ordinary citizens.

Stories are powerful. In Kenneth Burke's terms, they provide "equipment for living."[2] From the myriad details of history, powerful narratives guide readers' attention in the real world, helping them filter input and select relevant details. Stories guide readers to overlook alternative details, to ignore anomalies. They shape perception and apprehension. And here's the problem: this powerful founding story is not a full depiction of the growth of democracy in the British colonies and early United States. Rather, it is a victor's tale, designed to finish off by erasing from the nation's collective historical memory a very real battle with a robust alternative model of democratic theory and practice that was flourishing – much to the Framers' consternation – in the early nation. This alternative democracy, which we can think of as vernacular democracy, originated in the daily practice of ordinary colonists, many of whom came to the colonies from Britain having been enclosed out of commons. This more colloquial practice of democracy generated and motored the American Revolution; and despite the fact that the political elite of the late British colonies who supported independence seemingly embraced this participatory and equalitarian practice of democracy, in the later years of the Revolution they pulled away, seeking in their words to "tame" the democratic enthusiasm and power of ordinary American citizens even as they drew on that power (renamed "sovereignty") to authorize the representative federal republicanism they proffered as a containment device for commons democracy. Because of the mesmerizing force of our founding narrative about democracy, historians and literary historians have hardly noticed these alternative forms of vernacular democracy that are literally hiding in plain sight. Once you know to look for them, however, you'll begin seeing them everywhere in the political literature and fiction of the British colonies and the early United States.

Vernacular democracy has its roots in several cultural strands. Let's start with the commons, which have received little attention in British colonial and early US history, not least because a tradition of American exceptionalism (firmly tethered to the triumphalist story of the Framers' founding) asserting that, because of the natural bounty and free availability of land for common folk in the colonies and early republic, ordinary citizens did not suffer from the stark wealth disparities between commoners and aristocrats that characterized class relations in Europe during the colonial era. This is how America came to be known as the "land of the common man." Yet it is also true, as the historian Allan Kulikoff details in his book *From British Peasants to Colonial American Farmers*, that many of the early British settlers in the colonies – commoners who came on their own dime as well as the many who came under indentures as servants – came to the Americas steeped in commoning traditions, traditions that concerned the sharing and management not just of natural resources like firewood and pastures but of domestic and civic resources as well; and these same people brought along a political sensibility tempered by decades of resistance to enclosure efforts in England.[3]

The history and traditions of commoning in Europe are complex and still poorly understood. Commons culture is improvisational, locally based, and locally inflected, making generalizations difficult. In her study of commoners and common right in eighteenth- and early nineteenth-century England, the historian J. M. Neeson describes commoning as "possession without ownership."[4] The legal historian Stuart Banner alternately describes it as a "third form" of ownership, existing *between* public and private. Neeson notes that "we know relatively little about common right and less about commoners" and points, like Banner, to the imaginative constraints that come from "an age such as ours when land is owned exclusively and when enterprise is understood to be essentially individual, not cooperative."[5] Another block to historical study comes in the fact that commoners didn't amass libraries, nor did they leave extensive writings *to* libraries. Thus, historians studying commoners depend crucially on contemporary accounts of their *adversaries*, people trying to enclose them out of newly private lands, who saw them as impediments to "progress," the antithesis to individual enterprise: as poor, dirty, lazy, and primitive. These opponents – members of elite property-holding classes benefiting from enclosure – came to hate commoners with what Neeson describes as an "almost xenophobic intensity," frequently characterizing former commoners – cottagers, squatters, and vagrants alike – as something like a race apart, beyond the pale of modern politics and economic progress.[6]

In her sympathetic account of common right, enclosure, and social change in eighteenth-century England, Neeson argues that, for eighteenth-century commoners, the traditions and practice of commoning fostered alternative economic, social, and political outlooks among its practitioners, based not in individual accumulation and surplus but in familial and community sufficiency. Common rights of pasturage and forage offered employment to some and subsistence for many. It was a "vital part of the economy of women and children" and could significantly increase a family's resources and income.[7] The sharing of common natural and cultural resources encouraged frugality, collaboration, and mutuality: "Time spent searching for wild strawberries, mushrooms, whortle berries and cranberries for the vicar, or catching wheatears for the gentry, was time well spent not only in the senses of earning money but also in the sense of establishing connection" both with landscapes and within social orders.[8] Commoning cultivated both intimacy and expertise with natural resources even as it created networks that satisfied mutual needs in the larger community. An economy grounded in gifts and exchange, it served in crucial ways as insurance for poorer folk, a back-up resource when other avenues failed. Thus, enclosure changed not only the physical landscape of the countryside with fences and hedges; it transformed the social order of the communities that had coexisted in common, erecting social new barriers between "haves" and "have-nots" and fragmenting commoners into smallholders, cottagers, dependants, beggars, vagrants, and criminals.

Many early colonists in the British American colonies came seeking access to a livelihood and way of life no longer accessible to them in England. They brought with them the practices and traditions of commoning they had been raised in and had fought to save. British commoners were not alone in this endeavor. Stuart Banner emphasizes that "the earliest European colonizers in many parts of the present-day United States held much of their productive land in common. They farmed in common fields, grazed their animals in common pastures, and gathered wood and other natural resources from common wasteland."[9] To this day, holders of private land must post "do not trespass" signs if they do not want people hunting for wildlife on their property – so deep and nevertheless hidden is the logic of commoning in US law. Neeson asks us to consider how the collectivism of commoning created what she describes as a "social efficiency" – a value too easily overlooked by historians focused on modern capitalism's singular emphasis on economic efficiency and growth.[10] Alongside Neeson's emphasis on how commoning creates social value, Banner emphasizes the political value it creates among its practitioners, who gain meaningful experiences of self-governing as they participate in negotiating community resource allocation.

A second strand informing vernacular democracy comes from the complex brew emerging between the Protestant Reformation's rejection of Catholic church hierarchy and the modern political science of contract theory that came in the wake of the Protestant Reformation. Martin Luther's attempt to reform Catholic practice beginning early in the sixteenth century aimed to empower ordinary believers, by translating the Bible from Latin into vernacular languages so it could be studied without the intermediation of church authority and by encouraging communities of true believers that they could practice their faith by self-congregating, forming their own church communities. The social logic of the Reformation changed Europe, unleashing theological as well as class rebellion.

On the heels of the Reformation, modern social contract theory emerged from influential seventeenth-century thinkers like Thomas Hobbes, who grounded his social contract theory as an antidote to life in the State of Nature, famously "nasty, brutish and short." John Locke soon rejected Hobbes's depiction of the State of Nature. For Locke, men were equal under natural law, a pre-political but importantly not pre-moral state of liberty where all are free to pursue their own interests. The harmony of the State of Nature, according to Locke, was jeopardized by man's inevitable selfishness – attempts to steal property or to enslave fellow men. To control such inevitable selfishness, men agreed – consented and compacted – to form governments, to unite into commonwealths.

Early in the seventeenth century, a group of Protestant nonconformists fled for the Netherlands, seeking its protections for religious freedom. Soon, though, to guard their cultural as well as religious integrity, they decided to leave Leiden for the British colonies. They obtained a contract from Virginia Company stockholders who financed their trip expecting to be repaid by the colonists' profits. These were the Pilgrims, forty-one people who traveled on the *Mayflower*. They were accompanied by sixty-one non-Separatist commoners – merchants, craftsmen, orphans, and indentured servants. Their destination was the Hudson River. When they landed further north, however, near Cape Cod in present-day Massachusetts, the non-Separatists on the ship refused to be governed by the Virginia Company contract. To save the joint enterprise, the forty-one adult men (including two indentured servants) crafted and signed what we now know as the Mayflower Compact. This legal document, binding all ship members into a "civil Body Politick," was framed so that this group could together "enact, constitute and frame such just and equal Laws, Ordinances, Acts, Constitutions and Offices, from time to time, as shall be thought most meet and convenient for the general good of the Colony, unto which we promise all due submission and obedience."[11] Here, we see a convergence of theological and civil self-governing logics underpinning a self-managing and importantly diverse community. The Mayflower Compact owes a certain debt to the Calvinism and covenant theology of its Pilgrim signers. Soon a broader array of Protestant groups, from Quakers and Anabaptists to Methodists and Baptists, would enter the British colonies, whose self-covenanting sensibilities and socially egalitarian practices and ideals would inform developing practices of vernacular democracy across the colonies.

Plymouth Plantation demonstrated its commitment to equalitarian self-governing by instituting rules for both common labor and common store. These rules drew on the open field system of England, before enclosure, where the area of settlement was administrated as a communal good, shared by all. This was not an anomaly of idealism in a colonial outpost. Back in England, just a few years later, the Levellers, another group of nonconforming dissenters, would proffer an egalitarian religious and political vision grounded in agrarianism, emphasizing the natural rights of men and advocating for the translation of British Law from Latin into the common English, along with popular suffrage. Hot on their heels came the Diggers, who termed themselves "true levellers" and who would distinguish themselves from their competitors by advocating for property held entirely in common and promoting what we can now think of as an ecological relationship between man and nature. They earned their name by tearing down fences and hedges so that people could return to cultivating land in common.

Plymouth Plantation formally abandoned its "Common Course and Condition" in 1623, redressing its chronic lack of food stores by assigning private plots for agriculture and letting each family provision itself. As William Bradford summarizes, this decision

> had very good success, for it made all hands very industrious, so as much more corn was planted than otherwise would have been by any means the Government or any other could use .... The women now went willingly into the field and took their little ones with them to set corn; which before would allege weakness and inability; whom to have compelled would have been thought great tyranny and oppression.[12]

For Bradford, Plymouth's experiment repudiated Plato's advocacy for communistic society in *The Republic*. For historians following Bradford, this episode has been good enough proof that Plymouth's early rejection of common fields set America securely on the modern liberal path toward private property and accumulation.

Yet this sacking of commoning in the British colonies is pinned to common field cropping, as if practice in Plymouth and elsewhere didn't continue to include the exercise of common right in wetlands, coastal areas, and forests, rivers, and oceans, as if commoning couldn't exist alongside practices of private property, as if logics of commoning could not evolve as times moved forward. We can get a sense of the dimensions of ongoing commoning traditions in the British colonies from a later observer, Hector St. John de Crèvecoeur, whose *Letters from an American Farmer* and *Eighteenth-Century Sketches*, both written in the run-up to the American Revolution, widely document the vernacular practices of commoning among ordinary

British American colonists.[13] We could thumbnail the practices Crèvecoeur describes as a combination of self-provisioning and mutual support. He shows how colonists emphasized the sharing of both natural resources (like seeds, firewood, and herbal remedies) and labor and creative resources (like traditional folk ballads, or sharing beds and fires with strangers, local traditions for peacekeeping and fairness, or serving in militia). In this way, his writings about the colonies also detail the third important cultural strand of vernacular democracy that flourished in the late colonies, that of *neighboring*.

Crèvecouer's *Letters from an American Farmer* is most famous today for a widely anthologized passage, "What is an American?" This passage, which concludes "The American is a new man, who acts on new principles, he must therefore entertain new ideas and form new opinions," celebrates two signposts of the familiar American democratic story – America as ethnic melting pot and the American as a self-interested individual who is able to advance economically through a combination of his own enterprise combined with the bounty of the New World. Reading only this passage, though, diverts readers from the larger message of Letter 3: Farmer James's interest is less in individual self-making than in the neighborliness fostered in the American colonies, which collectively enables individual self-advancement. As Farmer James proudly notes, "We know, properly speaking, no strangers." To illustrate, he tells the story of Andrew the Hebridean. The emotional climax of this letter comes on the day that Scottish immigrant erects his house. His neighbors come together to build Andrew's house in a single day, a festive event that Andrew spends marveling at his new neighbors' generosity of labor and goodwill. Farmer James summarizes this communal event as America's boon to its European settlers. His term for this is "municipal blessing" – a blessing that marks the new American's ascension into self-making political and economic *community*.

The historian Barbara Smith elaborates on the window Farmer James offers here onto the practice and sensibility that traversed the British colonies. In her account, "migration to North America often put a premium on social connections that could help people weather the challenges of a new environment."[14] Puritans arrived in New England aspiring to be "knit together" in covenantal community. Quakers came to the Eastern Seaboard, Pennsylvania and New Jersey in particular, as a Society of Friends. High mortality rates everywhere led colonists to new practices for replacing lost kinship networks. These practices of "neighboring" made local social interconnections not just a fabric of life but an ethic. Smith argues that the ubiquity of neighborly ethics across the colonies was a base that allowed the Patriot movement to abstract and network local Patriot committees into a larger, "continental" movement: a democratic revolution. For middling and ordinary colonists, participatory political habits combined with economic and social principles grounded in neighborliness. Local experiences with religious, legal, and political self-determination enabled them to envision, propel, and support a revolutionary battle for political independence from the king and parliament, *and* to simultaneously declare their interdependence – their common cause as Patriots. Thomas Paine famously denominated this shared revolutionary sensibility as *Common Sense*. He heralded the revolutionary act of ordinary people contracting together in "a bond of solemn obligation, which the whole enters into, to support the right of every separate part, whether of religion, personal freedom, or property."[15] Echoing Locke in his assertion that a "government of our own is our natural right," Paine urged his fellow colonists to seize the crucial opportunity of self-constituting as an independent nation, precisely through their contractual affirmation of mutual support: "A firm bargain and a right reckoning make long friends."[16] Here, modern political theory joined with vernacular democratic practices held in common by ordinary colonists to found a new nation.

We justly celebrate the ideal of political equality that funds the American Revolution. We've paid less attention to the Patriots' insistence that political equality could only be maintained through equalitarian economic and banking policies. The political elite supported the interdependence of economic and political equality in the run-up to the Revolution; but they began to pull back from economic equalitarianism in the 1780s, aspiring, once it seemed the newly created United States would prevail in its war for independence, to create an economy that would vault the new nation into international prominence. The historians Woody Holton and Terry Bouton have detailed how the Framers thus began enacting the very kinds of taxes and economic policies that the Patriots had risen up against England for imposing in the 1760s and 1770s.[17] In response, ordinary Patriots protested these new policies across the nation, most famously in Massachusetts' so-called Shays rebellion. In the face of popular pushback, the political elite sought to reassure foreign creditors that popular government would not be a threat to their investments, searching for ways to erect what they called "barriers against democracy." The new Federal Constitution, ensuring for structures of representation rather than direct political participation, was one important maneuver in this battle.

Another maneuver was a new effort to portray vernacular democratic practices – the very practices expressed in protests against these draconian economic policies as well as in the Revolution itself – as pre-political, primitive, even savage: a danger to and not the boon of the new self-governing nation. For example, in the months before the Constitutional Convention in 1787, a group of Yale-educated New Englanders known as the "Hartford" or "Connecticut Wits" – David Humphreys, Joel Barlow, John Trumbull, and Lemuel Hopkins – published a mock-epic poem skewering the protests being staged by democratic Patriots. *The Anarchiad*, which appeared in the *New Haven Gazette* in twelve installments from October 1786 to September 1787, warns of a "darkness" that threatens to overwhelm the "new-born state" and describes the dangers posed by badly dressed "mobs in myriad" who "blacken all the way," "shade with rags the plain," and "*discord* spread."[18] The poem vilifies two key actors in the protest, Daniel Shays and Job Shattuck, as demonic and evil as well as criminally lawless. The "Wits" don't bother to rehearse the protesters' specific complaints about aggressive foreclosure and regressive taxation policies that they believed were benefiting wealthy speculators to the disadvantage of ordinary people (many of them veterans of the Revolution whose livelihoods had suffered specifically because of their military service). Instead, the "Wits" characterize the protest as an eternal battle between evil and good, between savagery and civilization. The poem's happy ending comes when Hesper (who manifests Venus, the "bringer of light") confronts the filthy and badly dressed mob and summons the nation's sages to assemble in Philadelphia and rescue the nation from the lawless rabble (and presumably too their poor taste in clothes!).

Insofar as historians note the battles between vernacular democratic practices and the Framers' attempts to contain them, they have tended to assume that the ratification of the Federal Constitution closes the chapter on vernacular democracy in the United States. It doesn't. Ordinary folk continued to rely on their local practices of democratic association well into the early years of the nation, operating under the notion that they were completely capable of self-governing, despite attempts by the political elite to school them into submitting to their political betters. (As Benjamin Rush famously framed this argument, "It is often said, 'that the sovereign and all other power is seated *in* the people'. This idea is unhappily expressed. It should be – 'all power is derived *from* the people'." Rush drove home the point of the distinction: "They possess it only on the days of their election.")[19] One of the earliest clear expressions of ongoing local vernacular democratic association came in the immediate aftermath of Ratification, when Alexander Hamilton ushered through Congress the first federal tax, on whiskey, which he promised would provide revenue to offset the Revolution's war-bond debt and help with foreign creditors. Western Pennsylvania – where President Washington first aimed to begin collecting the tax – fought it because of the particular hardship it imposed on the region's poorest inhabitants. There, whiskey was not just a drink. For poor farmers, it was a fundamental means of self-finance. Wheat was too expensive to transport across the mountains, but even poor tenant farmers could convert grain to profit by distilling and transporting whiskey. As the historian William Hogeland summarizes, "a liquid commodity both literally and figuratively, the drink democratized local economies." He observes that whiskey "connected popular finance theories with small-scale commercial development that, though marginal, had the potential to free rural people of debt and dependency."[20] Large producers could pay the tax and still make money, but tenuously solvent smallholders would forfeit this key source of revenue. Without it, they feared having to sell their lands to large landholders. So, smallholders and tenants viewed this tax as an attempt to undercut their hard-won economic independence. They protested through legal means. When those means failed, they organized extralegally, as a "regulation," a protest of the people against unfair government.

To put down what Hamilton enduringly characterized as a rebellion, Washington called up more militia troops than he had commanded during the Revolution, a force of almost 13,000 men. The rebellion was over before the troops arrived, with key agitators heading even further west to avoid arrest. The spectacle of a federal militia squashing a local tax protest – US citizens formally designated as enemies of the United States – was yet another part of the political elite's maneuvering to "tame" vernacular democracy. If regional inhabitants had imagined that vernacular and representative democratic practices could peacefully coexist in the newly federalized nation, the message of Washington's militia was a forceful negative.

The spectacle Hamilton engineered via the Whiskey "Rebellion" fundamentally reset the terms for understanding vernacular democracy in the new nation. Henceforth, these practices were officially understood as primitive, illegal behaviors located largely in the nation's backcountries and frontiers, uncivilized activities that demanded federal policing for the good of the nation; and here is when "reading democracy" gets really interesting, because early US authors found these ongoing clashes interesting and worth portraying.

Hugh Henry Brackenridge, a lawyer, journalist, and eventually, novelist, had been a central player in the Whiskey Rebellion. He arrived in Pittsburgh in 1781 and founded the *Pittsburgh Gazette*. He was elected to the Pennsylvania State Assembly in 1786, a seat he soon lost for supporting the Federal Constitution. His subsequent involvement in the Whiskey Regulation nearly cost him his life: Alexander Hamilton had Brackenridge square in his sights when he rolled into Pittsburgh in 1784 to prosecute the traitor ringleaders. Unfortunately for Hamilton, the key piece of evidence against Brackenridge turned out to be useless and Brackenridge's own account of how he spent his time trying to dampen the fury of the protesters and persuade them to a more reasonable course ultimately seems to have persuaded Hamilton.

Brackenridge published two different accounts of the event, the first a nonfictional *Account of the Insurrection* (1795) and the second a fictionalized, rollickingly picaresque, multivolume novel, *Modern Chivalry* (1792–1816).[21] Seldom read for the very fact of its length, the novel plays out endlessly and episodically a variety of confrontations between vernacular and representative democratic practices, mostly turning on the misadventures of two key characters, the stuffy and self-important Captain Farrago and his ever-wayward servant Teague O'Regan. It posits vernacular democracy as a vital partner to formal democratic institutions. The novel combines episodes of political contention and debate with humor, exploring conflicts that emerge in the process of political representation between local actors and between governments and citizens. It offers a range of ideas about what democratic practice might include; and it frames as productive and even crucial the tensions produced between direct democratic local traditions and federal representative order. Brackenridge uses the often ridiculous political sketches of his novel thematically. Through them he suggests opening up the Constitution's mechanistic model to a more comprehensively organic representational practice by harnessing precisely the expansive, often chaotic, but always inventive dynamics of local democratic radicalism for both local *and* national political work. Despite the novel's silliness, Brackenridge asks readers to take the political practices of ordinary westerners seriously, as an important resource for the new country's project of self-governance. He insists that the heritage of vernacular democracy should be nurtured and balanced with the aims of formal, representative constitutionalism rather than vilified or mocked. *Modern Chivalry* wittily and pleasurably drives home the point that a democracy of laws alone will exclude to its detriment the disruptive and dynamic energies of ordinary people.

Mason Locke Weems came to very different conclusions about vernacular democracy, which he promoted through his wildly popular, highly fictionalized biography of the nation's first president, *The Life of Washington* (1809).[22] There, Weems spins out what would become the prototype for our familiar story of democracy. It is a story that encourages ordinary citizens to look away from each other in the project of self-government, taking their guidance instead from political elders. Weems models patriotism not as coequality but as deference to leaders through the sentimental tale of

a dead president whose most admirable quality was his childlike self-subordination to father figures.

Weems's depiction of Washington appeals to privately oriented feelings, proposing the civic cultivation of private feelings as a *replacement* for public action. Readers' patriotism will manifest in their self-cultivated admiration for and emulation of the dead president. The chapter that recounted the "birth and education" of the nation's first president foregrounds little George's relation to his own father, the grandfatherly Mr. Washington. Little George may be mischievous, but his saving grace comes always in his devotion to father figures. Everyone is familiar with the story of the cherry tree and little George's inability to lie to his father. It is not the only story that remedies monkey business by "remembering the father." In another episode, Weems recounts how little George's habitual identification with fatherly authority led him shamelessly to tattle on schoolmates for fighting. Weems offered a former classmate reminiscing about how George would upbraid his classmates:

> Angry or not angry, you shall never, boys, have my consent to a practice so shocking! shocking even in *slaves* and *dogs*; then how utterly scandalous in little boys at school, who ought to look at one another as brothers. And what must be the feelings of our tender parents, when, instead of seeing us come home smiling and lovely, as the JOYS OF THEIR HEARTS! they see us creeping in like young *blackguards*, with our heads *bound up, black eyes*, and *bloody clothes*! And what is all this for? Why, that we *may get praise*!! But the truth is, a quarrelsome boy was never sincerely praised![23]

In this speech, George invokes brotherly feeling – fraternity – by appealing to the "tender" feelings not of those brothers but of their parents. It is by this same logic, one that substitutes hierarchy for equalitarianism, that George justifies hauling in the master to end conflict rather than allowing boys to settle their disagreement democratically among themselves. Weems's schoolboy George teaches readers what to do with the disorderly habits of vernacular democracy, reminding "boy" citizens not to negotiate their own disagreements but to subordinate themselves instead to the higher wisdom of their loving master, teacher, father, or president (who has their best interests at heart).

Like Brackenridge, James Fenimore Cooper was interested in the legacy of vernacular democracy in the late colonies and the early United States. Yet, like Weems, Cooper did not advocate for its ongoing role in the early nation. Rather, he used his first novel to portray its decline. *The Pioneers* (1826), enduringly analyzed by myth and symbol critics as an account of the conflict between "nature and civilization" and by environmental critics as a depiction of man's inherent greed and wastefulness, becomes something more nuanced and historical when read with questions of vernacular democracy in mind.[24] From this angle, Cooper's novel, sent in the 1790s, appears less as a simple, mythic account of "man's" transition from the "state of nature" into "civilization" and more a carefully historicized account of how European settlers on the frontier distributed access to shared goods and constructed vernacular systems of social order, "fair play," or "the peace." It also shows how these local residents reacted to the federal imposition of a top-down and more systematized ("modern") legal system, engineered through the combined force of state and federal government as well as private capital.

Cooper's plot highlights Judge Marmaduke Temple's plans to develop his land in upstate New York. His plans to map, fence, and manage environmental abundance for his own profit drives a new perception of scarcity among people already inhabiting the area. The Judge's plans, combined with his ability to influence their implementation both with his own money and access to state politics, will affect residents' customary access to natural goods. It will also curtail their customary abilities to communally administer goods and justice. What Cooper outlines is a form of enclosure, a term seldom used to describe processes more typically explained with terms like "modernization" and "economic development" in the early United States.

Some recent historians have begun paying attention to similarities between the kinds of pressures created by game laws and enclosure in England with those on the laboring and non-propertied classes in the British American colonies and the early United States. They focus attention on the competition of big money to control access to land and wealth, creating severe limits most especially for Native Americans but also for poor whites in the colonies and early republic. As Joanna Brooks underscores in her book *Why We Left*, the history of the United States is not an exception to but instead a long episode in the lessons of "dislocation and disposability that have characterized modernity."[25] Poor white settlers – whose parents had perhaps come to the Americas as indentured servants, convicts, or debtors, and whose families had perhaps been displaced from competencies by enclosure – had hard choices to make when land jobbers and surveyors came on behalf of wealthy owners in the early United States. Current residents could move west, abandoning their improvements and rejecting the new conditions imposed by landowners. Or they could stay, giving up customary practices of self-government. Cooper's novel details that hard choice, and in the end his hero, Natty Bumppo, packs up and leaves.

The novel's drama pivots around two "trials." In the first, Judge Marmaduke Temple and two local residents, Natty Bumppo and Oliver

Edwards, all shoot at a deer on Christmas Eve and debate who it should go home with, relying on vernacular democratic traditions of fairness. In the second, Natty is hauled into court to be tried before Judge Temple by the new formal processes of state law for shooting another deer, this one out of season. Differently from the decorum and hierarchy that govern the state trial, in the first those involved argue informally and before the eyes of the community – here the Judge's daughter and his slave Aggy – to determine the disposition of the deer. They invoke competing informal traditions (like a coin flip or a barter), settling the dispute informally. The novel demonstrates through a variety of scenes that the results of these communal face-to-face, case-by-case adjudications are as morally and environmentally sound as any judgments reached by the rules of formal state law. Thus, the novel dramatizes how local traditions of self-governance are losing out to newer "modern" rules of property and management principles. Just as the novel traces the vanishing of game, trappers, and crucially Native Americans from upstate New York, *The Pioneers* details the vanishing rights of European-descended residents to navigate and allocate their immediate resources among themselves. Natty's voice as an environmental conservationist has long been celebrated in this novel. Paying attention to Cooper's interest in vernacular democracy means we can also see his message about how, in losing control of natural resource commons, ordinary people also lost democratic agency and key rights to self-govern.

The staging of Cooper's novel indicates these local rights to self-governing were sunsetting by the end of the eighteenth century. Maybe that's what he hoped for, but the facts on the ground don't support his projection. Alongside Cooper, political leaders and key US intellectuals and writers were crafting a story about the fading of vernacular democratic practice. Yet Alexis de Tocqueville, whose voyage through the United States in 1831 resulted in what has become a classic text, *Democracy in America*, emphasized the ongoing prominence of vernacular democracy – he calls it association – in his sweeping study of US political society.[26] Tocqueville argues that this locally nurtured spirit of liberty, one that has nothing to do with the formal governing institutions, is what most distinguishes the character of US democratic practice:

> The inhabitant of the United States learns from birth that he must rely on himself to combat the ills and trials of life; he is restless and defiant in his outlook toward the authority of society and appeals to its power only when he cannot do without it. The beginnings of this attitude first appear in school, where the children even in their games, submit to rules settled by themselves and punish offenses which they have defined themselves. The same attitude turns up again in all the affairs

of social life. If some obstacle blocks the public road halting the circulation of traffic, the neighbors at once form a deliberative body; this improvised assembly produces and executive authority which remedies the trouble before anyone has thought of the possibility of some previously constituted authority beyond that of those concerned. Where enjoyment is concerned, people associate to make the festivities grander and more orderly. Finally, associations are formed to combat exclusively moral troubles: intemperance is fought in common. Public security, trade and industry, and morals and religion all provide the aims for associations in the United States. There is no end which the human will despairs of attaining by the free action of the collective power of individuals.[27]

For Tocqueville, democracy doesn't depend on sovereign citizens and their political representatives; it depends on citizens' ability to cultivate democratic subjectivity through participation in collective problem-solving. This practicing interdependence is what generates the "spirit of liberty." Democratic power, in Tocqueville's depiction, is a common-pool resource that is still robustly abundant in the early United States.

At the end of *The Pioneers*, Cooper has Natty pack up his advocacy for vernacular democratic practices and head west. Just so, frontier novels well into the nineteenth century acknowledge the presence of such vernacular democratic practices and ideals, embodied not, as for Cooper, in solitary individuals but in larger collectives, from outlaw gangs to entire frontier settlements. Not that novelists saw this as a good thing. Largely, frontier novels represented the egalitarian communities they featured as expressing (at best) naïve ideals that were in the process of being forgotten or (at worst) as a form of savagery or organized criminality that needed to be repudiated and overcome for the settlement to "mature" and win its admission as a state to the nation. In this increasingly durable plotline, we see the continuing resonance of Hamilton's strategy in the Whiskey Rebellion, even generations later. Yet the sheer repetition of these frontier novel plotlines suggests that the vernacular democratic practices and idealism the political elite aimed to curtail continued – even robustly. Real-world political conflict over the terms of developing democracy in the context of national expansion thus conditions the emergence of the fictional frontier narrative well into the nineteenth century. While the official story may have won out in our civics education, it's worth reviewing these struggles over democratic idealism and meaning in the literature of the British colonies and the early United States because it lets us see democracy as something more common, less official, more robust, less distant, more organic, less formal – as something that maybe, even today, in the United States continues to be struggled over outside the lines of and beyond the view afforded by our official story of democracy.[28]

Notes

1. For a good discussion of this more nuanced reading of American "democracy," see Terry Bouton, *Taming Democracy: "The People," The Founders, and the Troubled Ending of the American Revolution* (New York: Oxford University Press, 2007).
2. Kenneth Burke, "Literature As Equipment for Living," in Burke, *The Philosophy of Literary Form* (Berkeley: University of California Press, 1973), 293–304.
3. Allan Kulikoff, *From British Peasants to Colonial American Farmers* (Chapel Hill: University of North Carolina Press, 2000).
4. J. M. Neeson, *Commoners: Common Right, Enclosure and Social Change in England, 1700–1820* (Cambridge: Cambridge University Press, 1993), 1–2.
5. Ibid., 6–7.
6. Ibid., 32.
7. Ibid., 177.
8. Ibid., 182.
9. Stuart Banner, "The Political Function of the Commons: Changing Conceptions of Property and Sovereignty in Missouri, 1750–1850," *American Journal of Legal History* 41, no. 1 (1997): 61–93.
10. Neeson, *Commoners*, 321.
11. William Bradford, *Of Plymouth Plantation: 1620–1647*, ed. Samuel Eliot Morison (New York: Modern Library, 1967), 76–77.
12. Ibid., 120–121.
13. Hector St. John Crèvecoeur, *Letters from an American Farmer and Sketches of Eighteenth-Century America* (New York: Penguin, 1963).
14. Barbara Smith, *The Freedoms We Lost: Consent and Resistance in Revolutionary America* (New York: New Press, 2010), 56.
15. Thomas Paine, *Common Sense*, in *Thomas Paine: Collected Writings*, ed. Eric Foner (New York: Library of America, 1995), 43.
16. Ibid., 34, 43.
17. Woody Holton, *Forced Founders: Indians, Debtors, Slaves and the Making of the American Revolution* (Chapel Hill: University of North Carolina Press, 1999), and also Holton, *Unruly Americans and the Origins of the Constitution* (New York: Hill and Wang, 2008); Bouton, *Taming Democracy*.
18. David Humphreys, Joel Barlow, John Trumbull, and Lemuel Hopkins, *The Anarchiad: A New England Poem, 1786–1787*, ed. Luther G. Riggs, Scholars Facsimiles and Reprints (Gainesville: University Press of Florida, [1861] 1967), 6.
19. Benjamin Rush, "Address to the People of the United States," January 1787, https://histcsac.wiscweb.wisc.edu/wp-content/uploads/sites/281/2017/07/Benjamin_Rush.pdf.
20. William Hogeland, *The Whiskey Rebellion: George Washington, Alexander Hamilton, and the Frontier Rebels Who Challenged America's Newfound Sovereignty* (New York: Simon and Schuster, 2010), 67.
21. Hugh Henry Brackenridge, *Incidents of the Insurrection*, ed. Daniel Marder (New Haven, CT: College and University Press, 1972); *Modern Chivalry*, ed. Claude M. Newlin (New York: American Book company, 1937).

22. Mason Locke Weems, *The Life of Washington*, ed. Marcus Cunliffe (Cambridge, MA: Belknap Press, 1962).

23. Ibid., 16.

24. James Fenimore Cooper, "The Pioneers," in Cooper, *The Leatherstocking Tales*, Vol. 1. (New York: Library of America, 1985).

25. Joanna Brooks, *Why We Left: Untold Stories and Songs of America's First Immigrants* (Minneapolis: University of Minnesota Press, 2013), 21.

26. Alexis de Tocqueville, *Democracy in America* (1835), trans. George Lawrence; ed. J. P. Mayer, vols. 1–2 (New York: Harper & Row, 1969).

27. Ibid., Vol. 1, pt. 2, chapter 4, 189–190.

28. For more on this author's work on American Democracy, see also Dana D. Nelson, *Commons Democracy: Reading the Politics of Participation in the Early United States* (New York: Fordham University Press, 2016); and Nelson, "Representative/Democracy: Presidents, Democratic Management, and the Unfinished Business of Male Sentimentalism," in Cathy N. Davidson, ed., *No More Separate Spheres!* (Durham, NC: Duke University Press, 2002), 325–352.

PART II

Readings in Early America

7

KATHLEEN DONEGAN

Accident, Disaster, and Trauma
Shattered in Early America

Despite the commanding force of settler colonialism in the seventeenth and eighteenth centuries, early America was often written as a disaster. For settlers, there was fear at every turn, and those fears often came to pass in lived experiences that were formerly unimaginable: sudden famine, mass mortality, racial warfare. Nature itself turned against them in wholly unfamiliar ways. In response, colonists wrote much of their early history as a record of collapse. Within their ruinous "true relations" they both revealed and confronted a separation from their former selves. They claimed, rightly, that no one unexposed to the New World could understand the desperation that so often governed, and at many times defined, colonial life. The experience of becoming colonial veered dangerously away from the experience of being unconditionally English. After all, there was no context for their Englishness except for what they built with poor materials and weak hands. When disaster came, their suffering became so deeply aligned with their colonial condition that the two merged to create a new identity. What happened to colonists? They suffered hardship – and either succumbed, endured, or retaliated. They were also violent – much more violent than they thought they would be. Their attempts to represent this deadly combination of suffering and violence became what we can name as the earliest colonial American literature – a literature of catastrophe.

It begins with the writings from the first English settlements. George Percy wrote of the fort at Jamestown, "There were never Englishmen left in a forreigne Countrey in such miserie as wee were in this new discovered Virginia."[1] The first Virginia settlers landed in 1607, and by 1609 they were starving, under siege by the Powhatan, and driven into a crumbling fort that was quickly becoming a graveyard. Of the barely surviving men, Percy wrote that "a lecture of miserie" hung on every face.[2] In Plymouth, settlers soon sickened, due in part to wading through brackish water as they continually made their way from ship to settlement, settlement to ship, for supplies, respite, and visits to women and children who could not, or would not, come ashore. When the first ferocious winter came, they were so weakened that they were "scarce able to bury their dead."[3] In Barbados, many did not survive the "seasoning" that settlers passed through as their English bodies attempted to acclimate to the West Indian tropics. They were wracked with disease, debauched in their habits, and careless with their dead. Corpses floated in the rare stagnant water, and still they drank from it. Not that anyone should have been surprised. Since the beginning of English attempts to colonize Roanoke in 1585, that place had been settled, defeated, rescued, deserted, held in wait, deserted again, settled again, in need of rescue again, and finally found abandoned. The last colony's 115 people simply disappeared. If settlement was the first step of English intrusion onto Native American land, it was a step so unsteady that all former grounding gave way beneath it.

Yet English settlers were far from the only ones to suffer from colonial incursion. Indeed, they were more often the source of suffering. Native Americans across the global south had already experienced the unbridled spread of disease, enslavement, and destruction from Spanish colonizers for almost a century. Now, under English colonialism, another geopolitical arena was in violent upheaval as a new colonial force became intent on negating and unseating Native peoples and power. Indigenous deaths from European diseases alone led one historian to call colonists the "beneficiaries of catastrophe."[4] The colonial world also created, and was created by, the transatlantic slave trade. Approximately 12.5 million people were kidnapped from their homes in Africa, chained, sold, and transported by force to the Americas to labor for life. Not only was their freedom taken from them; they were also robbed of their names, their languages, their histories, their cultures, their homelands, their genealogies, their very claim to the human condition. Even if one survived all this, one suffered a social death.[5] It is staggering that people withstood an exclusion so deep, a loss so profound. If we claim that settler colonists wrote a literature of disaster, we must also account for the disaster they wrought.

In these encounters and their aftermaths, early American life remade people who aimed to find coherence despite its fragmenting forces. What follows are stories of how some of them shattered.

Accident: Shipwreck and the Theater of Survival

Although we often think of early Americans as looking West, they more often looked East, not toward the forest but toward the sea. They were an ocean-going people, and the Atlantic was the context for the exchanges on which they depended – people, news, goods, and connection to European life. If many ships arrived safely, however, many were also wrecked. Throughout the seventeenth and eighteenth centuries, personal narratives of wrecking and casting away, of capture and captivity at sea, grew in both number and popularity. These texts expose a far more disorderly aspect of colonial mobility, one in which the inciting incident was accident and the primary practice was survival. Widely circulated in their day, these narratives have sunk unremembered into the archive – perhaps because they portray "American" arrivals in a foundering, rather than founding, mode.

One of the most popular early texts printed in Philadelphia was written by the Quaker Jonathan Dickinson, who tells the harrowing story of how, en route from Jamaica, his company shipwrecked off the coast of Florida. The banner of Dickinson's narrative is deliverance. His claim: everywhere we were threatened, and everywhere we were saved. However, a far more intricate drama unfolds in the colonial arena he describes than the standard of deliverance admits. The accident prompts the crew to engage in acts of mimicry, emergency, and feigned identity that uncover the complexity of their colonial identities, both in fact and in fantasy. Theirs was an extraordinary colonial performance.

On June 7, 1692, an earthquake hit Port Royal and most of the city sank into the sea. Jonathan Dickinson's business survived, but its physical, social, and economic context did not. After struggling to recover for four years in the ruins, Dickinson hired a boat. Its mixed crew of twenty-six passengers sailed out of Port Royal bound for Philadelphia, under a protective convoy and into waters violently agitated by the twin dangers of hurricanes and privateers. Their barkentine was named *Reformation*, and they no doubt hoped it would be a means of deliverance from the scene of disaster; but the ways of deliverance turned out to be far more complicated than the group anticipated. Soon threatened by the French, separated from their convoy, and battered by a hurricane, the *Reformation* was wrecked off the coast of Florida. The bodies that crawled up onto that shore were certain of nothing but their own peril.

When still in the midst of their wreckage, the group was accosted by two Native men, who came, according to Dickinson, "running fiercely and foaming at the mouth … . Their countenance … very furious and bloody."[6] Clearly, there was to be no succor here. When these two men left to deliver news of the wreck to the rest of their people, the castaways engaged in an uncommon act of emergency government. They would pretend they were Spanish. When the Native people returned "in a very great number all running and shouting," the ruse was tried:

> they rushed in upon us and cried *Nickaleer Nickaleer*. We understood them not
> at first: they repeating it over unto us often. At last they cried *Epainia* or

Spaniard, by which we understood them that at first they meant *English*; but they were answered to the latter in Spanish yea to which they replied, *No Spainia no*, but all cried out *Nickaleer, Nickaleer*.[7]

The Jobes, the small coastal group upon whose lap the sea had thrown the Dickinson company, knew the colonial Spanish well. Of the English, they had encountered bad rumors, lost sailors, and reason enough for scorn. So, after looting whatever was salvageable from the wreck, including whatever clothes were still on the colonial Jamaicans' backs, they pressed the astounded crew again with their question: "They asked us again, *Nickaleer, Nickaleer*? But we answered by saying *Pennsylvania*."[8]

In their accidental arrival, their colonial identity is put fully into flux. The word *Nickaleer* becomes a leitmotif of the text. The Dickinson group translates it to mean "English" but the designation is a marker of their own colonial hybridity. After all, what noncolonial English person would ever recognize themselves in that word? When posed as a question, "Nickaleer?" spells danger. The castaways answer with the perfect non sequitur: "Pennsylvania." They leave their colonial destination as an empty and cryptic space, to be read by their interlocutors without further explanation. Panicked that their Spanish pantomime has been transparent, they clearly hope that being "Pennsylvania" is far enough away from being "Nickaleer" to save their skins. This is the problem of identity for these unwilling arrivals. The big question – "Who Are You?" – is variously rendered as a threat, as a performance, as a neologism, as a riddle, and as a nasty trick. Certainly, it is a question that requires a cagy, if risky, answer. "Nickaleer, Nickaleer": it is put to them as a constant refrain, as Native Americans sometimes ominously and sometimes mockingly put the colonists' identity to the test.

The company's Spanish role-playing is never fully successful; instead, it garners deep suspicion and frank anger among Native groups. During their stay at the village of St. Lucie, the castaways who have dark hair are identified as potentially coming from Havana or St. Augustine, but those with light hair are counted as "no Spaniards."[9] Native people are well-versed in the types of people in colonial Spain, so that "Spaniard" can mean from either Spain, Havana, or St. Augustine. Bodies are various and nameable, but some bodies just don't make the cut. Beyond the body's appearance, its actions can also testify to national identity. Two mariners, separated from the rest of the shipwrecked band and sensing themselves threatened by an approaching Native man, fall down on their knees and begin crossing themselves in mimicry of Spaniards on the verge of death. When they are returned to the group, they boast of their sudden inspiration and their convincing performance. In another scene, though, Natives call the Nickaleer's bluff, saying that, since most of them seem to be Spanish, they might look forward to witnessing the murder of some real English castaways being held captive nearby. The killing never takes place, but the group's sudden hush seems to confirm what the Native people suspect. For "the whole night following [we] were troubled with ... two young Indians, who at times would be abusing one or other of us, singling them out and asking if they were not *Nickaleer* or English? If they said, nay, then they would hit them a blow or more with a truncheon, which they had; and said they were."[10]

The great threat, as Dickinson puts it, is that "we should be discovered to be what these people did suppose we were," a convoluted assessment of identity for sure.[11] In the context of the accident, these strategies of impersonation are more than a gimmick. The homelessness of wreckage brings an unsettling loss of self in its wake. When self-recognition slips away, you become homesick – for yourself. You long to claim the objects of your own familiarity but do not dare to betray this desire, which would be to betray yourself. It was this way for Dickinson, who restrained himself when he saw an English name carved on the shaft of a knife; who shuddered silently when he heard one Native man curse, "English son of a bitch"; who trembled when he saw Native women nurse his infant child wrapped in deerskin; and who nonetheless traveled his way up the Florida coast naked and Nickaleer. It was a different way for Caesar, a young enslaved boy, who stayed for a long while with a cacique who was resolved not to part with him. For Solomon Cresson, who was "mightily in one Indian's favor," went arm and arm with him, and wore his cloak all through their stay.[12] For the enslaved woman Hagar, who arrived at St. Augustine with her baby dead and strapped to her back. For the Jamaican colonist Penelope who, "being big with child, by the Spaniards Perswasion," simply decided to stay.[13] Shipwreck made everyone and everything seem accidental. On the one hand, colonial identity was left in the lurch while, on the other hand, it was busy being reassigned, resisted, and reformed.

Disaster: Collapse and Catastrophe at Jamestown

For the Dickinson party, accidental arrival demanded a fearful play for survival among a diverse cast of characters. For others, shipwreck, while plunging the world into chaos, ended in something more salvageable. So it stood with the famous ship the *Sea Venture*. The flagship of a convoy bringing new provisions, laws, leaders, and men to the suffering colony in Virginia, it was separated from its fleet in a hurricane. Its 150 passengers and crew members battled the storm for three days before the ship violently crashed off the island of Bermuda. The people were cast away on a shore that was not unknown but was everywhere feared. It was called by mariners "The Isle of Devils," but when the leaders took account, not a single person had perished. The island was unpopulated; fat wild pigs roamed the land; the weather was ideal; the food plentiful. Instead of hazarding their fortunes, their arrival led to the founding of a new colony. Over the next ten months, the men constructed two pinnaces that they named the *Deliverance* and the *Patience*. When the vessels were seaworthy, they set sail for Jamestown.

If the wreck of the *Sea Venture* turned out to be a propitious accident, though, what they found in Jamestown was unmitigated disaster. The company arrived at Jamestown fort in May 1610. When they saw the gates swinging from their hinges, the palisades torn down, the empty houses burned, they were wary. When they saw the barely surviving survivors, they were stunned. In the winter of 1609, Jamestown's settlers had entered what has become known as their "starving time." Of the approximately 500 men in Virginia at the start of that winter, only 60 survived. They now looked with hollow eyes at the hale Englishmen who entered their ruined garrison. Meanwhile, the colonists were as far from being Englishmen as one could imagine. Their governor George Percy remembers the unspeakably brutal experience "which noe man [can] trewly descrybe butt he which hathe Tasted the bitternesse thereof."[14] Tasting bitterness took many forms that winter. After consuming all the horses, dogs, and cats in the fort, they turned to eating vermin. Then to sucking leather. Then to licking the blood off dying men. Corpses were dug up from the ground for food. They ate the unburied too.[15] Never before were Englishmen left in such misery. One came into the public space and raged that, if there was a God, "he wolde not Suffer his Creatures whome he had made and framed to indure those miseries."[16] Others, mere skeletons, ran across the grounds of the fort crying, "We are starved! We are starved!"[17] These words of fury and frenzy, hanging in the putrid air, defined a colonial scene that would have been inconceivable to the colonists' former selves and yet was inescapably true.

Crisis was not new to Virginia. In the first disastrous winter, famine struck and disease ran rampant; only 38 of 104 settlers survived. Supply ships from London turned out to be useless. Just days after the First Supply came in, someone accidently set fire to the fort, destroying all the new supplies, the old provisions, and the fort itself. The Second Supply left behind more mouths to feed than food to feed them with. The men, according to John Smith, were soon sick, lame, bruised, and useless, capable of nothing but complaint.[18] The Third Supply was led by the lost *Sea Venture*, the ship that held the cargo the colonists so desperately needed. After it was wrecked, the rest of its fleet arrived in Virginia, depositing 300 uncontrolled men who sowed chaos. In this unruly time, John Smith lost his command and with it the crucial trade and temporary truce that he and Wahusonacock, the paramount chief of the Powhatan confederacy, had made. Smith's substantial influence – his ability to improvise in the colonial contact zone while imposing discipline within the fort – had kept the colony in corn. Only eight people died during his presidency. However, with Smith gone, Powhatan relations precarious, the men defiant, and leadership as weak as could be, there loomed a disaster worse than anything that had come before.

Between the time Smith was driven from Virginia in October 1609 and starvation set in that winter, both suffering and violence intensified. Settlers turned against the Powhatan with a growing fury, and Powhatan retribution took ever harsher forms. When colonists in an outlying fort rampaged through Native villages, warriors responded by killing nearly half of them and posing a deadly threat to any who ventured past the palisade. When men came to one Native town demanding food, they were killed and propped up in the forest, their mouths stuffed with bread. When the deposed president John Ratcliffe came with more than a dozen men into Werowcomoco roughly demanding trade, the men were killed and Ratcliffe was flayed alive with mussel shells, his flesh thrown into a fire before him. All the while, terrified stragglers from the colony's outposts fled into Jamestown while Native people laid it under siege. Anglo-Powhatan relations had entered a state of disaster, guaranteeing the direst outcome for the now-starving settlers. Emaciated and feral, pinned inside their fort – their misery defined them. Nothing they knew could hold what they'd become.

Enter Sir Thomas Gates who had set out on the *Sea Venture*, survived the wreck, founded Bermuda, and still carried the appointment of Governor of Virginia. He took in the disaster at Jamestown and realized that his limited provisions could not last more than a few weeks. Yet, in those few weeks, he instituted military rule among the surviving but destroyed men. Speaking ill of the leaders got a bodkin driven through your tongue. Maligning the Virginia Company carried a death sentence. Thus, even after the settlers' misery was discovered, disaster continued to stretch into deadly discipline, tight rations, and ticking time. Finally, it was clear that the colony must be abandoned. When the time came to board the boats and turn their backs on what remained of Jamestown, Gates had to prevent the survivors from blazing it. This, it turned out, was a prudent decision. On their way out to sea, by chance and to their great surprise, they encountered a ship carrying Thomas West, Lord de la Warr. West, newly appointed Governor of Virginia for life, was the latest hope for rescuing the colony. At that unexpected meeting, his first act as commander was to turn the retreating boats around, back to Jamestown. Now, they were set on revenge. Now, the disaster of Virginia was to be wreaked upon the Powhatan.

The lead-up to what many call the First Anglo-Powhatan War had already begun because, by inducing famine in the fort, the Powhatan had all but extinguished the colony; but when de la Warr began to order colonial battalions to ravage Native villages, the war raged. In an attack against the Paspahegh, the defeated George Percy (the man who had presided over the starving time) led a troop into their village. The men burned corn, desecrated temples, destroyed houses, and put the people to waste. The destruction was complete. A few horrified survivors remained: one warrior and the "queen" of Paspahegh with her children. The warrior was handled with dispatch. They cut off his head. The woman and children, however, were a different story, as they were well-known to the colonists. The choice was made to bring them back to Jamestown, but the men in the boat grew restive. Why had these people been allowed to live? A quick and deadly counsel was held, and it was decided. The children were thrown into the water and shot. This act did more than countermand all rules of engagement known to Native people. It testified to how settlers' abject suffering had roiled into intense violence, their unspeakable fatality into murder so ruthless it goes unrecorded even in our histories.

The English had slaughtered their enemies on the killing fields of Ireland, but this was different. The violence of Jamestown did not strengthen the colonists' English identities; it shattered them. It shattered them because they could no longer fulfill the divine promise and national will that they succeed in colonizing the New World as Englishmen, that they rise there naturally because of their inherent superiority, that they civilize a wilderness just as they were civilized themselves. Instead, person and mission merged with the disaster. Even when London propagandists claimed, "the ill and odious wound of Virginia"[19] was recovered, that wound stays open to this day, every time we prefer the Mayflower story as a narrative of national origins. Because it was not Plymouth but Virginia that began colonial America – with a blow, a collapse, a catastrophe.

Trauma: Furious Histories

For all the disorientation, loss, suffering, and violence in early colonial America, a few things were clear. The "wilderness" was to be cleared. The land was to be made profitable. The "country people" were to be overpowered. Everything was to be dominated. Effecting that domination drove settlers' twin missions to defeat Natives, who held the ground, and to enslave Africans, who would be forced to work it. So Native dispossession and African enslavement became the experiential, cultural, and historical traumas that defined settler colonialism and made possible its expansion over centuries. Violently stripping away the anchors of their enemies' existence as sovereign people, colonists created programs of destruction that proved their New World dream to be what it was: a recurring global nightmare. For Native and African Americans, trauma – the experience of loss and pain so extreme that it could not be assimilated – haunted their former self-determination, even as they resisted subjugation through everyday resistance, war, and rebellion.[20] So brutal were Native and African experiences in the colonial world that they came to hold, in the words of one theorist, "an impossible history within them," a history that still calls for recovery.[21] Atrocity resists summary. Its histories do not allow for closure, and this rejection of closure causes dominant narratives to rupture, to splinter, to become unsettled in the reckoning. Here, then, are two narratives that, in their atrocity, depict events in two long colonial histories that refuse to be smoothed out: one of unbridled warfare against the Pequot of New England, and the other of un/common trauma inflicted on enslaved people of the Caribbean.

The background of the Pequot War concerned the lucrative fur and wampum trade in the Connecticut River Valley. Through the 1630s, competition there grew increasingly aggressive. As the valley became more volatile, Dutch, English, Pequot, Narragansett, and surrounding tribes all watched the situation closely. Relationships among these groups were complex, but above all, it was the powerful Pequot the English wanted to break. As soon as English colonists had an opportunity to set terms in the trade, those set for the Pequot were so severe, amounted to such extortion, that one historian concludes: "No nation could abide by such terms and maintain its sovereignty."[22] Pequot sovereignty did not interest the Puritans. On May 1, 1637, the General Court at Hartford issued a declaration: "It is ordered that there shall be an offensive war against the Pequot."[23] So, against their formidable, but in their eyes illegitimate, enemy, the Puritans marched.[24] As instruments of God's vengeance, the appointed military captains, John Mason and John Underhill, were charged to inflict pain on the entire Pequot nation, to reduce them to total submission. At dawn on May 26, 1637, these captains with a force of 77 settlers and backed by almost 250 Mohegan and Narragansett allies commenced their attack on the Pequot fort at Mystic.

Inside a ring of closely set young tree trunks was a two-acre village, full of wigwams with narrow lanes between them. In these wigwams, more than 400 people lay sleeping. They were families: about a third of them are warriors, the rest were women, children, and elders. A barking dog broke the night's silence; then a single voice called out. Suddenly the air exploded in a chaos of gunfire. People were ripped awake, their minds racing from confusion, to alarm, to panic. In his narrative of the attack, John Mason writes that he "heard a Dog bark and an Indian crying *Owanux! Owanux!* Which is Englishmen! Englishmen!"[25] As John Underhill tells it: the "volley given at break of day, and themselves fast asleep, bred in them such a terror, that they brake forth in a most doleful cry."[26] Another source calls that cry "hideous and pittifull."[27]

As the English stormed the fort, half of those who got through its narrow entryways suffered casualties. Others tried to slash their way through the village but the lanes were too tight, the wigwams too close. Already they were stumbling over corpses. The Pequot fought back, hard. "Most courageously did these Pequots behave themselves," Underhill remarks. Referring to himself, Mason then writes of a fatal decision:

> The Captain told them that We should never kill them after that manner: The Captain also said, WE MUST BURN THEM; and immediately stepping into the Wigwam where he had been before, brought out a Fire-Brand, and putting it into the Matts with which they were covered, set the Wigwams on Fire. When it was thoroughly kindled, the Indians ran as Men most dreadfully Amazed. And indeed such a dreadful Terror did the ALMIGHTY let fall upon their Spirits, that they would fly from us and run into the very Flames, where many of them perished.[28]

Underhill reports: "Many courageous fellows fought most desperately, so as they were scorched and burnt with the very flame, the fire burnt their very bowstrings, and so perished valiantly: mercy they did deserve for their valour, could we have had opportunity to have bestowed it."[29] Yet that opportunity for mercy was neither sought nor found. According to Underhill, "The fort blazed most terribly ... many were burnt, both men, women, and children." Those who were forced out of the fort were "entertained with the point of a sword; downe fell men, women, and children."[30] In less than an hour, more than 500 people were killed. Pequot men who later arrived at the fort "beholding what was done, stamped and tore the Hair from their Heads."[31] The massacre broke the tribe.

Underhill records the aftermath: "Great and dolefull was the bloudy sight ... to see so many soules lie gasping on the ground, so thicke in some places, that you could hardly passe along." Then the captain puts a question: "It may bee demanded, Why should you be so furious (as some have said) should not Christians have more mercy and compassion?"[32] Amazingly, he gives Native Americans the last word on this. The Narragansett and Mohegan, allied in this battle with the English, never entered the fort but formed an outer ring around it. From there, they watched in awe and in horror. According to Underhill: they "greatly admired the manner of English mens fight : but cried *mach it, mach it* ; that is, it is naught, it is naught, because it is too furious, and slaies too many men."[33] Here, even in the accounts of the assailants, shock, grief, trauma, and protest are all visible. Even in these texts most sternly committed to justify bringing full terror down upon the Pequot's heads, even among these very men so dead set on extermination, there exists a record of horror.

The war continued and, at its conclusion, the Pequot were devastated. Of the survivors, some went to other tribes, where they were treated harshly. Some were killed, their heads and hands returned to the English as trophies. Others were pressed into service by colonists. Still others were sold into a more distant slavery, transported to the West Indies and traded there for Africans to bring back to New England. None were allowed to call themselves Pequot, not even to speak the word. The name Pequot – as a place, a people, a history, an identity, even as a name for a refugee, a survivor, a slave – the name itself would be eradicated. For in the work of utter conquest, it was not enough simply to destroy an enemy. You had to wipe their name off the face of the earth.

This exchange of Pequots for Africans inaugurated New England's slave trade with the Caribbean; but English colonists had established slavery from the moment they settled in the West Indies not a dozen years before. Present from the beginning, African and Afro-Caribbean enslavement in British West Indies grew rapidly after the introduction of sugar culture in the 1640s, as labor moved from white servants and enslaved Natives to bonded Africans. While in the 1650s, the latter made up 20 percent of the population, by the early eighteenth century, they comprised 80 percent of the inhabitants in the British West Indies.[34] The concentration of enslaved Black laborers was even greater on the big sugar islands; in 1750, in Jamaica, African-descended people outnumbered whites by a ratio of ten to one.[35] This demographic dominance was a function of greed, not of natural growth. Mortality rates on West Indian plantations were so high that the continued large-scale importation of people from Africa was necessary to maintain the industry that grew up around the back-breaking work of sugar production. Between the origin of the British transatlantic slave trade in 1562 until its abolition in 1807, more than 3.2 million ships embarked for Africa, most disembarking into the slave markets of the West Indies.[36] In the eyes of traders and buyers, the people they carried were not people but cargo, commodities.

For all the figures around slavery that it is possible to reconstruct, numbers give us a false sense of comprehending a system whose effects remain immeasurable. Immeasurable, but not without testimony. One of the most powerful accounts comes from Mary Prince, born into slavery at Brackish-Pond, Bermuda in 1788: *The History of Mary Prince, A West Indian Slave*. In stark language, Prince describes her treatment under four owners, as she passed "from one misery to another, and from one cruel master to a worse."-[37] At eighteen, separated from her family, she was sold from "one butcher to another" and brought to Turk's Island.[38] There, she labored in the salt works from the dark of the morning, through the day of punishing sun, to the dark of the night. Standing for hours in the salt water, enslaved laborers' legs were covered with boils, eating down "to the very bone." This killing work was not punishment enough; Prince recounts being stripped, tied, and lashed until her back was "raw with gashes." "Yet there was nothing very remarkable in this," she writes, "for it might serve as a sample of the common usage of the slaves on that horrible island."[39] In telling of her life on Turk's Island, Prince's narrative frequently incorporates the experiences of other enslaved people, giving voice to the everyday horror of their lives. Through these acts of witness, she allows her reader a wincing glimpse into a system that was total, and that was the engine of the colonial world.

Prince turns from herself to Daniel, whose hip was injured from the grueling work so that he could not keep pace with the others. As a consequence, his enslaver regularly tied him down and whipped him until raw, then threw buckets of salt water over him who was all one open wound. "[T]he man writhed on the ground like a worm, and screamed aloud with agony," but not a muscle of his torturer's face moved.[40] Daniel could never heal but lived with always lacerated flesh. Maggots crawled in the gashes. Slain yet alive, he haunted the others; he became "an object of pity and terror to the whole gang of slaves, and in his wretched case we saw, each of us, our own lot, if we should live to be as old."[41] The people saw their terror materialized in his splayed body and saw what might be the alternative to their always imminent death in the shape of the undead man. Prince turns to Ben who, hanging from the whipping place with a pool of blood beneath him, had a bayonet driven straight through his foot. To Sarah, an elderly and disabled woman, who was whipped and then thrown in the brambles, upon which she was so "grievously wounded, that her body swelled and festered all over, and she died a few days after." To her own mother who, when Prince suddenly encountered her on Turk's Island, was "gone from her senses" and did not know her daughter. It is both too much and too little to tell. Prince knows herself to be testifying for these people who lived in grief: "In telling my own sorrows, I cannot pass by those of my fellow-slaves – for when I think of my own griefs, I remember theirs."[42] The autobiography as a form of the self becomes collective in practice, its goal not simply to speak but to speak out and speak for. "I know what the slave knows," Prince declares.[43] "This is slavery. I tell it."[44]

Sometimes Prince can only tell the repeating trauma of enslavement by falling into language that repeats itself. Work, work, work. Weep, weep, weep. Lick, lick. Sick, sick. The trials, the trials. Again and again.[45] This linguistic repetition stands in for the repetition of physical and psychic pain that seems endless and that destroys language's capacity to represent beyond reverberation. Torture is always in the present; the "round hundred" lashes are experienced as a hundred moments of one. This is another mark of trauma: the past refuses to stay past but is constantly recurring. At these moments of repetitive enunciation, the narrative lingers where language fails. The repeated words do more than emphasize; they hold open places where the body's knowledge exceeds the power of words. Portraying a sadistic world where extraordinary violence becomes ordinary, where the stretched time of pain is both the realest thing and the most unreal, Prince can stop time for her readers, sometimes by repetition, sometimes by exclamation, and sometimes by command. When Prince finally gains her "sweet" freedom, she is able to speak beyond the pain she inhabited for so long. "Stop ... and hear what I have to say," she demands.[46] "I will say the truth."[47] The opportunity to command a white audience to hear the truth of enslavement firsthand was extremely rare, but the weight of "what the slave knows" was felt everywhere, even if colonists denied it. The repeating trauma of colonization for both Native and African Americans did not prevent either group from resisting or persisting. It did create a colonial world of extreme and ongoing violence, in which colonists' fundamental refusal to acknowledge the personhood of those they persecuted allowed them to shatter lives, again and again.

Accident, disaster, trauma. Together, they created a literature that separated what existed before colonial encounters from what arose in their aftermath. The latter is often a record of loss and violence, wherein human experiences of becoming colonial shook the foundations of former selves. It was, in the words of one scholar, "a new world for all," a world often defined by precarity, confusion, brutality, and unsettlement.[48] Certainly, continuities and cultural survivals persisted among Europeans, Natives, and Africans; and certainly modes of feeling, of understanding, and of expression were distinct among these groups who lived in such different states. Yet those ways of being also became entangled in a process of creolization that, if it was productive of new discourses, was also infused with something more than everyday cultural mingling. It was infused with the catastrophe that arose from the crisis of colonial settlement, in which the recurrence of acute conditions created a profoundly unstable world. It was not only the hazard of material events but also the inability to comprehend them that created this atmosphere of unsteadiness. Both factors, external and internal, led to a state of self-otherness that shaped coloniality and its literature.

Notes

1. George Percy, "A Trewe Relaycon of the Proceedings and Occurantes of Momente," in *Captain John Smith: Writings with Other Narratives of Roanoke, Jamestown, and the First English Settlement of America*, ed. James Horn (New York: Literary Classics of the United States, 2007), 993.
2. Ibid., 1101.
3. William Bradford, *Of Plymouth Plantation, 1620–1647 by William Bradford, Sometime Governor Thereof*, ed. Samuel Eliot Morison (New York: Alfred A. Knopf, 2002), 95.
4. John M. Murrin, *Beneficiaries of Catastrophe: The English Colonies in America* (Washington, DC: American Historical Association, 1997).
5. Orlando Patterson, *Slavery and Social Death: A Comparative Study* (Cambridge, MA: Harvard University Press, 1982).
6. Jonathan Dickinson, *Jonathan Dickinson's Journal, or God's Protecting Providence, Being the Narrative of a Journey from Port Royal in Jamaica to Philadelphia*, ed. Evangeline Walker Andrews and Charles McLean Andrews (New Haven, CT: Yale University Press), 6.
7. Ibid., 7.
8. Ibid., 8.
9. Ibid., 27.
10. Ibid., 28.
11. Ibid., 35.
12. Ibid., 17.
13. Ibid., 68.
14. Percy, "A Trewe Relaycon," 1099.
15. Joseph Stromberg, "Starving Setters in Jamestown Colony Resorted to Cannibalism," Smithsonian.com (April 30, 2013), www.smithsonianmag.com/history/starving-settlers-in-jamestown-colony-resorted-to-cannibalism-46000815/.
16. Percy, "A Trewe Relaycon," 1002.
17. Ibid., 1101.
18. John Smith, "The General Historie of Virginia, New-England, and the Summer Isles," in *Captain John Smith*, ed. Horn, 341.
19. Robert Johnson, *Nova Brittania, Offering Most Excellent Fruits by Planting in Virginia* (London, 1609), n.p.
20. James C. Scott, *Weapons of the Weak: Everyday Forms of Peasant Resistance* (New Haven, CT: Yale University Press, 1985).
21. Cathy Caruth, *Trauma: Exercises in Memory* (Baltimore: Johns Hopkins University Press, 1995), 5.
22. Ronald Dale Karr, "'Why Should You Be So Furious?' The Violence of the Pequot War," *The Journal of American History* 85, no. 3 (1998): 900.
23. Elizabeth Hubbell Schenck, *History of Fairfield County, Connecticut* (New York: J.J. Little and Company, 1889), xi.
24. Karr, "'Why Should You Be So Furious?'," 907.

25. John Mason, "A Brief History of the Pequot War," (1736), ed. Paul Royster, *Electronic Texts in American Studies*, Paper 42, 7, http://digitalcommons .unl.edu/etas/42.

26. John Underhill, "Newes from America; Or, A New and Experimentall Discoverie of New England; Containing, A Trve Relation of Their War-like Proceedings These Two Yeares Last Past, with a Figure of the Indian Fort, or Palizado," (1638), ed. Paul Royster, *Electronic Texts in American Studies*, Paper 37, 32, http://digitalcommons.unl.edu/etas/37.

27. Philip Vincent, "A True Relation of the Late Battell fought in New England, between the English, and the Salvages: With the present state of things there," (1637), *Electronic Texts in American Studies*, Paper 35, 8, http://digitalcommons .unl.edu/etas/35.

28. Mason, "A Brief History," 8.

29. Underhill, "Newes from America," 35.

30. Ibid.

31. Mason, "A Brief History," 11.

32. Underhill, "Newes from America," 35.

33. Ibid., 38.

34. "Slavery in the Caribbean," *International Slavery Museum*, www.liverpoolmu seums.org.uk/ism/slavery/archaeology/caribbean/.

35. Richard S. Dunn, *A Tale of Two Plantations: Slave Life and Labor in Jamaica and Virginia* (Cambridge, MA: Harvard University Press, 2015), 4.

36. "Transatlantic Slave Trade-Estimates," *Slave Voyages* (Emory University, 2019), www.slavevoyages.org/assessment/estimates.

37. Mary Prince, *The History of Mary Prince*, ed. Sarah Salih (New York: Penguin, 2000), 16.

38. Ibid., 20.

39. Ibid., 19 ("bone"), 20 ("gashes"), 20 ("common usage").

40. Ibid., 21.

41. Ibid.

42. Ibid., 22.

43. Ibid., 21.

44. Ibid., 38.

45. Ibid., 20 ("work"), 16 ("weep"), 15 ("lick"), 22 ("sick"), 13 ("trials"), 17 ("again").

46. Ibid., 34.

47. Ibid., 38.

48. Colin G. Calloway, *New Worlds for All: Europeans and the Remaking of Early America* (Baltimore: Johns Hopkins University Press, 2013).

8

JONATHAN BEECHER FIELD

Settler Kitsch
The Legacies of Puritanism in America

Interstate Fight Songs

The legacies of Puritanism in America seem to be nowhere and everywhere at the same time. On one hand, very few current US citizens belong to churches that William Bradford or John Winthrop would recognize as such. On the other hand, for much of the twentieth century, signage for the Massachusetts Turnpike featured a logo that was a Pilgrim hat with an Indian arrow through it. In the judgment of highway officials, this image evidently served as an iconic representation of Massachusetts. It is also an example of a legacy of Puritanism I am calling settler kitsch. Kitsch, of course, is a term made famous by the art critic Clement Greenberg in his essay "Avant-Garde and Kitsch." In 1939, Greenberg inveighed against the proliferation of lowbrow art mass-produced for a mass audience. Greenberg's frame of reference is such that contemporary readers will be surprised by some of the artifacts he categorizes as kitsch, but the concept does offer a way to understand an aesthetic process that makes unspeakable moments of history palatable. Throughout the twentieth century and into the twenty-first, there is a proliferation of images that work to reduce the violent, genocidal encounters between England settlers and New England Natives to cartoonish horseplay. This transformation echoes what Tuck and Yang refer to as "a set of evasions, or 'settler moves to innocence.'"[1] Transformations like these are the most persistent legacies of New England Puritanism one is likely to encounter in everyday life.

Another legacy of Puritanism works in tandem with settler kitsch, which is the persistent notion that Puritans are why we can't have nice things, which is to say sexy things. When present-day activists use the hashtag #freethenipple to chastise social media platforms like Instagram or Tumblr for restricting sexually oriented content, they frequently blame "puritans" for these repressive policies.[2] Many contemporary US citizens, like to think of themselves as sexually liberated and uninhibited, or at the least do not identify with the sexual mores they associate with Puritans. Unfortunately, disavowing this presumed legacy of sexual repression makes it easy for present-day settlers also to disavow the Puritan heritage of settler colonialism. As such, in the twenty-first century, it is very difficult to take Puritans seriously, because of their prudish reputation. In turn, it is easy to reduce the violence of settler colonialism to something like a Tom & Jerry cartoon. As such, the most salient legacies of American Puritanism today are not an intellectual genealogy that runs something like Eliot to Edwards to Emerson to Eliot to Ellison to Ellis. Instead, Americans today engage with a Puritan past through phenomena like #freethenipple and settler kitsch.

As such, the legacies I am detailing here do not represent an intellectual history of Puritan legacies as they unfold across time. Rather, this is a sketch of cultural history of specters of Puritanism in the twenty-first century. For one thing, Perry Miller, Sacvan Bercovitch, Amanda Porterfield, Bryce Traister, Max Weber, and others have already done that intellectual history work in various forms, and for another, those narratives are limited in the heuristic values they bring to more relevant contemporary cultural formations like sexy Pilgrim costumes, settler-themed Thanksgiving saltshakers, and Wednesday Addams's oration in the *Addams Family Values*.[3]

Against the conception of legacy as a patrimony that follows biological lines of inheritance, this chapter considers the ramifications of a Puritan legacy that is simultaneously for everybody and for nobody. Rather than tracing genealogies from Winthrop's city on a hill to Reagan's city on a hill, or from Mary Rowlandson's captivity in the seventeenth century to Patty Hearst's in the twentieth, I will explore how Americans imagine the legacy of Puritanism as something like the lead blanket you wear at the dentist, weighing us down and preventing us from becoming our true uninhibited selves. Like the lead blanket, too, contemporary imaginations of Puritanism can also work to shield us from things we might prefer not to confront. This ambivalent connection to a colonial past allows many US residents to remain comfortable with the uncomfortable realities of the settler colonial violence perpetrated by Puritans in a portion of the continent that became part of the United States.

It is likely that most US residents complete their education through the high school or college level without reading a word published by a seventeenth-century Puritan colonist, except maybe Winthrop's phrase "city on a hill." It would be hard to find any contemporary American church with a theology, liturgy, or polity that closely resembles the churches of Puritan New England. It is easy, however, to find assertions that this or that aspect of contemporary US culture is a legacy of the Puritanism embraced by some of the settlers of one corner of North America in the seventeenth century. For example, online activists, organized under the hashtag #freethenipple, who feel that Instagram or Facebook should allow the unfettered display of female breasts, often point to the "puritanism" that informs these restrictions. Lina Esco, who initiated the free the nipple movement, opined in a *Time* editorial "I came up with 'free the nipple' because it's engaging and funny – and the fuel we needed to start a serious dialogue about gender equality. The shaming of the female nipple is a direct reflection of how unevolved this puritanical country is."[4] One of the more famous incidents associated with this movement was Scout Willis's topless foray through downtown Manhattan. She posted pictures on Instagram, which suspended her account, leading *New York* magazine's *The Cut* to recap "after puritanical Instagram banned her account … Willis has taken her protest to Twitter."[5]

In an article supporting this movement, *Maxim* magazine cited "chipping away at puritanism" as one of its benefits.[6] Examples of this association between twenty-first-century repression and seventeenth-century religion are easy to find. Yet the religious lives of the people at Instagram enacting these restrictions are unlikely to have anything at all to do with the theology and ecclesiology English settlers brought to New England in the seventeenth century. More broadly speaking, contemporary media often invoke the specter of puritanism as a repressive force. When *Playboy* founder Hugh Hefner died in 2017, he was eulogized as an antagonist of the puritanism that consumed mid-twentieth-century America.[7] Journalists routinely describe Hefner's fellow high-profile pornographers, Bob Guccione and Larry Flynt, in similar terms.

Ironically, the modern association of the first white settlers of New England with censorship and repression comes in large part from a confrontation between a Baltimore journalist and a New Jersey postal inspector. Anthony Comstock was born in Connecticut and made his home as an adult in New Jersey. In 1873, he founded the New York Society for the Suppression of Vice and lobbied successfully for the passage of the "Comstock law," which criminalized using the US mail to distribute materials containing obscenity, contraception information, and contraceptives or sex toys. He finagled an appointment as a special postal inspector and bragged about the tonnage of obscene material he destroyed over the course of his career. As Rochelle Gurstein details in an essay titled "Puritanism As Epithet," Emma Goldman was eloquent in her association of Comstock and Comstockery with puritanism.[8] In her 1910 essay "The Hypocrisy of Puritanism," Goldman observes: "Puritanism no longer employs the thumbscrew and lash; but it still has a most pernicious hold on the minds and feelings of the American people. Naught else can explain the power of a Comstock. Like the Torquemadas of ante-bellum days, Anthony Comstock is the autocrat of American morals."[9]

Comstock's definition of obscenity was expansive – he referred to George Bernard Shaw as an "Irish smut dealer" – and included medical textbooks as well as manuals intended to provide sexual education for married women. His censorship attracted the ire of Baltimore's H. L. Mencken, who attributed Comstock's activity to puritanism. Mencken's work is larded with disparaging references to puritans as the source of distinctly American neuroses about sex. Famously, he defined puritanism as "the haunting fear that someone, somewhere, may be happy." Most notably, in a 1915 essay titled "Puritanism as a literary force," Mencken decried the puritan pathologies he saw afoot in Comstockery, which included the "throttling influence of an ever alert and bellicose Puritanism, not only in our grand literature, but also in our petit literature, our minor poetry, even in our humour." Mencken expounds on this theme at length, lamenting that "the typical American maker of books becomes a timorous and ineffective fellow whose work tends inevitably toward a feeble superficiality. Sucking in the Puritan spirit with the very air he breathes, and perhaps burdened inwardly with an inheritance of the actual Puritan stupidity, he is further kept on a straight path of chemical purity."[10] More broadly, for Mencken,

> The Puritan's utter lack of aesthetic sense, his distrust of all romantic emotion, his unmatchable intolerance of opposition, his unbreakable belief in his own bleak and narrow views, his savage cruelty of attack, his lust for relentless and barbarous persecution – these things have put an almost unbearable burden upon the exchange of ideas in the United States, and particularly upon that form of it which involves playing with them for the mere game's sake.[11]

Mencken's furor at the Puritan critics who kept, for instance, Dreiser's *The Titan* from getting its due evidently prevents him from tracing early modern Calvinism to twentieth-century literary culture with any clarity, which is a shame, for "From Calvin to Comstock" would make for interesting reading. Ironically, it was the New Jersey–based Comstock who inspired the formation of the Boston-based Watch and Ward Society, the organization responsible for the phrase "banned in Boston." However, traditional accounts of this form of censorship (and marketing) often bypass Comstock's influence and attribute censorship efforts in the late nineteenth and early twentieth century to the English men and women who settled Boston in the mid-seventeenth century. None of this is to say that John Winthrop would have welcomed the publication of, say, *Ulysses*, but the anachronism inherent in this question points to the difficulty of making this kind of connection.

This connection between Puritanism in colonial New England and censorship in the twentieth-century United States is somewhere between tenuous and spurious, but Mencken's agitating helped establish it as conventional wisdom. In her 1915 essay "Comstockery in America," Planned Parenthood founder Margaret Sanger writes: "It is the Comstock laws which produce the [illegal] abortionist and make him a thriving necessity while the lawmakers close their Puritan eyes."[12] Writing in 1998, Rochelle Gurstein characterizes Morris Ernst's 1937 account of the court decision allowing the publication of *Ulysses* in the United States as celebrating a "crushing defeat for the forces of puritanism."[13] Not surprisingly, the New York Society for the Suppression of Vice protested this verdict.

This association popularized by Mencken is persistent, and the mean men from Boston in big hats have been invoked in nearly every high-profile censorship case over the last century or so. A 1973 *New York Times* article compiled reactions to the recent obscenity ruling against Kurt Vonnegut, Jr.'s *Breakfast of Champions*. The novelists Ross Macdonald, Joyce Carol Oates, and John Updike all blamed the decision on "puritanism" in one form or another, with Oates commenting: "When America is not fighting a war, the puritanical desire to punish people has to be let out at home."[14] In her 1988 reappraisal of Vladimir Nabokov's *Lolita*, Erica Jong opined: "It was not only that 'Lolita' dealt with forbidden obsessions; 'Lolita' was, above all, literary. American puritanism is more comfortable with sex when it stays in the gutter than when it rises to the level of art."[15] Jong, herself, was the author of the 1973 novel *Fear of Flying*, which one of her defenders described as "a huge international best seller and a widely debated emblem of the sexual coming of age of women in Puritan America?"[16] (It is worth noting that Jong's novel is set in the 1970s, and its heroine is a Jewish woman who lives on the Upper West Side of New York City.)

Beyond the question of regulating (female) nudity and censoring sexually explicit content, puritanism figures more generally as a label for a distinctly American asceticism and joylessness. In a review of a concert by the legendary Boomer troubadour Jimmy Buffett, a *Los Angeles Times'* critic observed: "In many of his songs, he celebrated adventure and travel, recoiling from the strait-laced life and the Puritan ethic."[17] A 2017 *Vice* article offered a timeline of "All the Times in American History That Authorities Tried to Stop People From Dancing," beginning with Puritan minister Increase Mather's *Arrow Against Vain and Promiscuous Dancing* and continuing through the 1984 Kevin Bacon film *Footloose*.[18] This timeline is notable for its gaps, especially the ones separating the 1684 publication of Mather's text, the 1845 founding of (Baptist) Baylor College, and the 1984 release of *Footloose*. When the first Baptists arrived in Puritan Massachusetts, the

Puritan leaders responded by whipping them.[19] Three hundred years, 1,750 miles, and a sectarian divide separate Mather's *Arrow* from the town in Oklahoma that inspired *Footloose*. If there is a connection between Increase Mather's repression and Kevin Bacon's resistance, the legacy of Puritanism must be a durable and robust one.

Yet it is difficult to point to any current religious establishment in the United States and make a case that it has a strong connection to the Bible Commonwealth established by English settlers four centuries ago. In some cases, institutions and/or physical structures founded as Puritan churches in the seventeenth century now operate under Congregational or Unitarian management.[20] The "About Us" section on the webpages of these churches can make for interesting reading, as the current church leadership seeks to claim the historic cachet of Puritan founding, while disavowing every aspect of perceived Puritan doctrine. For instance, the heirs of the church that Thomas Hooker founded in Cambridge in 1633 put it like this:

> [For more than 375 years,] First Church has welcomed searchers and seekers, pilgrims and pioneers to share on the journey of faith that guided is by God's grace, every step of the way. Though we celebrate a rich and robust history and tradition, we are called to live out our faith in the present, to make what is ancient fresh, and to make our ideals for the future relevant in the here and now. Here is just a snapshot of our earlier years ...[21]

The website of the First Parish of Concord, a Unitarian church in Concord, states:

> In 2004, the First Parish in Concord gave a large collection of its historic records to the Concord Free Public Library. The recent processing of this rich material provides a natural opportunity to take stock of the long history of Concord's Unitarian-Universalist church, which was first gathered in 1636 in Cambridge, Massachusetts. Its first ministers, Peter Bulkeley and John Jones, were formally installed in 1637, in Cambridge.[22]

The phrasing of this passage suggests that Peter Bulkeley and John Jones were Unitarians. They were not. Elsewhere, I have detailed the uneasy perch of John Winthrop outside of the First Church of Boston as material evidence of this ambivalent disavowal, but there are many other places to find this posture, which is more of an awkward side hug of Puritan history than a full embrace.[23] The alleged prudishness of New England Puritans distances them from the present moment culturally as much as temporally. They are repressed; we are not. They hate sex; we aspire to a healthy relationship with our bodies and sexualities. As Rochelle Gurstein observed in 1994, "For almost a hundred years now, the charge of Puritanism has guaranteed the accuser the prestige of being on the side of progress, free speech and sexual emancipation."[24] At the same time, these filiations can be complex, in that, for some, alignment with a Puritan legacy is a point of pride, as in the Society of Mayflower Descendants.

The legacy of Puritanism, then, is difficult to pin down. This complexity should not be surprising, for, under any circumstances, legacies are complicated things. In its most common sense, a legacy connotes a welcome inheritance that passes from generation to generation and is a gift of wealth or property or, more abstractly, culture. For instance, the University of Chicago is the legacy of a generous gift from John D. Rockefeller. There are several ways that Puritan legacies depart from this model. A legacy can be a burden rather than a boon. In 2018, the *Chicago Maroon* published an article titled "UChicago's Legacy of White Supremacy."[25] A legacy, for good or for ill, can disappear and reappear generations later. Inspired in part by Jordan Stein's argument about queer temporalities, this chapter considers legacies as entities that can move laterally, disappear, and reappear in a different time and place, with new context and new meaning.[26]

One advantage to this approach is that it moves the work of understanding legacies of Puritanism in the present day out of a chain of direct biological inheritance. Genealogy and early American history have a deeply intertwined – some might say incestuous – history. The New England Historical and Genealogical Society remains an important resource for scholars as well as genealogists. The General Society of Mayflower Descendants, on its webpage, stipulates: "If you are interested in joining us, *you will need to provide evidence of your lineage from one of the Mayflower Pilgrims. Anyone who can prove this ancestry may join.*"[27]

Settler Kitsch

Historically, many conversations about the first white settlers of New England have hinged on these questions of biological heredity that we see in the membership requirements for the Mayflower society. Here, rather than debating evidence that might or might not establish a set of links from Increase Mather to Cotton Mather to Instagram's posting regulations, I am interested that Americans continue to make connections like these, whether they are true or not. The persistent legend that Americans inherited their prudishness from the Puritans has an impact on how many Americans think about the most significant material legacy of the Puritans, which is the land they took from Indigenous people and bequeathed to further generations of settlers. Unlike the first settlers, today's settlers are groovy and liberated, and therefore oppose what the Puritans supposedly stood for, even as they reap the benefits.[28]

If we were to look for a rupture between conventional filiopietism for Puritan forebears and the more ambivalent embraces we see today, Nathaniel Hawthorne offers a promising site of investigation. The novelist claims, but does not own, this legacy. Hawthorne famously had a genealogical connection to one of the judges who hanged alleged witches in Salem, and his unease with this legacy is one of the first things students reading *The Scarlet Letter* learn about Hawthorne. More pointedly in his shorter fiction, we can see Hawthorne satirizing Puritan mores, even as he relies on this inheritance for the theme of his most famous work. In stories like *Young Goodman Brown* and *Endicott and the Red Cross*, Hawthorne does the work of separating the values of these settlers from the kinder and gentler mores of nineteenth-century New England. These two stories in particular expose hypocrisy with the kind of ham-fisted irony you might find in a high school creative writing class, but they help to begin to produce the idea that the settlers of New England were cartoons. He does not use the word, but D. H. Lawrence's 1923 characterization of *The Scarlet Letter* as a "colossal satire" suggests he might concur with the notion of Hawthorne's work as proto-kitsch.[29] While Hawthorne dismisses the values of his settler forebears, he does little to disavow their salient material legacy to him, which is putatively legal possession of the continent of North America.

The Scarlet Letter's framing narrative of the discovery of an actual, material A works to authenticate Hester's story. As such, the frame works to suggest that the Puritan patriarchs were really as stern and judgmental as we like to imagine them. There is a lot more going on in the novel than this, but the title of the novel and its plot revolve around the punishment for Hester's sexual sin. Detached from the context of the novel, a scarlet letter has become a familiar way to refer to almost any kind of sin or shame, usually undeserved. The issue here is not if this use of the phrase misreads Hawthorne's novel but the material Puritan roots of the scarlet letter suggest that it is men like John Winthrop and Thomas Hooker who are responsible for the scarlet letters that surround us today, in places as disparate as the 2010 film *Easy A*, not to mention the ongoing conversations about a mid-1990s affair between President Clinton and an intern.

It is easy to understand the logic and ideology of the process of dispossession enacted by the first waves of Puritan and Pilgrim settlers by reading primary sources. For instance, John Cotton, in his farewell speech to the first wave of Puritan settlers in 1630, imagines an exchange where the settlers trade their "spirituals" (knowledge of Jesus Christ) for the Natives' "temporalls" (the continent of North America).[30] As any contemporary evangelical Christian can tell you, it is not customary to invoice your converts for the cost of their salvation. However, very few contemporary US residents derive their understanding of the settlement of New England by reading sermons from the 1630s. Instead, the images that circulate of Pilgrims and Puritans doing this work of dispossession work at the level of cartoons, because the echoes of their prudish repression make it impossible for us to take them seriously. As such, the popular imaginary of New England's settlement looks more like a Warner Brothers cartoon than a violent and genocidal conflict.[31]

One easy place to see this dynamic is in Thanksgiving cards. Images of young white children adopting Pilgrim hats or Indian headdresses more or less interchangeably amplify the sense of the holiday as a cultural encounter that ended in reconciliation and friendship. Various presidents declared various days of thanksgiving, but Thanksgiving's contemporary form as a national holiday celebrated on the fourth Thursday of November owes its genesis to an 1863 proclamation by Abraham Lincoln, who saw the day as a way to promote reconciliation in the midst of the Civil War. Lincoln's proclamation does not invoke the Pilgrims explicitly, but the material forms of this celebration typically evoke the 1621 gathering William Bradford chronicles in *Of Plimoth Plantation*. The idea of this encounter as a good moment for historical cosplay is buttressed by the ease of making these costumes. Even today, many schoolchildren in the United States make Pilgrim hats and/or Indian headdresses as an activity in the days leading up to Thanksgiving. The proliferation of these benign images makes it difficult to recover the actual violence that attended this process of settlement. If you consider how difficult it is to imagine a diorama of the Trail of Tears populated with Hummel figurines, you can see how settler kitsch works.

After generations of scholars of American Puritanism who frequently treated New England's Indigenous inhabitants as an afterthought, there has been scholarship seeking to do more to articulate the facts of the encounter between Native and settler in New England. Francis Jennings's *The Invasion of America* and Jill Lepore's *The Name of War* were early gestures in this direction, while, more recently, Kathleen Donegan's *Seasons of Misery*, Jean O'Brien's *Firsting and Lasting*, Christine DeLucia's *Memory Lands*, and Lisa Brooks's *Our Beloved Kin* work in a variety of ways to enrich and complicate our understanding of New England settler colonialism and, more importantly, to give names, faces, and voices to New England's Indigenous inhabitants. Even as this heroic scholarly work continues, settler kitsch remains a staple of US mass culture. There are boudoir photographers happy to arrange a Thanksgiving-themed pinup photo session, while the vitamin company Muscle Milk uses videos of a "sexy pilgrim" to promote their dietary supplements.[32] The sexy pilgrim trope is a peculiar space where perceptions of Puritan prudishness and the ideology of settler colonialism intersect. One of the peculiarities of contemporary sexual discourse is that what is not sexy is sexy because it is not sexy. The icon of the sexy librarian is perhaps the most familiar version of this notion, but it also operates with the sexy pilgrim, exemplified in Figure 8.1 by Marilyn Monroe sporting a blunderbuss.

If the Marilyn Monroe pinup works to celebrate her sex appeal to demonstrate that her sexiness transcends unsexy things like a turkey, a blunderbuss, and a Pilgrim costume, Demi Moore's appearance as Hester Prynne in the 1995 film adaptation of *The Scarlet Letter* does Marilyn one better by having Demi's sex appeal transcend an entire unsexy society. As the tagline on the poster proclaims, WHEN INTIMACY IS FORBIDDEN, AND PASSION IS A SIN, LOVE IS THE MOST DEFIANT CRIME OF ALL.

For several decades, college and professional sports mascots that appropriate Native names and iconography have been a topic of contention. Some

Figure 8.1 Marilyn Monroe in abbreviated Pilgrim costume, with a blunderbuss and turkey for accessories, 1950. In the mid-twentieth century, Pilgrim-themed pinups were surprisingly popular.

universities, notably Stanford and Dartmouth, dropped their Native mascots in 1972 and 1974 respectively, while other programs, both collegiate and professional, continue to use Native mascots in spite of ongoing criticism. For a variety of reasons, the history of a Puritan as an unofficial mascot of Harvard University has attracted less attention, but the intersection of these icons as illustrations for football programs offers a classic example of the work of settler kitsch in the twentieth century. Harvard (unofficially represented by a Puritan) and Dartmouth (the "Indians" until 1974) play one another every year in football (Figure 8.2). The illustrators of the programs for these football games often chose to illustrate the covers with images of a cartoon Indian and a cartoon Puritan involved in some sort of violent shenanigan. A recurring trope in these images is a Native arrow passing harmlessly through the big hat of the Puritan settler. The big hat is intrinsically comical, but the way arrows never seem to harm settlers is a droll way to represent the fundamental futility of Native resistance to settler aggression.

A more elaborate instance of settler kitsch is on display in the Thanksgiving pageant scene in the 1993 film *Addams Family Values*. This movie is a sequel to a movie based on a television show that is in turn based on popular cartoons by Charles Addams that appeared in the *New Yorker* from 1937 to 1988. In the sequel, Wednesday Addams (Christina Ricci) is at summer camp, and the campers are putting on a play about Thanksgiving as the culmination of their time at camp. The event goes according to plan until Wednesday Addams arrives, identifies herself as "Pocahontas" of the Chippewas, and delivers a speech to her fellow campers dressed as Pilgrims, which culminates in a declaration that she will scalp them and burn their village. Wednesday does tell the audience that the Pilgrims have stolen Native land and that the Natives will not fare well in the future, but this critique is impossible to take at face value – Ricci is playing a cartoon character who is herself playing Indian in the stylized, two-dimensional context of a summer camp theatrical. The violence, such as it is, is unsettling, but, again, it is cartoon violence like that we see in football programs of earlier decades or in animated cartoons. It is violence that hurts nobody and truth presented in a way that will not make anyone uncomfortable.

A final complication of settler kitsch comes in something I am calling the dialectics of Native erasure. In 1989, the Massachusetts Turnpike Authority agreed to remove the arrow from the iconic Mass Pike signs described at the opening of this chapter. The hat on the logo is a Pilgrim hat – a big black hat with a buckle on the front, of a sort one would never wear unless it was part of a Pilgrim costume. There is no head inside the hat – so it exists as a kind of free-floating signifier of an aspect of Massachusetts heritage. The arrow, I would argue, is supposed to be hard to take seriously. Of the ways

Figure 8.2 Dartmouth vs. Harvard football programs, 1946, 1953. Many American college football programs of this era featured illustrations presenting conflicts between the opponents' mascots. With Dartmouth's Indian mascot and Harvard's unofficial Puritan mascot, many of their programs featured images of cartoonish violence between settlers and Natives.

Massachusetts motorists might well be concerned about suffering a violent death behind the wheel, but arrows are low on the list of potential causes. When Steve Martin wears the comedy prop that has two halves of an arrow attached to a headband allowing him to simulate being shot with an arrow, the point is not to simulate that he has been shot but that he is trying too hard to be funny. As such, arrows are funny, because this symbol of Native resistance to English settlement is deemed laughably puny. After all, Jared Diamond told all the dads back in the 1990s that Guns, Germs, and Steel were responsible for settlement.

The impetus for this move came from a surprising source, for a surprising reason. According to a UPI article, a second-grade class in Amherst, Massachusetts, mounted a letter-writing campaign urging officials to get rid of the arrow. While institutions like Stanford and Dartmouth disavowed Native iconography out of respect for Indigenous objections, the change to the Mass Pike logo happened because the teacher of this class, Barbara Skolnick Rothenberg, "thought it conveyed a message of violence and aggression, with the violence directed towards the Pilgrims."[33] The ensuing logo retains the Pilgrim hat but omits the arrow (Figure 8.3).

A cartoonish representation of the violent struggle for lands that Native Americans called home is a problematic choice for a road sign, but this solution is not a solution and is worse in some ways. The hat stands alone, and rather than representing conflict, the unscathed Pilgrim hat suggests that the Natives were never there. This is an example of the dialectics of Native erasure – when Indigenous history, culture, or people appear in an encounter with settler culture, these representations make people uncomfortable, because they are a reminder that one group of people stole a continent from another group of people, and killed many of them in the process. As this theft moves from something actively celebrated by settler culture – as in the giant statue of Hannah Dustan clutching the scalps of the Native women and children she took for the bounty they carried – to something settler culture is vaguely uneasy with, the easiest solution is to remove the evidence of the Native presence in the first place.

Figure 8.3 Until 1989, the signs for the Massachusetts Turnpike featured a Pilgrim hat with an arrow through it. The current Mass Turnpike Authority logo retains the hat but omits the arrow.

Even as we recognize the kitschy elements of Marilyn's Monroe's turkey hunter or Demi Moore's Hester Prynne, or wince at the artwork on old football programs, this ambivalent contemporary posture toward Puritan legacies establishes a difference between Us (USA!) and Them (mean men in black hats). This halfhearted disavowal produces an ongoing appetite for caricatures of Puritans and Puritanism, which serve not only for the fathers of the Daughters of the Mayflower but also, more generally, for the nation at large. This ambivalent othering produces a return of repressed origins in cartoonish form, most notably in the context of celebrations of Thanksgivings but also in innumerable fictions, memorials, celebrations, mascots, histories, and more. This transformation of Puritanism into a kind of cartoonish distortion I am calling "settler kitsch" as a way of naming the evasions, disavowals, and moves to innocence that accompany the work of Native dispossession enacted by the Puritan settlers of New England in the seventeenth century and beyond. An American inability to take the Puritans seriously because they were stuffy and prudish offers a way for settlers to distance themselves from the violent realities of settler colonialism that attended the propagation of the Puritan faith in New England. This is the most salient legacy of American Puritanism in the twenty-first century.

Notes

1. E. Tuck and K. W. Yang, "Decolonization Is Not a Metaphor," *Decolonization: Indigeneity, Education, and Society* 1, no. 1 (2012): 1.
2. It is worth noting that the capricious and opaque enforcement of content policies on social media platforms has had a calamitous impact on the safety and prosperity of many entrepreneurs who use these media, including models, photographers, and sex workers.
3. Although they have a different name, the Pilgrims are part of the legacy of Puritans. Especially in the United States, the terms overlap. "Puritan" refers broadly to English Calvinists who became disenchanted with the Church of England's stipulated religious practice. The name "Puritan" began as a derisive term for English Calvinists who objected to the more ornate aspects of Anglicanism. Some of these Puritans chose not to conform with these Anglican liturgical guidelines, instead practicing a more austere and sermon-focused worship. These Christians were called "nonconformists." Some of these nonconformists, including the settlers who traveled to Plymouth on the *Mayflower*, chose to separate from the Anglican church, on the grounds that it was irredeemably corrupt. These were called "separating nonconformists." Other English Christians, including the main body of the settlers of the Massachusetts Bay Colony, chose not to conform but held out hope that their example would inspire the Church of England to follow a more righteous path. The Puritans who settled in and around Boston can be deemed small-p

pilgrims, in that they were on a religious journey. The English settlers of Plymouth who arrived on the *Mayflower* are known as Pilgrims, with a capital P. There are important differences between these two types of nonconformism and major differences between the settlement and history of Plymouth Colony and the Massachusetts Bay Colony, but both settlements contribute to the conceptions of Puritanism in circulation today, and this chapter considers both.

4. Lina Esco, "'Free the Nipple' Is Not About Seeing Breasts," *Time*, September 11, 2015, time.com/4029632/lina-esco-should-we-freethenipple/.

5. Allison P. Davis, "Scout Willis Stages Topless Protest in New York," *The Cut*, May 29, 2014, www.thecut.com/2014/05/scout-willis-stages-topless-protest-in-new-york.html.

6. Kayleen Schaefer, "The 7 Unexpected Benefits of Supporting 'Free the Nipple'," *Maxim*, December 14, 2015, www.maxim.com/maxim-man/7-unexpected-benefits-supporting-free-nipple.

7. Laura Mansnerus, "Hugh Hefner, Who Built the Playboy Empire and Embodied It, Dies at 91," *New York Times*, September 27, 2017, www.nytimes.com/2017/09/27/obituaries/hugh-hefner-dead.html.

8. Rochelle Gurstein, "Puritanism As Epithet," *Salmagundi* no. 101–102 (1994): 102.

9. Emma Goldman, "The Hypocrisy of Puritanism," in *Anarchism and Other Essays*, 3rd rev. ed. (New York: Mother Earth Publishing Association, 1917), 2, www.marxists.org/reference/archive/goldman/works/1917/puritanism.htm.

10. H. L. Mencken, "Puritanism As a Literary Force," in *A Book of Prefaces* (New York: Knopf, 1918), 275.

11. Ibid., 201–202.

12. Margaret Sanger, "Comstockery in America" (1915), The Margaret Sanger Papers Project, New York University, www.nyu.edu/projects/sanger/webedition/app/documents/show.php?sangerDoc=303242.xml.

13. Rochelle Gurstein, *The Repeal of Reticence: America's Cultural and Legal Struggles Over Free Speech, Obscenity, Sexual Liberation, and Modern Art* (New York: Hill and Wang, 1998), 207.

14. Robert A. Wright, "Broad Spectrum of Writers Attacks Obscenity Ruling," *New York Times*, August 21, 1973, www.nytimes.com/1973/08/21/archives/broad-spectrum-of-writers-attacks-obscenity-ruling-frank-speech.html.

15. Erica Jong, "Summer Reading; Time Has Been Kind to the Nymphet: 'Lolita' 30 Years Later," *New York Times*, June 5, 1988, www.nytimes.com/1988/06/05/books/summer-reading-time-has-been-kind-to-the-nymphet-lolita-30-years-later.html.

16. Benjamin R. Barber, "Violating Our Puritan Soul," *New York Times*, March 28, 1993, https://timesmachine.nytimes.com/timesmachine/1993/03/28/047993.html?pageNumber=365.

17. Mike Boehm, "Buffett Is the Perfect Party Host: Parrot Heads Surface Out of Season to See Laid-Back Hero Preach Spring Break Ethos with No Intrusion from Real World," *Los Angeles Times*, October 11, 1993, www.latimes.com/archives/la-xpm-1993-10-11-ca-44522-story.html.

18. Anna Codrea-Rado, "All the Times in American History That Authorities Tried to Stop People from Dancing," *Vice*, March 6, 2017, www.vice.com/en_us/article/nzmkn8/laws-against-dancing-nightlife-history-timeline.

19. Jonathan Beecher Field, *Errands into The Metropolis: New England Dissidents in Revolutionary London* (Lebanon, NH: University Press of New England, 2009), 75–83.

20. The contemporary US churches with the closest doctrinal connections to early American Puritanism are probably Dutch Reform churches operating in the Midwest.

21. "About Us," First Church in Cambridge website, www.firstchurchcambridge.org/about-us/first-church-history.

22. "History of First Parish," First Parish in Concord website, http://firstparish.org/wp/about/our-stories/history-of-first-parish/.

23. Jonathan Beecher Field, "Puritan Acts and Monuments," in Bryce Traister, ed., *American Literature and the New Puritan Studies* (Cambridge: Cambridge University Press, 2017), 164.

24. Gurstein, "Puritanism As Epithet," 95.

25. Aram Ghoogasian, "UChicago's Legacy of White Supremacy," *Chicago Maroon*, January 27, 2018, www.chicagomaroon.com/article/2018/1/27/uchicago-legacy-white-supremacy/.

26. Jordan Stein, "American Literary History and Queer Temporalities," *American Literary History* 25, no. 4 (2013): 855–869, https://doi.org/10.1093/alh/ajt043.

27. Emphasis in original. See the Mayflower Society's webpage: www.themayflowersociety.org/join.

28. This chapter uses the term "settlers" to refer to occupants of land originally inhabited by Natives. When it is necessary to differentiate those who did the original work of settling, I use the term "original settler."

29. D. H. Lawrence, *Studies In Classic American Literature*. Available online: http://xroads.virginia.edu/~HYPER/LAWRENCE/lawrence.html.

30. John Cotton, "Gods Promise to His Plantation," (1630), ed. Reiner Smolinski. *Electronic Texts in American Studies*, Paper 22, http://digitalcommons.unl.edu/etas/22.

31. There is a literal Warner Brothers cartoon where Porky Pig is the captain of the *Mayflower*, but his encounter with the Indigenous people of New England is relatively peaceful. See the listing on IMDb: www.imdb.com/title/tt0032909/.

32. See "Muscle Milk's Sexy Pilgrim," YouTube, January 13, 2010, https://youtu.be/DJJhJkjBmWw.

33. UPI Archives, "Kids Pluck Arrow from Pilgrims' Hat," UPI.com, November 23, 1989, www.upi.com/Archives/1989/11/23/Kids-pluck-arrow-from-Pilgrims-hat/4156627800400/?fbclid=IwAR2jgCz6vwriGxa4goX218wgxcaw1n8w9Rhc8_UEX7Uk2r-dPuByqhbqDIU.

9

PAUL DOWNES

Like a Prayer
The Anti-Slavery Petition in the Era of Revolution

> The arguments of these black petitions will reverberate through the era
> of the Revolution, and beyond.
>
> Sidney Kaplan[1]

It has often been claimed that early America's principal contribution to
literary culture took the form of revolutionary political writing. Paine's
Common Sense; Jefferson's *Declaration*; the *Federalist Papers*; and
Washington's Farewell speech, among others, helped to define a distinctly
American oratorical style and invented a set of ringing republican phrases
that continue to inform popular political discourse in the twenty-first century. Yet, as we know all too well, this much-celebrated archive was the
product of a decidedly limited circle of "Founding Fathers" who not only
failed to include women in their definition of the citizen but also succeeded in
protecting a system of racialized enslavement that had been growing expo-
nentially throughout the eighteenth century. Those of us who continue to
teach and write about these texts sometimes proceed by pointing out the
paradoxical relationship between the founders' rhetoric of "liberty" and the
nascent nation's utter dependency upon the enormous wealth produced by
slave labor. Another approach has been to follow Frederick Douglass's
example and attempt to discern a latent egalitarian anti-racism hidden within
the misread and misapplied lines of the founding texts themselves. This
chapter offers a different approach by considering how a particular genre
of political writing practiced by African Americans during the revolutionary
period might help us to reinvent what counts as "founding" American
thought. Can we read late eighteenth-century anti-slavery petitions by
Black Americans alongside the *Declaration of Independence*, for example,
not just to show where the latter fell short or where it might, eventually, lead
us but to acquire new insights into the relationship between equality and
sovereignty in a democratic community?

Since at least the publication of Herbert Aptheker's monumental *Documentary History of the Negro People in the United States* in 1951, scholars have been aware of a series of petitions sent in the 1770s to the authorities in Massachusetts, Connecticut, and New Hampshire explicitly pleading for intervention to protect Black Americans from slavery and its associated injustices.[2] These anti-slavery petitions were the first written expressions of a specifically Black collective political voice in what would become the United States. As Harry Reed explains, "The self-affirming quality of the black petitions during the revolutionary period is unmistakable. Contained in the petitions is the beginning process of self-identity and naming the people ... creating a conception of a people but also a community of common interest and the potential for united action."[3] Reed makes a significant claim about Black identity here, but maybe we can build upon his observation by asking if these petitions also contribute to constructing an *American* "community of common interest." This task will require us to think a little more about the generic specificity of the petition – its history and its rhetorical conventions – in order to appreciate how such revolutionary era interventions might have been doing even more than at first appears.

The petition, or "prayer," addressed to the sovereign has a complex and multifaceted history in seventeenth-century England and the American colonies, and it played an important if underappreciated role in the political culture of the revolutionary period. Yet the petition also appears to have developed a renewed appeal in twenty-first-century online political culture, as rapidly evolving media technology and widespread popular dissatisfaction with the corporate monopoly on governmental policy-making have combined to intensify the reach and appeal of the online petition. Scholarly studies and celebrations of the Founding Fathers and their "sacred" documents show no sign of abating, but perhaps contemporary democratic thought and practice have as much to learn from revolutionary-era anti-slavery petitions as from the Declaration of Independence – as much to learn, perhaps, from an enslaved Black Bostonian named FELIX as from Thomas Jefferson or James Madison.

From "Grace" to "Right": A Brief History of the Republican Petition

Colonial Americans were inveterate petitioners, and the various legislative mechanisms available for petitioning state and local governments helped to facilitate an unusually participatory political culture among white, male property owners in the prerevolutionary American colonies.[4] The culture of petitioning may also have been responsible for *expanding* political participation in the prerevolutionary era. In Connecticut, for example, as Stephen

A. Higginson explains, "not only the enfranchised population, but also unrepresented groups – notably women, felons, Indians, and, in some cases, slaves – represented themselves and voiced grievances through petition."[5] The petition, in other words, has a strong case to make for being considered as the preeminent genre of American political writing.

Although American colonists might trace their right to petition back through Blackstone's monumental *Commentaries on English Law* and the 1689 Bill of Rights, all the way, by some accounts, to the Magna Carta, much of the force and appeal of the colonial-era petition derived from the explosion of petitioning in mid-seventeenth-century England.[6] English radicals, as one contemporary put it, were "seized with the petitioning disease" in the 1640s and 1650s,[7] and in the aftermath of Charles I's surrender, insurgent royalists joined in the activity too, asking the Long Parliament in 1648 to affirm their right to present the "just desires of the oppressed in a petitionary way (the undoubted right of the subject) and the very life of liberty itself."[8] From our perspective, however, the most interesting development in the history of the petition concerns the growing disparity between two distinct forms of petition: the petition of grace and the petition of right. As Richard L. Bushman explains, "A petition of grace was an appeal to the generosity of the crown for an exercise of power on the petitioner's behalf," whereas, "a petition of right was based on law [and] the appeal was not for grace, but to the remedy of wrongs done contrary to law."[9] A petition of right would be granted, in other words, "not out of royal generosity, but out of respect for the subject's rights."[10] As republican radicalism gained traction in the first decades of the English seventeenth century, so the appeal of the petition of grace (and of its characteristic rhetoric of supplication) gave way to a more insistent and demanding deployment of the petition of right, both inside and outside parliament. After the death of Charles I, petitions to parliament did not cease, but they began to take on a peculiarly mixed and, in some respects, incoherent tone, "presented, like instructions, as the voice of the sovereign people, oddly supplicatory but at the same time demanding."[11] The increasing popularity of forceful petitions of right, even as Cromwell's revolution achieved temporary success, inevitably raised the thorny question of where, precisely, sovereignty was to be found in post-monarchic England. Should a petition, in other words, be thought of as an address to or from the sovereign power? Was it a prayer or a command? Was the petition's formal addressee being asked to dispense or enforce a right that did or did not belong to the petitioning people? As Edmund Morgan explains, "The right to petition seems a strange sort of right under a government based on popular sovereignty ... Why does anyone need a right to pray, beg, or supplicate, especially if the power thus implored is supposed to be inferior to the supplicants?"[12]

In America, antipathy toward the more subservient rhetoric of the petition of grace intensified throughout the eighteenth century.[13] Nevertheless, in the wake of the Coercive Acts, and even as revolutionary fervor began to spread, some frustrated Americans continued to believe that appeals to King George, using the conventional language of the petition of grace, would succeed in reversing parliament's vindictive and "tyrannical" trade policies. This wave of petitioning to the crown culminated, for the Americans, in the 1774 "loyal address to his Majesty" from the First Continental Congress, calling for a repeal of the Intolerable Acts. "To the King's most excellent majesty," the petition begins; "Most gracious sovereign . . . We your majesty's faithful subjects . . . by this our humble petition, beg leave to lay our grievances before the throne."[14] After listing some of these grievances, the colonial subjects, once again, addressed their king directly: "To a sovereign who glories in the name of Briton the bare recital of these acts must, we presume, justify the loyal subjects, who fly to the foot of his throne and implore his clemency for protection against them."[15] This is not, to state the obvious, revolutionary language. All that American radicals despised in the monarchical form of government was captured by the fawning obsequiousness required of such conventional petitions of grace, and when the petition met with nothing but silence, those who had long dismissed the very idea of such a petition were not at all surprised. The 1774 Petition was seen by many at the time, and has certainly been dismissed by most since, as either the final performance of humiliation on the part of excessively loyal subjects or merely an empty gesture, designed to demonstrate that all avenues to peaceful resolution had been pursued prior to rebellion. The year before the petition was sent, the *Massachusetts Spy* referred to the "degrading" "whine and cry" of petitioning the king, and Committees of Correspondence in various parts of the colonies spoke of the continued recourse to petitioning as "the most ridiculous idea that ever entered into weak heads" and "an insult to the understanding of mankind."[16]

In the place of these "degrading" petitions, republican revolutionaries offered what William Warner has described as "the first instance of the most distinctive genre of modern political writing, the popular declaration."[17] In *Protocols of Liberty*, Warner retells the story of American independence as a passage from petitioning to declaring that proceeded via a crucial intermediary form – the *Votes and Proceedings* of the Massachusetts revolutionary Committee of Correspondence – that exploited a "hybrid structure" and established its authority "through its incorporation and redirection of two traditional constituents of the petition, the statement of rights and the list of infringements and grievances."[18] In addition, however, and crucially from our perspective, these new revolutionary addresses replaced "the deferential address to authority with an egalitarian address to fellow citizens."[19] From the republican point of view that Warner ventriloquizes, the outdated petition, characterized by "a mutually acknowledged asymmetry of power" and "rooted deep within the constitution of the monarchical form of government," only served to reaffirm "the covenant between ruler and ruled by asking for protection and vowing allegiance." Petitioners, unlike the new patriots, "lower[ed] themselves in humility before the petitioned as they would in prayer,[20] and such bowing and scraping, as Whitman and Emerson, among others, would later affirm, was not what defined a "real" American. "There was a time when [petitioning the king] was proper," wrote Thomas Paine in *Common Sense*, "and there is a proper time for it to cease";[21] and cease, as we know, it did, in 1776: "In every stage of these oppressions," wrote Thomas Jefferson in the *Declaration of Independence*, "we have petitioned for redress in the most humble terms: our repeated petitions have been answered only by repeated injuries." The United States became an independent, sovereign nation, in other words, precisely by shifting from one genre of political writing (the "degrading" petition of grace) to another (the "sacred" Declaration of Independence) and by simultaneously getting up off its knees and assuming its place "among the powers of the earth."

There's something not quite right about this story, though, because for certain Americans the era of the petition, even the era of the petition of *grace*, did not come to an abrupt end in the 1770s. In fact, as we have seen, the tradition of collectively oriented Black political writing in America begins, right here in the 1770s, by deploying the language of the petition of grace (as well as, in some instances, that of the petition of right) at precisely the moment when white republican Americans imagined they had left such language behind. At once revolutionary in their demand for political equality and archaic in their recourse to the rhetoric of submission, Black anti-slavery petitions were peculiarly out of joint in revolutionary America, and we might well ask how such compromised texts could have any chance of entering into the canon of founding American political documents. What I want to suggest, however, is that it is precisely this out-of-jointedness that gives the revolutionary-era anti-slavery petition its critical purchase. In offering a view of the limitations of the (white) republican founding, it opens up a conceptual path to another, more inclusive American democracy to come. These petitions remind us to think about the valuable persistence of the postrevolutionary petition of right and, more surprisingly, about the continued significance of the discredited petition of grace as a counterintuitive

Like a Prayer

source of post-republican (and post-liberal) political possibilities. The anti-slavery petition, as we shall see, effected a subtle redeployment of the rhetoric of deference as part of an effort to bring about a more radical revolution than the one most Americans thought they were engaged in.

The Radicalism of FELIX's Anti-Slavery Petition

Hundreds of Black men and women submitted petitions to local and state governments in the eighteenth century, and they addressed an enormous range of individual issues, many of which were indirectly related to the injustices of slavery.[22] By focusing on the January 6, 1773 petition to "His Excellency Thomas Hutchinson, Esq., Governor; To the Honorable His Majesty's Council, and To the Honorable House of Representatives in General Court assembled at Boston" from someone who simply signs themselves "FELIX," I want to draw attention to the first example we have of a Black American publishing a document that explicitly articulates a collective political voice working for an end to slavery for all Black Americans. Harry Reed suggests that petitions such as this one pioneered the work of representing a preexisting collective even as they emanated from individuals who were actively working to *produce* that very sense of community (hoping "to influence other blacks to join them in a show of unity").[23] At first glance, however, it is hard not to be put off by the extent to which FELIX's petition unreservedly inhabits the language of obeisance and humility bequeathed to it by the conventions of the monarchical petition of grace. FELIX refers to the "humble petition" of the author and those for whom he speaks (the "many Slaves, living in the Town of Boston, and other Towns in the Province") and proceeds to ask that the "honorable" address-ees "be pleased to take [the slaves'] unhappy State and Condition" under their "wise and just consideration."[24] Asking that he and his fellow black Americans be "made free," FELIX follows standard petitionary protocol by declining (or, we might say, performing a reluctance) to tell the sovereign directly what to do: "We presume not to dictate to your Excellency and Honors," writes FELIX, "being willing to rest our cause on your humanity and justice; yet would beg leave to say a word or two on the subject."[25]

How should we evaluate the language of deference that FELIX inherits from the tradition of the petition of grace and that he uses here to address those who continue to uphold the system of slavery in America? What can we do with the unnerving experience of listening to African Americans politely asking for consideration from their white victimizers? One approach would be to recall Harry Reed's suggestion that these petitions "may be the earliest political documents containing what black literary critics refer to as encoding in black language."[26] Or, as Jacqueline Bacon and Glen McClish put it, what we might look for in the language of the Black petitions is a form of "signifying" in Henry Louis Gates, Jr.'s sense.[27] Citing Kenneth Burke on the "rhetoric of courtship" ("the use of hierarchical language to imply the possible reversal of roles of superior and inferior, thus destabilizing the existing power structure"), Bacon and McClish note "an exaggerated tone of goodwill," in the early Black petitions, "that highlights the irony of their implicit message."[28] Such an approach seems highly plausible, and indeed it might be argued that, throughout its history, in England and the colonies, the petition of grace was always an elaborately disguised form – a wolf of right dressed up in the deferential language of a sheep of grace. "The acceptable talk of royal protection," suggests Bushman (with respect to the debate over the wording of the 1764 petition from Massachusetts to King George in opposition to the impending Stamp Act), "trembled on the edge of resentment and threat."[29] According to this interpretive protocol, the petition's explicit performance of obeisance pales in significance next to its implicit assertion of original right and extra-political authority. "We think ourselves very happy," writes FELIX, "that we may thus address the Great and General Court of this Province, which great and good Court is to us, the best Judge, under God, of what is wise, just and good."[30] How can we not want to hear what Frederick Douglass would later call "scorching irony" in such excessively deferential language?[31]

For all their appeal, however, attempts to rewrite early Black petitions as forceful petitions of right cleverly disguised as obsequious petitions of grace are still in danger of subsuming the revolutionary Black petition within the more general (republican) discourse of natural right and popular sovereignty, with its accompanying disdain for any traces of (monarchical) deference. This approach might, for example, fall into the trap of suggesting that Black political actors were simply a step or two behind white revolutionaries, stuck having to speak the language of prayer and submission until "their time" came to inherit the discourse of republican self-determination. This is an inadequate way of reading the revolutionary-era anti-slavery petition, not least because it misses the specificity of American slavery as a form of political disempowerment. If white Americans in the 1770s were increasingly invested in a theory of sovereignty that demanded the recognition (rather than asked for the gift) of natural, prepossessed rights, Black Americans like FELIX found themselves in a situation of drastic, and in some respects *unprecedented*, rightlessness. How many Black men are there in Massachusetts, FELIX asks, whose lives are "embittered with this most intolerable reflection," namely, "That, let their behavior be what it will, neither they, nor their children to all generations, shall ever be able to do, or to possess and enjoy anything, no, not even *Life itself*, but in a manner as the *Beasts that perish*."³² As white Americans were celebrating at what is sometimes thought of as the birth of the modern idea of "human rights," Black Americans were becoming increasingly aware of the possibility that rights conceived as such (as "natural" or "human") might also have contributed to the construction of radically "rightless" individuals who were not included in the human community at all. American slavery, in other words, had produced what ought to have been a scandal for republican political philosophy: a human being without even what Hannah Arendt called "a right to have rights."³³ "We have no property!" FELIX continues, "We have no wives! No children! We have no city! No Country!"³⁴ Black Americans *had*, in other words, nothing. This extraordinary moment invokes the classically Lockean association between possession and political right, only to raise the specter of an absolute state of rightlessness that republican orthodoxy was unable even to recognize. (And, of course, FELIX's first-person plural reference to having "no wives" suggests yet another layer of rightlessness, a Black female rightlessness, hovering behind that state of dispossession described by the petition – as if it were possible to be excluded even from the community of the absolutely rightless.)

Possession of *anything*, FELIX suggests, might constitute the beginnings, *perhaps*, of political identity and political right. Yet lacking anything to possess (including, as we know, even *themselves* as enslaved subjects), it is not at all clear that these Black Americans *have* a self that could *have* rights; and this unique state of political and psychic dislocation could not but generate a unique political thought. Lacking a city or a country, the Black men and women described in the petition from FELIX anticipate those abandoned figures of twentieth-century political exclusion, whose "calamity," Arendt explained, is "not that they are deprived of life, liberty and the pursuit of happiness [as the Declaration of Independence would have it] ... but that they no longer belong to any community whatsoever."³⁵ The phenomenon of American slavery, in other words, ought to have awakened eighteenth-century revolutionaries to what Arendt says only came into focus in the second half of the twentieth century, namely that,

> Equality, in contrast to all that is involved in mere existence, is not given us, but is the result of human organization insofar as it is guided by the principle of justice. *We are not born equal*; we become equal as members of a group on the strength of our decision to guarantee ourselves mutually equal rights.³⁶

Arendt's provocative insight flies in the face of the Declaration of Independence's most famous phrase, a phrase that continues to generate veneration among American historians and politicians of all stripes, even from those who are willing to expose the appalling racism of this document's authors.[37] If Arendt is right in saying that the horrific condition of the twentieth century's stateless and rightless peoples owes something to the limitations of eighteenth-century natural rights discourse, then we ought to consider the possibility that these limitations were registered in the moment of the American founding precisely where Black Americans put their demand for justice into writing. The justice that Black Americans sought in 1773 could not rely on republican America's declaration of "natural" or "human rights" and the accompanying fantasy of popular, pre-political sovereign authority that such a discourse presumed (although this was certainly a discourse that some early Black petitioners were willing to use).[38] In other words, speaking not *from* but *to* a position of sovereign authority, FELIX is forced to inhabit the language and the political rhetoric of the petition of grace even in the midst of what was otherwise being celebrated as a radically republican social and legal transformation. Rather than simply lament this as one more sign of the humiliating effects of racism and enslavement, though, I want to suggest that this discursive limitation is precisely what simultaneously allows FELIX to slip an alternative to republican orthodoxy into the founding scene of American democracy. If we want to identify traces of a more egalitarian future in the texts of the founding – an opening onto democracy to come in the canon of political writing produced during the revolutionary era – then we *have* to include the petition of FELIX among the nation's indispensable founding documents, and we have to subject it to careful and inventive rereadings.

So what critical insight can be gleaned from the tainted "monarchic" language of the petition of grace that FELIX seems to have been forced to deploy? How can we hear the future speaking through such apparently archaic gestures and formulations? I want to propose that the conventions of the petition of grace, while they may seem (from a republican perspective) to belong to a superseded historical moment, nevertheless hint at a set of political ideas that can inform ongoing critiques of liberal humanist orthodoxy. If, as Arendt suggests, rights and equality come back to us from an organized human community that we bring into being (via "our decision to guarantee ourselves mutually equal rights"), then those rights, in an important sense, do not belong to us in advance.[39] They are not, *pace* Jefferson, inalienable. And if such rights do not belong to us in advance, then we have to acknowledge that, in some very particular sense, all our rights come to us from elsewhere, via a detour through one or another kind of absolute or *sovereign* other, whether that other takes the form of a benevolent monarch or a precariously organized collective. It is this admittedly somewhat difficult notion of a sovereign otherness (or sovereign supplement) at the origin of whatever rights and equality we may enjoy that is registered in the conventional supplicatory rhetoric (the *prayer*) of the petition of grace. The sovereign addressee of the petition of grace, whoever or whatever that addressee may be in any given instance, gives a face of one kind or another to this radical other upon whom (or upon which) our human or any other kind of rights depend.[40] This is not how conventional republicanism theorizes human rights, but it is, I would argue, how petitioners like FELIX might help us to theorize rights for a post-racist democracy to come.

If the invocation of a natural, pre-political, and radically individualized sovereign "right" opens up the possibility for some beings to be stripped of every right (and of their membership in any community of rights-bearing individuals), then we need to be able to conceptualize what Arendt calls a "right to have rights" that would be oriented toward a radically unpredictable community to come. This is a challenging concept, not least because it tries to break with the language of rights that has dominated political thought and practice for the last 300 years. Yet a revolutionary-era anti-slavery petition like that of FELIX helps us to understand this notion of a right to have rights, precisely because of the ways in which it exposes and responds to the contradictions and limitations of the conventional concept of rights. FELIX speaks with and through the language that "he" is both forced to use (by republican orthodoxy) and that "he" simultaneously appropriates from the tradition of the petition of grace – the language of the petition as prayer: "Devoid of all predicative content," writes Hamacher, "devoid of the power to produce out of itself what is desired, the *euché* [prayer] is ... the language of 'unqualified mere existence'."[41] Or, as FELIX puts it in 1773, "We pray for such relief [that] to us will be as Life from the dead."[42] If we cannot say for sure whether FELIX's petition is a prayer (and hence, from a white republican perspective, an example of an outmoded and humiliating political gesture) or "*like* a prayer" (and, as such, spiked with the intellectual and political force of a "signifying" gesture), that is because its power then and now coincides with this very undecidability. To read FELIX's petition is to reactivate this revolutionary indeterminacy.

FELIX's petition reminds us that any call for the observance of rights that one does not have is, in some sense, a call for something more like an intervention of grace – an appeal to a sovereign figure that does not immediately coincide with the "people" in whose name the petition is made. The Black petitioners may have "no city" and "no country," but, writes FELIX, "we have" something; "we have a Father in Heaven, and we are determined, as far as his Grace shall enable us ... to keep all his commandments."[43] This explicit invocation of (Christian) grace in the midst of FELIX's petition marks its deployment of complex and overlapping religious and political concepts. If the conventional petition of grace identifies sovereign power with its direct addressee (i.e. it is to the king's grace that the monarchic petitioner appeals), here, in the petition of FELIX, grace appears to be displaced, off to one side or watching over the communication between the petitioner and the petitioned. Another petitionary scene, that is to say, haunts or shadows the one explicitly invoked by FELIX, and a divine authority to initiate a more violent resistance to slavery is very slyly introduced in the next sentence: Not only do the African American petitioners pledge to keep God's commandments, even in their "degraded contemptuous life," but, "Especially will we be obedient to our Masters, so long as God in his sovereign Providence shall *suffer* us to be holden in Bondage."[44] What could easily sound like a version of conventional petitionary obeisance and self-deprecation (we will obey our masters) instead serves to remind white Americans that another (post-secular?) sovereignty occupies and commands the political field shared by blacks and whites. God the sovereign gives a face and a name to the precarious possibility of peaceful coexistence for black *and* white people in an America to come; but that same divine figure also inscribes the possibility of violent revolutionary dissolution: divine sovereignty (or what we might also call the sovereignty of a democratic American people to come) could at any moment sanction destructive resistance to slavery and the racist hegemony that supports it. The radical possibilities that always lurked within the petition of grace (the opening it gave for the king's subjects to appeal beyond the established political order for redress from acts of injustice) return here via the petitioners' appeal to God "in his sovereign providence." Hence, at precisely the moment when white republican Americans were ready to consign the petition of grace to the dustbin of monarchic history, FELIX invokes it on behalf of an American equality to come. Who, we might want to ask, was more attuned, in this moment, to the future of the United States – or to the future of democracy?[45]

If divinely sanctioned revolutionary violence is invoked by FELIX, however, so too, as we have noted, is a future state of peaceful coexistence. At the end of the petition, FELIX "humbly beg[s] leave" to add one more thing: "We pray for such Relief only, which by no possibility can ever be productive of the least wrong or injury to our Masters; but to us will be as Life from the dead."[46] Here again, we might be tempted to hear only the pitiable traces of a quasi-monarchic deference, a wholly extravagant goodwill directed at those who had enslaved the petitioners and the millions of other victims of Atlantic slavery. Perhaps, though, it's worth reading such lines at face value and recognizing the extraordinary appeal to nonviolence they inscribe. This nonviolence speaks to the very possibility of the emergence of community out of a state of absolute violence (the "state of nature" of slavery) and, as such, anticipates the philosophy of nonviolence espoused by Martin Luther King almost 200 years later. The commitment to nonviolence in the form of the petition's hope that the end of slavery will not coincide with wrong or injury done to those who had once held slaves may certainly be read as another sly (coded) threat, or it may be read as merely a pragmatic and resigned adherence to form; but FELIX's invocation of a nonviolent revolution might also be a way of recognizing the theoretical possibility, difficult as it is to accept, that genuine or peaceful community can emerge out of radical antagonism. Such a position might easily be assimilated to a religious (Christian) idealism, but it can also be thought of as offering its own resistance to idealizing narratives of communal foundation. That community might develop out of antagonism contradicts all those narratives (ethno-nationalist, fundamentalist) that would found community only on a prior, essential identity (even the identity of belonging to what is imagined to be a fixed and pregiven "human" being). As a political theory, nonviolence proposes that a peaceful community need not proceed from or depend upon an absolute purging of violence from its origin; nonviolence refuses to identify community with the assertion of an originary purity, an originary state of unequivocal justice. It is the violence of idealism, in other words, that a certain understanding of nonviolence opposes, and that opposition can be heard in FELIX's closing "hope," as it can in the writings of Dr. King. "Nonviolent resistance is not a method for cowards," wrote King, "it does not seek to defeat or humiliate the opponent, but to win his friendship and understanding ... The end is redemption and reconciliation. The aftermath of nonviolence is the creation of the beloved community, while the aftermath of violence is tragic bitterness."[47]

Yet are we still left with residual discomfort about the ritual humility that characterizes the petition of grace and that clings to FELIX's petition like the stain of racist subservience? Is there any way to reread and redeem the bowing and scraping of the anti-slavery petition of grace? I think so. The deference and humility performed by the conventions of the petition of grace return, perhaps, every time we register our allegiance to each other in a democratic collectivity of aspirationally equal citizens. Our equality demands a certain humility, even if that humility no longer bears an obvious relationship to the language of the monarchic petition of grace. Celebrating and calling for more democracy, for democracy now, we inherit not so much Jefferson's faith in an equality we were all individually born with as FELIX's faith in and dependence upon the wisdom and justice of each other. This is the justice of a sovereign other(ness) to which – or to whom – we continue to offer the obeisance of a petition of grace every time we stand aside and hold the literal or political door open for *whoever* comes along, every time we give up space and time to the sovereign *whoever* whose arrival gives us what none of us alone could ever have had. The petition's humility, understood thus, has a theoretical edge to it that we might not want to disown and that we might even call, borrowing the phrase from Cornel West's discussion of Martin Luther King, "radical humility."[48]

Notes

1. Sidney Kaplan, ed., *The Black Presence in the Era of the American Revolution, 1770–1800* (New York: New York Graphic Society, 1973), 27.
2. Herbert Aptheker, ed., *Documentary History of the Negro People in the United States* (New York: Citadel Press, 1951).
3. Harry Reed, *Platform for Change: The Foundations of the Northern Free Black Community, 1775–1865* (East Lansing: Michigan State University Press, 1994), 12.
4. Stephen A. Higginson, "A Short History of the Right to Petition Government for the Redress of Grievances," *The Yale Law Journal* 96, no. 1 (1986): 142–166, 144.
5. Ibid., 153.
6. The 1689 English Bill of Rights vindicated and asserted the "ancient rights and liberties" of the English, including "the right of the subjects to petition the king." See the text of the Bill on the website of The Avalon Project at Yale Law School: http://avalon.law.yale.edu/17th_century/england.asp.
7. Quoted in David Zaret, *Origins of Democratic Culture: Printing, Petitions, and the Public Sphere in Early-Modern England* (Princeton: Princeton University Press, 2000), 221.
8. Quoted in ibid., 87.
9. Richard L. Bushman, *King and People in Provincial Massachusetts* (Chapel Hill: University of North Carolina Press, 1985), 46.
10. Ibid., 46–47.
11. Edmund S. Morgan, *Inventing the People: The Rise of Popular Sovereignty in England and America* (New York: W.W. Norton, 1988), 225.
12. Ibid., 225.
13. "The extravagant diction of the seventeenth century gave way to a more moderate tone of voice," Bushman writes, as "petitions came to incorporate what can be called a Lockean spirit [whereby] the king was obligated to protect the people's rights just as much as they were obligated to obey and serve." Bushman, *King and People*, 51.
14. See Edwin Wolf, "The Authorship of the 1774 Address to the King Restudied," *William and Mary Quarterly* 22, no. 2 (1965): 189–224, for a transcription of the final engrossed copy of the petition as well as earlier drafts.
15. Ibid., 221.
16. Quoted in Pauline Maier, *From Resistance to Revolution: Colonial Radicals and the Development of American Opposition to Britain, 1765–1776* (New York: W. W. Norton, 1972), 213.
17. William Warner, *Protocols of Liberty: Communication, Innovation, and the American Revolution* (Chicago: University of Chicago Press, 2013), 53.
18. Ibid.
19. Ibid.
20. Ibid., 55–56.

21. Thomas Paine, *Common Sense*, ed. Edward Larkin (Peterborough, ON: Broadview, 2004), 69.
22. Approximately 3,000 of these petitions have been collected by the *Race and Slavery Petitions Project* at the University of North Carolina at Greensboro as part of the Digital Library on American Slavery: https://library.uncg.edu/slavery/petitions/.
23. Reed, *Platform for Change*, 12.
24. Aptheker, *Documentary History*, 6.
25. Ibid.
26. Reed, *Platform for Change*, 12.
27. See Jacqueline Bacon and Glen McClish, "Descendants of Africa, Sons of '76: Exploring Early African-American Rhetoric," *Rhetoric Society Quarterly* 36, no. 1 (2006): 1–29, 7. For "signifying," see Henry Louis Gates, Jr., *Figures in Black: Words, Signs, and the "Racial" Self* (Oxford: Oxford University Press, 1987).
28. Bacon and McClish, "Descendants of Africa," 7.
29. Bushman, *King and People*, 50.
30. Aptheker, *Documentary History*, 7.
31. Frederick Douglass, *Selected Speeches and Writings*, ed. Philip S. Foner (Chicago: Chicago Review Press, 2000), 196.
32. Aptheker, *Documentary History*, 6. Of the radically rightless, Hannah Arendt says, "blessings and doom are meted out to them according to accident and without any relation whatsoever to what they do, did, or may do." See Arendt, *The Origins of Totalitarianism* (New York: Meridian, 1994), 296.
33. See Arendt, *The Origins of Totalitarianism*, 296.
34. Aptheker, *Documentary History*, 6.
35. Arendt, *The Origins of Totalitarianism*, 295. Oddly, the closest precursor to these newly rightless and stateless peoples of the twentieth century is not, for Arendt, the victim of Atlantic slavery, but the ancient Greek slave: "This [right-lessness] was to a certain extent the plight of slaves," she writes, "whom Aristotle therefore did not count among human beings" (297).
36. Ibid., 301, emphasis added.
37. The Pulitzer prize-winning historian Joseph P. Ellis devotes a powerful section of his 2018 book, *American Dialogue: The Founders and Us* (New York: Knopf, 2018), to detailing Jefferson's sickening sense of racial superiority and his tragic failure to emancipate the slaves he owned before his death; but Ellis sees nothing but hope in Jefferson's famous phrase. "The claim that 'all men are created equal,'" writes Ellis, "has assumed many mystical meanings, but all of them are incompatible with slavery, and there is no reason to believe that Jefferson was oblivious to that fact" (21).
38. See, for example, the April 20, 1773 petition presented to the General Court via the representative of the town of Thompson, Massachusetts: "we cannot but expect your house will again take our deplorable case into serious consideration, and give us that ample relief which, *as men*, we have a natural right to." Aptheker, *Documentary History*, 8.
39. Which is to say that we do not "have" these rights, as Werner Hamacher has provocatively written. See Hamacher, "The One Right No One Ever Has," trans. Julia Ng, *Philosophy Today* 61, no. 4 (2017): 947–962.

40. The need for rights, Hamacher argues, testifies to nature or reason's reliance upon a "supplemental law," "added to the law of nature and reason," a law that "cannot be subjected to the principle of possession … but rather is independent of this principle and superior to it without having its *own* logic of ownership at its disposal." Hamacher, "The One Right," 953.

41. Hamacher, "The Right to Have Rights (Four and-a-Half Remarks)," *South Atlantic Quarterly* 103, no. 2/3 (2004): 343–356, 355.

42. Aptheker, *Documentary History*, 7.

43. Ibid., 6.

44. Ibid., 6–7, emphasis in original.

45. Orlando Patterson quotes Tacitus expressing typical noble disdain toward the freedman of Claudius who became the tyrannical governor of Judea: "With all manner of brutality and lust, he exercised the power of a monarch in the spirit of a slave." The freedman's name was FELIX. See Orlando Patterson, *Slavery and Social Death: A Comparative Study* (Cambridge, MA: Harvard University Press, 1982), 306.

46. Aptheker, *Documentary History*, 7.

47. "Pilgrimage to Nonviolence," in Martin Luther King, Jr., *The Radical King*, ed. Cornel West (Boston: Beacon Press, 2015), 49–50.

48. Cornel West, "Introduction," in King, *The Radical King*, 3.

10

RAMESH MALLIPEDDI

Varieties of Bondage in the Early Atlantic

Indian King: For your part, Sir, you've been so noble, that I repent the fatal Difference that makes us meet in Arms. Yet though I'm young, I'm sensible of Injuries; and oft have heard my Grandsire say, That we were Monarchs once of all this spacious World, till you, an unknown People, landing here, distress'd and ruin'd by destructive Storms, abusing all our charitable Hospitality, usurp'd our Right, and made your Friends your Slaves.

Bacon: I will not justify the Ingratitude of my Forefathers, but finding here my Inheritance, I am resolv'd still to maintain it so, and by my Sword which first cut out my Portion, defend each Inch of Land, with my last drop of Blood.

Aphra Behn, *The Widow Ranter; Or, the History of Bacon in Virginia: A Tragi-comedy* (1690)[1]

On February 17, 1627, Captain Henry Powell landed in Barbados with forty Englishmen and ten African slaves, captured en route from a Portuguese prize ship, to settle the island for his sponsor, William Courteen, owner of a prominent London-based Anglo-Dutch merchant firm. Two months later, Powell sailed to Dutch Guiana on the South American mainland to trade with Arawak Indians for seeds and plants needed for the colony. The Arawaks, Powell later recalled,

> had a desire to goe with me as free people to manure those fruits and that I should allow them a piece of Land, the which I did and they would Manure those fruits and bring up their children to Christianitie and that wee might driue a constant trade between that Iland and the Mayne for there was manie more of the Indians of that place that had a desire for to Come for the Iland the next yeare if I would come there againe.[2]

Keeping their side of the bargain, thirty-two Arawaks, including several women and children, voluntarily migrated on the *William and John* to the fledgling English colony with seeds and cuttings of tobacco, sugarcane, cotton, plantains, potatoes, cassava, corn, and pines to assist and instruct the English in farming provisions and staples. In May 1627, John, Henry Powell's brother, arrived from England on the *Peter* with a cargo of seventy-nine additional servants. Relying on the labor of indentured white servants, African slaves, and the horticultural expertise of Arawak Indians, the colonists cut down wood near the coast, built houses, and established five plantations within a year, executing their sponsor's desire to "plant and possess" the island. A year later, James Hay, earl of Carlisle, secured a proprietary grant from Charles I to Barbados and dispatched his own group, precipitating a protracted struggle for control with the rival claimants, the Courteen syndicate. Because of internecine strife, Henry Powell left Barbados in the 1630s, but a decade later, he discovered, to his dismay, that a former governor had enslaved the Arawak Indians, in violation of the original agreement. Powell therefore petitioned the colony's governor to secure the release of five remaining Arawaks – Yow, an Indian woman, her three children, as well a young boy named Barbadoes – from bondage.

By concentrating rather exclusively on colonial North America and equating bondage with African slavery, existing accounts of the early Atlantic have obscured the centrality of Indigenous people in the hemispheric Americas. The story of Arawak migration and enslavement, recounted by several witnesses involved in the original expedition, attests to the diversity of labor regimes that undergirded colonial ventures in the early English Atlantic. Although Barbados became a major sugar colony after the mid-seventeenth century, relying primarily on the work of Black slaves, the labor systems in early years were racially heterogenous, comprising English indentured servants, Native Arawaks, and African slaves. In fact, the workforce in the first months of settlement was predominantly English and Native American, not African. Moreover, the status of Arawaks – who relocated to Barbados to grow and trade in agricultural products – is more akin to English planters than to white indentured servants or African slaves, although a law enacted by Governor Henry Hawley and his council in July 1636 decreed that "Negroes and Indians, that came here to be sold, should serve for life, unless a contract was before made to the contrary," effectively reducing Native Americans to slavery.[3] Enslavement presumably meant the loss of land Arawaks owned and cultivated at the Indian Plantation, one of the five estates originally created by the arrivants. In Barbados and other New World colonies, plantation societies were thus built on expropriated Native lands and the coerced labor of Indigenous and African peoples.

Yet racialized subjection in the English Atlantic continues to be associated overwhelmingly, if not exclusively, with Africans, in part because of the

magnitude and colossal significance of African chattel slavery to the plantation complex in particular and to the institutions of capitalist modernity in
general. A generation of historians have documented the centrality of the
African slave trade and Black slavery to the rise of the Industrial Revolution;
modern systems of credit, insurance, and finance; the birth of consumer
societies; and racial ideologies. Consequently, in several influential
accounts, slavery in the Atlantic is synonymous with African bondage
in the cultivation of tobacco, sugar, and cotton on plantations. To be
sure, workforces in the Atlantic became increasingly Africanized in the
eighteenth century, but laboring people in the early years of settlement
were by no means monochromatic; rather, they were, in Gary Nash's
classic account, red, white, and black. The productive activities that
subject peoples were engaged in were equally diverse and heterogenous.
Perhaps, more significantly, Indigenous enslavement remains largely
overlooked in the scholarship not only because of numerical inferiority
but because of demographic differences. Slave populations imported
from Africa were preponderantly male and toiled in fields. In contrast,
the traffic in Indigenous people primarily consisted, as the historian
Andrés Reséndez has argued in *The Other Slavery*, of women and
children who were employed in ancillary occupations. More generally,
Spanish colonists employed Natives in mining, artisanal work, and
tributary labor systems such as encomiendas and repartimientos.
Native Americans worked as domestic servants, nurses, fishermen, hunters, footmen, and food gatherers on English plantations in the early
Caribbean, providing auxiliary or socially reproductive services that
made economic production possible. The subjection of Indians to such
"extremely varied labor practices" has made these other slaveries largely
invisible.[4] Reséndez's claim is partly borne out by contemporary practices of Indian enslavement in early Barbados. For instance, the enslaved
Arawaks Henry Powell tried to rescue from bondage were mainly
women and children. Likewise, the Indian slaves Richard Ligon encountered during his stay on the island from 1647 to 1650 were women
engaged in household work: "As for the *Indians*, we have but few, and
those fetched from other Countries; some from the neighboring Islands,
some from the Main, which we make slaves: the women who are better
versed in ordering the Cassava and making bread, than the *Negroes*, we
imploy for that purpose, as also for making Mobbie." Indeed, the
Native American Yarico, one of the most famous women in Ligon's
History, is a "slave in the house" and brought over, like the Arawaks
who boarded the *William and John*, as a free woman from "near the
Sea-coast, upon the Main."[5]

This chapter concentrates on a range of literary and extraliterary sources – plays, proto-ethnographic texts, the early novel, and pamphlets – to investigate the complicated histories of territorial dispossession and labor extraction. As England's colonial priorities gradually shifted in the seventeenth century from commerce and trade to agriculture and settlement, the seizure of Native lands and expropriation of Indigenous and African labor became normalized. Indians were by no means a vanishing presence. Rather, the enslaved Indian – restrained by fetters, weighed down with baskets of gold and silver, emerging from or driven into cavernous mines, and tortured on the rack for hoarding gold and silver – was ubiquitous in the period's mediascape. Moreover, Indian subjection was a powerful rhetorical tool in England's own struggle against Spain, Europe's foremost colonial power in the Atlantic, whose vast territorial empire was built on the conquest of Native people. As the English moved from the quest for gold and establishing trading outposts to planting and agrarian settlement, their distinctive programs for possession through improvement were worked out in opposition to the methods of Spanish colonists. Paul Cohen has argued that Atlantic history, in its current form, "is primarily an Anglo-American paradigm, well-suited to the specificities of British patterns of commercial exchange, overseas settlement, and colonial policy in North America," and, as such, accords little space to Native Americans and their experiences of territoriality.[6] In this context, attention to the different histories of bondage in the hemispheric Americas – especially to the connected histories of African servitude and Native American unfreedom – illuminates the centrality of INDIGENEITY to dispossession, the evolution of legal codes, and systems of compulsory labor in the early Atlantic.

Mobile Contact to Sedentary Attachment

England established its first permanent colony in Chesapeake in 1607, but the nation was a relatively late entrant to colonizing ventures in the Atlantic. During the previous century, England's continental counterparts – the Spanish, the Portuguese, and the Dutch – had established a formidable commercial and territorial presence in the North Atlantic Ocean, the Antilles, and the South American mainland. In decades prior to Columbus's voyage to Hispaniola, the Iberian nations possessed thriving sugar industries on the West African coastline. Portugal occupied the island of São Tomé (1470) in the equatorial Gulf of Guinea and cultivated sugar with African captives brought over from Lisbon. Likewise, Spain acquired the Canaries in 1475 and found in those islands a thriving sugar industry. The Iberians transferred to the Americas models of commercial agriculture first developed on the West Coast of Africa. Hence, Eric Williams considered their agrarian ingenuity – the use of enslaved labor to grow staples in equatorial lands – an event of world-historical significance, one that marked "the transition from the Middle Ages to the modern era."[7] In fact, sugar manufacture in Hispaniola commenced with the cuttings of cane that Columbus transported from the Canaries on his second voyage in 1493, and, by 1558, the Spanish Antilles were producing 60,000 *arrobas* of sugar. The Spanish instituted a highly diversified extractive system, exporting pearls, indigo, cacao, Mexican cochineal (dyestuff), and hides. Concurrently, the Portuguese Crown in 1506 set up "royal factories" along the Brazilian coast to exploit timber (especially brazilwood, an important source of red dye used in textile manufacturing), but their economic activities extended to mineral, floral, and human resources, including Amerindian slaves, animal skins, and parrots. Following the union of the Portuguese and Spanish Crowns in 1580, Lisbon became the slave-trading capital of the Western world, and Brazil the most important producer of sugar in Europe.

The discovery in 1546 of vast silver deposits in Zacatecas, Mexico, and a year earlier in the Andean mountain ranges of Potosí, Peru, however, profoundly altered the nature of the Iberian enterprise in the Americas, transforming the Spanish Indies into a silver-based empire. The decisive significance of precious metals to the Spanish Empire is underscored by Vasquez's astonishment at the abundance of gold and silver in the opening scene of John Dryden's history play, *The Indian Emperour* (1665):

> Me thinks we walk in dreams on Fairy land,
> Where golden Ore lies mixt with common sand;
> Each downfal of a flood the Mountains pour,
> From their rich bowels rolls a silver shower.[8]

Gold is the motor force of unfolding dramatic conflict. At the end of the play, Pizarro and his fellow commanders torture Montezuma and the Aztec high priest on the rack for hiding "Gold, from Christian hands, by stealth."[9] Indeed, after the mid-sixteenth century, nearly 80 percent of the value of colonial exports from the Spanish Main consisted of silver, and the region accounted for a quarter of the Crown's annual revenue. These mineral-rich regions in the viceroyalties of New Mexico and Peru were densely populated with Indigenous people, but following a royal prohibition in 1542 on enslaving Indians, the conquistadors devised tributary systems – such as the repartimiento and the encomienda – to procure labor. However, in the wake of massive depopulation occasioned by disease and mistreatment, the colonists turned to Africans. Between 1595 and 1640, Portuguese merchants transported 250,000 to 300,000 Africans to Spanish America, some of whom worked alongside Indians digging silver in Peru.

Racial slavery is often associated with agrarian work on the periphery, or with mining and excavation in cavernous, subterranean spaces of the countryside, in regions far removed from metropolitan centers; but a distinctive feature of Spanish America is the ubiquitousness of African slaves in the urban centers of the viceroyalties of New Spain and Peru, Mexico City and Lima, where Blacks, both bound and free, were employed as retainers, artisans, and household servants. During his travels through Mexico City in 1625, the Dominican priest Thomas Gage, who lived for twelve years in Mexico and Central America and whose *English-American* provided one of the first eyewitness accounts of the region, noticed Spanish gentlemen having in their "train of black-more slaves some a dozen, some halfe a dozen waiting on them, in brave and gallant Liveries, heavy with gold and silver lace, with silke stockins on their black legs, and roses on their feet, and swords by their sides."[10] The historian J. H. Elliott estimates that the population of Blacks in the urban centers of Lima, Mexico City, Quito, Cartagena, and Santa Fe de Bogotá ranged anywhere between 10 and 25 percent.[11]

The English Crown was only minimally involved in overseas affairs throughout the sixteenth century, when the Iberian powers had already acquired formidable empires. In the absence of sustained state support, England's colonial activities in the heyday of Iberian expansion in the Americas were confined to trade, privateering, and exploration, undertaken mostly by private adventurers. In 1562, John Hawkins embarked on the first of several slaving voyages, transporting nearly 300 slaves from West Africa to Spanish plantations in Hispaniola. A decade later, between 1572 and 1573, Francis Drake raided Spanish treasure fleets, ambushing with the help of escaped slaves (Cimarrones) a mule train carrying bullion on the Isthmus of Panama. Subsequently, Walter Raleigh attempted to establish a colony on the island of Roanoke and also set out on a quest for gold to Guyana. These trading and piratical exploits of Elizabethan sea dogs, though motivated by private gain and often ending disastrously, were instrumental in creating the myth of the British Empire as an empire of the seas, in contrast to the land-based empires of ancient Rome and contemporary Spain. For instance, in his canonical topographical poem "Cooper's Hill" (1642), published on the eve of the Civil War, John Denham considers trade, not war, the mainstay of the English imperial enterprise:

As a wise king first settles fruitful peace
In his own realms, and with their rich increase,
Seeks wars abroad, and in triumph brings
The spoils of kingdoms, and the crowns of kings.
Thames to London doth at first present
Those tributes, which neighbouring counties sent,
But as his second visit from the east,
Spices he brings, and treasures from the west.
Finds wealth where 'tis, bestows it where it wants,
Cities in deserts, woods in cities plants.
Rounds the whole globe, and with his flying towers
Brings home to us, and makes both Indies ours;
So that to us no thing, no place is strange
While thy fair bosom is the world's exchange:[12]

The speaker here acknowledges war and trade as engines of national prosperity but subordinates the "spoils of kingdoms" and "crowns of kings" gained in military conquests to the "treasures," spices, and wealth bestowed by maritime trade, in an effort to extol the virtues of commercial exchange. Indeed, the free, unfettered Thames is the emblem of England's developing global power, extending from the East to the West. Likewise, in Edmund Waller's "Panegyric to the Lord Protector" (1655), the source of England's wealth is not the backbreaking toil involved in excavating gold but the effortless movement of overseas commerce:

To dig for Wealth we weary not our Limbs,
Gold (tho' the heaviest Metal) hither swims:
Ours is the Harvest where the Indians mow,
We plough the Deep and reap what others sow.[13]

Notwithstanding these attempts to construct imperial identity oceanically rather than territorially, English colonists under James I increasingly concentrated their efforts on settlement, establishing colonies in North America and the West Indies, first in Jamestown (1607) and Plymouth (1620) and then in St. Christopher (1624), Barbados (1627), Nevis (1628), and Antigua (1632), all in the Lesser Antilles. The early overseas endeavors were mostly sponsored and supported by a group of prominent courtiers, merchants, and landed gentlemen – including Sir William Courteen, Maurice Thompson, James Hay, Robert Rich, Samuel Vassall, James Drax, and Martin Noell – who obtained charters from the Crown for the planting of export staples.[14] In seeking to found agrarian settlements, the English passed, in the historian K. R. Andrews's apt words, "from mobile contact to sedentary attachment, from haunting by sea to plantations by land."[15] Collectively, these efforts, as

Anthony Pagden has observed, signaled a desire to abandon "the quest for Indian gold, characteristic of Spanish-style kingdoms, for that of 'colonies' or 'plantations'; places, that is, which would be sources not of humans or minerals, but of agriculture and commercial wealth."[16]

Unlike Spanish possessions in Hispaniola, Mexico, and Peru, the Lesser Antilles lacked a large Indigenous population that could be subdued. Hence English planters recruited white indentured laborers for plantation work. Indeed, the majority of the workforce during the tobacco era (1627–1640) consisted of white servants, who bound themselves for a fixed term (between three and ten years) in exchange for costs of passage, shelter, clothing, and food, at the end of which they received a "freedom due" of $10 and a parcel of land. Several socioeconomic factors in the first decades of the seventeenth century – including the widespread enclosure of arable land, rising prices, and declining wages – forced Englishmen to seek employment abroad. When the rate of voluntary emigration failed to meet the growing labor demands of the colonists, the English state began to ship vagrants, convicts, and war prisoners. In particular, Oliver Cromwell's military campaigns in Ireland and Scotland in the 1640s and 1650s produced a windfall. Historians have estimated that more than 10,000 war prisoners were shipped off to Barbados to labor on plantations.

White servants, mostly young men and hailing from landless, impoverished families, were virtually treated as chattels, inasmuch as they were purchased, sold, and traded like commodities. As Simon Newman has observed, "servants were used as collateral for loans," "taxed as property," and "constituted the most easily transferable embodiment of capital."[17] Moreover, in the absence of customary rights or legal norms that governed relations between masters and their farm apprentices in the metropolis, Caribbean planters often punished their indentured laborers mercilessly. Thus, Ligon writes, "I have seen an Overseer beat a Servant with a cane about the head, till the blood has followed, for a fault that's not worth the speaking of . . . Truly, I have seen such cruelty there done there to Servants, as I did not think one Christian could have done to another."[18] Unable to endure unremitting physical abuse, indentured laborers, according to Father Andrew White's firsthand account, "conspired to kill their masters and make themselves free."[19] A decade later, during Ligon's stay on the island, white laborers attempted, although unsuccessfully, to "fall upon their Masters, and cut all their throats, and by that means, to make themselves [not] only free men, but Masters of the Island."[20]

The transition from tobacco to sugar after 1645 coincided with a shift in the labor regimes, as African slaves surpassed white bound servants to become the colony's dominant workforce, in part owing to the labor-intensive nature of sugarcane cultivation. While tobacco required one slave per ten acres, sugar needed one for every two acres. In Portuguese Brazil, cultivation and manufacture were separate operations, where, relying on squads of about ten slaves, tenants cultivated cane on small units (ranging from ten to fifteen acres) leased from a *senhor de engenho* (lord of the mill) and carried their produce to the *senhor*'s sugar works to be processed, receiving in turn about half the sugar as their share. Sugar plantations in the English Caribbean, unlike Portuguese Brazil, were integrated units, combining the functions of field and factory. To be economically viable and financially efficient, a planter needed cane fields averaging between 100 and 200 acres. The infrastructure of sugar works – a mill, boiler, curing house, and other physical equipment – required a considerable capital outlay that was beyond the means of smallholders. Consequently, a group of elite planters monopolized land ownership in Barbados, displacing thousands of independent farmers who dominated the early decades of settlement. The number of planters in Barbados dropped from 11,200 to 745 between 1640 and 1660. At the same time, the colony's slave population increased fourfold, from 5,600 in 1645 to 20,200 in 1655. In 1650, Barbados exported 3 million pounds of sugar, making it the richest colony in colonial America.

The "sugar revolution" in Barbados was thus accompanied by a demographic revolution, with African captives beginning to outnumber whites. In 1661, the Barbados assembly enacted a comprehensive slave code, "An Act for the Better Ordering and Governing of Negroes," categorizing Africans as chattels, slaves as their masters' property. As such, they could be freely bought and sold, entailed with real estate, bequeathed as inheritance, and subjected to private punishments with impunity. The slave's social death – her genealogical isolation, lack of communal belonging, and erasure of personal identity – is the obverse of legal death. As Elsa Goveia notes, "the legal nullity of the slave's personality, except when he was to be controlled or punished, was the greatest obstacle to his adequate personal protection."[21] Defined as property, slaves could not legally own property, enter into contractual agreements, or litigate on their own behalf. These legal deprivations found their formal expression in the "law of evidence," according to which "any free person could give evidence for or against a slave," yet "the evidence of slaves [could not be] not admitted for or against free persons in the British islands."[22]

Given the existence of various involuntary labor regimes, historians have debated whether chattel slavery constituted a unique racialized system of labor extraction or just one form of bound labor among others. Simon Newman has argued that early modern English understandings of unfree labor "existed on a continuum and encompassed white vagrants, convicts, and prisoners of war, bound Scots, Irishmen, Englishmen, as well as African slaves and pawns in West Africa, and African slaves in Barbados." As such, "in terms of the daily experience of workers, slavery was not different from other systems of forced labor."[23] The economic historians John McCusker and Russel Menard insist that labor markets, not racial ideologies, shaped planter choices because, rather than preferring African slaves over white servants, "planters took what workers they could get."[24] By contrast, David Eltis has maintained that, in investigating why Europeans considered certain groups "suitable for enslavement," "economic motivation should be assigned a subsidiary role in the rise and fall of the exclusively African-based bondage that Europeans carried across the Atlantic." English planters in Barbados experimented with various forms of unfree labor, yet there were no "African indentured servants" or "English slaves." The determining factor, according to Eltis, was not the relative profitability of servile labor over indentured labor but "the inability of colonists to conceive of Europeans as chattel slaves."[25]

Indigenous Reproductive Labor

Both canonical and revisionist accounts of the interconnections between racism and slavery equate bondage with African servitude, but enslaved Indigenous people too were vital to the rise and establishment of Atlantic colonies. Barbados did not have a Native presence at the time of settlement, but Indian slaves on the island were brought over either from neighboring colonies or from the Spanish Main. Europeans preferred the supposedly tractable Arawaks from Dutch Guiana to the Lesser Antillean Kalinagos, who were considered ferocious and militaristic. Barbados was also an important destination for Native American war captives from South Carolina and New England, especially following major conflicts such as the King Philip's War (1675–1678).[26] The trade in Indians was a central economic feature of South Carolina during the first fifty years of its founding, when between 30,000 and 50,000 Native slaves were exported to the colonies on the Eastern Seaboard and the Caribbean. In fact, Barbados enacted a law in 1676 prohibiting the importation of Indians.[27] Whether procured from mainland colonies or the Greater Caribbean, Indians were employed primarily in domestic service, food cultivation, and provisioning. To purchase Indian captives, English colonists seem to have tapped into already-existing networks of Indigenous enslavement. According to George Warren's 1667 *An Impartial Description of Surinam*, Indians executed male war prisoners "with the most barbarous Cruelties," while "Women and Children they preserve[d] for Slaves, and [sold] them for Trifles to the

English."[28] For instance, upon acquiring an estate from Major William Hillard, Colonel Modyford, Ligon's patron, received 500 acres of land, sugar works, as well as "Houses for *Negroes* and *Indian* slaves, with 96 *Negroes*, and three *Indian* women, with their Children; 28 Christians." Ligon credits Indian women with the "best skill" at removing chegoes (tropical vermin) that often infected the colonists. Planters employed Native women in culinary work to prepare cassava bread and mobbie, and the men as footmen and fishermen who, "with their own bows and arrows they will go out; and in a day's time, kill as much fish, as will serve a family of a dozen persons, two or three days."[29]

It would be incorrect to underestimate the significance of hunting, fishing, and culinary labor. During the early days of settlement, planters grew commercial staples to the exclusion of food crops, frequently forcing the inhabitants to the brink of starvation. In 1631, the Colonial Privy Council in London received a "humble petition of the Planters and Adventurers to the Caribbee Islands, as by the Earl of Carlile present in Councell of the greate distresse wherein the said Planters and theire servants, were at this present by reason of the greate want of bread, and other victualls there."[30] Although, in later decades, Africans raised some vegetables and root crops in their gardens, planters mostly relied on imported foodstuffs to feed themselves and their workforces, especially on small, densely populated colonies like Barbados. The colonists' single-minded pursuit of profit in commodity agriculture was undertaken at the expense of provisioning, as Ligon was well aware: "though the Island [of Barbados] stands as all Islands do, environed with the Sea, (and therefore is not like to be unfurnished of that provision [fish]) yet, the Planters are so good husbands, and tend their profits so much, as they will not spare a *Negro's* absence so long, as to go to the *Bridge* and fetch it."[31] In this context, Indigenous labor in food gathering and preparation became all the more essential. Indeed, as Carolyn Arena has recently argued, the presence of Natives as domestic servants, cooks, nurses, fishermen, and hunters provides "evidence for the diversity of labor activities of Indian slaves in Caribbean colonies rather than a specialized set of economic contributions."[32] Yet the gendered, socially reproductive enslaved Indian labor remains undervalued because it is not economically productive. Likewise, hunting and fishing required considerable Native expertise and skill, but since for Europeans they are primarily recreational or gentlemanly – rather than strictly productive – pursuits, the labor involved in them is often disavowed, if not rendered invisible.

Indian slavery was also one of the potent rhetorical vehicles in the English state's efforts to legitimize claims to Native lands in the Atlantic, especially under the Cromwellian Protectorate (1653–1659). Commercial agriculture in the English Caribbean flourished without extensive support from the early Stuarts. As the nation was embroiled in the Civil War, English planters and merchants relied on the Dutch, the foremost commercial power of the day, for slaves, supplies, shipping, and finance, but after Charles I's execution in 1649, the English Republic became increasingly assertive in colonial affairs. In 1651, the Navigation Act was enacted by the Rump Parliament to curtail Dutch maritime supremacy. The English Protectorate also challenged the Spanish Empire in America by embarking on a military campaign – known in contemporary parlance as the Western Design – to capture San Domingo in Hispaniola. The undertaking was simultaneously a military offensive and a multimedia event. The entire mediascape – theatrical entertainments, print literature, and iconography – was deployed to promote the Protestant cause against Catholic Spain. Thomas Gage, in his 1654 memorial, urged Cromwell to undertake the expedition, since "the Lord [made his] highnesse, as our protector, so also a protector of those poore Indians, which want protection from the cruelties of the Spaniards."[33] In 1656, John Phillips translated Bartolomé de Las Casas's *Relación de la destrucción de las Indias* as *The Tears of the Indians*. Accompanied by graphic visual imagery of Native American martyrdom at the hands of Spanish conquistadors, Phillips dedicated the work to Cromwell, laying "prostrate before the Throne of [his] Justice, above Twenty Millions of the Souls of the slaughtered Indians."[34] Two years later, William Davenant staged *The Cruelties of the Spaniards in Peru* (1658), whose opening scene reveals "the natives, in feathered habits and bonnets carrying, in Indian baskets, ingots of gold and wedges of silver."[35] The Peruvian miners are brutalized and their prince is tortured by the Spanish, before being rescued by English forces. In all these versions, England's military campaign is not designed to capture the famed Indies riches that made the Habsburg Empire so formidable but to avenge the sufferings of hapless Indians.

Yet the most ambitious argument to simultaneously contest the legal basis of Spanish suzerainty and deprive Native Americans of their territorial rights was advanced in "A Manifesto of the Lord Protector," attributed to Cromwell's Latin Secretary, John Milton, and published on the eve of the invasion:

> They [the Spaniards] pretend to have a double title, one founded upon the pope's gift, and another upon their having first discovered those places … But such an imaginary title [of first discovery], founded on such a silly pretence, without being in possession, cannot possibly create any true and lawful right. The best right of possession in America is that which is founded on one's having planted colonies there, and settled in such places as had

either no inhabitants, or by the consent of the inhabitants, if there were any; or at least, in some of the wild and uncultivated places of their country, which they were not numerous enough to replenish and improve; since God has created this earth for the use of men, and ordered them to replenish it throughout.[36]

"The Manifesto" disputes the religious authority of papal edicts (or the power of Alexandrine Bulls) to confer titles on Catholic monarchs as well as the putative rights of first discovery. Perhaps, more significantly, it elaborates a distinctively English model of sovereignty (*imperium*) and property (*dominium*). The legitimate basis for territorial possession in the Americas is not military conquest but agrarian labor; not forcible appropriation but cultivation and improvement. By settling "uninhabited" lands and improving "wild and uncultivated" places, English colonists become the rightful possessors of land. In advancing these claims, "The Manifesto" outlined, nearly three decades before John Locke's *Two Treatises on Government*, an "agricultural model" of colonization. Yet, in positing the legal canard of *terra nullius*, "The Manifesto" seems oblivious to the possibility that Indigenous people's relationship to land might be governed by use rather than personal right, or that collective sovereignty over land might have precedence over individual ownership.[37]

Black Labor, Native American Frontier

Notwithstanding the patriotic fervor that accompanied the Western Design, Cromwell's army failed to capture San Domingo and took Jamaica, another Spanish possession, instead. After the 1650s, Jamaica, located in the Greater Antilles, and the South American colony Suriname (not to mention South Carolina) became principal destinations for the Barbadian planter diaspora.[38] The expanding English Caribbean imperial frontier – and the racial violence undergirding that expansion – is the subject of Aphra Behn's novella *Oroonoko* (1688), in which a Black prince, captured in Guinea and transported as a slave to Surinam, organizes an insurrection after discovering his wife Imoinda's pregnancy, in an effort to prevent their unborn child from enslavement. The planters capture Oroonoko and brutally dismember him as a deterrent to fellow slaves. Behn's novella remained popular via Thomas Southerne's dramatic adaptation, *Oroonoko; A Tragedy* (1695), whose final act also features a scene of punishment, where the governor and his associates chain Oroonoko to the ground, his arms and legs stretched out, and whip him. Juxtaposing the figure of the tortured Native American Montezuma in Dryden's *Indian Emperor* with that of the Black African prince in Southerne's *Oroonoko*, Elizabeth Maddock Dillon has suggested that, while the tortured Indian king embodies the loss of "territorial sovereignty" and "the usurpation of land," Southerne's Oroonoko, as a "figure of labor," theatrically performs "an economically oriented role."[39] Thus, the colonization of Native American land forms the basis for the expropriation of African slave labor.

Yet the conflict over land between Native Americans and English frontiersmen in Behn's own New World play, *The Widow Ranter*, based on Nathaniel Bacon's armed rebellion against Governor Sir William Berkeley in colonial Virginia, suggests the simultaneous – rather than successive – histories of territorial dispossession and labor extraction. Tobacco cultivation in Virginia commenced, as it had in Barbados and St. Christopher, in the 1620s, when nearly 20,000 Indians lived in small villages in the Chesapeake tidewater region. With the rapid expansion of commercial agriculture, annual tobacco exports increased from a million pounds in the 1620s to more than 20 million pounds by 1680. During the same period, nearly 75,000 English people migrated to the colony, more than half of them as indentured servants.[40] After 1680, the labor force was increasingly Africanized, with the colony's Black population approaching 20,000 in 1700.[41] The planters' discovery and exploitation of the region's agricultural potential inevitably led to frenzied competition for and encroachment of Native lands, especially as freed servants aspired for land ownership. The Indian king's complaint, quoted in this chapter's epigraph, registers the logic of settler colonial usurpation and the gradual erosion of Indigenous entitlement to land. The conjoined histories of the African prince in Behn's novella *Oroonoko* and that of the Indian king in her play *The Widow Ranter* reveal the interconnected yet distinct histories of racialized bondage and territorial dispossession. Indeed, the continued expansion of plantation agriculture in the early Atlantic, supported by African chattel slavery, had, as its inevitable corollary, the diminution of Native American territorial sovereignty.

Notes

1. Aphra Behn, *The Widow Ranter; Or, The History of Bacon in Virginia: A Tragicomedy* (London, 1690), 13–14.
2. "The Humble Petition of Capt. Henry Powell to the Right Honourable Daniel Searle," (ca. 1652), in V. T. Harlow, ed., *Colonising Expeditions to the West Indies and Guiana* (London: Hakluyt Society, 1924), 37–38.
3. William Duke, *Memoirs of the First Settlement of the Island of Barbados and Other Carribbee Islands* (London, 1743), 19.
4. Andrés Reséndez, *The Other Slavery: The Uncovered Story of Indian Enslavement in America* (Boston: Houghton Mifflin Harcourt, 2016), 10.
5. Richard Ligon, *A True and Exact History of the Island of Barbados* (Indianapolis: Hackett Publishing Company, [1657] 2011), 106, 107.

6. Paul Cohen, "Was There an Amerindian Atlantic? Reflections on the Limits of a Historiographical Concept," *History of European Ideas* 34, no. 4 (2008): 388–410, 392.

7. Eric Williams, *From Columbus to Castro: The History of the Caribbean, 1492–1969* (New York: Vintage, 1984), 13.

8. John Dryden, *The Indian Emperour, or The Conquest of Mexico by the Spaniards*, in *The Works of John Dryden*, ed. John Loftis and Vinton A. Dearing, 9 vols. (Berkley and Los Angeles: University of California Press, 1967), 9.1.27–30.

9. Dryden, *Indian Emperor*, 5.2.8.

10. Thomas Gage, *The English-American, His Travail by Sea and Land, or, A New Survey of the West-India's* (London, 1648), 60. First quoted in J. H. Elliott, *Empires of the Atlantic World: Britain and Spain in America, 1492–1830* (New Haven, CT: Yale University Press, 2006), 101.

11. Elliott, *Empires of the Atlantic World*, 100.

12. John Denham, "Cooper's Hill," lines, 205–218, in *Expans'd Hieroglyphics: A Critical Edition of Sir John Denham's Cooper's Hill*, ed. Brendan O Hehir (Berkeley and Los Angeles: University of California Press, 1969), 124.

13. Edmund Waller, *A Panegyric to My Lord Protector*, lines 61–64, in *The Poems of Edmund Waller*, ed. G. Thorn Drury, 2 vols. (New York: Charles Scribner's Sons, 1901), 2:12.

14. L. H. Roper, *Advancing Empire: English Interests and Overseas Expansion, 1613–1688* (New York: Cambridge University Press, 2017).

15. K. R. Andrews, "The English in the Caribbean, 1560–1620," in K. R. Andrews, N. P. Canny, and P. E. H. Hair, eds., *The Westward Enterprise: English Activities in Ireland, the Atlantic, and America, 1480–1650* (Detroit: Wayne State University Press, 1978), 123.

16. Anthony Pagden, "The Struggle for Legitimacy and the Image of Empire in the Atlantic, c. 1700," in Nicholas Canny, ed., *The Oxford History of the British Empire, Vol. 1: The Origins of Empire: British Overseas Enterprise to the Close of the Seventeenth Century* (New York: Oxford University Press, 2001), 34–54, 36.

17. Simon Newman, *A New World of Labor: The Development of Plantation Slavery in the British Atlantic* (Philadelphia: University of Pennsylvania Press, 2013), 75.

18. Ligon, *True and Exact History*, 94

19. "A Brief Relation of the Voyage unto Maryland, By Father Andrew White, 1634," in Clayton Colman Hall, ed., *Narratives of Early Maryland, 1633–1684* (New York: Charles Scribner's Sons, 1910), 34.

20. Ligon, *True and Exact History*, 96.

21. Elsa Goveia, *The West Indian Slave Laws of the 18th Century* (Barbados: Caribbean University Press, 1970), 34.

22. Ibid., 34.

23. Newman, *A New World of Labor*, 3.

24. John McCusker and Russel Menard, "The Origins of Slavery in the Americas," in Mark M. Smith and Robert L. Paquette, eds., *The Oxford Handbook of Slavery in the Americas* (New York: Oxford University Press, 2010), 276, 281.

25. David Eltis, "Europeans and the Rise and Fall of African Slavery in the Americas: An Interpretation," *The American Historical Review* 98, no. 5 (1993): 1399–1423, 1401, 1422.

26. Allan Gallay, *The Indian Slave Trade: The Rise of the English Empire in the American South, 1670–1717* (New Haven, CT: Yale University Press, 2003); Margaret Allen Newell, *Brethren by Nature: New England Indians, Colonists, and the Origins of American Slavery* (Ithaca, NY: Cornell University Press, 2016).

27. Linford D. Fisher, "'Dangerous Designs': The 1676 Barbados Act to Prohibit New England Indian Slave Importation," *William and Mary Quarterly* 71, no. 1 (2014): 99–124.

28. George Warren, *An Impartial Description of Surinam* (London, 1667), 26.

29. Ligon, *True and Exact History*, 67, 106.

30. *Acts of the Privy Council of England, Colonial Series*, ed. Sir William Almeric FitzRoy, James Munro, and W. L. Grant, 2 vols. (London, 1908–1912), 1:159.

31. Ligon, *True and Exact History*, 83.

32. Carolyn Arena, "Indian Slaves from Guiana in Seventeenth-Century Barbados," *Ethnohistory* 64, no. 1 (2017): 65–90, 74.

33. "Some briefe and true observations concerning the West–Indies, humbly presented to his highnesse, Oliver, lord protector of the commonwealth of England, Scotland, and Ireland, [by mr. Thomas Gage]," "State Papers, 1654: December," in *A Collection of the State Papers of John Thurloe, Vol. 3: December 1654–August 1655*, ed. Thomas Birch (London: Fletcher Gyles, 1742), 46–63, www.british-history.ac.uk/thurloe-papers/vol3/pp46-63.

34. John Phillips, *The Tears of the Indians: Being an Historical and True Account of the Cruel Massacres and Slaughters of above Twenty Million of Innocent Peoples; Committed by the Spaniards* (London, 1656), 2.

35. William Davenant, *The History of Sir Francis Drake*, 1:5–6, in Janet Clare, ed., *Drama of the English Republic, 1649–60* (Manchester: Manchester University Press, 2002), 244.

36. "A Manifesto of the Lord Protector … Wherein is shown the reasonableness of the cause of the Republic against the depredations of the Spaniards. Written in Latin by John Milton and Frist Printed in 1655, now translated into English (1738)," in Rufus Wilmot Griswold, ed., *Prose Works of John Milton*, 2 vols. (Philadelphia: Herman Hooker, 1845), 2:467–477, 474, 475.

37. For an excellent recent treatment of these questions, see Alan Greer, *Property and Dispossession: Natives, Empires and Land in Early Modern North America* (New York: Cambridge University Press, 2018).

38. Justin Roberts, "Surrendering Surinam: The Barbadian Diaspora and the Expansion of the English Sugar Frontier, 1650–75," *William and Mary Quarterly* 73, no. 2 (2016): 225–256.

39. Elizabeth Maddock Dillon, *New World Drama: The Performative Commons in the Atlantic World, 1649–1849* (Durham, NC: Duke University Press, 2014), 97–98, 98.

40. Allan Kulikoff, *Tobacco and Slaves: The Development of Southern Cultures in the Chesapeake, 1680–1800* (Chapel Hill: University of North Carolina Press, 1986), 23–35.

41. T. H. Breen, "A Changing Labor Force and Race Relations in Virginia, 1660–1710," *Journal of Social History* 7, no. 1 (1973): 3–25.

11

SANDRA SLATER

The Erotics of Early America

Throughout the age of exploration, European notions of gender not only clashed with Native conceptions of gendered identities but also caused tension among Europeans themselves. The very notion of a *terra incognita* inspired men from Spain, France, and England to embark on journeys of discovery, exploration, and conquest. Tales of monstrous sea creatures, mer-people, and frightful storms scared away all but the bravest men who understood themselves as exceptionally courageous. The resulting hyperbolic masculinity of European explorers is legendary. Men like Hernán Cortés, Samuel de Champlain, John Smith, and others became emblazed in the annals of history as heroic. They saw themselves that way, too, which resulted in strong personalities determined to carve out wealth from North America but also impose their own visions of civilization, culture, and identities on Indigenous societies.

European constructions of gender identities in the early modern period greatly affected the ways in which European explorers both behaved and represented their encounters in what they called the New World. Codes of conduct dictated that women be fully clothed, chaperoned, and subservient to men, thereby circumscribing and delimiting female access to power and claims on individuality or independence that might follow. Laws of couverture essentially deprived women of any legal identity beyond that of daughter or wife. Most European explorers who commanded expeditions moved in prestigious circles, usually associated with monarchies and courts. In these elite worlds, genteel manners and expectations fell heavily upon women who defied conventions of society. These hierarchies of gendered power also reflected expectations that men devote themselves to hard labor or, if a gentleman, leisurely pursuits such as hunting. Always in command of themselves and their households, men ordered society.

In North America, Indigenous communities approached gender far differently and less hierarchically, preferring instead to assign complementary roles to men and women. Divisions of labor respected women as essential contributors to daily life and therefore Native women enjoyed greater access to personal freedoms, political expression, and sexual liberty. In Indigenous ordering of life, men hunted, fished, and engaged in necessary warfare, while women dedicated themselves to agricultural production, household labor, childrearing, and the various obligations that come in processing meat and skins from hunting expeditions. European men struggled to understand these variant cultural norms and frequently expressed anger that Native men lazily enjoyed hunting while the women were "drudges" who did most of the labor. Hunting for survival and sustenance was beyond the comprehension of gentlemen explorers who placed all Native behaviors within their own paradigms of understanding. They were often in sharp contrast, which resulted in escalated oppression and violence against Native peoples identified as "uncivilized" or "barbarous." It is through these misunderstandings and moments of conflict that we can best understand how Europeans and Natives thought, acted, and understood the world around them. Often thought of as a "middle ground," where worlds collided, the early modern Atlantic was a site of cultural misunderstanding, adaptations, oppressions, and often violence.

European men understood themselves as conquerors of not only the Atlantic Ocean but all of nature itself. Europeans, especially British adventurers, envisioned the New World as a womanly form, unspoiled by civilization or man and ready to be penetrated and conquered. Nature has traditionally been personified as various female embodiments: a fearful mysterious wilderness, a gentle providing mother, or a fertile virgin.[1] The constructs of the wilderness as a ferocious and prohibitive femininity fortified male notions of exceptionalism; despite her aggression, even she could be conquered. Explorers who dared venture into the wilderness containing unknown peoples, monsters, and secrets elevated their personal and social status, often dramatizing, intentionally or not, the various dangers associated with the voyage and the unknown terrain that awaited at the end of that arduous journey. The English explorers' expectations of monstrous beings and uncontrollable women both intrigued and frightened them. Seeking to distance European identity from that of Natives, many employed tropes of deviant female sexuality, wantonness, and a lack of natural law as indicators of inadequacies.[2] No matter how brutal, nothing feminine could ever compete with masculinity as the apex of authority and power.

The gendered metaphor related to Mother Nature as a benevolent figure providing nourishment and life to those who worked with her was a less prevalent, though certainly an important, construction. Early European arrivals to North America found themselves frequently in dire straits when needing to cultivate the land and produce sustainable agriculture and crops. English settlers in Jamestown and Massachusetts remarked and frequently criticized the Native way of relating to the land as not something to be "improved upon" but something to be respected. It was a symbiotic connection demanding knowledge, care, and long-term investment. Even the first Thanksgiving included the "three sisters" of colonial agriculture: beans, squash, and maize. The earth and her crops were women, all related, all valuable.

Unsurprisingly, literary writing tended to employ more gendered metaphors than did other genres like travel and voyage narratives. Marc Lescarbot, a harsh critic of contemporary French society, saw the New World in mythical and gendered language. Toward the end of his second volume, he portrayed land sexually: "Thus does one seek for land as for his well-beloved, who sometimes repulses her lover rudely enough."[3] The land was a young woman, a modest lover. Sexually suggestive, though not quite so crude as Raleigh's portrayals, Lescarbot's statement confirms that connections between land, gender, and sex were present in the mentalities of the French explorers. If land is inherently sexualized, then untouched or virginal land of the New World represented male domination in the form of possession and cultivation. However, Lescarbot's metaphoric intimacy is not a product of force or conquest but rather of a marriage of sorts. Enamored with the idea of a French golden age generated from a return to the soil and farming, Lescarbot also saw the New World as a maternal provider. He implored his audience to "consider her; let us put our hands into her bosom and see if her maternal dugs [breasts] will yield milk to nourish her children, and what more may be hoped for from her."[4]

The most sexually aggressive depiction of North America was that of a virgin. Conveniently ignoring the presence of millions of Native Americans, explorers personified the New World as a young virgin, pure and malleable. Her conquest and possession by men (explorers) have long been taken as the symbolic exploitation of femininity. Scholars have long discussed Sir Walter Raleigh's highly sexual references in his *Discoverie of Guina*, in which he discusses penetrating the virgin forests of the New World. Similarly, Christopher Columbus referenced the earth as a breast complete with the Indies as a nipple.

Anxieties over women's bodies were present in all the colonizing nations of the sixteenth and seventeenth centuries. The ascension of Elizabeth I to the English throne revived debates about the nature of women, their disposition, and their ability to govern, thereby raising questions about the dominant gender paradigm of late Tudor England.[5] Although occupying a traditionally masculine role as head of state, Elizabeth I was able to create a persona as a virtuous monarch married to the English nation. Paradoxically, this androgynous persona relied on discourses of women's roles and appropriate femininity to survive. Sir Walter Raleigh felt it necessary to declare to the Natives of Guiana that he served a Queen "who was the great cacique of the north, and a virgin."[6] At all times, Elizabeth embodied both the male political figure and the female dutiful wife, chaste and pure, wife to a nation, and mother to all citizens.[7]

Growing awareness of colonial "new worlds" complicated the psychological landscape of Elizabethan England. Within English culture, negotiations of gender norms and behaviors reflected this tumultuous period of social and global alteration. One might even say that the age of exploration prompted a broad crisis of gender within imperial exploration cultures and their colonial theaters. Many men of this era sought to contain the aspirations of women symbolically and actually actuated by Elizabeth's long reign. Using natural law as a reference point, male politicians, social commentators, and theologians marginalized women who behaved outside the prescribed roles ordained by biology and Christian theology.[8] This reactionary reimposition of conventional gender roles found particular expression in New World colonial scenes and further encouraged these male arbiters of convention to broadly understand their role as policing other domains of ethnic, sexual, religious, linguistic, and Indigenous expressions of difference.

Generally, English women only appear in the documents of Puritan America in death or deviancy. Deeds worthy of the annals of history included piety, purity, and appropriate behavior, as women subordinate to God and the dominant men in their lives were usually seen through the lens of motherhood and a godly wife. Seventeenth-century Massachusetts Bay governor Thomas Dudley recalled the death of the "daughter of Mr. Sharpe, a godly virgin."[9] It was through her sexual purity and adherence to social expectations of womanhood that "she well deserve[s] to be remembered."[10] Male approval came only after a life lived in piety, no longer tempted by sin. Likewise, the daughter of John Ruggles passed away at the age of eleven, but she deserved mention due to her expression of "so much faith and assurance of salvation."[11] When Mrs. Skelton "fell into a fever" and passed away she received remark due to the fact that "she was a godly and a helpful woman, and indeed the main pillar of her family" who would be "weak and helpless since her death."[12] It is important to note that in these passages the women are referred to as either daughters or wives, never by their own names or individual identities.

Wayward women received attention from Massachusetts Bay chroniclers. Usually written about sexual or theological sins, accounts of deviant women affiliated them with Satan. Addressing the multiple preachers who failed to successfully lead the Massachusetts Bay Colony, Roger Clap criticized the false teachings propagated by the Antinomians that "led away ... silly women, laden with their lusts."[13] This "snare of the Devil" appealed to women who lacked the spiritual and physical fortitude to resist.[14] The concept of women's susceptibility to the seduction of Satan permeates early American writings. The Puritans feared the allure of evil and expressed difficulty in understanding women as separate entities from Satan. Women, along with Satan, spoiled the Garden of Eden for Adam and all mankind. Women's sexuality threatened men's stability and thus men associated female passion and sexuality with evil.

French colonists were particularly preoccupied with what they took to be excessive practices of nudity among Indigenous women.[15] Although critical of Native sexual practices, Samuel de Champlain, found the Native women physically appealing. He considered them "pleasing and pretty, both in figure, complexion and feature, all in harmony."[16] He admired the way they "bedeck[ed] and bedizen[ed] their daughters" who already possessed a natural beauty.[17] The pertness of their breasts drew much praise as they hung "down very little except when they are old."[18] This observation should be understood in conjunction with the English perceptions of African women whose similar sexual freedoms and relative nudity invited scorn without praise. Europeans considered elevated breasts, due in part to the prevalence of corsets, to be a "marker of refinement, courtliness and status."[19]

That European explorers found Native women attractive and sexually appealing contradicted an ideology of savagery that otherwise diminished where it did not deny their membership in the human family. If the women were indeed "savages," and thus subhuman, as early modern Europeans expected, then European male attraction civilized them. Given the expected modesty of dress in Europe, the French were mentally unprepared to encounter the sex appeal of Native women but were quite approving of Frenchmen marrying Indian women. To bolster the population in the New World, the French government openly encouraged interracial marriage in the earliest years of exploration and settlement.[20] There is little indication that those who openly acted upon their attraction to Native women and married them received scorn from the French people. Clearly, Indian women who married Frenchmen and adapted to French society posed no challenge to conceptions of masculine identity. If anything, their beauty made them objects of lust, possessions that could be claimed without a compromise of ideology about savagery and civilization.

Though Frenchmen considered Native women attractive, their sexual availability was troubling. Champlain, despite his obvious appreciation for the beauty of young Native women, was appalled by "a shameless girl" in the Carmaron (or Karenhassa) village who "came boldly up to [him], offering to keep [him] company."[21] According to his writings, he "declined with thanks" and sent her "away with gentle remonstrances."[22] The degree of sexual expression afforded to single Native women, who practiced this freedom without fear of social reprisal, alarmed European observers. Several observers commented on the courtship and marriage rituals that accompanied women's sexual freedom among several suitors before deciding to marry one of them.[23] It is unclear whether the sexual freedom or the power of choice women exerted troubled these men the most. It was a combination of these patterns of behavior that combined to make Native women targets of religious conversion in the settlement era of New France.[24] Clearly, Indian women only received acceptance through assimilation and marriage into European civilization.

Comparatively, Pocahontas represented the counterpart to the lascivious Native woman. While she received a tentative acceptance in English society through complete assimilation and rejection of Native culture, her marriage to John Rolfe still needed justification to Virginian and English society. No matter how "English" she became, she was still an Indian. Pocahontas's relationships with John Smith and John Rolfe inspire historians to think about gender and the ways Native women either reinforced or challenged European masculinities. She provided validation for the English program of recasting gender among Native women. From the colonizer's perspective, the success and effective Europeanization and Christianization of Pocahontas supported the English divinely ordained impetus to colonize and Christianize. While in English captivity, Pocahontas received training in English customs, civility, and religion. Among her teachers was the "twenty-eight-year-old widower John Rolfe."[25] Far from admitting devotion and affection, Rolfe framed the marriage as a personal sacrifice for the good of Christianity and the colony. The letter also reveals the misconceptions and stereotypes of Indian women as lusty deviants capable of leading good Christian men astray. Rolfe insisted that his desire to marry was in "no way led with the unbridled desire of carnall affection."[26] He feared that the "vulgar sort who [measure] all mens actions by the base rule of their own filtinesse" would mock him and would think of his marriage as an ends to sexual and sensual gratification.[27] Clearly beneath him in quality, as "her manners [were] barbarous, her generations accursed, and so discrepant in all nurtriture form," Rolfe committed the ultimate sacrifice in marrying her.[28] Pocahontas served as both a cultural broker and a commodity. The English viewed her as a piece of effective propaganda for the colonial project.

Though there are several recorded marriages between Europeans and Native women, especially in New France, there were far more instances of sexual violence against Native women throughout the colonies, especially in New Spain. Violence perpetuated against Native women in the New World received both indirect acceptance and strong religious condemnation. Conquistadors received the most attention for their sexual aggression, especially from the Franciscans who accompanied them. The English and French criticized the behavior of Spanish men in Mesoamerica as unmanly and barbaric. That women, through sexual violation, became the pawns in this contest of masculinities is not surprising but should not be ignored. From the earliest beginnings of colonization, Native women were the recipients of violent sexual aggressions.

Michele de Cuneo, an Italian voyager with Columbus to the Caribbean, recorded a detailed description of his rape of a Native woman. Viewing her as lusty and the actions as a form of conquest, recognition of sexual assault is exchanged for an account of seduction. He wrote:

> While I was in the boat, I capture a very beautiful Carib woman, who the Lord Admiral [Columbus] gave to me. When I had taken her to my cabin she was naked – as was their custom. I was filled with my desire to take my pleasure with her and attempted to satisfy my desire. She was unwilling, and so treated me with her nails that I wished I had never begun. But – to cut a long story short – I then took a piece of rope and whipped her soundly, and she let forth such incredible screams that you would not have believed your ears. Eventually we came to such terms, I assure you, that you would have thought she had been brought up in a school for whores.[29]

Several elements here illuminate the male psyche of explorers. That Columbus "gave" this woman to Cuneo assumes that Columbus, as Admiral, owned her. As an inhabitant of the land he conquered, he could dispose of her how he saw fit. This dehumanization of female sexuality operated to advance the masculine endeavor of conquest. The flagrancy of this sexual violence excited Cuneo. He understood the rape as a game, with his possession as a toy. According to the historian Stephanie Wood, "Cuneo twists the rape into a scene of seduction, titillating his European male audience back home, knowing full well that the 'Carib' woman's version of events would never come to the fore."[30] Cuneo intentionally framed the tale to sexualize the New World without regard to the woman involved. Thinking of his male European audience, Cuneo discusses this rape as a metaphor for colonization. This is consistent with the tendency of early modern literature to employ nature and virgin lands as titillating imagery designed to induce men to leave European and be among the first to enter the New World, establishing dominance and ownership. In this same vein, Cuneo aligns Native women with the New World – both awaiting the penetration of the European male. Though offering token resistance, both would eventually be grateful and benefit from the European presence.

Assaults on Native women resulted in an emasculation of their husbands, fathers, and brothers who found it difficult to protect them. An experience in Hispaniola powerfully demonstrates the tension between Native and European men who used the women as pawns and in acts of aggression. In La Navidad, Guillermo Coma commented: "Bad feeling arose and broke out into warfare because of the licentious conduct of our men towards the Indian women, for each Spaniard had five women to minister to his pleasure ... the husbands and relatives of the women, unable to take this, banded together to avenge this insult and eliminate this outrage."[31] When Columbus arrived back to the fort, he found it burned and all the remaining Spanish soldiers dead. For these Spanish soldiers, Indian women functioned as concubines and whores not worthy of respect or marriage. More importantly, this denigration of Indian women deeply offended Indian men who wanted to protect the virtue of their relatives.

Women themselves often acted in ways to foil the sexual advances of the Spanish. The Florentine Codex reveals that many women of the Aztec city of Tenochtitlan "covered their faces with mud and put on ragged blouses and skirts" in an effort to seem less appealing to the conquistadors who desired "beautiful women, with yellow bodies."[32] This behavior indicates quite clearly that Native women feared sexual assault and sought ways to outwit their attackers. What is certain is that conquistadors viewed Native women as free for the taking either with consent or against their will.

Colonial settlers also feared potential sexual violence against English women by Indigenous people. This was especially true for the New England Puritans, who associated the wilderness with Satan and thought of Natives as Satan's minions. Puritan conceptions of women having weaker bodies and therefore being less able to resist the sexual threats of Satan, both literally and metaphorically, influenced seventeenth-century literature. The captivity narratives of Mary Rowlandson and Hannah Dunston attest to the anxieties among Puritans over sexual purity, but there are no indications of any sexual violence from Natives against any European women during the period of conquest. The captivity narrative served to reintegrate English women into Puritan society but also as a testament to their ability to resist the temptations of the wilderness and maintain their salvation, especially under duress.

The narratives of Rowlandson and Dunston appeared during the latter seventeenth century when the captivity narrative became a well-published testament to Puritan holiness. However, the process really began during the Pequot War in the late 1630s. Captured in an Indian raid on Wethersfield, two Puritan women related their ordeal after their release. They arrived at Fort Seabrooke where the Puritan leaders led an "examination of the two maids" to determine if they had been compromised sexually. The eldest confessed that "they did solicite her to uncleannesse, but her heart being much broken and afflicted under that bondage" she repented day and night, constantly praying for deliverance.[33] She spent her "breath in supplication to her God ... which sweetened all her sorowes, and gave her constant hope."[34] The young woman likened herself to King David and the leaders agreed. Her refusal to forsake God and to relinquish her chastity, even in the midst of such trials, made her an example not only to Puritan women but to all Puritans. John Underhill, a witness to her confession, drew a lesson for all humanity. Her example demonstrated that "a great measure of sweet comfort and consolation ... in the time of trouble" is to be found in the soul "affected with the sense of Gods fatherly love."[35] His admonishment "better in the Lyons denne, in the midst of all the roaring Lyons and with Christ, then in a doune bed with wife and children without Christ" echoed his insistence that only through misery could faith be proven.[36] God showed his blessings and favoritism through tribulations, which the young woman had survived. Interestingly, her story is only told to the community through the male religious leaders. Divine truths may be gained by women, but the dissemination of righteous information was a masculine endeavor. Women's purportedly feeble intellect did not allow them to interpret their own religious experiences and thus they depended on men to relate their personal truths. While she could and did display all the virtues possible for a Christian woman, her story required mediation through male leaders and the transmission of this knowledge to other Puritan families via male interlocution.

Although Puritan leaders expressed consistent anxiety about Native sexuality and potential aggression, court records from early New England indicate that several Puritan men faced charges of rape in their own communities. For violent sexual crimes, courts mandated a series of punishments indicating the level of offense, though rarely were these punishments heavy. In Massachusetts, in 1642, Robert Wyar and John Garland were

> indited for ravishing two yong girls, the fact confessed by the girls, & the girls both upon search found to have bin defloured, & filthy dalliance confessed by the boyes; the Jury found them, not guilty, wth reference to the Capitall Law. The Cort judged the boyes to bee openly whipped at Boston, the next market day, & againe toe bee whipped at Cambridge on the Lecture day, & each of them to pay [five pounds] a peece to their master in service. It was also judged that the two girls Sarah Wythes, & Ursula Odle being both guilty of that wickedness, shall bee severely whipped at Cambridge in the presence of the Secretary.[37]

The complexity of the case and the role the girls play in their "ravishment" reflect the fragility of the New England court. Though technically rape was a capital crime, murky evidence could often result in both parties receiving punishments. For the crime of sexual violence against an unnamed girl in Massachusetts Bay in 1640, John Pope "was censured to bee severely whiped."[38] Although indicted for "his unchast attempt upon" this one girl, the court also accused him of "dalliance maydes, & rebellios or stubborne carriage against his master."[39] Though his myriad of sexually aggressive crimes against several women in New England demanded a severe penalty, his "stubborne carriage" exacerbated his crimes and indicated an unrepent-ant criminal, proud to his master, and unrepentant for his sexual deviancy. An indentured servant was likely to receive harsher punishments from the courts.

The courts also addressed cases of bestiality. George Spencer's story of bestiality offers a window into the world of sexual crime in early New England. In 1641, a dead pig was born deformed in New Haven. The piglet "had no haire on the whole body ... and of a reddish white collour like a childs; the bead most straing, itt had butt one ye in the middle of the face, and that large and open, like some blemished eye of a man."[40] The eye of this "monster" resembled that of George Spencer who many suspected of "unna-tureall and abominable filthynes with the sow." Sent to prison for the suspected bestiality and other "miscarriages" Specer faced continual ques-tioning by the New Haven court and various magistrates and ministers in New Haven. Faced with accusations of his other "miscarriages," Spencer freely admitted to "miscarryages to his mar, and lying, and that he had scoffed att the Lords day, calling itt the Ladys day, butt denyed other scoffing, wicked, and bitter speeches witnessed against him, and other formr acts of filthynes, either with Indians or English."[41] Sentenced to death, as was the sow, the court encouraged him to spend the "small remainder of his time in the acknowledgmt of his owne formcr sinfull miscarriages, together with the abominable lewdness he had committed with the sow there present, and his desperate obstinacie in such fearefull denyalls."[42] Spencer served as a warning to the rest of the colony, a shame to be blighted.

Legal codes also extended to sodomy. European notions of sodomy and its inherent evils derived largely from a strong Christian influence and condem-nation of its practice. However, in Native society, gender performance defied the European dichotomy of male/female. European explorers responded with fear and violence. Several historians over the last twenty years have devoted their scholarship to the "berdache" also known as two-spirits, in North American Indigenous societies. The term "berdache" misrepresents and also unfairly simplifies what is truly a complicated terminology and has mistakenly received scrutiny for its Western origins as a derogatory term.[43] "Third gender" refers to either men who adopted feminine characteristics and/or women who embraced masculine occupations or behaviors. "Fourth gender" exclusively refers to women who adopted masculine characteristics. Another difficulty in assessing the behaviors and social practices of two-spirited peoples was the European insistence that all third or fourth genders were sodomites. This universal declaration needed no evidence. Without acquiring sufficient information to make this claim, Europeans aggressively persecuted even the most benign gender aberrance.

In the Spanish conquest of North America, conquistadors and missionaries zealously attacked the two-spirits, with the hope of total eradication. The experiences of Cabeza de Vaca in the American southwest also demonstrate the widespread prejudices two-spirited Natives faced from invading Europeans.[44] Discussing the Guaycones in Central American, de Vaca noted that "there are some among them who practice sodomy."[45] Inherent in his observation was the Castilian law that conflated sodomy and bestiality.[46] In a later passage, in which Cabeza de Vaca lists the many moral shortcomings of an unidentified tribe, he describes the presence of two-spirits as those engaging in "wicked behavior."[47] This wickedness was the unity of "one man married to another" who were "effeminate, impotent men."[48] Although they were "more muscular than other men and taller [suffering] very great loads," de Vaca still considered them "unmanly" because of their preference for the "task of women" rather than the "use [of] a bow."[49]

Sodomy had long been condemned in early modern Europe. When Balboa published *De orbe novo* in 1516, he recalled the presence of "men dressed as women and practicing sodomy" whom he "quickly threw some forty of these transvestites to the dogs," the first record of Spanish punishment of sodomy on the American continent. "Active" sexual partners received no punishment, while "passive" men died for their crimes against God and nature. Those men who penetrated other men still maintained their masculine status, while those who received penetration relinquished their masculinity in favor of the female role of recipient. The latter were castigated not only for sodomy but, moreover, for their perceived chosen emasculation. The French encountered sodomy as an act of emasculation in war. In Florida, under the command of René Laudonniére, a soldier witnessed how the Timicua "never left the site of battle without piercing the mutilated corpses of their enemies right through the anus with an arrow."[50] Through anal penetration, the Outina placed the conquered soldiers in the sexual posture of women. This overtly sexualized practice intentionally reenacted sodomy and emasculated their enemies. To lose in battle was to fail at your masculinity and right to dominance.

Hernán Cortés equally condemned the entire population of Mexico as sodomites. "We have learnt and been informed for sure that they are all sodomites and use that abominate sin," he claimed. His contemporary and fellow conquistador, Bernal Díaz del Castillo, echoed these concerns, writing, "all the rest were sodomites, especially those who lived on the coasts and in warm lands; so much so that young men paraded around dressed in women's clothes in order to work in the diabolical and abominable role."[51] He naturally associated transvestitism with sodomy and the compromised masculinity these men embodied. If they dressed in women's clothing, then they must be the recipient of penetration, hence becoming womanly in the process.

Gonzalo Fernández de Oviedo claimed emphatically that all in Indigenous America practiced sodomy. Within his lengthy denigration lies the overarching concern that two-spirited people posed a threat to appropriate masculinity and threatened the prevailing moral and social order adhered to by Europeans. He lamented that "they wear strings of beads and bracelets and the other things used by women as adornment; and they do not exercise in the use of weapons, nor do anything proper to men, but they occupy themselves in the usual chores of the house such as to sweep and wash and other things customary for women."[52] That berdache men rejected the glories of warfare in favor of housework outraged European men who could not envision a masculine pursuit more glorious or noble than war. Debauched sexuality came second to debased masculinity. These men not only defiled themselves by sexually receiving other men but adopted the habits of women, thus rejecting their inherent masculinity. Unlike Native women who sought to embrace masculinity, "berdache" and two-spirited people openly rejected masculinity, a decision more odious. European men viewed two-spirited men as having renounced their manhood, their greatest asset, and instead choosing and privileging femininity.

Same-sex desire provoked the severest scorn from English religious and laymen alike. En route to America, Francis Higginson recalled that the Puritans discovered "five beastly Sodomitical boys which confessed their wickedness, not to be named."[53] Owing to the severity of this act, the Puritans "referred them to be punished by the Governor ... who afterwards sent them back ... to be punished in Old England, as the crime deserved."[54] The boys reappear in the Company Records of Massachusetts Bay and it is clear that no one knew quite how to punish them. In 1629, after they returned from New England to England, the court could not decide whether to refer their case to the Judge of the Admiralty or issue a warrant.[55] They reappear in the records several days later and the court decided they should be "legally discharged" from the company responsible for the colonies.[56] The colonies could not be affiliated with such crimes and maintain their religious integrity.

New England faced other challenges to religious piety through inappropriate sexual behavior, most infamously in the adventures of Thomas Morton. Though not a case of perceived sodomy, Morton embodied all the sexual and sensual pleasures so terrifying to Puritans. Spending only a few months in Plymouth in 1622, he returned to the colony in 1624 with expectations for financial gain in his enterprises with Captain Richard Wollaston.[57] The two established Mount Wollaston as their plantation.[58] According to Bradford, they erected a "maypole, drinking and dancing about it many days together, inviting the Indian women for their consorts, dancing and frisking together like so many fairies or furies" not to mention "worse practices" Bradford fails to detail. The maypole was incredibly phallic and historically erected in celebrations of spring and fertility. Morton transgressed the normative behavior expected in the Plymouth colony by engaging in drunkenness and wanton sexuality with Native women and enjoying a degree of frivolity the austere Separatists despised. Sins of the flesh indicated vanity and self-indulgence, deviant behaviors that provoked the local population: Mount Wollaston became Merrymount.

Puritans struggled with the variety and prevalence of corporeal sins in the colonies. Although Puritans believed women more apt to sin due to their weak physical natures that invited intrusion from Satan, men also faced challenges to their souls, largely through vanity or sexual sins. Men who embraced vanity often opened the door to a multitude of sins associated with the pervasive category of "pride," which included masturbation or "self-love." Robert Cushman described prideful men as "wicked" and "given over of God to vile lusts."[59] Richard Baxter paralleled the insistence that pride led to "carnal minds, which is threatened with death."[60] In another sermon, Baxter admonished Christians to "always be suspicious of carnal self-love" because it "is the burrow or fortress of sin."[61] Thomas Shepard of Massachusetts Bay described his own youthful folly and sin of pride.[62] He, too, saw pride as an entrée into sexual sins. Shepard wrote of his years at Cambridge as a time when "foolish & proud," he gave himself over "to lust & pride & gaming & bowling & drinking."[63] While bowling may not be among the gravest of sins, it paved the way for sexual "deviancy."

Michael Wigglesworth also saw pride as an avenue to sexual sins. His poetry often associates the sin of Sodom with the sin of pride. In *God's Controversy with New England*, Wigglesworth criticizes the second generation of New England Puritans and accused them of separating themselves and New England from the initial values of their Puritan fathers and also from God. Wigglesworth wrote:

> Yea many grow to more and more excess;
> More light and loose, more Carnall and prophane.
> The sins of Sodom, Pride, and Wantonness,
> Among the multitude spring up amain.
> Are these the fruits of pious Education;
> To Run with greater speed and Courage to Damnation?[64]

The association between pride and sexual deviance reflects Wigglesworth's own personal struggles. His autobiography often reads like a verbal self-flagellation against his lack of humility and, occasionally, his inability to control masturbation and nocturnal emissions.[65] Sexual sins indulged the flesh and resulted from narcissism. Through written confession, both Wigglesworth and Moody repented and renewed their faith, a core tenet of Puritanism. Self-discipline and perseverance fought against fleshly inclinations to sin. As Theodore Dwight Bozeman argues, self-control was critical to Puritanism. "Propounded and refined over several decades in a steady barrage of sermons, personal counsels, and books," the mandate of control over the earthly body "was central to the new pietism" of Puritanism in early New England.[66] Desires of the flesh also served to remind writers of the constant battle between indulgence and humility, a battle understood to enable penitents to suffer for the glory of God. In these ways, sufferings enacted holiness.

For Michael Wigglesworth, masturbation was the embodiment of vanity and self-love. He linked pride with sexual impropriety in his journal and poetry and often felt that his predilection toward pride and vanity resulted in estrangement from Christ and would ultimately lead to his damnation. Wigglesworth lamented in 1653 that "Pride I feel still again and again abounding, self-admiration, though destroying my self daly."[67] Wigglesworth then proceeds to explain that the source of his self-contempt is masturbation. "Ah Lord I am vile," he writes, "I desire to abhor my self (o that I could!) ... I find such unresistable torments of carnal lusts or provocation unto the ejection of seed that I find my self unable to read anything to inform me about my distemper because of the prevailing or rising of my lusts."[68] Two days later, he recorded that

> Last night a filthy dream and so pollution escaped me in my sleep for which I desire to hang down my head with shame and beseech the Lord not to make me possess the sin of my youth and give me into the hands of my abominations.[69]

For Wigglesworth, pride and carnality, eternally linked with Satan, led to more minor but not inconsequential social sins and personal transgressions against students and neighbors.

Thomas Shepard wrote of becoming drunk at a feast. When he regained consciousness, on the Sabbath no less, he found himself "sick with [his] beastly carnage."[70] In his drunkenness, he had evidently engaged in a sexual experience with a fellow male student, which left him with "much sadness of hart."[71] In the wake of his same-sex intimacy, Shepard related his renewed dedication to God owing to "the terror of God's wrath" and his fear of "death & the flames of God's wrath."[72] Humility deriving from fear was an acceptable form of piety. He had reached the "height of pride" and needed to repent. Later in life, Shepard recalled his youth with praise for the "good things" he had "received of the Lord," including deliverance from "loose company."[73] Shepard wrote that he

> oft resisted the Lord and neglected secret prayer, and care of his ways a long time and followed by bowling loose company until I came to that height of pride that for their sakes I was once or twice dead drunke and lived in specula- tive wantonness (yet still refrained from grosse acts of sin which some of my own familiars were to their horror and shame overtaken with) yet at this very time of worst and under wrath the Lord dealt most graciously with me, and made my last act of drunkenness the beginning of more serious thoughts of making my peace with God.[74]

Given his early confession of sexual impropriety and drunkenness, it is likely these are the same incident. Shepard's repetition reflects not only repentance and a willingness to humble himself in the eyes of God; he also considers this a pivotal moment on which he frequently reflected. He associated pride with his deepest regret and his most shameful of sins.

Whether given to pride, vanity, lust, nudity, bestiality, same-sex desire, or any other manner of sexual demonstration, the exploration and settlement of North America was clearly predicated on gendered identities and clashing cultures. Europeans brought with them a variety of well-ingrained expect- ations for an ordered society hardened by the influence of Christianity and generations of solidified gendered identities in Europe. However, the "New World" presented a plethora of opportunities to impose "civilization." The chaos of settlement was far removed from the gentle nourishing maternal figure or the young innocent virgin. Instead, the New World was ferocious, violent, and full of conflict between Europeans and Natives but also among Europeans themselves, who struggled to impose order in the wilderness, often unsuccessfully.

Notes

1. Westling, 33, 27; James Axtell, "Europeans, Indians, and the Age of Discovery in American History Textbooks," *The American Historical Review* 92, no. 3 (June 1987): 624.
2. Jennifer L. Morgan, "'Some Could Suckle over Their Shoulder': Male Travelers, Female Bodies, and the Gendering of Racial Ideology, 1550–1770," *William and Mary Quarterly* 54, no. 1 (1997): 170.
3. Marc Lescarbot, *The History of New France*, vol. 3, ed. W. L. Grant (Toronto: The Publications of the Champlain Society), 308.
4. Lescarbot, *History of New France*, 246.
5. Kathleen M. Brown, *Good Wives, Nasty Wenches and Anxious Patriarchs: Gender, Race, and Power in Colonial Virginia* (Chapel Hill: University of North Carolina Press, 1996), 13.
6. Sir Walter Raleigh, "Discovery of Guiana," *Hakluyt: Voyages and Discoveries*, ed. Jack Beeching (New York: Penguin, 1972), 388.
7. Brown, *Good Wives*, 21.
8. Michael S. Kimmel, "From Lord and Master to Cuckold and Fop: Masculinity in 17th Century England," in Kimmel, *The History of Men: Essays on the History of American and British Masculinities* (Albany: State University of New York, 2005), 125–142.
9. Thomas Dudley, *The Life and Work of Thomas Dudley, the Second Governor of Massachusetts*, Jones, Augustine, and Oliver Wendell Holmes Collection (Boston: Houghton, Mifflin and Co, 1899), 327, https://lccn.loc.gov /99002120.
10. Ibid.
11. Ibid., 329.
12. Ibid., 339.
13. Roger Clapp, *The Memoir of Capt. Roger Clapp* (ca. 1630) (New York: BiblioLife, 2009), 360.
14. Ibid.
15. Samuel de Champlain, "Voyages," in *The Works of Samuel de Champlain: 1608–1620*, vols. 1–7 (Toronto: Champlain Society, 2013), 4: 104–105; Lescarbot, *History of New France*, 15.
16. Ibid., "Voyages" (1619), 3:136.
17. Ibid., 3:135. In "Voyages" (1632), Champlain again remarked at how the women were "well formed, plump, and of a dusky hue on account of certain pigments with which they rub themselves, which make them look olive-coloured" (4:53). This beauty, with no reference to color, reveals the degree to which race was not an element in New France relations. While it could be argued that they perhaps suspected the Natives of being naturally fair-skinned, but who chose to darken their skins, I disagree. Cartier's expectations of the land of Saguenay included a description of the people who Donnacona, the Iroquois leader in Quebec, described as fair and light-skinned. Jacques Cartier, *The Voyages of Jacques Cartier*, ed. Ramsay Cook (Toronto: University of Toronto Press, 2017).
18. Champlain, "Voyages" (1619), 3:136.
19. Morgan, "Male Travelers, Female Bodies," 172 n. 14.

20. Marcel Trudel, *The Beginnings of New France, 1524–1663*, trans. Patricia Claxton (Toronto: McClelland and Stewart, 1973).
21. Champlain, "Voyages" (1619), 3:47.
22. Ibid.
23. Cartier, *Voyage*, 182. Champlain, "Voyages" (1613), 2:48–49; Champlain, "Voyages" (1619), 3:137–139; Champlain, "Voyages" (1632) 4:53–54. There are some discrepancies as to what age these sexual liaisons began. Most sources indicate between eleven and fifteen years of age, most settling upon a husband in their early twenties.
24. See again Carol Devens, *Countering Colonization: Native American Women and Great Lakes Missions, 1630–1900* (Berkley: University of California Press, 1992) and Karen Anderson, *Chain Her by One Foot: The Subjugation of Women in Seventeenth-Century New France* (New York: Routledge, 1993).
25. Helen C. Roundtree, *Pocahontas's People: The Powhatan Indians through Four Centuries* (Norman: University of Oklahoma Press, 1996), 59.
26. John Rolfe, *Narratives of Early Virginia, 1606–1625*, ed. Lyon Gardiner Tyler (New York: Charles Scribner's Sons, 1907), 240.
27. Ibid., 243.
28. Ibid.
29. Stephanie Wood, "Sexual Violation in the Conquest of the Americas," in Merril D. Smith, ed., *Sex and Sexuality in Early America* (New York: New York University Press, 1998), 11.
30. Ibid.
31. Ibid., 13.
32. Ibid., 17.
33. John Underhill, *Newes from America; Or, A New and Experimentall Discoverie of New England; Containing, A Trve Relation of Their War-like Proceedings These Two Yeares Last Past, with a Figure of the Indian Fort, or Palizado*, ed. Paul Royster, Digital Commons at the University of Nebraska, 28–29, https://digitalcommons.unl.edu/etas/37/.
34. Ibid.
35. Ibid., 30.
36. Ibid., 31.
37. *Records of the Court of Assistants of the Colony of the Massachusetts Bay*, vol. 2 (1630–1692), ed. John Noble (Boston: County of Suffolk, 1904), 115, Archive .org, 121, https://archive.org/details/recordscourtassoocrongoog.
38. Ibid., 92.
39. Ibid., 92.
40. *New Haven Court Records*, umich.edu, 63, www.google.com/#q=New+Haven+court+records+colonial.
41. Ibid., 65.
42. Ibid., 72.
43. Will Roscoe, *Changing Ones: Third and Fourth Genders in Native North America* (New York: Palgrave Macmillan, 2000), 17; Roscoe, *Living the Spirit. A Gay American Indian Anthology* (New York: St. Martin's Griffin, 1988).
44. Roscoe, *Changing Ones*, 4.
45. Cabaza de Vaca, *The Narrative of Cabeza de Vaca* (Lincoln: University of Nebraska Press, 2003).

46. Ibid., 107. It was not unusual for European observers to bundle sins in describing the Natives they encountered. Pedro Cieza de Léon discussed that sodomites in Peru also practiced cannibalism. See Walter Williams, *The Spirit and the Flesh: Sexual Diversity in American Indian Culture* (New York: Beacon Press, 1992), 135.
47. Ibid., 132.
48. Ibid.
49. Ibid.
50. Jacques Le Moyne de Morgues, reprinted in Rene Laudonnière, *Three Voyages*, ed. and trans. Charles E. Bennett (Gainesville: University of Florida, 1975), 31.
51. Bernal Díaz del Castillo, reprinted in Juan Ruiz de Arce, *La memoria de Juan Ruiz de Arce: Conquista del Perú, saberes secretos de caballería y defensa del Mayorazgo. Textos y documentos españoles y americanos* (Madrid: Iberoamericana Editorial Vervuert, 2002), 32. Díaz also commented on the proliferation of clay idols in which sodomy was depicted.
52. Michael Horswell, "Towards and Andean Theory of Ritual Same-Sexuality and Third Gender Subjectivity," in Pete Sigal, ed., *Infamous Desire: Male Homosexuality in Colonial Latin America* (Chicago: University of Chicago Press, 2003), 74.
53. Francis Higginson, "A True Relation of the last Voyage to New-England, declaring all circumstances, with the manner of the passage we had by sea, and what matter of country and inhabitants we found when we came to land; and what is the present state and condition of the English people that are there already (1629)," in Alexander Young, ed., *Chronicles of the First Planters of the Colony of Massachusetts Bay 1623–1636* (1846) (New York: Da Capo Press, 1970), 231.
54. Ibid.
55. Ibid., 90.
56. Ibid., 94.
57. Morton fell into a questionable crowd while in England, especially his friendship with Humphrey Rastall, who was suspected of being a pirate. It seems that Rastall and Wollaston were also acquainted. Philip Ranlet, *Enemies of the Bay Colony* (New York: University Press of America, 2006), 9. See also William Heath, "Thomas Morton: From Merry Old England to New England," *Journal of American Studies* 41, no. 1 (2007): 136–168.
58. William Bradford, *Of Plymouth Plantation* (New York: McGraw Hill, 1981), 226.
59. Robert Cushman, "The Sin and Danger of Self-Love, Described in a Sermon Preached at Plymouth, in New England (1621)," *Early English Books Online*, database, 5.
60. Richard Baxter, "The Sinfulness of Flesh-Pleasing," *The Digital Puritan*, 2, http://digitalpuritan.net/richard-baxter/.
61. Baxter, "Directions for Hating Sin," *The Digital Puritan*, 5, http://digitalpuritan .net/richard-baxter/.
62. Thomas Shepard, "Thomas Shepard's *Confessions*," in *Publications of the Colonial Society of Massachusetts*, vol. 58, ed. George Selement and Bruce C. Woolley (Boston: The Society, 1981).

63. Thomas Shepard, *The Autobiography of Thomas Shepard*, ed. Nehemiah Adams (Boston: Pierce and Parker, 1832), 20–21.

64. Michael Wigglesworth, *God's Controversy with New England*, Digital Commons at the University of Nebraska, 98, https://digitalcommons.unl.edu /cgi/viewcontent.cgi?article=1036&context=etas.

65. The historian Brian Carroll made connections between Wigglesworth and Joseph Moody, whose own coded diary, written a generation after Wigglesworth's, more conspicuously records Moody's frequent sexual frustration, masturbation, and nocturnal emissions. Though less concerned with pride than Wigglesworth, both authors anxiously reflect on the effect of unregulated sexuality on their souls. Brian D. Carroll, "'I Indulged My Desire Too Freely': Sexuality, Spirituality, and the Sin of Self-Pollution in the Diary of Joseph Moody, 1720–1724," *William and Mary Quarterly* 60, no. 1 (2003): 155–170. See also Philip McIntire Woodwell, ed., *Handkerchief Moody: The Diary and the Man* (Portland, ME: Colonial Offset Printing Company, 1983).

66. Dwight Bozeman, *The Precisianist Strain: Disciplinary Religion and Antinomian Backlash in Puritanism to 1638* (Chapel Hill: Ommohundro Institute and University of North Carolina Press, 2004), 105.

67. Michael Wigglesworth, *Diary of Michael Wigglesworth*, Colonial Society of Massachusetts, 4, www.colonialsociety.org/node/911.

68. Ibid., 4.

69. Ibid., 5.

70. Shepard, *Autobiography*, 22.

71. Ibid., 22.

72. Ibid., 23.

73. Ibid., 71.

74. Ibid., 71–72.

PART III

Early American Places

12

CAROLINE WIGGINTON

Indigenous Colonial America

Early American literature is Indigenous American literature. As the Muscogee Creek and Cherokee literary scholar Craig Womack influentially declares in *Red on Red*, Indigenous American "literatures are the *tree*, the oldest literatures in the Americas, the most American of American literatures ... Without Native American literature, *there is no American canon*."[1] This chapter provides a partial history of Indigenous American literatures in which its texts constitute the tree of, rather than mere branches upon, the early American literary canon. While it takes 1830 or so as its end point, that year has been chosen because it is what many deem the conclusion of the early American period, and not because by then the colonial period was over for Indigenous Americans. Native peoples in the Americas still live under settler colonialism as their territories are still occupied and they are still marginalized populations confronting assaults on their sovereignty and existence. Note that I use *Native* and *Indigenous* interchangeably throughout the chapter. *Native* is generally common – though not in every field – in Native American and Indigenous studies (NAIS) in the United States. For many, *Indigenous* invokes a more global context and is now frequently preferred outside the United States, including in Canada along with First Nations, Inuit, and Métis. When possible, NAIS advocates using a people's or tribal nation's own name for itself. Doing so helps avoid eliding the specificities of diverse Indigenous peoples: there are more than 570 federally recognized nations and many more non-recognized nations in the United States alone. Moreover, using Indigenous peoples' specific names for their communities functions as an implicit reminder that the borders and networks of settler colonial nation-states are not the same as those of Indigenous nations. Therefore, this chapter's geographic scope is the entire hemisphere. Its recurrent turn to English-language writings produced in the Eastern Seaboard of North America reflects my disciplinary training and expertise and should not be taken to suggest the absence of other Indigenous American texts and traditions.

Shaping an Indigenous American literary history in which its texts are the tree necessitates considering Indigenous approaches and forms and avoiding the automatic use of European ones. Much recent work in Native and early American studies, including that of Lisa Brooks (Abenaki), Matt Cohen, and Phillip Round, presents new approaches to American literary history, grounded in its Indigenous contexts. Foregrounding Native graphic, communicatory, and print practices, they identify by turns an "indigenous American literary tradition," wherein Native-authored alphabetic writing links to awikhigan (an Abenaki word "originally describ[ing] birchbark messages, maps, and scrolls"); a networked wilderness, wherein paper on a maypole and animal traps in the forest are publication events communicating messages to Native and non-Native audiences alike; and a Native bibliography that merges the timelines of North American print cultures with Native adoption of and education in alphabetic and syllabic textualities in order to engage in legal and political writing under colonization.[2] As Round observes, this rethinking of American literary history is warranted because its "trajectory . . . has been from the beginning intimately tied to the indigenous cultures of this continent."[3] Collectively, the work of those like Brooks, Cohen, and Round underscores that there is no early American literature without Native peoples.

Their work often makes this argument by applying and then reframing and interrogating Eurocentric terms like *writing, publication, literacy,* and *book.* In doing so, they simultaneously suggest the potency and the inadequacy of colonialist concepts. Their potency is clear: Eurocentric terms have legal, political, and cultural authority, and refusing their use in Indigenous contexts has resulted in psychic and material harms to Native communities and peoples, including land theft, cultural denigration, denial of sovereign rights, forced sterilization, and child abduction. Referring to a Haudenosaunee (Iroquois) wampum belt as a book, for example, concisely indicates to many that the object holds knowledge and meaning, that with literacy it can be read, and that its creation and circulation were acts of authorship and publication. One effect of acknowledging wampum belts' bookishness is an affirmation of their status in court cases that seek to determine the timing, nature, and continuing obligations of diplomatic agreements between Haudenosaunee and settler colonial nations. Another is their inclusion in the category of Haudenosaunee literature. Yet the inadequacy of Eurocentric terms is also clear to those who know about wampum. *Book* does not succinctly evoke the extralinguistic, visual, ceremonial, and oral aspects of reading a wampum belt. It does not denote the potential animacies of the belt's shell and sinew components. If *book* is the only term we use, it may limit how we read and understand these texts.[4]

The simultaneous potency and inadequacy of colonialist terms call into question the efficacy of familiar literary genres like poetry, the novel, auto-biography, and so on, in organizing a history of Indigenous American litera-tures. Genres have been important to literary studies because they help us identify, compare, evaluate, and interpret texts. When we know a genre's norms, we can understand how a particular text follows, transgresses, and reshapes expectations. When we understand a genre's evolutions across time and place, we can locate a text in the genre's development and we can make suppositions about audience and purpose. Most of us know how to read a poem, more or less. We watch for rhyme, rhythm, wordplay, and stanza and line breaks. We expect poetry to be complex and to reward careful appraisal, and we admire its artful creators. However, as with *book*, *poem* may mask or divert us from other ways of understanding an Indigenous text, even when it looks like a poem.

If colonialist terms and genres are potent but inadequate, how then to organize an Indigenous American literary history? In the above discussion, poetry and the other genres are nouns, but genre is not always classified that way. In some approaches, genre names what a text does or, as rhetorician Carolyn Miller explains, its "social action"; she argues that a "sound defin-ition of genre must be centered not on the substance or the form of discourse but on the action it is used to accomplish."[5] An action-based understanding of genre accords with certain scholarship in Native studies. In his important essay "Rhetorical Sovereignty: What Do American Indians Want from Writing?," Scott Richard Lyons (Leech Lake Ojibwe) concerns himself not so much with what writing is but with what writing ideally does by confirm-ing what his title implies: American Indians want writing to perform rhet-orical sovereignty, where rhetorical sovereignty is "the inherent right and ability of peoples to determine their own communicative needs and desires in the pursuit of self-determination."[6] This self-determination serves the people as a collective, rather than individuals or the state. "Sovereignty," he explains, "is the guiding story in our pursuit of self-determination, the general strategy by which we aim to best recover our losses from the ravages of colonization: our lands, our languages, our cultures, our self-respect ... [T]he pursuit of sovereignty is an attempt to revive not our past, but our possibilities."[7] In linking writing with the enactment of collective, future-focused self-determination, Lyons's essay links to other theorizations of Native sovereignty. As Daniel Heath Justice (Cherokee) underscores, a foundation of Indigenous nations and peoples is kinship: "[our] kinship isn't a status thing; it's dynamic, ever in motion. It requires attentiveness; kinship is best thought of as a verb rather than a noun, because kinship, in most indigenous contexts, is something that's *done* more than something that simply *is*."[8] Indigenous kinship contexts and practices, he underscores, are not universal but particular to particular peoples. Rigorous and ethical scholarship must recollect and respect the differences among the hundreds and hundreds of Indigenous nations and cultures.

If writing, sovereignty, and kinship are activities Indigenous nation-peoples do and they do these community-sustaining activities in ways that are at times comparable but always dynamic and specific, then perhaps Indigenous genres may be approached as categories of action as well. What are the genres of doing in Indigenous American literatures? How do those genres support performances of autonomy, sovereignty, and peoplehood? How do certain genres of doing facilitate comparisons across form and across cultures and communities? How do genres of doing support considering the specificities of histories, aesthetics, and peoples? The remainder of this chapter surveys some of Indigenous American literatures' genres of doing and then briefly considers the implications of those categories for early American literary studies.

To Record

One thing that Indigenous American literatures do is record information. Incan khipu is one notable example. Long before the arrival of Spanish conquistadores in South America, administrators of Tawantinsuyu, or the Incan Empire, used a cord-and-knot-based system for recording information like census data and tributes. When juxtaposed with precolonial khipu, postcontact khipu records and testifies to the dramatic changes wrought by Spanish violence and colonization upon the Incan population and economy and, by extension, its political organization. Khipu thus records something other than bureaucratic and statistical snapshots that may seem irrelevant to Indigenous American literatures; it records a way of thinking about and organizing information specific to the Incan Empire and its Andean neighbors. It chronicles changes and responses to colonization. That khipu was the form of Incan record-keeping also suggests that numeracy, tactility, and sequence are all components of Incan literary aesthetics. The presence of migrated and adapted versions of these components in other forms of literature written and produced by Incans' descendants signals moments of recording and accounting. Thus the magisterial thousand-plus-page manuscript *Nueva corónica y buen gobierno* by Felipe Guaman Poma de Ayala, an Indigenous Peruvian born in the final years of the Incan Empire, may be understood as a paper text that enfolds numeracy, tactility, and sequence alongside alphabetic script and illustration to make an account. Organized in a series of sections within sections – its smallest unit (perhaps its knots) often an intricate drawing followed by a page or more of writing, sometimes multidirectional – *Nueva corónica* makes an account of precolonial and postcontact historical leaders, practices, and events, including Spanish mistreatment of the region's Indigenous peoples.[9]

Another example of an Indigenous literature that records can be found in a text authored by the Mahican Hendrick Aupaumut about his 1790s diplomatic expedition. He journeyed on behalf of US Secretary of War Henry Knox to the Native nations of what are now parts of New York, Pennsylvania, and Ohio. Though the full text is a narration, as reflected by its title *A Short Narration of My Last Journey to the Western Country*, embedded within it are many transcripts of speeches made by Aupaumut and the Native leaders with whom he met. In one sequence of transcripts, toward the end, Aupaumut notes that the Mohawk leader Joseph Brant sent an emissary to a diplomatic council, warning the attendees to trust neither Aupaumut nor the United States. Through his emissary, Brant suggested that the journey of Aupaumut and his "Companions" through the region was not truly friendly: they were taking a covert census so "that the White people may judge how many men will be sufficient to fall upon the Indians." Aupaumut's *Short Narration* records his response to these accusations:

> But let us look back in the path of our forefathers, and see whether you can find one single instance wherein, or how my ancestors or myself have deceived you, or led you one step astray. I say Let us look narrowly, to see whether you can find one bone of yours lay on the ground, by my deceitfulness, and I now declare that you cannot find one such instance … But you look back and see heaps of your bones, wherein the Maquas [Mohawks] have deceived you repeatedly.[10]

This moment in Aupaumut's narration records not only a diplomatic conversation but also competing claims about accounting itself: Brant accuses Aupaumut of being on a reconnaissance mission in service of waging war against the region's Native nations; Aupaumut responds by asking his audience to tally and compare the number of their "bone[s] … on the ground" attributable to him versus the Mohawks. For Aupaumut, bones function as quantifying metonyms for deceptions and fatalities. In this instance, then, Indigenous literature records literally and figuratively in order to guide Native peoples in making decisions about their present and future alliances and friendships.

To Narrate

Another thing Indigenous American literatures do is narrate. Narration may rely on recording but crucially it organizes and establishes connections, often chronological, correlational, or causal, between a set of items and events. Khipu is again a notable example, though aspects of narrative khipu remain opaque to historians and anthropologists, as the Spanish colonial government banned khipu in the late sixteenth century and thereby largely eradicated certain aspects of khipu literacy. Contemporary scholars continue to speculate about what some khipu narrate, even as those same khipu testify to the existence of Incan narrative practices and even as the Incas' descendants have maintained and developed relationships to khipu. Many other nonalphabetic Indigenous narrative forms existed in the precolonial and postcontact Americas. The Codex Zouche-Nuttall, for example, in part recounts the life and reign of the eleventh-century Mixtec leader Lord Eight Deer Jaguar Claw. Painted on deerskin and bound accordion-style in the fifteenth century, this vibrant text uses pictorial and iconic ideograms to narrate Lord Eight Deer's decades of military and political achievements. It sits on a literary continuum with Codex Mendoza, created in the following century after the Spanish Conquest. This later codex resembles a European manuscript book and interweaves Mesoamerican ideographic form with Spanish alphabetic translations and explanations. It demonstrates the interanimation of different writing practices in order to sustain a genre.[11]

At times, Indigenous literatures narrate in order to enact another purpose. For example, petitions and related legal documents, produced for imperial and US courts and governments, often hinge on acts of narration. The Creek diplomat and trader Coosaponakeesa (also known as Mary Musgrove Mathews Bosomworth) penned a series of memorials in the 1740s and 1750s to support petitions sent to colonial administrators. Justifying her demand for recognition of her property rights to three coastal islands and monetary restitution for debts incurred on behalf of the Georgian colony, the memorials knit together her familial and personal histories with the founding and future of Georgia and its ongoing dependence on the Creek nation as well as, by extension, her diplomatic expertise. In a crescendo of outrage near the end of her 1747 memorial, she draws together the threads of her narration:

> AND Lastly your Memorialist cannot Help repeating with an equal Mixture of a Real Grief of Heart, and Indignation; that her Injuries and Oppressions have been such, as she believes; have been scarce paralleled under a British Government. Language is too Weak to Represent her present Deplorable Case; She at present Labours under every sence of Injury; and Circumstance of Distress; Destitute of even the Common Necessaries of Life, being Insulted, Abused, contemned and Dispised by those ungratefull People who are indebted to her for the Blessings they Injoy.[12]

This paragraph concludes and interprets the preceding narration as a tale of unparalleled injustice. British abuse of colonial power is not only a betrayal of treaties but a personal assault upon Coosaponakeesa. The denial of her petitions, she implies (and elsewhere states outright), would be an unwise decision as alienating her undermines the stability of Georgia due to her authority within the powerful and independent Creek nation. She appropriates a colonialist form – in this case a manuscript memorial – to produce a narration that serves personal and national sovereignties. The rhythms of British legalese structure her narrative and thereby support and preserve her narrative.[13]

Similarly, a 1788 petition of the Montaukett Nation on Long Island makes its case through narration, but here that narration adopts biblical rather than legal language. Presaging the narration with the suggestion that what will come is merely an aside requiring their audience's "Condescention and Patience to hear," the Montauketts recall a precolonial past, when the "Great and good Spirit above" had provided them with a "great Continent & he fill'd this Indian World, with veriety, and a Prodigious Number of four footed Beasts, Fowl without number and Fish of all kinds great and Small, fill'd our Seas, Rivers, Brooks, and Ponds every where." European colonists "found [them] Naked and very poor Destitute of every thing," the petition continues ironically, "only this we had good and a Large Country to live in, and well furnished with Natural Provisions." Owing to their "Learning, Knowledge, and Understanding," the colonists easily grasped the Montaukett land's "goodness." "But alas," the story ends, "by our Fore Fathers Ignorance [of English literacy and property ownership practices] and Your Fathers great Knowledge, we are undone for this Life." This petition's narration is no aside but a bold and bitter lament that aligns Montauk with an innocent Eden and colonists with a serpent who brings about the nation's fall not through temptation but through fraud and manipulation. The petition's concluding request for livestock seems paltry compensation for all that has been taken, and New York's government would be ungenerous in denying their request.

Whether enfolded into petitions or not, when Indigenous literatures narrate they are creating connections between items and events, just as all narrative texts do. These literatures demonstrate what items and events Indigenous peoples choose to remember, how they choose to connect them, and in what form and in what situations they choose to narrate. Produced for non-Indigenous audiences, Codex Mendoza, Coosaponakeesa's memorials, and the Montaukett petition suggest that, for colonialist audiences, Indigenous literatures appropriate and modify European forms in order to preserve histories, share their perspectives on colonial violence and loss, and present pragmatic and visionary tactics for shaping their futures.

To Map

If narration frequently articulates chronological and causal relationships, mapping represents spatial and communal ones. Indigenous American literatures are rife with texts that map. Because settler colonialism seeks to eradicate Native peoples, cultures, autonomies, and territorial rights so that settler colonists can permanently occupy Indigenous lands and secure their resources, mapping is a critical practice of Indigenous American literatures. Acknowledging and documenting territories and relationships between nations and kin aids Native peoples in surviving and resisting efforts to alienate them from their homes and to disrupt their sovereignties. Mappings performed by Indigenous literatures also offer a crucial evidentiary source for contemporary communities seeking acknowledgment of historical and ongoing territorial rights.

The mediated and autobiographical *A Narrative of the Life of Mrs. Mary Jemison* (1824) is a text that maps. Jemison was born to a Euro-American family and captured by Shawnee warriors as a girl in 1755. Soon after, she was adopted into the Seneca nation, and she remained Seneca until her death, refusing to abandon her new nation and growing family. She told her story to the Christian minister James Seaver when she was about eighty. In her account, she remembers how she negotiated with regional Native and non-Native leaders at the Big Tree Council in 1797 to receive a "piece of land reserved for my use" in upstate New York.[14] In subsequent chapters, she notes how portions of her reserved land were chipped away by natural and human disaster, just like portions of her family: two of her sons were murdered by a third, John, who was himself killed during a quarrel. Each time the text returns to her land, she provides the natural boundaries until, at the end of her published narrative, she has just twenty-two acres. Describing what's left, she writes, "The land which I now own, is bounded as follows: – Beginning at the center of the Great Slide [a section of the Genesee River] and running west one mile, thence north two miles, thence east about one mile on the Genesee river, thence south on the west bank of the Genesee river to the place of beginning." She also notes that future "income" generated from her "reserved" land should be "equally divided amongst the members of the Seneca nation."[15] As an elderly woman with no living children who was a citizen of a matrilineal Native nation – property rights, clans, and genealogies are traced through the women – she told her life story in a way that indicates cognizance of both the importance of written documents to the US government and a desire to fulfill her responsibilities as a Seneca matriarch to her entire nation. Her text maps in language where her reserved land was and is so that it can always be known and found even after her death and even after its sale.

While texts like Jemison's map in ways that preserve the boundaries and locations of Indigenous lands, other Indigenous literatures map in ways that preserve the relationships between or constituting places. The weavers of certain early nineteenth-century Mohegan wood-splint baskets adorned them with pink and green four-lobed medallions and arcing stockades lined with dots.[16] To the untrained eye, such motifs can seem solely decorative, but in fact they have cartographic valences. The stockade is a Mohegan symbol for the Trail of Life motif; it recalls the east–west journey of the sun and spirits as well as the east–west journey made by some parts of the Mohegan community when they left their nation's lands in what had become Connecticut in order to help found a new Native nation and refuge, Brothertown. Thus such baskets map a relationship between two geographically separated parts of Mohegan and, in linking them to the reliably cyclical circulations of the sun and the spirit, suggest their enduring connection.

Similarly, *Life of Black Hawk, or Mà-ka-tai-me-she-kià-kiàk* (1833) relates that Black Hawk's great-grandfather led the Sauk nation westward from the Great Lakes after receiving instruction from the Great Spirit. They arrived at "a village near Green Bay" and

> held a council with the Foxes [Meskwaki], and a national treaty of friendship and alliance was concluded upon. The Foxes abandoned their village and joined the Sacs … [T]hey soon became as one band or nation of people … [After a period on the Ouisconsin River, t]hey all descended Rock river, drove the Kaskaskias from the country, and commenced the erection of their village, determined never to leave it. At this village I was born.[17]

This portion of Black Hawk's *Life* maps the original homelands of the Sauk nation; the historic routes of their migration to the Rock River, a tributary of the Mississippi River in present-day Illinois; their geographic and communal convergence with the Meskwaki; and their settlement in the principal village, Saukenak. The text identifies Saukenak as both Black Hawk's natal home and a sacred refuge for a combined people. When subsequent portions of Black Hawk's *Life* describe the nation's temporary and forced departures from Saukenak and citizens' persistent determination to return, what results is a textual mapping placing Saukenak at the center. The position of Saukenak at the map's center is accentuated not only by Black Hawk's willingness to wage war for it but by Sauk women's resolve in returning and planting corn, even when their homes were destroyed by white squatters, their fields fenced, and all that remained were "small patches" upon which to "raise something for our children to subsist upon."[18] In mapping the historic routes to and forced removals from this central place, Black Hawk's *Life* honors and preserves its sacred importance and counters US expansionist cartography that identify this place and others as something other than Sauk territory. Black Hawk's *Life*, Jemison's *Narrative*, and the Mohegan basket demonstrate that, when Indigenous texts map, they can also document and animate relationships within and between places and communities. Doing so complements the work of other genres of doing, like narrating, and serves the presents and futures of Native peoples.

To Teach

Another Indigenous American literary genre of doing is teaching. Native communities' oral literatures are largely recognized as imbued with teachings for all their citizens, both children and adults. In *The Truth About Stories: A Native Memoir*, Thomas King contends that "the truth about stories is that's all we are."[19] In a key example, he demonstrates that creation stories, whether Native or non-Native, teach fundamental ways of understanding and interacting with the world. Comparing the Judeo-Christian creation story of an omnipotent and solitary god who punishes his human creations, Adam and Eve, for disobedience with an Indigenous creation story of a woman named Charm whose impetuous curiosity results in the cocreation of the earth by her, water animals, and her twin children on the back of a turtle, he wonders, "What if the creation story in Genesis had featured a flawed deity who was understanding and sympathetic rather than autocratic and rigid? Someone who, in the process of creation, found herself lost from time to time and in need of advice, someone who was willing to accept a little help with more difficult decisions?"[20] His questions imply that cultures listening to and adhering to Indigenous stories like the one he tells about Charm learn lessons about flexibility, humility, nonhierarchical leadership, and partnership with human and nonhuman beings, and that these lessons are structural to their communities.

Oral Indigenous literatures can also teach new lessons to audiences outside of a community. In 1781, the Cherokee diplomat Nanye'hi gave a speech to American treaty commissioners led by General Nathanael Greene. Nanye'hi had gained the status of Ghigua (Beloved Woman) by demonstrating leadership and wisdom, and she showcased those qualities in her talk, recorded in the treaty commission proceedings:

We did never concern in the [for]mer Treaty, which has been broken, but we do
in this, and on our account, who are your Mothers, let it never [be] broken. You
know Women are always looked upon as nothing; but we are your Mothers;
you are our sons. Our cry [is] all for Peace; let it continue because we are Your
Mothers. This Peace must last forever. Let your Womens sons be Ours, and let
our sons be yours. Let your Women hear our Words.[21]

Her speech instructs the treaty commissioners to recognize that women are
significant because they are mothers. The mothers of both nations, Nanye'hi
indicates, demand peace and they will therefore accept the men of both
nations as their shared sons. She structures unity through women's bodies,
maternity, and investment in enduring peace, making Cherokee-US diplomacy a merging of families and reciprocities. War and conflict would be akin
to fratricide, a selfish and unnatural act. Her words teach her audience about
nation-to-nation bonds and obligations and conclude by appealing to the
white American women to "hear" the force of the Cherokee women's message as well.

Mohegan minister and leader Samson Occom's *A Sermon Preached at the
Execution of Moses Paul, an Indian* (1772) teaches a mixed Native and non-
Native audience. His sermon, which went through numerous printed editions throughout New England and beyond, segments and re-segments the
"great concourse of people" attending to his words and explicates the
biblical passage Romans 6:23: "For the wages of sin is death; but the gift
of God is eternal life through Jesus Christ our Lord." In the beginning, he
urges Christians to pray for Moses Paul's spiritual salvation and non-
Christians to acknowledge Paul's crime stems from universal human
"frailty."[22] Next, he addresses everyone and insists all sin and all can be
saved. Toward the end, he addresses Paul directly: "You are the bone of my
bone, and flesh of my flesh."[23] Though Paul's execution is imminent, Occom
reassures him that there is still time to repent and ascend to heaven. Eternal
life, Occom explains to Paul specifically and all indirectly, "is offered upon
free terms": "He that hath no money may come; he that hath no righteous-
ness, no goodness may come, the call is to poor undone sinners; the call is not
to the righteous, but sinners calling them to repentance."[24] Occom then turns
briefly to ministers, enjoining them to "combine together" and call upon all
their followers to "rise up against sin and satan," and finally concludes by
addressing "*My poor kindred*," the "Indians," and exhorts them to abjure
alcohol. Drunkenness is the foolish act of rational beings, as it lowers
humanity beneath "beasts" and "devils": "He disfigures every part of him,
both soul and body, which was made after the Image of God."[25] Occom's
sermon parses his audience and presents targeted observations about the

implications of the opening passage from Romans. As listeners and readers understand his lessons for them and for others, all of the lessons, including those addressed to others, recohere to emphasize the main point of universal sin and universal salvation, but with different valances for different audiences. Native, Black, impoverished, and otherwise oppressed and disregarded persons receive lessons about their capacity for rationality and self-determination, about their divine creation, and about the equal merit of their natures and souls. Complacent white Christians receive messages about the falsity and hypocrisy of an exclusive Christianity and about their complicity in sinfulness through injustices enacted on their neighbors, especially in providing alcohol to Native peoples.

When Indigenous literatures teach, they showcase the established and emergent knowledge and values of a particular community. They reveal how a community understands its complicated and competing obligations to its members as well as the larger world, including nonhuman beings. In early America, they could provide guides to all peoples, Native and non-Native, for how to respond to rapidly and radically shifting colonial contexts. In *Why Indigenous Literatures Matter*, Daniel Heath Justice posits that we should value Indigenous stories because of their capacity to teach. What they teach are urgent lessons in how to be human, how to be good relatives and good ancestors, and how to live together, none of which are obvious or easy: "if ... 'human' is a learned process rather than simply a state of being, so, too, is kinship."[26]

To Express

Recording, narrating, mapping, teaching: such genres of doing may suggest that Indigenous American literatures are universally earnest and practical, rather than emotive and creative. Not so. Wit and artfulness suffuse these literatures, and another thing they do is express emotion and imagination. Non-scriptive texts utilizing bead- and quill-work and moose-hair embroidery, for example, may express delight and reverence for the natural world through representational and nonrepresentational combinations of pattern, texture, and color. Many Kānaka Maoli, or Indigenous Hawaiians, inked tattoos on their skin. The design and placement of these tattoos might express menace, triumph, or pride in one's skills as a warrior. Just as knowledge of Incan khipu forms and styles assists in analyzing colonial Andean literatures, understanding how, why, and when particular nations and cultures used non-scriptive literatures to express emotions can guide the reading of scriptive texts authored by these same communities.

Sometimes, however, Indigenous American literatures wear their hearts on their sleeves. Pequot activist and minister William Apess's *An Indian's Looking-Glass for the White Man* (1833) conveys rage and disgust at the genocidal and hypocritical predations of white Christian nations upon Native ones. In a powerful passage, worth quoting in full to display how each sentence helps build toward a crescendo of righteous fury and personal dignity, Apess guides his reader in creating an image of the world's population gathered together:

> Assemble all nations together in your imagination, and then let the whites be seated amongst them, and then let us look for the whites, and I doubt not it would be hard finding them; for to the rest of the nations, they are still but a handful. Now suppose these skins were put together, and each skin had its national crimes written upon it – which skin do you think would have the greatest? I will ask one question more. Can you charge the Indians with robbing a nation almost of their whole Continent, and murdering their women and children, and then depriving the remainder of their lawful rights, that nature and God require them to have? And to cap the climax, rob another nation to till their grounds, and welter out their days under the lash with hunger and fatigue under the scorching rays of a burning sun? I should look at all the skins, and I know that when I cast my eye upon that white skin, and if I saw those crimes written upon it, I should enter my protest against it immediately, and cleave to that which is more honorable. And I can tell you that I am satisfied with the manner of my creation, fully – whether others are or not.[27]

Apess uses the first person and directly addresses his audience. Though white skin and white nations remain separate from the "you" he addresses, that direct address shifts his fury away from a distant and historical target and aims it at his audience, positioning it as both jury and criminal in a court of moral judgment. His horror over the severity of the misdeeds of colonization and slavery – atrocities the United States continued for decades if not a century or more after the publication of *Indian's Looking-Glass* – sets in stark relief his "satisf[action] with the manner of [his] creation." It is better to be oppressed and despised as an inferior race by thieves and murderers than to be a prideful citizen of a despotic nation.

The poetry of Ojibwe author Jane Johnston Schoolcraft (Bamewawagezhikaquay) may at times express rage but more often evinces sorrow, joy, and love of her home and family. When writing in English, she consistently rhymes and employs varied stanza lengths, meters, and figurative language; when writing in Anishinaabemowin, she seems beguiled by how this polysynthetic language, in which smaller morphemes are creatively assembled into long words, produces echoing resonances of sight and sound through a poem. Thus the language alters not only what she writes but the style and

form of how she writes it. A series of poems she wrote in 1827, upon the
sudden death of her two-year-old son William, combine these variations in her
style even as they express again and again her immense grief over her child's
loss and her desire for consolation. In one example, entitled "Resignation,"
she writes:

> How hard to teach the heart, opprest with grief,
> Amid gay, worldly scenes, to find relief;
> And the long cherish'd bliss we had in view,
> To banish from the mind – where first it grew!
> But Faith, in time, can sweetly soothe the soul,
> And Resignation hold a mind control;
> The mind may then resume a proper tone.
> And calmly think on hopes forever flown.[28]

This poem meditates on how her consolation might emerge through emotional
"control" rather than "banish[ment]" of remembered "bliss." Once she
establishes "Resignation" through Christian "Faith," she can "resume" lin-
gering with the ghosts of her "hopes." Pulling on both the skilled soundplay of
her Anishinaabemowin poetry and the forms of English-language poetry, the
poem dramatizes the process. In peppering her lines with consonance – the first
line's "h" and "t" sounds and the seventh line's "m," the alliterations of
"sweetly soothe the soul" and "forever flown" – she anticipates through the
repetition of sounds a time when she can repeatedly and "calmly" think on
lost possibilities. Yet, by breaking her thoughts into a series of iambic pentameter
couplets rife with punctuation, she suggests an impatience with her lurching if
predictable progress. Texts like Schoolcraft's demonstrate that, just like many
other traditions, Indigenous literatures express emotions, imaginations, and
ideas that may, on the one hand, feel intimately distinctive to a person or
community and, on the other, invite conversation and understanding.

To Survive

One final thing that Indigenous American literatures do is survive. Non-
Native archives and books are rife with Native texts that, due to their
preservation by settler colonists, survive and resist efforts to eradicate
Native presence. Often collected under duress and in order to validate settler
colonial claims to territory and resources, such texts nevertheless remain an
important repository of Indigenous voices and experiences. In 1624, John
Smith published a record of Powhatan words and their English equivalents at
the end of *The Generall Historie of Virginia*. In the early 1700s, Spanish
officials in Florida circulated letters containing Apalachee refuges' narratives

of violence and enslavement during a war between Spanish and English forces in the southeast. The Hudson's Bay Company Archives houses Peter Fidler's 1801 hand-drawn paper map of the Rocky Mountains and upper Missouri River. Fidler's map is not an original but rather a copy of a map drawn in the snow by Blackfeet leader Ac ko mik ki, to which Fidler has appended his phonetic translations of Blackfeet names and information about Indigenous populations in the region. Mary Rowlandson's *Sovereignty and Goodness of God* (1682) is replete with teachings about how to find food and engage in the exchange of labor and goods in Nipmuc territory during a period of scarcity. The Black preacher John Marrant's 1785 conversion narrative recounts Cherokee expressions of curiosity about his emotional piety during his captivity by them. Such texts, often penned by or nested within the writings of settler colonists, are examples of Indigenous literatures that survive. It may be easy to dismiss them as representations of Native peoples rather than the creations of Native agency, however partial, masked, and altered by others. Yet, as Michael Witgen reasons, "The evidence capturing the Native perspective ... is often readily available. This is not necessarily a matter of reading European texts against the grain. It is, rather, more simply a matter of reading texts written by Europeans without privileging the[ir] fantasies of discovery."[29] When it comes to Indigenous literatures that survive, readers can carefully and ethically excavate what other genres of doing – recording, narrating, mapping, teaching, expressing – their presence performs.

Indigenous American literatures do many things. They record. They narrate. They map. They teach. They express. They survive. Yet they do other things as well, including pray, evaluate, worship, translate, persuade, and communicate. They are also multifunctional. Examples in this chapter have shown texts engaging in narration to teach, creating maps to record, and so on. Approaching Indigenous American literatures through genres of doing should not produce rigid classifications. Instead, these genres may aid readers in identifying and exploring cross-form, cross-temporal, and cross-cultural resonances. This holds true for considering Native texts from multiple traditions alongside each other and also in the case of Native and non-Native texts. Finding resonances across nations and practices should not blind scholars to textual and cultural specificities, however. As Chadwick Allen insists, it is imperative that comparative and juxtapositional readings focus on the "staging of purposeful Indigenous juxtapositions" that retain rather than ignore "local specificity."[30] Indigenous American literatures' genres of doing may help stage questions and perspectives on what and how these literatures do things for their creators, communities, and audiences, past, present, and future.

Notes

1. Craig S. Womack, *Red on Red: Native Literary Separatism* (Minneapolis: University of Minnesota Press, 1999), 7.
2. Lisa Brooks, *The Common Pot: The Recovery of Native Space in the Northeast* (Minneapolis: University of Minnesota Press, 2008), 13, xxi; Matt Cohen, *The Networked Wilderness: Communicating in Early New England* (Minneapolis: University of Minnesota Press, 2009), especially 3–7, 29–49; Phillip H. Round, *Removable Type: Histories of the Book in Indian Country, 1663–1880* (Chapel Hill: University of North Carolina Press, 2010), 5.
3. Round, *Removable Type*, 5.
4. Penelope Myrtle Kelsey, *Reading the Wampum: Essays on Hodinöhsö:ni' Visual Code and Epistemological Recovery* (Syracuse: Syracuse University Press, 2014), xii–xviii.
5. Carolyn R. Miller, "Genre As Social Action," *Quarterly Journal of Speech* 70 (1984): 151.
6. Scott Richard Lyons, "Rhetorical Sovereignty: What Do American Indians Want from Writing?," *College Composition and Communication* 51, no. 3 (2000): 447–468, 462.
7. Ibid., 449.
8. Daniel Heath Justice, "'Go Away Water!': Kinship, Criticism and the Decolonization Imperative," in Craig S. Womack, Daniel Heath Justice, and Christopher B. Teuton, eds., *Reasoning Together: The Native Critics Collective* (Norman: University of Oklahoma Press, 2008), 150.
9. Felipe Guaman Poma de Ayala, *The First New Chronicle and Good Government: On the History of the World and the Incas up to 1615*, trans. Roland Hamilton (Austin: University of Texas Press, 2009); Galen Brokaw, "*Khipu* Numeracy and Alphabetic Literacy in the Andes: Felipe Guaman Poma de Ayala's *Nueva Corónica y Buen Gobierno*," *Colonial Latin American Review* 11, no. 2 (2002): 275–303. See also "The Guaman Poma Website," at Det Kongelige Bibliotek: www.kb.dk/permalink/2006/poma/info/en/front page.htm.
10. Hendrick Aupaumut, "A Short Narration of My Last Journey to the Western Country," in Paul Lauter, ed., *Heath Anthology of American Literature*, vol. A, 7th ed. (Boston: Houghton Mifflin, 2013), 905.
11. For the Codex Zouche-Nuttall, see the British Museum holding: www .britishmuseum.org/research/collection_online/collection_object_details.aspx? objectId=662517&partId=1. A digital edition of the Codex Mendoza is available online: https://codicemendoza.inah.gob.mx/inicio.php?lang=english.
12. Coosaponakeesa (Mary Musgrove Mathews Bosomworth), "Memorial (1747)," in Lisa L. Moore, Joanna Brooks, and Caroline Wigginton, eds., *Transatlantic Feminisms in the Age of Revolutions* (New York: Oxford University Press, 2012), 122.
13. For a contemporary example of an Indigenous author using colonialist legal rhythms to structure a literary text, see Layli Long Soldier, *Whereas: Poems* (Minneapolis: Graywolf Press, 2017).
14. James Seaver, *A Narrative of the Life of Mrs. Mary Jemison*, ed. June Namias (Norman: University of Oklahoma Press, 1992), 120. Jemison or perhaps Seaver

downplays her canny skills during this council. Jemison refused a set acreage determined by a survey and instead demanded that natural boundaries be used to designate her reserved land. US governmental negotiators believed that her plot would come to no more than 150 acres; it was almost 18,000. See James Hadden Smith, *History of Livingston County, New York, with Illustrations and Biographical Sketches of Some of Its Prominent Men and Pioneers* (Syracuse, NY: D. Mason & Co., 1881), 75.

15. Seaver, *A Narrative of the Life of Mrs. Mary Jemison*, 156.
16. See the image "Mohegan Wood-Splint Basket," in Kristina Bross and Hilary E. Wyss, eds., *Early Native Literacies in New England: A Documentary and Critical Anthology* (Amherst: University of Massachusetts Press, 2008), 51.
17. Black Hawk, *Life of Black Hawk, or Mà-ka-tai-me-she-kià-kiàk: Dictated by Himself*, ed. J. Gerald Kennedy (New York: Penguin, 2008), 12–13.
18. Ibid., 60.
19. Thomas King, *The Truth About Stories: A Native Memoir* (Minneapolis: University of Minnesota Press, 2008), 2. King does not name the tradition from which he takes the story, but a version of it is shared by many Indigenous peoples of the eastern half of North America, often referred to in Indigenous communities as Turtle Island.
20. Ibid., 27.
21. Nancy Ward (Nanye'hi), "Speech to the U.S. Treaty Commissioners (1781)," in Moore, Brooks, and Wigginton, *Transatlantic Feminisms*, 180.
22. Samson Occom, *The Collected Writings of Samson Occom, Mohegan: Leadership and Literature in Eighteenth-Century Native America*, ed. Joanna Brooks (New York: Oxford University Press, 2006), 178.
23. Ibid., 188.
24. Ibid., 189.
25. Ibid., 191–192.
26. Daniel Heath Justice, *Why Indigenous Literatures Matter* (Ottawa: Wilfrid Laurier University Press, 2017), 74.
27. William Apess, "An Indian's Looking-Glass for the White Man," in Bernd C. Peyer, ed., *American Indian Nonfiction: An Anthology of Writings, 1760s–1930s* (Norman: University of Oklahoma Press, 2007), 76–77.
28. Jane Johnston Schoolcraft, *The Sound the Stars Make Rushing Through the Sky: The Writings of Jane Johnston Schoolcraft*, ed. Robert Dale Parker (Philadelphia: University of Pennsylvania Press, 2007), 125.
29. Michael Witgen, *An Infinity of Nations: How the Native New World Shaped Early North America* (Philadelphia: University of Pennsylvania Press, 2012), 15.
30. Chadwick Allen, *Trans-Indigenous: Methodologies for Global Native Literary Studies* (Minneapolis: University of Minnesota Press, 2012), xix.

13

ALLISON BIGELOW

Colonial Latin America

Writing in 1624, the English adventurer John Smith (1580–1631) described "three of the foulest acts" recently committed in the Bermuda colony. In one example, a rooster owned by a man accused of "buggering a Sow" followed the farmer's lead with another pig, "so frequently tread[ing] the Pigge as if it had been one of his Hens, that the pigge languished and died within a while after, and then the Cocke resorted to the very same Sow (that this fellow was accused for) in the very same manner." As a consequence of cross-species sexual activity, Smith noted that a monstrous two-headed chicken was hatched "about the same time."[1]

Three years later, Bahia-born Franciscan friar Vicente do Salvador (1564–ca. 1636) described a similar crossing of the species line in Pernambuco. Salvador related the story, told to him by "uma mulher de crédito" (a woman of credit), in which a new mother awoke to find a snake sucking at her life-giving body. The snake nursed at her chest "com tamta brandura que ela cuidava ser a criança" (with such tenderness that she thought it was her child). After witnessing the act for several nights, the woman told her husband about it. The next night, he lay in waiting for the snake. When it arrived, he killed it, putting an end to the serpent's "engano" (deceit).[2]

Passages like these lend themselves to comparative analysis. Smith and Salvador wrote at the same time about similar issues of human–animal relationships, but they did so in different regions of the Americas, in different languages, and without knowledge of each other's existence. Their representations of life in Bermuda and Brazil, two extended Caribbean regions that were dramatically and forever transformed by the same large-scale socioeconomic and biopolitical forces, including the transatlantic slave trade, Columbian exchange, and colonial violence, invoke similar stories of female victims of nature gone awry.[3] Yet their texts reach different moralizing and historical conclusions. Smith suggests that Captain Nathaniel Butler's (ca. 1577–ca. 1639) mismanagement led to bestiality, monstrous births, and crimes like rape, sodomy, and murder, while in Salvador's domestic scene,

218

paternal power excises the Satanic snake from the marital bower. By putting Smith and Salvador's similarities and differences in dialogue, comparative analysis can reveal insights into the historical and symbolic elements embedded in both texts.

At different moments and to different degrees, this framework of similarity and difference has influenced important comparative hemispheric scholarship. As a contribution to this volume's reflection on the history and future of methods in early American literary studies, and to interrogate the extent to which texts from Latin America might be productively brought into conversation with works from North America, spaces that were already connected through Caribbean ports, this chapter analyzes major critical paradigms and methodological approaches to colonial hemispheric studies. Early North America was home to a diverse linguistic landscape, including Indigenous languages that ranged from Abenaki and Catawba on the Eastern Seaboard to Sioux and Tunica languages in the Midwest and Mississippi Valley, as well as the languages of rival European empires, such as Dutch, French, German, and Spanish. Because the English and Iberian empires carved up the largest territorial and linguistic stretches of the New World, I focus on overlaps and divergences in Anglo and Iberian American literatures.[4] While histories of the "hemispheric turn" often begin with Herbert Bolton (1870–1953) and trace his influence through works like Louis Hanke's *Do the Americas Have a Common History?* (1964), this chapter prioritizes scholarship published within the past decade and, in doing so, provides examples from primary sources that readers of this volume could use in future research projects.[5]

Comparative Frameworks in the Literatures of the Americas

In the years leading up to the Columbian quincentenary, and in the wake of that monumental moment of reflection, comparative scholarship has enriched our understanding of the deep interconnections and critical differences between and among diverse regions, literary publics, and linguistic communities of the early Americas. Writing in 1990, a quarter-century after Hanke interrogated the limits of hemispheric history, Gustavo Pérez Firmat convened a group of scholars to ask *Do the Americas Have a Common Literature?* In his introductory essay, Pérez Firmat identified four main threads of comparative scholarship: generic, genetic, appositional, and mediative.[6]

These four permeable methods continue to inform comparative hemispheric scholarship, in part because recent work emphasizes how a focus on the Spanish Americas, as the literary scholars Kirsten Silva Gruesz and Rodrigo Lazo explain in a special issue of *Early American Literature* (2018), "represents an *orientation*" rather than "a new subfield or a prescription for a single methodology" (emphasis in the original). As they go on to note, attending to Spanish-language publications offers a "transtemporal" way to continue to shift the field "away from its original New England and English-language focus." Because the United States is the world's second-largest Spanish-speaking country, and because Latinx student enrollments are increasing throughout colleges and universities in the country, Gruesz and Lazo argue that focusing on the Spanish Americas can encourage new directions in research and teaching by "calling forth a differently usable past appropriate to contemporary conditions" – one in which the present shapes our study of the past and the past sheds light on our world today.[7]

While Spanish America has played a central, if at times reductive or oppositional, role in comparative scholarship, hemispheric research on early Anglo and Iberian American literatures includes works written and performed in languages like Aimara, *bozal*, Nahuatl, Quechua, and Portuguese, as well as comparisons of Indigenous literacies, Afro-Indigenous contact, and transpacific exchanges.[8] This more expanded approach helps to address a core tension in comparative studies. Despite well-intended efforts to read across borders – a kind of transnationalism before nation-statehood – hemispheric scholarship that rotates upon a two-point, Anglo-Iberian axis occasionally reinforces the kinds of binaries that it seeks to complicate, such as North and South, or Protestant and Catholic.

In contrast, hemispheric frameworks treat Spanish, an imperial instrument when viewed from the perspective of sixteenth- and seventeenth-century actors, and a persecuted language when viewed from the perspective of the contemporary United States, as one of many early American languages. It does not take pride of place. Nor does its current role in US scholarly and public life influence research agendas about the colonial era. The intellectual stakes, theoretical underpinnings, political commitments, and classroom practices of comparative inter-American methods therefore differ from Spanish American orientations, although the two models could productively converge in the future. Toward that end, and to communicate the possibilities and pitfalls of comparative scholarship to early Americanists who might wish to incorporate these methods and orientations into their research and teaching, this chapter discusses primary sources from Spanish and Portuguese America, as well as secondary works about hemispheric issues, including Indigenous languages, narratives of "discovery," and African diasporic voices.

The works surveyed in what follows reflect current conversations about modes of comparison – a term that scholars across the disciplines are revising. To that end, Eliga Gould, David Kazanjian, and Juliet Hooker, assessing comparative research in Atlantic history, political theory, and literary studies, have analyzed how the binaries created by traditional comparative scholarship contribute to diverse methodological challenges in early inter-American studies. In an influential essay on intertwined anglophone and hispanophone Atlantic societies, Gould argues that conventional comparisons, which study "societies that are geographically or temporally remote" and tend to "accept national boundaries as fixed, to take the distinctiveness of their subjects as a given, and to assume that the subjects being compared are, in fact, comparable," cannot account for ever-shifting forms of exchange in the early Atlantic world. Kazanjian, studying Atlantic regions whose actors never came into contact, makes a similar point. Because comparison traditionally "presumes a stable and objective point of comparison . . . as well as units of comparison," comparative scholarship can flatten the complexities of aesthetics, ideas, and cultures as they shift over time. Hooker extends the issue, finding that the evaluative structure of comparison often "becomes an exercise in ranking" that constructs the kinds of "differences it purports to ask" and distracts us from the substantive questions that we ought to analyze. All three scholars therefore present alternative modes of comparison, entangled (Gould), appositional (Kazanjian), and juxtapositional (Hooker), which align with Pérez Firmat's models of mediative, appositional, and generic scholarship.[9]

The similar work conducted across the disciplines, although called by different names, suggests how comparative hemispheric research can address what the literary scholar Eric Slauter identifies as "a trade deficit" between Atlantic literature and history, wherein literary scholars "import more from historians than they export to them," and even those "who believe they are doing historical work" find themselves "out of touch with what counts as advanced work in history." [10] Unlike in Atlantic studies, colonial Latin American history, especially in Mesoamerica, has long been informed by textual analysis of Native-language sources, making almost indistinguishable historicist research by literary scholars and discursive analysis by historians, to say nothing of work in ethnohistory, religion, and visual or material cultures.[11] A comparative hemispheric approach to early American literature – including oral traditions, literacies, and writing systems – necessarily engages similarities and differences across texts and contexts. Because historians and literary scholars of Latin America use the same tools to negotiate similar methodological issues, such as fragmented colonial archives, inter-American scholarship might offer a solution to the "trade deficit" problem in Atlantic studies. In what follows, I outline the sources and approaches that enable this critical multidisciplinary research.

Generic Comparisons

The first approach, generic, takes shared textual properties, aesthetic modes, or thematic concepts, such as religious women's poetry, representations of Indigenous communities, or theories of racial mixture, and situates them within inter-American contexts. For example, a generic comparison of colonial Iberian linguistic practices would analyze how writers surveyed Indigenous languages in, say, Mexico and Brazil, and how those writers used linguistic elements to make larger claims about Indigenous cultures, practices, and worldviews. Such a study might begin in 1576, when the Portuguese historian Pero de Magalhães Gândavo (ca. 1540–ca. 1580) outlined a one-to-one relationship between Indigenous alphabets and civilizations. Gândavo reported that coastal languages belonged to the same family, which "carece de três letras – scilicet, não se acha nela F, nem L, nem R, coisa digna de espanto, porque assim não têm Fé, nem Lei, nem Rei; e desta maneira vivem sem Justiça e desordenadamente" (lacks three letters – namely, F, L, and R, which is worthy of notice because they have neither Faith, nor Law, nor Rex; and in this way they live without Justice and in disorder).[12]

Eleven years later, the Portuguese scientist Gabriel Soares de Souza (ca. 1540s–1591) went beyond Gândavo's claim, arguing that the lack of the letter "F" prefigured failed missionary efforts in Tupinambá communities because "não têm fé em nenhuma coisa que adorem nem os nascidos entre os cristãos e doutrinados pelos padres da Companhia não têm fé em Deus Nosso Senhor, nem têm verdade nem lealdade a nenhuma pessoa que lhe faça bem" (they do not have Faith in anything that they adore. Those born among Christians and educated by Jesuit priests have no faith in God our Father. They do not know truth nor do they have loyalty to any person who does them good).[13] In the seventeenth century, these arguments were recirculated by the sugar planter Ambrósio Fernandes Brandão (1555–1618), author of Os diálogos das grandezas do Brasil (1618?), and the criollo historian Vicente do Salvador, quoted at the beginning of this chapter.[14] These authors believed that letters and their sounds revealed broader truths about Indigenous lifeways and worldmaking.

Writers throughout the Americas observed that Indigenous languages lacked phonetic features common to Indo-European tongues, but they reached different conclusions about the relationship between language and custom. The Franciscan friar Diego de Landa (1524–1579), bishop of Yucatán, observed that, because Yucatec Maya did not use the letters D, F, G, Q, R, or S, many words sounded alike, and Spanish speakers struggled to write and pronounce them. For this reason, they added letters to distinguish words like *tan* (chalk) from *than* (speech), today written as *t'aan*.[15] Like writers in Brazil, de Landa compared the local language with his own; but unlike his Brazilian contemporaries, he did not convert linguistic evidence into a larger thesis about the state of Native society, nor was he influenced by authors who did so. These overlaps and divergences offer opportunities for further research, such as the role of religious orders in shaping colonial assessments of Native languages and differences in Spanish and Portuguese approaches to the collection and interpretation of linguistic data.

Recent examples of generic scholarship include Hooker's *Theorizing Race in the Americas* (2017), which charts a "hemispheric genealogy of racial thought" through the work of intellectuals and politicians like Frederick Douglass (1818–1895), Domingo Faustino Sarmiento (1811–1888), W. E. B. Du Bois (1868–1963), and José Vasconcelos Calderón (1882–1959), and the literary critic Lisa Voigt's *Writing Captivity in the Early Atlantic World* (2012), which analyzes English-, Spanish-, and Portuguese-language sources to show how information gathered by prisoners and captives shaped imperial operations on the ground and in imaginative terms.[16]

Genetic Comparisons

The second approach, genetic, traces causal relations between specific publications, discursive forms, and readership communities across geopolitical and linguistic lines. For instance, a genetic study might analyze the imaginative chronology through which the English polymath and imperial apologist Richard Hakluyt (1553–1616) excerpted portions of the *The Historie of Cambria, now called Wales* (1584), written by the Anglican clergyman David Powel (ca. 1549/1552–1598), to revise the story of American "discovery" such that "it is manifest that the countrey was by Britaines discovered long before Columbus led any Spanyards thither."[17] To support his claim, Hakluyt juxtaposed Powel's work with the words of the Spanish historian Francisco López de Gómara (ca. 1511–ca. 1566), who described wooden and metallic crucifixes in Cozumel ("Acuzamil") and Campeche ("Xicalanco"). After seeing the pre-Columbian crosses, "arguyen algunos que muchos Españoles se fueron a esta tierra quando la destruction de España, hecha por los Moros en tiempo del rey don Rodrigo" (some argue that many Spaniards came to this land after the destruction of Spain by the Moors in the time of King Rodrigo). López de Gómara's secondhand arguments fashioned a pre-Christian precedent for Spanish colonialism by linking the conquista and reconquista. In Hakluyt's hands, though, the passage evidenced an English triumph that predated Spanish occupation, one of many rhetorical strategies that anglophone authors used to legitimize the English empire and dismiss Spanish claims of New World possession.[18]

Indigenous writers like El Inca Garcilaso de la Vega (1539–1616) and Felipe Guaman Poma de Ayala (ca. 1535–ca. 1616) also revised the narrative of Colón's "discovery," although they did so for different reasons and with different evidentiary forms.[19] According to El Inca, around 1484, one Alonso Sánchez left his home in Huelva, in the southernmost corner of Andalucía, passed through the Canary Islands, and was shipwrecked on the island "que ahora llaman Santo Domingo" (which they now call Santo Domingo). Enacting this framed narration some 130 years later, El Inca describes how Sánchez and five survivors eventually returned to Spain and told their story to a Genovese man, Cristóbal Colón (1451–1506). When they passed away, in Colón's home, the Admiral resolved to give "el nuevo mundo y sus riquezas a España" (the New World and its wealth to Spain), now inscribed in his rhyming coat of arms ("A Castilla y a León / Nuevo Mundo dio Colón" [To Castilla and León / the New World was given by Colón]). Both Hakluyt and El Inca refer readers to López de Gómara, but only El Inca explains why it was important to say what the Spanish historian did not: López de Gómara's distance from the time and place of events left him to rely on imperfect historical accounts rather than the authoritative family networks that El Inca commanded in "mi tierra" (my land).[20]

Over time, writers like the Puritan minister Cotton Mather (1663–1728) cited El Inca's decentering of Colón as proof of shaky Spanish claims to the New World. Then, Mather traced Indigenous toponyms like Nahumkeick to Hebrew roots rather than Algonquian etymologies, to show that Native peoples were not really native to the Americas.[21] By charting how authors across the Americas retell the story of Columbian "discovery," genetic scholarship reveals how the same authorities and tropes are used to achieve different political ends at particular historical moments.

Recent literary examples of genetic work include Emily García's (2017) study of Spanish-language publications in revolutionary Philadelphia, a critical meeting place for anglophone, hispanophone, and francophone ideas, and Anna Brickhouse's *Unsettlement of America* (2015), which traces how the stories of Indigenous actors, as told by authors like El Inca, were retranslated and repackaged by Anglo-American writers in order "to consolidate U.S. legal ascendancy over the indigenous lands of North America" at critical moments in nineteenth-century US history.[22]

Appositional Comparisons

The third approach, appositional, resembles the juxtapositional practices of generic criticism but does not identify a causal connection between texts. The readings of cross-species contact in Smith's *Generall Historie* and Salvador's *Historia do Brasil* that introduce this chapter illustrate an example of appositional scholarship. Other examples include the literary scholar Jillian Sayre's (2018) analysis of "the necropolitics of national feeling" in contemporaneous works from New England, Philadelphia, and newly independent viceregal centers of Latin America and David Kazanjian's *On the Brink of Freedom* (2016), which analyzes sovereignty and political movements in Yucatán and Angola. Anti-slavery proponents in these regions spoke different languages and operated separately, but their beliefs and experiences were shaped by a common Atlantic history of extraction and exploitation.[23]

Mediative Comparisons

The final approach in Pérez Firmat's system, mediative, treats texts that focus on inter-American issues or historical actors who lived hemispheric lives. The classic example is José Martí's (1853–1893) *Nuestra América*, which was published almost simultaneously in New York (January 10, 1891) and Mexico (January 30, 1891). Martí's essay uses the independence movement in still-colonial Cuba as a philosophical departure point for rethinking hemispheric connections and disjunctions and for articulating a curious racial logic in newly liberated Latin American countries. Martí declares, as only a writer who is not Indigenous or Afro-descendant can, "No hay odio de razas, porque no hay razas" (There can be no racial hatred because there is no such thing as race).[24]

Mediative studies have generally focused on actors and ideas that crossed national and linguistic lines. Future work could also consider spaces that were colonized by successive waves of European empires – that is, people whose lives became mediative by virtue of conquest. Such was the case of Jacob Jeosua Bueno Enriques, a Jewish resident of Santo Domingo. In 1658 or 1659, Bueno Enriques and silversmith Domingo Francisco were captured by French pirates and brought to Jamaica, a Spanish colony that was conquered in 1655 by Oliver Cromwell (1599–1658) in the name of the English Protectorate. During Francisco's visit to Bueno Enriques's home in Punta de Cagoe (Port Royal), a Spanish corruption of the Taíno toponym Caguay, Bueno Enriques asked his friend about island affairs.[25] Francisco described a copper mine that had been operational until the English conquest but was, in his estimation, still in good condition ("estaua en tiempo de los espagnioles pᵃ fabricar y quanto auia echio la esperiensa y la allaua buena"). Around 1661, Bueno Enriques traveled to London and met with an English-speaking Jewish man, Manoel da Fonseca, who worked for the Spanish ambassador Carlos de Batteville (1605–1670). The case drew the attention of Lord

Bellamy ("Melor Belemi"), who was eager for parliamentary officials to learn of copper deposits in the newly conquered colony. Bueno Enriques dictated his statement to one such official, offering to reveal sources of Jamaican copper in exchange for naturalization and the liberty to worship in the temple for him and his brothers, Joseph and Moises. He also sought new sources of wealth for himself: "q me daria negras bastantes pᵃ aser plantegas ho lo qᵉ yo quisiere" (that you give me enough Black women to make plantations or whatever I might want). With its multiple languages, religious networks, oceanic crossings, and gendered racial-economic exploitation, Bueno Enriques's story offers many possibilities for inter-American and transatlantic mediative analysis.[26]

In contrast, mediative texts by African diasporic writers explode categories like religious affiliations, cultural identities, and Atlantic worlds. For example, the transatlantic and hemispheric crossings of Olaudah Equiano (ca. 1745–1797) transport readers from Africa to Virginia and to England and from there to the francophone Mediterranean and Montserrat before landing in Philadelphia and Savannah, all in the first seven chapters of Equiano's twelve-chapter book.[27] Equiano's *Interesting Narrative* (1789), like the stories of Domingos Álvares (ca. 1709–ca. 1749/1750?) in Brazil and Juan Francisco Manzano (1797–1854) in Cuba, or the work of anti-slavery, anti-racist writers like Quobna Ottobah Cugoano (ca. 1757–ca. 1791), links him to hemispheric intellectual movements and cultural projects like Pan-Africanism.[28]

These voices force us to confront methodological challenges about categorization, identity, belonging, and the ways in which lived experience and the act of writing mediate these concerns. As the historian James H. Sweet argues, debates about Equiano's identity – namely, whether he was born in South Carolina or in Africa, and therefore whether he invented or drew from collective memory to write the opening chapter's account of the Middle Passage – represent a problematical but persistent scholarly effort to reduce complex cultural identities to binary terms, such as "African" (Igbo) or "American" (South Carolinian). The experiences of people like Equiano and Álvares, as mediated in first-person prose reports and documented in archival materials, instead reveal that "European taxonomies" could not "accommodate the complexities of African self-understandings or group imperatives."[29] Like the three other forms of comparison in Pérez Firmat's model, mediative scholarship not only puts categories like "English" and "Spanish," "African" and "American" into new light. It also invites us to rethink the colonialist assumptions that inform such classifications. As early American literary studies continues its slow shift away from New English philosophy and Puritan selves, interconnected forms of comparison – when performed in the ways outlined here – help us to escape from the binary categories that have long structured our field.

Comparison is not a panacea for these problems, but it can be part of the solution. The act of comparison, working in and between languages, requires literary scholars to slowly evaluate each word of a text and to situate particular discursive forms within contexts that take us into alternative archives and disciplines. Although comparativists continue to use the methods outlined by Pérez Firmat, we do so with an expanded corpus of sources from Indigenous, Africana, and Latinx communities. As demonstrated by the range of scholarly projects discussed in this chapter, these sources force us to address problems with traditional modes of comparison. To conclude, I briefly examine those problems and gesture toward critical new directions in hemispheric studies.

Conclusions

Technically, anything can be compared with anything else: medieval Middle Eastern poetry and contemporary francophone novels, the use of color in eighteenth-century Japanese silkscreens and *casta* paintings from colonial Latin America. The most valuable work, though, tells us something about the object of study that we could not learn without comparison. In colonial hemispheric studies, this value comes not only from our close readings of an expanded corpus but especially from our critical reckoning with methodological issues raised by those sources. For example, because of uneven colonial chronologies in Latin America (1492–1898) and British America (1607–1776), comparativists must think carefully about the dates that frame our research and conclusions, as well as the ideologies that undergird literary periodizations. Barbara Fuchs studies canonical texts in England and Spain to show how the traditional Hispanist periodization, which ends the *Siglo de Oro* with Cervantes in the early seventeenth century, marks "the beginning of the end for Spain," while a genealogy that highlights Shakespearean drama, printed in the same historical moment, evidences England's "incipient glory."[30] On the other side of the Atlantic, Sandra Gustafson explores the implications of periodization with a quiz that asks early Americanists to identify major historical and literary events of four traditional stopping points for the field – 1789, 1800, 1820, and 1830 – noting that there is "no answer for the 'right' date that could divide early from later American literature."[31] Selecting any of these years – or shaping the field around ideas like postcolonial colonialism – suggests particular aesthetic, cultural, philosophical, and political stakes.[32]

While literary scholars see the non-answers of periodization as productive intellectual points of departure, historians offer different responses to the problem of chronological asymmetry. John Huxtable Elliott's *Empires of the Atlantic World* (2006) accounts for the temporal separations of English and Spanish colonialisms by comparing similar moments in imperial history rather than similar eras. One cannot compare Mexico and Virginia in 1600, eighty years after the Spanish conquest of Tenochtitlan and seven years before the English imperial project began in Jamestown. Instead, he juxtaposes Spanish reports of 1519–1522 and English texts from the years 1607–1609, documenting how narrative similarities and differences invite us to revise traditional imperial historiographies of Iberian "conquest" and Anglo "commerce."[33]

Yet, as Elliott goes on to argue, despite similar rhetorical enactments of conquest, including legal justifications and negotiations with sovereign rulers Moctezuma (Montezuma) (ca. 1466–1520) and Wahunsenacawh (Wahusonacock) (1545–1618), the lettered accounts of Hernán Cortés (1485–1547) and Christopher Newport (1561–1616) reveal substantial differences in the experience of conquest. For example, at the time of the Spanish conquest, Tenochtitlan (Mexico City) was a major city, home to perhaps 150,000 residents, with approximately 500,000 people from different ethnic and linguistic groups living in the surrounding communities. Because of the Triple Alliance, a pre-Columbian agreement that united the cities of Tetzcoco, Tenochtitlan, and Tlacopan, ethnic Acolhuas, Nahuas, and Otomís were incorporated into Mexica imperial economic and political systems, including long-range metallic networks.[34] The pre-Columbian communities of Tsenacommacah (Eastern Virginia) likewise consisted of diverse ethnic groups, perhaps thirty in total, but these less concentrated polities operated under a paramount chiefdom, not an empire, and were united by a common Algonquian language. Although they, too, enjoyed long-range trade, coastal communities exchanged shell beads (*wampum*), not precious metals. According to Elliott, these two factors – Indigenous populations and mineral deposits – played determinative roles in Spanish and English colonial designs. Abundant mineral wealth that was processed by skilled Indigenous artisans who lived in densely populated lands "dictated an imperial strategy that had as its aim the bringing of Christianity and European-style 'civility' to these populations," while English imperialism, which used the same exploitative logic to justify its decisions, unfolded in regions with unique biopolitical and ecological conditions that were colonized under a different religious tradition and corporate structure.[35]

This, then, is the real promise and challenge for colonial comparative studies of the Anglo and Iberian Americas. Where we find rhetorical similarities in primary sources, from Newport and Cortés to Smith and Salvador and Equiano and Manzano, we find on-the-ground differences that are obscured by narrative styles, editorial practices, translations, paratextual elements, and publication formats, both in their own moments and as they shift over time. Comparative scholarship in the early Americas thus requires not only that we adopt a framework of similarity and difference but also, and especially, that we address still-unresolved, and perhaps ever-persistent, tensions between the two major disciplines that shape our field: history and literature. Colonial studies, by nature and necessity, has a foot in both areas. Future comparative research in literary studies, whether it utilizes the four major methods outlined in this chapter or orients itself in new ways, will need to account for the difference between lived experiences and the textual transmissions, enactments, and imaginations of those experiences. Doing so will enrich and expand our knowledge of the early Americas. In this way, a comparative approach that attends to the nitty-gritty nuances of language while treating texts as one of many forms of historical evidence, to be interpreted alongside data about climate, demographics, economics, material cultures, and related aspects of colonial life, can perhaps help to address the disciplinary "trade gap" between history and literature.

Notes

1. John Smith, *The Generall Historie of Virginia, New-England, and the Summer Isles* in *The Complete Works of Captain John Smith (1580–1631)*, 3 vols., ed. Philip Barbour (Chapel Hill: University of North Carolina Press for The Omohundro Institute of Early American History and Culture, 1986), 2:387 (folio 198).
2. Vicente do Salvador, *História do Brasil* (São Paulo: Edições Melhoramentos, 1975), 70.
3. Reports of sodomy in Bermuda resemble "similar aberrations ... recorded for the Pilgrim colony in Plymouth." Smith, *Complete Works*, 2:387 n. 1.
4. Sarah Rivett, *Unscripted America: Indigenous Languages and the Origin of a Literary Nation* (New York: Oxford University Press, 2017); Susanah Shaw Romney, *New Netherland Connections: Intimate Networks and Atlantic Ties in Seventeenth-Century America* (Chapel Hill: Omohundro Institute of Early American History and Culture for the University of North Carolina Press, 2014); Patrick M. Erben, *A Harmony of the Spirits: Translation and the Language of Community in Early Pennsylvania* (Chapel Hill: Omohundro Institute of Early American History and Culture for the University of North Carolina Press, 2012).
5. Louis Hanke, *Do the Americas Have a Common History?: A Critique of the Bolton Theory* (New York: Knopf, 1964). For a recent reappraisal, see Albert Hurtado, *Herbert Eugene Bolton: Historian of the American Borderlands* (Berkeley: University of California Press, 2012). For an assessment of the field from its Boltonian inception, see Ralph Bauer, "Early American Literature and American Literary History at the 'Hemispheric Turn,'" *Early American Literature*

45, no. 2 (2010): 217–233. For recent literature reviews, see Kirsten Silva Gruesz and Rodrigo Lazo, "The Spanish Americas: Introduction," *Early American Literature* 53 (2018): 641–664 and Rolena Adorno, "A Latin Americanist Looks at Early American Literature," *Early American Literature* 50, no. 1 (2015): 41–61.

6. Pérez Firmat, ed., *Do the Americas Have a Common Literature?* (Durham, NC: Duke University Press, 1990), 3–4. Edited volumes and special issues combine comparative modes. See Jorge Cañizares Esguerra, ed., *Entangled Empires: The Anglo-Iberian Atlantic, 1500–1830* (Philadelphia: University of Pennsylvania Press, 2018); Maria Windell and Jesse Alemán, eds., "Latinx Lives in Hemispheric Context" (Special Issue), *English Language Notes* 56, no. 2 (2018); Matthew Cohen and Jeffrey Glover, eds., *Colonial Mediascapes: Sensory Worlds of the Early Americas*, with intro. by Paul Chaat Smith (Lincoln: University of Nebraska Press, 2014); Ralph Bauer and José Antonio Mazzotti, eds., *Creole Subjects in the Colonial Americas: Empires, Texts, Identities* (Chapel Hill: University of North Carolina Press for the Omohundro Institute of Early American History and Culture, 2009).

7. Gruesz and Lazo, "The Spanish Americas: Introduction," 642, 645, 653. On usable comparative pasts, see Lois Parkinson Zamora, *The Usable Past: The Imagination of History in Recent Fiction of the Americas* (New York: Cambridge University Press, 1997) and Robert Blair St. George, *Possible Pasts: Becoming Colonial in Early America* (Ithaca, NY: Cornell University Press, 2000).

8. Marcia Stephenson, "From Marvelous Antidote to the Poison of Idolatry: The Transatlantic Role of Andean Bezoar Stones during the Late Sixteenth and Early Seventeenth Centuries," *Hispanic American Historical Review* 90, no. 1 (2010): 3–39; Birgit Brander Rasmussen, *Queequeg's Coffin: Indigenous Literacies and Early American Literature* (Durham, NC: Duke University Press, 2012); Breny Mendoza, "Colonial Connections," *Feminist Studies* 43, no. 3 (2017): 637–645; Dennis Herrick, *Esteban: The African Slave Who Explored America* (Albuquerque: University of New Mexico Press, 2018).

9. Eliga Gould, "Entangled Histories, Entangled Worlds: The English-Speaking Atlantic As a Spanish Periphery," *American Historical Review* 112, no. 3 (2007): 764–787, 766; David Kazanjian, *The Brink of Freedom: Improvising Life in the Nineteenth-Century Atlantic World* (Durham, NC: Duke University Press, 2016), 9; Juliet Hooker, *Theorizing Race in the Americas: Douglass, Sarmiento, Du Bois, and Vasconcelos* (New York: Oxford University Press, 2017), 11–13.

10. Eric Slauter, "History, Literature, and the Atlantic World," *William and Mary Quarterly* 65, no. 1 (2008): 135–166, 159.

11. Matthew Restall, "A History of the New Philology and the New Philology in History," *Latin American Research Review* 38, no. 1 (2003): 113–134.

12. Pero de Magalhães Gândavo, *Tratado da terra & história do Brasil*, ed. Leonardo Dantas Silva, 12th ed. (Recife: Editoria Massangana, 1995), 24.

13. Gabriel Soares de Sousa, *Notícia do Brasil*, ed. Luis de Alburquerque (Lisboa: Publicações Alfa, 1989), 218.

14. Brandão, *Os diálogos das grandezas do Brasil*, ed. Rodolfo García (Rio de Janeiro: Dois Mundos Editora, 1943), 275; Salvador, *Historia do Brasil*, 78.

Brandão concludes that Indigenous people consume manioc bread for nutrition, as instructed by Saint Thomas, and they eat human flesh "por vinganã."

15. Diego de Landa, *Relación de las cosas de Yucatán* (Mexico City: Consejo Nacional para la Cultura y las Artes, 1994), 111.

16. Hooker, *Theorizing Race in the Americas*; Lisa Voigt, *Writing Captivity in the Early Modern Atlantic: Circulations of Knowledge and Authority in the Iberian and English Imperial Worlds* (Chapel Hill: Omohundro Institute of Early American History and Culture for the University of North Carolina, 2009).

17. Richard Hakluyt, "The most ancient Discovery of the West Indies by Madoc . . ." *Principal Navigations*, 10 vols. (London and New York: J.M. Dent and Sons and E.P. Dutton & Co., 1927–1928), 5:79–80, 79.

18. López de Gómara, *La historia general delas Indias . . .* (Anvers: Juan Bellero, 1554), 63, Google Books; Gould, "Entangled Histories," 771.

19. Guaman Poma, enmeshed in a land dispute against Andean families, used his petition to Felipe III (1578–1621) to argue that news of the gold- and silver-rich Indies was announced during the reign of Rupert I, Elector Palantine (1309–1390). By synchronizing events like the birth of Christ in Bethlehem and the rule of the first Inca sovereign, Manqu Qhapaq, in Cuzco, Guaman Poma's multiple ways of recording history gesture toward the intertwined nature of the New World and the Old. Poma de Ayala, *Nueva corónica y buen gobierno*, ed. Franklin Pease G.Y., 3 vols. (Lima: Fondo de Cultura Económica), 1:38, 31.

20. El Inca Garcilaso, *Comentarios Reales de los Inca*, ed. Carlos Araníbar, 2 vols. (Mexico City: Fondo de Cultura Económica, 2004), 1: 12–13.

21. Cotton Mather, *Magnalia Christi Americana: or, the Ecclesiastical History of New-England . . .* (New York: Russell & Russell, 1967), 43, 67.

22. Emily García, "Interdependence and Interlingualism in Santiago Puglia's *El desengaño del hombre* (1794)," *Early American Literature* 53 no. 3 (2018): 745–772; Anna Brickhouse, *The Unsettlement of America: Translation, Interpretation, and the Story of Don Luis de Velasco, 1560–1945* (New York: Oxford University Press, 2015), 215. On new work in colonial translation, see Larissa Brewer-García, "The Agency of Translation in Colonial Latin American Studies: New Assessments of the Influence of Non-European Linguistic Intermediaries," in Santa Arias and Yolanda Martínez-San Miguel, eds., *Routledge Companion on Colonial Latin America and the Caribbean* (New York: Routledge, 2020), 379–392.

23. Jillian Sayre, "The Necropolitics of New World Nativism," *Early American Literature* 53, no. 3 (2018): 713–744; Kazanjian, *Brink of Freedom*.

24. José Martí, "Nuestra América," in Roberto Fernández Retamar, ed., *Política de Nuestra América* (Mexico City: Siglo Veintiuno, 1977), 37–44, 43.

25. B. W. Higman and Brian James Hudson, *Jamaican Place Names* (Kingston: University of the West Indies Press, 2009), 26.

26. National Archives, Kew, Colonial Papers 1/15, No. 74 (1661?), "Petition of Jacob Jeosua Bueno Enriques, a Jamaican Jew, to the King," 2 folios.

27. Olaudah Equiano, *The Interesting Narrative and Other Writings*, ed. Vincent Carretta (New York: Penguin, 1995).

28. Juan Francisco Manzano, *Autobiografía de un esclavo* (Madrid: Ediciones Guadarrama, 1975); Quobna Ottobah Cugoano, *Thoughts and Sentiments on the Evil of Slavery*, ed. Vincent Carretta (New York: Penguin, 1999);

James Sweet, *Domingos Álvares, African Healing, and the Intellectual History of the Atlantic World* (Chapel Hill: University of North Carolina Press, 2011); Elisa Larkin Nascimento, "Pan-Africanism and Latin America," in Kwame Dixon and Ollie A. Johnson, III, eds., *Comparative Racial Politics in Latin America* (New York: Routledge, 2018), 64–86.

29. James H. Sweet, "Mistaken Identities? Olaudah Equiano, Domingos Álvares, and the Methodological Challenges of Studying the African Diaspora," *The American Historical Review* 114, no. 2 (2009): 279–306, 281.

30. Barbara Fuchs, "Golden Ages and Golden Hinds; or, Periodizing Spain and England," *PMLA: Publications of the Modern Language Association of America* 127, no. 2 (2012): 321–327, 326, 324.

31. Sandra Gustafson, "What's in a Date? Temporalities of Early American Literature," *PMLA: Publications of the Modern Language Association of America* 128, no. 4 (2013): 961–967, 967.

32. Robert Yazzie, "Indigenous Peoples and Postcolonial Colonialism," in Marie Battiste, ed., *Reclaiming Indigenous Voice and Vision* (Vancouver: University of British Columbia Press, 2000), 39–49.

33. John Huxtable Elliott, *Empires of the Atlantic World: Britain and Spain in America, 1492–1830* (New Haven, CT: Yale University Press, 2006), 3–28, 406.

34. Barbara Mundy, *The Death of Aztec Tenochtitlan, the Life of Mexico City* (Austin: University of Texas Press, 2015), 1.

35. Gregory Waselkov, Peter Wood, and Tom Hatley, eds., *Powhatan's Mantle: Indians in the Colonial Southeast* (Lincoln: University of Nebraska Press, 2006), especially section 1, "Geography and Population"; Helen Rountree, ed., *Powhatan Foreign Relations, 1500–1722* (Charlottesville: University of Virginia Press, 1993).

14

MICHELLE BURNHAM

The Colonial Pacific

Where is the Pacific in colonial American literary studies? Nowhere, according to our anthologies, literary histories, syllabi, and scholarship, which all seem to agree that the Pacific enters American literary studies only well *after* the colonial period. The first volume of the *Norton Anthology of American Literature*, which reaches to 1820, does not include a single text from the Pacific. The *Heath Anthology*'s first volume, representing pre-1800 American literature, includes only one easily over-looked excerpt from Francisco Palóu's 1787 *Relación Histórica* (later translated as *Life of Junípero Serra*), which describes the establishment of the San Carlos Mission in Monterey Bay. Meanwhile, American literary histories – including the capacious 1994 *Cambridge History of American Literature* – are just as Atlantic-facing and continent-centered as their anthology counterparts. A search in the online database the *MLA International Bibliography* returns a meager six results for literary scholarship on the pre-1800 American Pacific.

Such orientations have similarly characterized the work of historians on early America – at least until Alan Taylor's 2001 *American Colonies*, which devoted a chapter to early California. Since then, the earlier Pacific has begun to garner greater attention by historians such as Matt Matsuda, David Igler, and David Armitage and Alison Bashford. Literary scholars of the colonial period have been far slower, however, to turn to early America's oceanic west. My point here is neither to beat up anthologies and literary histories, which already face an impossible task of inclusion and representation, nor to point a finger at scholars' choices. However, I do want to insist that the story of America we currently tell and teach is a very different one than it would be if we included the colonial Pacific. This chapter provides an overview of scholarship on the colonial Pacific to suggest what it looks like, why it is important, and how we might begin to go about incorporating it into our literary histories. In what follows, my focus is less on individual works than on broad and long contexts, in order to inspire scholars and students to recover and translate Pacific texts and traditions and to interpret them in a global, transoceanic context.

The irony to this Pacific oversight, of course, is that Christopher Columbus – whose descriptions of the West Indies now inaugurate nearly every anthology, syllabus, and history of American literature – believed himself to be describing locations in what we now call the Pacific Ocean. As I have argued elsewhere, because our narratives of American literature and culture have treated the Columbian moment as a starting point, the West Indies and the Americas immediately displace the East Indies and Asia from its story. The ensuing narrative trajectory – with its continental, national, and Atlantic foci – has blinded us to the fact that European maritime exploration continued in large part to be spurred by a persistent desire to access the East and the Pacific; it moreover did so long after Columbus, well through the long eighteenth century, including the American revolutionary period.[1]

A better narrative would conjoin these two parts of the globe, since the colonization of the Americas that followed in Columbus's wake was carried out in tandem with a persistent interest in reaching the desirable products of Asia. The American landmass physically blocked Europe's access to those goods and markets, even as the continent's mineral and human resources commercially lubricated that access. Peruvian silver, mined under brutal conditions by Indigenous peoples, was loaded onto ships that delivered it to China, where it was exchanged for commodities that traveled across the Pacific and the Atlantic. When we divide the Atlantic and Pacific oceans, and their continental counterparts of the Americas and Asia, into separate narratives, we obscure the global and transoceanic reach of this network and miss the larger literary and cultural history that helped to shape and respond to it. This dichotomy also prevents us from seeing that material maritime routes carried goods, bullion, and people between the Atlantic and Pacific worlds (as well as through the Indian Ocean) and that those voyages generated a great deal of writing that has often gone unaccounted for.

Historians such as Alison Games and Philip J. Stern have recently begun to challenge the long-standing dichotomy between an Atlantic and American world characterized by colonization on the one hand and a Pacific and Asian one characterized by trade on the other. Games insists that such an opposition obscures the "circular connections between trade and settlement" that help to place the English project of the Atlantic plantation colony in the context of the "trading world that produced it,"[2] while Stern calls into question "an Atlantic history that fails to account for either enduring connections with Asia or the myriad commercial, political, and legal regimes, like the Company, that recast the borders of the 'Atlantic' and 'Asia' in the first place."[3]

Interestingly, we can find much earlier efforts at this oceanic deconstruction within scholarship on the maritime dimensions of Spanish colonial history. Oskar Spate, writing in 1979 about the Spanish Pacific, rejected Immanuel Wallerstein's opposition between Spanish colonies in the Americas and Spanish trading posts in Asia because it "over-simplifies the variety of political relations involved."[4] As long ago as William Lytle Schurz's 1939 history of the Manila galleon trade, the "Spanish Orient" was described as "an adjunct of Spanish America."[5] More recently, in his 2014 global history of cotton, Sven Beckert notes that European "domination in Asia dovetailed with expansion into the Americas,"[6] as the maritime voyages of Columbus and Vasco da Gama paved the way for a global capitalist network that would be consolidated through corporations like the East India Company and its international counterparts around the globe.[7] Even Cortés planned multiple Pacific expeditions after his conquest of Mexico in efforts to access spices to the Asian west as well as cod fisheries in the American east, which he imagined reaching through a presumed transoceanic passage through the north that would lead to Newfoundland. Such a passage was a geographic fantasy, as was its fabled counterpart the great southern continent, but those fantasies were sustained by a global commercial desire that explains their persistence well into the eighteenth century.

This transoceanic reorientation demands a global perspective and context for a literary and cultural history that, in fact, already exists in many texts from the period. When John Donne refers in his 1633 poem "The Sunne Rising" to "both the India's of spice and Myne," for example, he is linking the spices of the Asian East Indies with the silver of the American West Indies in a single global vision of English commerce.[8] That vision also undergirded the promotional sermons Donne wrote for the Virginia Company, a corporation that – like its counterparts in Massachusetts, Dorchester, and Newfoundland – was established on a joint stock model drawn from the East India Company. These Pacific- and Atlantic-based colonial companies moreover featured many of the same leaders and investors.[9]

So many of the important changes that have transformed early American literary studies over the past thirty years – including de-canonization, literary recovery, transnationalism, multilingualism, transatlanticism, Indigenous studies, book history, and digital humanities – seem ready-made for identifying literary and cultural texts from and about the early American Pacific and for including and interrogating these into our histories in new ways. Our failure so far to do so is, I submit, less archival and linguistic than it is narrative, for we will not be able to read newly recovered (and translated) texts effectively unless we alter the temporal and spatial coordinates that have shaped American literary and historical narratives. The long history and wide geography of the Pacific is destined to remain invisible to colonial American studies until we allow Pacific texts, histories, and contexts to reshape our traditional narrative contours. The stakes for doing so go beyond canon expansion and intercultural complexity. In their edited volume on historical approaches to the Pacific world, David Armitage and Alison Bashford rightly insist that the Pacific "suggests a whole globe in a way that other oceans do not."[10] It's precisely this advantage that attention to the colonial Pacific brings to our study of early American literature and culture. Once we recognize its Pacific counterpart, the colonial American Atlantic may never look quite the same.

Centering the (Indigenous) Pacific

A Pacific-centered map of the world confronts us with an expanse of water so vast and visually dominating that we have to shift our gaze toward the map's edges to locate the continents that cluster closer to the center of traditional world maps. The fact that the Pacific is double the size of the Atlantic (and larger than all of the globe's land surface combined) is easily missed on more familiar Atlantic-centered maps, which not only exile the Pacific to the world's outer edges but slice it into two seemingly distant halves. Even without this visual cartographic division, the Pacific has typically been seen, as Adam McKeown notes, "more as a zone of fragmentation than as one of interaction" because of the challenge of finding unity amidst its size and diversity: as soon as we begin to track people and goods through its space, we are often taken "beyond the borders of the Pacific" in ways that resist a cohesively enclosed narrative.[11]

It is worth stopping to realize, however, that we carry this desire for cohesion and enclosure into our study of the Pacific from the narratives we have constructed about nations, continents, and other oceans. What if we turned this dynamic around? What if we embraced instead other models, drawn from Indigenous Pacific traditions, that offer new ways to narrate stories about nations, continents, and other oceans? In his influential essay "Our Sea of Islands" and the collection *We Are the Ocean*, Epeli Hauʻofa registers the centrality of water to Pacific Islanders, whose "universe comprised not only land surfaces but the surrounding ocean as far as they could traverse and exploit it, the underworld with its fire-controlling and earth-shaking denizens, and the heavens above with their hierarchies of powerful gods and named stars and constellations that people could count on to guide their ways across oceans."[12] This multidimensional vision invokes an Indigenous cosmology with layers of sky, land, and sea occupied by gods and spirits as well as humans.[13] Hauʻofa explains that nineteenth-century European imperialisms erased this "boundless world" of a Pacific sea of islands by boxing and ordering it.[14]

To this extent, "the Pacific" as we imagine it today is, as Spate has argued, invented by Europeans. What preceded this European invention is what Damon Salesa calls "native seas," many of which were large and complex.[15] He describes these as "cultured, practiced, spaces" not defined by the boundary between water and land;[16] in fact, they might instead be "nested in each other, or overlapped" or tied together through story. Such "native seas blanketed the Pacific, like a kaleidoscopic weave of maritime places, constantly being made and unmade, with Islanders holding all of it together with warp and weft-like voyages. It was a moving and changing map, like the ocean itself."[17] The historian Matt Matsuda echoes refusals like these to unify the Pacific. He observes that, while "unifying narratives" (such as New World "discovery," the triangular slave trade, or revolutions) have long organized our understanding of the Atlantic, they have been absent from accounts of Pacific history.[18] Yet this absence provides an opportunity to emphasize the Pacific's many overlapping and intersecting pasts; its history, like its geography, is "less a space with an abstract boundary than a series of interconnected places filled with lives and tales."[19] Armitage and Bashford argue that "we need new models and new narratives for writing the history of the Pacific" since the models that have shaped approaches to other oceans do not seem to accommodate the Pacific's size, complexity, and diversity.[20] I would extend this argument to suggest that we could benefit from such alternative narratives not just for the Pacific but for all the oceans with which it is connected, including the Atlantic. A transoceanic approach to early American studies – recognizing the long, ongoing connection between oceans – offers the best way to incorporate the Pacific into it.

The Pacific's spatial, geographic challenges are partnered in multiple ways with temporal, narrative ones. The timelines used in histories of the Pacific, for example, expose the limited perspectives from which those histories are told. When these timelines begin with European arrival – whether that is post-1500, or (more commonly) post-1700, or even post-1800 – they shrink, very often to the point of erasure, the rich complexity of the precolonial Indigenous Pacific, even as they erase the continued presence of Indigenous peoples and cultures in the Pacific today. Akira Iriye remarks that Eurocentric chronologies turn Pacific history into "simply a Pacific chapter of European or western history," bypassing an alternative that would "get away from a chronology that privileges geopolitics and consider the fates of the people who inhabit the ocean," allowing us to "give the many islands their due."[21] Salesa remarks that it took a full 400 years before all Pacific Islanders had encountered Europeans, for the "archipelagic and dispersed nature of Oceania meant that the arrival of Europeans after 1521 was locally dramatic, but regionally prolonged and haphazard."[22] Before their own arrival in it, Westerners tend to see in the Pacific only great watery distances and an overwhelming variety of languages, completely missing the "sea of islands" or "native seas" that were in fact integrated through long-distance trade and exchange. Salesa rightly remarks that "Pacific peoples were voyaging earlier, and much further than anyone else." Moreover, for these peoples, "history did not begin with the arrival of foreigners, as most non-indigenous histories do."[23] It is only from a European point of view that the Pacific appears as a latecomer to cartographic visibility and global commerce.

Human habitation of Australasia and Southeast Asia dates to approximately 40,000 years ago. The *Cambridge History of the Pacific Islanders* begins by acknowledging that "there can be no single, seamless history of the many peoples who inhabit the Pacific Islands" and asks, "is it not presumptuous to speak of 'Islanders' as if Pacific peoples spoke in a single voice?"[24] The volume simultaneously asserts that the connections between Pacific peoples are of greater importance than what might seem to be their "insularity."[25] As Salesa argues, trade relations characterized those connections long before European arrival, as they continued to afterwards, when Westerners were incorporated into existing networks even as they also disrupted them in profound and debilitating ways. Recovering earlier Indigenous knowledge and perspectives can be challenging, as revealed by efforts to understand precolonial Pacific navigation.[26] When scholars have speculated about the methods by and the reasons for which humans traveled across the Pacific's vast expanses, they have tended to assume that Indigenous voyaging was dangerous, daring, and driven by despair or threat. Archaeological evidence – as well as Indigenous knowledge systems and oral traditions – suggests, however, that such movement was routine, not that of "desperate drift voyagers, accidentally beached on new lands, or even desperate explorers driven by environmental change."[27] These voyages often left "sophisticated economic networks" in their wake,[28] although it is likely that "political and spiritual alliance" was an even stronger motivator than "material needs" for precolonial trade.[29]

Research indicates that Indigenous Pacific Islanders reached as far north as Hawai'i, as far south as islands in the subantarctic, as far east as the coast of South America, and as far west as Madagascar in East Africa. In 1976, an outrigger canoe voyage guided only by Indigenous navigational methods sailed from Hawai'i to Tahiti in "a feat believed impossible without instruments," while subsequent voyages reestablished "a connected Pacific" by reaching the shores of Canada and North America, Micronesia and Asia, and Rapa Nui in Aoteoroa.[30] Archaeologists have traced across these distances evidence of pottery, shells, jewelry, and other objects associated with a people referred to as the Lapita (after the location where this pottery was first discovered).[31] Belich appropriately calls this history "a staggering Neolithic globalisation"[32] and notes that such extensive Indigenous voyaging was already in decline by the time Europeans arrived in the Pacific, more or less after 1500. That arrival began the process of remaking the Pacific world through the long and brutal arms of European colonialism and imperialism.

That remaking extends to literary history as well. The Hawai'ian *Kumulipo* is a 2,000-line creation story that, in the words of Sujit Sivasundaram, provides a "deep history of the earth."[33] However, the poem/chant does not sit easily within Western disciplinary categories or literary genres, for it mixes and fuses religion, science, politics, and literature. As we engage with such texts, we should also honor Salesa's argument that "an ethical and full engagement with an indigenous past is through an indigenous present." He calls for increased attention to the work of Indigenous writers from both the past and the present, especially as the latter "knowingly work in a written tradition that is itself old, as well as an oral one that stretches back millennia."[34] Westerners have long written off as myth or legend stories in which humans, gods, and plants all converse with each other, or stories that sustain no distinction between the past and present.[35] These difficulties with how we recognize and read literary texts – and how we integrate them into a literary history – extend beyond genre to include other features of literary writing. For example, Western writing often casts Pacific Islanders as passive or inhuman beings who lack agency compared to their heroic European counterparts whose lives and stories are narratively constructed to serve the imperial visions of their home nations.

Violence and Resistance in the Pre-imperial Pacific

The information in the previous section makes it clear that, when the Portuguese, Spanish, Dutch, and other Europeans arrived in the Pacific, they entered into a long-flourishing world of trade and travel. At the same time, Europeans' presence in the Pacific was shaped by their experience in the Atlantic and Caribbean, as well as global contacts through Indian and Mediterranean maritime routes. These transoceanic contexts are crucial for shaping the recovery, integration, and understanding of Pacific texts into a global American literary history. Europe's entrance to the Pacific was driven by the desire for Asian spices like cloves, peppers, and nutmeg, which had long arrived in Europe through Venice and its visiting Chinese and Muslim merchants. In an effort to bypass that monopoly, Portugal sponsored Vasco da Gama's voyage, which reached Calicut, India in 1498, on a ship likely piloted by an Arab navigator with experience crossing the Indian Ocean between Africa and Asia. By 1511, Portugal consolidated its position in Asia through what Lisa Ford describes as Alfonso de Albuquerque's "brutal seizure of the Straits of Malacca." That act could be seen as a Pacific predecessor to Cortés's 1519 conquest of Mexico, which took place the same year as Magellan's Spanish-funded circumnavigation into and across the Pacific. A subsequent expedition, led by García Jofre de Loaísa in 1525, went to search for the *Trinidad*, lost on the Magellan voyage, while also pursuing Pacific commerce. Loaísa never found the ship, but when he reached the Philippines, he learned that the islands' people had already been trading with the Chinese, exchanging gold and pearls for silks and metals.

Evidence points to long-standing Chinese traffic in the region, including trade routes to East Africa operating as early as the tenth century. Such voyages were continued by the Chinese Muslim Admiral Zheng He, who commanded large, numerous, sophisticated, and busily populated ships that reached Ceylon, Indonesia, the eastern coast of Africa, and the Persian Gulf.[36] On one of those voyages, Zheng He transported a giraffe from East Africa to China's Ming court.[37] Zheng He also used Malacca as a base for his Indian Ocean voyages,[38] long before it was conquered by a series of European states – first Portugal, then the Netherlands, and finally England – for use as a Pacific trading hub. Meanwhile, beginning in the early sixteenth century, the Indigenous political groups of Malacca and the Spice Islands entered into what Bronwen Douglas describes as "expedient alliance or recurrent enmity with mutually hostile Portuguese, Spanish or Dutch colonial agents, avid for spices."[39]

Spanish profits in the Pacific were made by intercepting trade already being carried out by the Moros between China and the Philippines. Those profits from Asia were enabled by developments on the American side of the Pacific, where Spain established Panama City in 1518, a year before Magellan even left on his historic circumnavigation. A decade later, in 1528, Acapulco was established and then connected by trail in 1531 to Cuernavaca, where Cortés was located.[40] When a Spanish galleon arrived from Manila to Acapulco with a cargo of cinnamon in 1570, the annual galleon trade route was launched, which would continue until 1815. This route regularly sent Mexican silver through Manila to China, where it was exchanged for

Asian porcelain, silks, and furniture. Those products subsequently sailed to Acapulco, where they could travel by land into the Americas, as well as overland to Veracruz on the Gulf of Mexico, and then across the Atlantic to Seville. Through these networks, Kaoru Sugihara explains, "Latin American silver remained the main medium of exchange for economies on both sides of the Pacific well into the nineteenth century,"[41] while the Philippine port of Manila came to serve as a "pumping-station in a channel through which the silver of New Spain drew the luxuries of the Orient, above all Chinese silks, to America and to Seville."[42] This transoceanic commerce also encouraged transoceanic settlement, as many Chinese moved to Manila as shipbuilders and merchants, while crews of Chinese, Filipino, and Japanese sailors ended up in Mexico.[43] These encounters also brought Islam and Christianity into the Pacific, including Jesuit missionaries, whose efforts in Asia and the Americas were shaped by a global vision recorded in a substantial archive of written records.

A global American literary history of the colonial period would contain the kinds of texts suggested in the preceding paragraphs, including missionary letters and accounts, maritime voyage narratives, conquest histories, and commercial documents and records. At the same time, a global colonial American literary history should be contoured by the transnational, multi-lingual, and transoceanic contexts required to make sense of such texts. When Martín Íñiguez de Carquisano arrived at Guam in 1526, he was "hailed in good Spanish by a naked 'Indian'" who turned out instead to be "a surviving cabin boy from Magellan's *Trinidad*"[44] – the lost ship that Loaísa's expedition failed to find the year prior. For Atlanticists, this Pacific scenario may invoke the encounter, approximately a century later, of the welcome issued in English by Tisquantum, the Patuxet Native who had recently returned from England, to the "Pilgrim" settlers at Plymouth. It will also recall Cabeza de Vaca's contemporaneous description, in the narrative of his shipwreck and survival, of being misrecognized as an Indian by fellow Spaniards after he finally arrived, after traveling on foot for years across continental North America, in northern Mexico. The descriptions of Indonesia by the Portuguese apothecary Tomé Pires in his *Suma Oriental* during his 1512–1515 stay in Malacca, might similarly be read together with the 1588 descriptions of Virginia compiled by the English mathematician Thomas Harriot during his stay in Roanoke; similarly, the Venetian Antonio Pigafetta's account of Magellan's 1519–1522 voyage around the world provides a compelling Pacific counterpart to Columbus's Atlantic writings.

Joyce Chaplin has described the pre-imperial Pacific (a history that runs, she notes, from Balboa to Bligh) as a space that resisted European coloniza-tion and control until the nineteenth century;[45] "puzzled by the seascapes and landscapes they encountered, reduced to bare bodies that steadily lost teeth to scurvy," she remarks that "Europeans who ventured into the Pacific learned to think of that part of the globe as the realm of nature, a place of material forces that might someday be decoded by science."[46] However, it wasn't just geographical confusion and scurvy that caused European suffering and struggle in the early Pacific; it was the ongoing, active resistance of its Indigenous peoples.

Everywhere in the Pacific, Belich notes, Europeans "underestimated the resistance capacity" of Indigenous peoples.[47] They also under-observed and underreported it, perhaps because they simply could not register the grievances of Indigenous peoples; they categorized them more often as illegible riot than as valiant resistance, when they acknowledged them at all. This perspective is often repeated in later histories of the Pacific, such as William Lytle Schurz's early history of the Manila galleon trade, which tells the story of Magellan's navigation this way:

> The spices brought to Seville by Sebastián del Cano in the eighty-ton *Victoria* more than paid for all the initial cost of the entire expedition. Weighing heavily on the debit side was the life of Magellan, lost on Mactan of the Philippines, on the same day, it is said, that Francisco Serrão, the man who was almost his blood-brother, died in the nearby Moluccas.[48]

The narrative calculus of these two sentences write off the lives of two European humans as losses in the pursuit of profits from Pacific spices. The tragic heroism that drives the passage, however, requires the narrative exclusion of Indigenous peoples and their perspective from its story. Left untold is that Magellan was killed by Natives resisting his violent imposition of Christianity, while Serrão – who was seeking nutmeg, mace, and cloves in Ternate – died under mysterious circumstances that may have included poison.

It is true that European disaster was everywhere in the colonial Pacific. Cortés sent four expeditions into the Pacific in the 1530s, in search of a potential North American waterway; all ended in some combination of mutiny, shipwreck, murder, or disappearance.[49] The 1535 expedition of Simón de Alcazaba into Patagonia resulted in fully half of his company dead by drowning, killing, hanging, starving, or marooning.[50] Yet how we plot and narrate this suffering matters: if we see these as disastrous stepping stones on the path toward the triumph of European empire, we will fail to see them as episodes of repeated cyclical violence driven by European greed. The decade of the Cortés and Alcazaba expeditions also saw the great Inca revolt of 1536. It also saw the birth of Lautaro, the Indigenous Araucanian in what is today Chile, who, following his enslavement by the Spanish, organized and led a war of revolt against them, until he was killed in 1557. When Miguel López de Legazpi conquered the Ladrones (later renamed the Philippines) and created a settlement at Cebu in the 1560s, the Cebuans continued the resistance they first exhibited against Magellan. A 1567 expedition led by Álvara de Mendaña went into the Pacific in search of Solomon's gold, only to leave behind a series of increasingly tense and violent encounters with Natives across what are now called the Solomon Islands. Meanwhile, the Chinese led a revolt against the Spanish in Manila in 1574, assisted by the pirate Lim Ah Hong.[51] Resistance in the Philippines continued throughout much of the seventeenth century, as the Sultan Muhammad Kudarat led anti-Spanish and anti-Catholic rebellions.[52]

Pedro de Quirós, the pilot on a second Mendaña voyage in 1595, described their South Seas expedition as an "unrelieved tragedy" that included the bloody slaughter of several hundred Marquesans in an attempt to establish what would be the first European colony in the South Seas. For Spate, the expedition was characterized by the same "sickening cycle of friendly welcome, misunderstandings, sullen retreats, occasional reconciliations, robberies and killings" that accompanied other Spanish encounters with Indigenous peoples across the Pacific. After dying from a Native-inflicted wound, Mendaña was buried and disinterred before his body was placed on a frigate where his decomposed corpse was reportedly run aground on an unknown shoreline surrounded by a crew of dead men.[53] Spate observes that, throughout colonial Spanish America, "any economic life beyond sheer robbery depended on the exploitation of Indian labour."[54] Labor exploitation was accompanied by sexual abuse, as European men "killed, kidnapped, and raped women" all over the Pacific.[55] It is crucial to recover these histories and the agency of Indigenous peoples in them, even from within texts that fail to recognize or narrate them. When we change the perspective from which it is told, the colonial Pacific narrative shifts from tragic heroism to cyclical gothic.

Pirates, Corporations, and Books in the Transoceanic Pacific

By the sixteenth and seventeenth centuries, English privateering and Dutch trading voyages began to challenge Spanish and Portuguese dominance in the Pacific. Sir Francis Drake's 1577 voyage claimed territory for England he named Nova Albion, north of present-day San Francisco. Much more dramatic was his seizure of a Spanish ship filled with treasure, a feat that drew fascinated attention in England and began to threaten the dominance of Spain in the European Pacific. The Pacific continued to draw pirates, privateers, and buccaneers, where men like Dampier, Davis, Rogers, and Shelvocke used the island of Juan Fernández, off the coast of Chile, as a harbor.[56]

Meanwhile, the adventures and exploits of these men became popular reading material around the Atlantic world, including nonfiction narratives like Dampier's 1697 *New Voyage Round the World* and novelistic fiction such as Defoe's 1719 *Robinson Crusoe*, which is set on an Atlantic version of Juan Fernández Island.

These texts belong in a transoceanic literary history along with narratives like Carlos de Sigüenza's 1690 *The Misfortunes of Alonso Ramírez*. Published in Mexico City, *The Misfortunes of Alonso Ramírez* tells the story of a Spanish American carpenter from Puerto Rico who was taken captive and enslaved by Dampier in the Philippines. After traveling into the Indian Ocean with a crew of Africans, Filipinos, Chinese, and Americans, Ramírez was set free three years later on coastal Brazil, before an attempt to sail home to Puerto Rico resulted in shipwreck in the Yucatán. Fabio López Lázaro reads the text as a defense of Hispanic global and multicultural solidarity at a time when Spanish American culture dominated the New World. López Lázaro argues that Latin American colonial history should be situated within "Pacific, Asian, and European networks of contact and exchange and transoceanic communities of solidarity and power,"[57] a claim that could very well frame a global colonial literary history of the transoceanic Americas.

Pirates challenged the power of Portugal and Spain in the colonial Pacific, but that power was challenged in a more long-lasting way by the colonial corporation, which Lisa Ford describes as the Netherlands' "most important legal technology."[58] The Dutch East India Company (VOC) buttressed its commercial presence in the Pacific with military power, establishing treaties advantageous to the Dutch and then using violations of those treaties "as a pretext to seize Batavia and Amboina, to massacre thousands of people in the Banda Islands, and eventually to wrest control of key trading posts in the island archipelago, giving it effective control of the waterways of the Spice Islands."[59] These strategies of the Dutch (which amounted to something like a corporate global violence) would later be imitated, Ford notes, by the colonial trading corporations of the British and French.[60]

The economist John Maynard Keynes has moreover suggested that, in the British case, pirates and companies actually operated in tandem, through the Crown, to set the stage for commercial dominance. He observes, in his 1930 *Treatise on Money*, that the booty from Drake's capture formed

> the fountain and origin of British foreign investment. Elizabeth paid off out of the proceeds the whole of her foreign debt and invested a part of the balance ... in the Levant Company; largely out of the profits of the Levant Company was formed the East India Company, the profits of which during the seventeenth

and eighteenth centuries were the main foundation of England's foreign connections.[61]

English colonial corporations, which operated in both the Pacific and the Atlantic worlds, were therefore financially fueled by piracy, even as they were legally modeled off of Dutch predecessors.

The China and spice trades continued to draw into the Pacific ships, sailors, and goods from all over the world, and these only increased as competition between European powers for access to and control of desirable goods and markets in the Pacific stepped up in the second half of the eighteenth century. Long and ambitious voyages sponsored by German, French, Russian, and British explorers were propelled by a mixture of "scientific curiosity, imperial ambition, and the search for goods to trade with China."[62] The sandalwood and sea cucumber (or *bêche du mer*) trades developed, for example, as Western efforts to find goods that the Chinese would be willing to exchange for their highly desirable teas and spices. Meanwhile, the sailors on these voyages – who might be British, European, American, Chinese, or Lascars – often report brutal conditions on board ship, and some of them jumped ship in South Sea islands such as Fiji, Tonga, Samoa, or Hawai'i, where they sometimes became members of the households of important chieftains.[63] The competition between European powers in the Pacific played out as desire for control over and access to bodies for labor and for sex, as much as for markets and products.

Armitage and Bashford note that the Pacific is overwhelmingly imagined today as a "late eighteenth and nineteenth-century phenomenon" aligned with the Enlightenment, empire, and modernity.[64] That is because the Pacific has historically begun to matter and become legible only once the European presence there became more pervasive, when it also became easier to narrate that presence within a story of European empire. This period has been more exhaustively documented and discussed than earlier periods, and its imperial perspective has dominated those accounts; this chapter aims to redress this imbalance by focusing on earlier periods. The Russians have been less visible in these histories, although they also crossed the northern Pacific under the auspices of trading companies, especially in pursuit of sea otter over the course of the eighteenth century. Gwenn A. Miller has documented the Russian presence in what is now Alaska and its effect on Indigenous communities there.[65] By the early nineteenth century, the Russians moved as far south as Fort Ross in present-day California, where they arrived with Kodiak and Alutiiq Natives on whose hunting expertise they relied. In Fort Ross, these Indigenous groups from the north Pacific lived among, and sometimes married and had children with, Indigenous Kashaya peoples from northern California.

Yet even these activities on the Pacific's eastern edge were driven by commercial forces from its western edge. As Belich reminds us, China remained quietly dominant within this scene; in fact, all across the Pacific, the Chinese allowed "Europeans and their slaves to do the global dirty work. Europeans were happy to oblige, and diligently shipped furs, silver and American biota to Canton and Macau in return for silk, porcelain and, later, tea."[66] By the end of the eighteenth century, Russians were hunting sea otters in the subarctic Pacific, and Americans and Britons were hunting fur seals in the subantarctic – all on behalf of a fur market in China, during a period when China itself did little maritime voyaging at all. As Belich explains, "You did not need to move to globalise."[67]

While the connections between the Atlantic and the Pacific were fortified and multiplied in the second half of the eighteenth century by these material voyages, they were also strengthened by the publication, translation, and transmission of narratives about those voyages. It is important to remember that the eighteenth century was when writing about the Pacific boomed in Atlantic print culture in many forms: translations, abridgments, periodical publications, reprints. This was the era of the great circumnavigations by Cook and Vancouver, Bougainville and Lapérouse, and the publication of those narratives drove public interest in accounts of the Pacific by earlier voyagers and in other genres. We should not underestimate the power and effect of writing about the Pacific all over the Atlantic world. That writing inspired further voyages by monarchs and merchants alike, but it also inspired men to join crews in search of adventure and the possibility of profit. Ships themselves carried books with them into the Pacific. Alexander Dalrymple translated and published earlier Dutch and Spanish accounts into English, and Cook brought those books with him on his voyages. Russian and French Pacific narratives were also translated into English. Accounts of the Pacific made appearances all over the Atlantic in genres ranging from travel narratives to castaway accounts and novels. The records of missionaries in the Pacific also leave us a formidable and fascinating archive of texts, with their own complicated history of publication, reprinting, translation, and adaptation.

The search for a supposed great southern continent, along with the search for a presumed northwest passage, was finally abandoned by the end of the eighteenth century. Yet those geographical fantasies were fueled by commercial fantasies among European nations hoping to reach and exploit their imagined resources. The Pacific also fueled the production of literary fantasy, and there was almost as much traffic between the genres of travel narrative and fantasy as there was between the Atlantic and Pacific worlds. In his narrative of the 1519–1522 voyage of Magellan, Pigafetta describes birds that could only have "come from the terrestrial Paradise," and several of these birds were transported back to Seville even as the expedition lost so many ships and men in the Pacific.[68] By the eighteenth century, a number of novels set in the south Pacific, such as Robert Paltock's *Peter Wilkins* (1751) or the anonymous *Adventures of Hildebrand Bowman* (1778), featured birdlike women with wings who seduced lost sailors.

This chapter has aimed to offer a variety of ways to begin locating the Pacific within colonial American studies. In doing so, it aims to displace the assumption that the Pacific only arrives in American literary history with the well-known nineteenth-century fiction of Herman Melville or the non-fiction of Richard Henry Dana, Jr. That assumption – and the literary and cultural histories that rely on it – reproduces narratives whose perspectives give us a Pacific seen only from the continental US Atlantic shore, a perspective from which it looks like a distant and exotic destination for common seafarers or privileged adventurers who live a continent away, on the shore of a different ocean. The first European ship to catch a whale in the Pacific was the British *Emilia*, which did so in 1789 off the coast of Chile.[69] This event took place sixty years before the novels of Melville. Even more revealingly, it took place more than 170 years after the arrival of Magellan in the Pacific. Our literary anthologies and histories – and the narratives they implicitly or explicitly tell – need to reach into Indigenous, international, and multilingual colonial pasts. By acknowledging and accommodating the global dimensions and alternative perspectives of those pasts, readers, students, and scholars can create new, critical, transoceanic narratives for early American literary studies.

Notes

1. See my *Transoceanic America: Risk, Writing, and Revolution in the Global Pacific* (Oxford: Oxford University Press, 2019).
2. Alison Games, *The Web of Empire: English Cosmopolitans in an Age of Expansion, 1560–1660* (Oxford: Oxford University Press, 2008), 181, 12.
3. Philip J. Stern, *The Company-State: Corporate Sovereignty and the Early Modern Foundations of the British Empire in India* (Oxford: Oxford University Press, 2011), 3.
4. O. H. K. Spate, *The Spanish Lake* (Minneapolis: University of Minnesota Press, 1979), 220.
5. William Lytle Schurz, *The Manila Galleon* (1939; repr. New York: E.P. Dutton, 1959), 21.
6. Sven Beckert, *Empire of Cotton: A Global History* (New York: Knopf, 2015), 35.
7. For a longer discussion of Beckert's study in relation to a global transoceanic framework for American literary studies, see my *Transoceanic America*, 11–12.
8. Quoted in Spate, *The Spanish Lake*, 279.

9. For a discussion of the role of the company in transoceanic colonialism and American literary and cultural history, see my article, "Global America," in Kristina Bross and Abram Van Engen, eds., *A History of American Puritan Literature* (Cambridge: Cambridge University Press, 2020), 122–144.

10. David Armitage and Alison Bashford, eds., *Pacific Histories: Ocean, Land, People* (New York: Palgrave Macmillan, 2014), 6.

11. Adam McKeown, "Movement," in ibid., 143.

12. Epeli Hauʻofa, "Our Sea of Islands," in Hauʻofa, *We Are the Ocean*: Selected Works (Honolulu: University of Hawai'i Press, 2008), 31.

13. Donald Denoon, ed., *The Cambridge History of the Pacific Islanders* (Cambridge: Cambridge University Press, 1997), 117.

14. Hauʻofa, 34.

15. Damon Salesa, "The Pacific in Indigenous Time," in Armitage and Bashford, *Pacific Histories*, 44.

16. Ibid., 45.

17. Ibid., 49.

18. Matt K. Matsuda, "Afterword: Pacific Cross-Currents," in Armitage and Bashford, *Pacific Histories*, 327.

19. Ibid., 328.

20. Armitage and Bashford, *Pacific Histories*, 6.

21. Akira Iriye, "A Pacific Century?," in Armitage and Bashford, *Pacific Histories*, 100, 101.

22. Salesa, "The Pacific in Indigenous Time," 36.

23. Ibid., 33, 36.

24. Denoon, *Pacific Islanders*, 3, 4.

25. Ibid., 5.

26. This same problem applies to Indigenous gender relations, which, as Patricia O'Brien notes, were "a central organisational category in every society, but in varying ways" across the Pacific. Those relations have, however, become tangled inside of "colonial historical layers" that have actively obscured and complicated them, creating mythologies of female sexual availability produced at the vectors of desire, violence, and fantasy. Patricia O'Brien, "Gender," in Armitage and Bashford, *Pacific Histories*, 286.

27. Denoon, *Pacific Islanders*, 48.

28. Ibid., 50.

29. Matt K. Matsuda, *Pacific Worlds: A History of Seas, Peoples, and Cultures* (Cambridge: Cambridge University Press, 2012), 24.

30. Ibid., 22.

31. Salesa, "The Pacific in Indigenous Time," 34.

32. James Belich, "Race," in Armitage and Bashford, *Pacific Histories*, 263.

33. Sujit Sivasundaram, "Science," in Armitage and Bashford, *Pacific Histories*, 240.

34. Salesa, "The Pacific in Indigenous Time," 40, 39.

35. Denoon, *Pacific Islanders*, 14.

36. Spate, *The Spanish Lake*, 145.

37. Matsuda, *Pacific Worlds*, 45.

38. Spate, *The Spanish Lake*, 87.

39. Bronwen Douglas, "Religion," in Armitage and Bashford, *Pacific Histories*, 199.

40. Spate, *The Spanish Lake*, 64.

41. Kaoru Sugihara, "The Economy since 1800," in Armitage and Bashford, *Pacific Histories*, 171.
42. Spate, *The Spanish Lake*, 104.
43. McKeown, "Movement," 147.
44. Spate, *The Spanish Lake*, 90.
45. Joyce E. Chaplin, "The Pacific before Empire, *c.* 1500–1800," in Armitage and Bashford, *Pacific Histories*, 54.
46. Ibid., 64–65.
47. Belich, "Race," 271.
48. Schurz, *The Manila Galleon*, 18.
49. Spate, *The Spanish Lake*, 65–66.
50. Ibid., 96.
51. Matsuda, *Pacific Worlds*, 61.
52. Ibid., 62.
53. Spate, *The Spanish Lake*, 129–132.
54. Ibid., 79.
55. O'Brien, "Gender," 283. O'Brien insists on recognizing women's agency in this history, observing that they were "historical actors" and not mere "victims to external male-driven forces" (285).
56. Spate, *The Spanish Lake*, 119.
57. Fabio López Lázaro, *The Misfortunes of Alonso Ramírez: The True Adventures of a Spanish American with 17th-Century Pirates* (Austin: University of Texas Press, 2011), 8.
58. Lisa Ford, "Law," in Armitage and Bashford, *Pacific Histories*, 218.
59. Ibid., 219.
60. Ibid., 219.
61. Quoted in Spate, *The Spanish Lake*, 264.
62. McKeown, "Movement," 148.
63. Denoon, *Pacific Islanders*, 144.
64. Armitage and Bashford, *Pacific Histories*, 15.
65. Gwenn A. Miller, *Kodiak Kreol: Communities of Empire in Early Russian America* (Ithaca, NY: Cornell University Press, 2015).
66. Belich, "Race," 266.
67. Ibid.
68. Antonio Pigafetta, *The First Voyage around the World (1519–1522): An Account of Magellan's Expedition*, ed. Theodore J. Cachey, Luigi Ballerini, and Massimo Ciavolello (Toronto: University of Toronto Press, 2007),176.
69. McKeown, "Movement," 148–149.

15

CASSANDER SMITH

Caribbean America

The Caribbean, or West Indies, as it is more often termed, is a vital part of what Karin Wulf has called the "vast early America."[1] The region provided important strategic advantages for European nations endeavoring to expand their imperial reach across the Atlantic ocean. It was a central destination and point of origin for the circulation of goods (i.e. sugar and rum) and the forced migration of enslaved people on which the production of those goods depended. The Caribbean also maintained an intimate connection to the American mainland through war, religion, social ties, and trade. When Quaker missionaries "invaded" Boston in the late 1650s, they arrived from Barbados, where they had been living and preaching. During the infamous 1692 Salem witch trials in Massachusetts, accusers named an enslaved woman from Barbados as the catalyst for the crisis, and the town's minister was a Barbados transplant. There was an especially strong relationship between the plantation societies that sprang up in the southern colonies, and those of the Caribbean, so much so that one historian dubbed South Carolina and Georgia the "offspring" of Barbados.[2] During the Revolutionary War, the Caribbean was a central conduit through which American colonists secured supplies from France and Spain and was itself contested space among European forces. Our understanding today of the colonial American mainland and the Caribbean as discrete entities owes a great deal to that war which created a political divide. Rich, white planters in the Caribbean were forced to choose between a British metropole and their colonial counterparts on the mainland. All of this is to say that the Caribbean was central in the formation of early America.

The key to understanding the Caribbean and its literary significance within the context of the present volume is to think about it as both an imaginary and concrete space. Conceptually, the Caribbean materialized out of Christopher Columbus's voyages. Thinking he had reached the spice lands of South Asia (mainly India), he referred to as Indians the Lucayan and Taíno he encountered first in the Bahamas and then Cuba and Hispaniola. When the Spanish realized that Columbus had actually led them to a different continent, they named the region West India or "Indies," in opposition to India in the east. The moniker by which we commonly refer to the region today, the Caribbean, comes from the Carib, a dominant Indigenous group at the time of Columbus's voyages. Columbus writes in his journals that other Native nations feared the Carib because they purportedly ate human flesh. The English word *cannibal* is a cognate of *Caribbean*. Columbus's voyages and those of subsequent explorers were consequential in how Europeans perceived the Americas generally and the Caribbean specifically. Equally consequential were those encounters with Taíno, Carib, and other Indigenous populations and later Black Africans in the material world, which informed how Europeans wrote about, or imagined, the region.

As a concrete space, the Caribbean, like the American mainland, was a battle ground for empire. In the seventeenth and eighteenth centuries, the Spanish, British, and French were the three major European imperial presences there. It was also a testing ground for those proto-nationalist urgings in America that came to a head in 1776. In this respect, the Caribbean functioned as a crucial transnational space shaping ideas that circulated throughout the early Americas related to cultural identities, slavery and abolition, trade, and religion, among other issues. Ultimately, the writings in and about the early Caribbean illustrate the ways in which those in early America sought to understand and differentiate colonial and (proto-)national agendas. Those writings, importantly, also present a counternarrative to American colonialism and nationalism. This chapter offers an overview of that literature, outlining the contours of a Caribbean America. Given the limited space here, the discussion homes in on the British Caribbean.

Britain established its first colonies in the early seventeenth century, claiming Bermuda, which they named Somers Isles, in 1612, St. Christopher (or St. Kitts) in 1623, and Barbados in 1627. By 1636, they also had settled Antigua, Nevis, and Montserrat. In 1655, they wrestled Jamaica from Spain. For a brief period, beginning in 1629, they claimed Providence, in the heart of the Spanish Caribbean. Trade companies and merchants pushed the settlement of these islands through the same invasive and often violent strategy of settler colonialism employed in Plymouth, Massachusetts Bay, Jamestown, and elsewhere in the British American mainland. The primary aim was profit. Two notable exceptions are Jamaica, which was occupied, at least initially, by military force as part of a larger plan to challenge Spanish American dominance, and Providence, which was largely a Puritan experiment designed to counter Plymouth Colony.

Representations of these places and of the Caribbean more generally appear in a wide range of texts, comprising viewpoints from those living throughout Britain and the American locations of its expanding empire. The texts constitute a variety of genres, including plays, poems, novels, travel narratives, commercial brochures, religious treatises, memoirs, and slave narratives. The perspectives that the texts propagate are just as diverse as the genres in which they appear, and they illustrate the sociopolitical and cultural consequences of a way of thinking about the early Caribbean in America, or what scholars call a "Caribbean imaginary." This chapter maps out three such consequences: one related to the Caribbean's commercial potential; a second involving its reputation as an unhealthy, immoral wasteland; and a third that addresses the Caribbean's central role in the transatlantic slave trade and other forms of forced labor. The chapter ends with a brief discussion about the ways in which material world encounters, beyond the Caribbean imaginary, were circumscribed by, but also contested, commonly accepted ideas about the region, which in turn destabilized American efforts to articulate national and colonial projects.

Profiting in the Caribbean

In the tradition of Columbus, British travelers and American settler colonists alike imagined the Caribbean as a space of immense commercial possibilities that both enriched and threatened its American neighbors. Consequently, discussions of the region's economic viability and its usefulness to the American mainland shape the literature. To be sure, English colonization of the Caribbean began rather inauspiciously. In 1609, a hurricane knocked off course a ship heading for Jamestown. The ship crashed off the shore of Bermuda. Some 150 crew members and passengers survived for nearly a year on the island before rigging two pinnaces and sailing on to Jamestown. One of those passengers, William Strachey, wrote an account of their ordeal a year later. In that account, he notes that, upon first realizing they had shipwrecked off Bermuda, he and the others were disheartened, having heard reports that the islands were "dangerous." He writes that Bermuda "be so terrible to all that ever touched on them, and such tempests, thunders, and other fearful objects are seen and heard about them that they be called commonly 'the Devil's Islands.'"[3] His opinion of the archipelago soon changes as the survivors find adequate succor over the year. Though prone to stormy weather and possessing poor soil quality, which he describes as "dark, red, sandy, dry, and uncapable," Strachey argues, the islands of Bermuda contain an assortment of fish, fowl, tortoises, and wild boars. Strachey comes to know by "experience" that Bermuda is "as habitable and commodious as most countries of the same climate and situation."[4]

Strachey's observations align with those of John Smith, who muses about Bermuda, "it may as truly be said of those Ilands as ever it was said of the Rhodes, that there is no one day throughout the 12 moneths, but that in some houre thereof, the sun looks singularly & cleere upon them."[5] Most often noted for his narratives about the early years of Jamestown and his encounters with Pocahontas, Smith was finishing a brief term as the colony's governor when the Bermuda shipwreck occurred. In 1612, based on the reports from those castaways about the plentiful resources on Bermuda, colonial administrators organized its permanent settlement. The idea, as Smith notes, was that Britain's first colony in the West Indies would be "beneficiall ... and helpful to the Plantation of Virginia."[6] This is an early indication of how American settlers envisioned the Caribbean as a staging ground from which they could strengthen their commercial interests on the mainland.

The literature represents in a similar vein other British-controlled Caribbean islands. Texts render Barbados as especially viable. In his 1657 narrative *True and Exact History of the Island of Barbadoes*, Richard Ligon writes as he approaches the island:

> Being now come in sight of this happy Iland, the neerer we came, the more beautifull it appeared to our eyes ... There we saw the high, large, and lofty Trees, with their spreading Branches, and flourishing tops, seem'd to be beholding to the earth and roots, that gave them such plenty of sap for their nourishment, as to grow to that perfection of beauty and largenesse.[7]

Throughout the narrative, he painstakingly describes the natural resources, the people, and the economy of the island, declaring ultimately that "they that have industry ... may make it the Ladder to clyme to a high degree, of Wealth and opulencie."[8]

Beyond Barbados's material resources, Britain saw it as a strategic base in the Caribbean from which they could exploit the resources of their other Caribbean holdings, namely Jamaica. They seized Jamaica from Spain in 1655 as consolation prize during Oliver Cromwell's failed Western Design. As part of this military campaign to oust Spain from the Caribbean by conquering its islands one by one, Cromwell expected Barbados to provide the military expedition with additional men and supplies. Thomas Modyford, a Barbados planter who would become governor of Jamaica, wrote to Cromwell in 1654 that Barbados would be "the magazine of all necessaries" for a Western Design.[9] The capture of Jamaica, at the time a minor outpost of the Spanish American empire, did little to weaken Spain in the region. Nevertheless, the General Robert Venables described Jamaica in 1655 as "a very good Island." In 1774, the historian Edward Long insisted "it is easy to conceive ... how vastly profitable [Jamaica] is to the mother-country in every view." He proclaims ultimately that it would be an "enormous and irreparable" loss "should [Jamaica] ever devolve into the hands of any other power."[10]

The commercial potential of the Caribbean was ever present in the British American textual imagination as illustrated in James Grainger's massive poem *The Sugar Cane*. Published in 1764, the poem celebrates the British Empire and the success of West Indies sugar plantations, particularly on St. Kitts. "Thrice happy he, to whom such fields are given!" Grainger writes. "For him the Cane with little labour grows." He echoes the idea that planters can get rich with little effort because of the soil's fecundity. "This land, for many a crop, will feed [the planter's] mills'/ Disdain supplies, nor ask from compost aid."[11]

As Grainger's verse suggests, planters took for granted that they could exploit the islands' potential with relative ease in part because they, like their counterparts on the American mainland, typically wrote Indigenous populations out of the narrative. Smith and Strachey point out that Bermuda was vacant in 1609. While acknowledging that Barbados provided hunting grounds for neighboring Indigenous nations, Ligon still represents it when the English arrive in 1627 as unoccupied, "overgrown with Wood, as there could be found no Champions ... for men to dwell in; nor found they any beasts to inhabit there, only Hogs."[12] The English clergyman and former Catholic priest Thomas Gage, too, insisted that the British could easily seize the Spanish Caribbean, beginning with spaces sparsely populated. In a letter to Cromwell in 1654, Gage urged Cromwell to begin his invasion with Hispaniola (present-day Haiti and Dominican Republic) as "not one quarter of it [is] inhabited, and so more easie to take."[13] Gage's 1648 travel narrative *The English-American*, about his exploits in Spanish America between 1625 and 1637, informed Cromwell's Western Design. He did not factor in the political agency of those very present Indigenous and Maroon communities that helped Spain foil British plans.

Not only do these early writers render the land as empty but they also perceive it as unsullied, virginal in its purity. When Sir Walter Raleigh advocated for colonization of Guiana in his *Discovery of the Large, Rich, and Beautiful Empire of Guiana*, published in 1596, he declares that "Guiana is a Countrey that hath yet her Maydenhead, never sackt, turned, nor wrought ... It hath never been entred by any armie of strength, and never conquered or possesed by any Christian Prince."[14] His image of an empty, untouched land, which assumes a gendered hue, effaces the Orenoqueponi and other Natives he encounters there. Travelers to the American mainland echoed Raleigh's rhetorical strategy for describing Guiana. In 1616, for example, John Smith describes New England as vacant, virginal, and gendered, "her treasures hauing yet neuer beene opened, nor her originals wasted, consumed, nor abused."[15] Thomas Morton, in his 1632 *New English Canaan*, writes similarly of the region that it is a "faire virgin," long neglected and awaiting settlement.[16]

Fictional representations of the Caribbean also render it as a space prime for conquest as reflected in Daniel Defoe's *Robinson Crusoe* in 1719 and its gendered counterpart *The Female American*, published anonymously in 1767. In both novels, the main character colonizes an island deemed vacant despite evidence of inhabitancy. *The Female American* in particular centers on a female castaway named Unca Eliza Wakefield, who with relative ease claims the religious grounds of an Indigenous community and then proselytizes them. Her conquest yields spiritual more so than commercial gains, rewriting within a Caribbean context the narrative about England's first permanent settlement in America, Jamestown. Unca Eliza is biracial; she is the fictional daughter of Virginia's first governor and a Native princess, evoking the Pocahontas myth. She is both American and English, a transnational figure. When she is castaway on an unidentified island in the Atlantic – while heading to England – she employs her multicultural abilities to survive and conquer the island. Her conquest, though, eschews the violent precepts of settler colonialism (at least that appears to be the novel's ethics), suggesting a more utopian outcome, one in which cultures assimilate peacefully. She adapts to her new island situation, while converting her Native neighbors to Christianity. There is no warfare or bloodshed. Her Native converts accept her teachings with little opposition, which makes her colonial experiment more reminiscent of the narratives about Massachusetts Bay and the early efforts of John Eliot than Jamestown. She does not seek wealth or commercial advantage. Even when the opportunity for rescue presents itself at the end of the novel, she chooses to live among her new converts, living out a kind of spiritual imperialism. She carves out a place for women in empire (and nation) building and reconstitutes American identity as both transnational and transracial.

The Caribbean Unclean

Representations of the Caribbean's commercial viability in early American texts provide stark contrast to a second common mode of representation, that of the region as a cesspool of disease and immorality. In terms of the presumed physical consequences, as often as writers noted the material resources in the region, they just as often fretted about the tropical climate. Their anxieties reflected an idea dating back to antiquity that the nature of a place dictates the cultural and bodily constitutions of the life-forms that reside in it. To some extent, Columbus's voyages challenged climate-based theories of human difference. Still, in the seventeenth and eighteenth centuries, would-be travelers to the Americas feared that the climate there would compromise their health. John Josselyn, writing about his travels through New England in 1638 and 1663, argues that an imbalance occurs when bodies accustomed to more temperate climates encounter hotter climates that are "limbecks [alembics] to our bodies." He writes, "forraign heat will extract the inward and adventitious heat consume the natural, so much more heat any man receives outwardly from the heat of the sun, so much more wants he the same inwardly."[17]

Even more than the cooler climates of the American mainland, travelers feared the heat of the Caribbean. After acknowledging that in Jamaica people are not plagued by the typical ailments found in Europe, like smallpox, Thomas Trapham notes "Jamaica therefore as part of the Indies hath its endemical evils,"[18] and Richard Towne urges English transplants to the region to allow for a period of "seasoning" in which their bodies become acclimated to the new climate.[19] Hector St. John de Crèvecoeur, in his 1782 *Letters From An American Farmer*, differentiates between the gentler climates of the American mainland and the "debilitating nature" of the Caribbean sun that quickly corrodes the bodies of white planters. He writes:

> Here are always to be seen a great number of valetudinarians from the West Indies, seeking for the renovation of health, exhausted by the debilitating nature of their sun, air, and modes of living. Many of these West Indians have I seen, at thirty, loaded with the infirmities of old age; for nothing is more common in those countries of wealth, than for persons to lose the abilities of enjoying the comforts of life, at a time when we northern men just begin to taste the fruits of our labour and prudence.[20]

To assuage fears and promote English settlement in Jamaica, the English soldier-turned-priest Edmund Hickeringill proclaims, "I never came in more temperate climes than those of Jamaica, Hispaniola, St. Kits, Barbadoes, etc."[21] He does not contradict climate theory but argues that the Caribbean falls into a temperate zone that is as habitable as "Virginia, New England; nay as Portugal, Spain, Italy or any other confines upon the Mediterranean Sea ... though fam'd to be the world's Garden."[22] Hans Sloane, too, challenges the idea that the West Indies poses a unique health risk. "For my own part," he says, "I never saw a disease in Jamaica, which I had not met with in Europe, and that in people who never had been in either [East or West] Indies."[23]

Rather than the climate, English writers linked ailments to people's daily habits and overindulgences. "For how shall it otherwise happen," muses

Towne, "than that dropsical disorders must ensue when the body is predisposed for their production by the natural constitution of the air, and at the same time the Quantity of the Blood is increased, and the solids enervated by Intemperance."[24] When describing the consumption of Rum in Barbados, Ligon quips, "The people drink much of it, indeed too much; for it often layes them asleep on the ground, and that is accounted a very unwholsome lodging."[25]

Ligon's remark about drunkenness speaks to a general perception, by the mid-seventeenth century, that all of the West Indies was plagued by immorality and lawlessness, due in large part to the rise of profitable sugar plantations that made Caribbean landowners the richest in British America. Visitors to the islands determined that the region's planter inhabitants were awash with money and material excesses (including rum) to the detriment of moral concerns. Among the maternal worries for Sarah Gray Cary, living in Boston in 1790, was that her son, living in Grenada, would be led astray by "a set of companions whose gross manners and way of life are a reflection upon human nature."[26] She warns her son, "One moment of intoxication is sufficient to overthrow every good resolution."[27] To their neighbors up north, the West Indies lacked a spiritual core and vision; the islands were a hodgepodge of Judaism, Catholicism, African religions brought by enslaved Black Africans, and Quakerism. The hedonism that New England Puritans associated with the West Indies contrasted with their own sense of spiritual purpose. Writing from Barbados, a minister conveys to John Winthrop in Massachusetts his uneasiness about living among the "great profaness ... and great hearsies" of Barbados. He "begs" Winthrop's help "at the throne of grace."[28] In 1660, the Puritan minister John Norton urges all of New England "always to remember, that originally they are a Plantation religion, not a plantation of trade."[29] The Caribbean mediated for American colonists ideas about commerce and morality. They asserted moral differences even as they solidified trade relationships between the two regions.

The Caribbean's reputation for immorality strengthened with the rise of pirate culture beginning in the latter half of the seventeenth century and moving into the next century. Alexander Exquemelin, in his *Bucanniers of America*, published in English in 1684, presents gruesome tales about pirates such as Henry Morgan, who sail around the Caribbean terrorizing (mostly) Spanish soldiers and settlers as they raid the coffers of European empires. Writing under the pseudonym Charles Johnson, Daniel Defoe (it is widely believed) published a more extensive history of Caribbean piracy in 1724. He describes piracy as pathological, "infesting the West-Indies."[30] The region becomes a breeding ground for pirates, Defoe says, because of the "many small inlets, Lagoons and Harbours" scattered throughout the area that provide "natural Security," or cover, preventing military ships from finding and capturing the criminals. Exquemelin's and Defoe's accounts are largely responsible for how we think about "pirates of the Caribbean" today.[31]

States of Unfreedom

Piracy was one lens through which onlookers saw the Caribbean as a particularly violent space in the seventeenth and eighteenth centuries. The transatlantic slave trade was another. As a third common mode of representation, the Caribbean was ground zero for debates about slavery and other forms of unfreedom in early America. It developed a reputation for brutal oppression, while the American mainland appeared more benevolent and humane in opposition. The Caribbean's reputation was stoked early on by texts such as Aphra Behn's 1688 novella *Oroonoko*, which tells the story of an African prince who is tricked into slavery in Surinam and, as a slave, leads a revolt. When invoking the slaves, the title character declares the slaveholders are "below the wildest savages." He asks those enslaved, "shall we render obedience to such a degenerate race, who have no one humane virtue left, to distinguish 'em from the vilest creatures? Will you, I say, suffer the lash from such hands?"[32] The colonial leadership suppresses the rebellion and executes Oroonoko in a grotesque act of drawing and quartering his limbs. Behn does not advocate for the abolition of the slave trade; rather, she calls attention to the ways in which certain colonial entities in the West Indies carry out the practice using methods that are uncivil and lawless.

In 1800, amid heated debates in Britain and the United States about the abolition of the slave trade, William Earle takes up a similar project as Behn with his novel *Obi or the History of Three-Fingered Jack*. The novel is based on the real-life deeds of a Black African man who escapes enslavement in Jamaica and entrenches himself in the mountains, from where he leads a short-lived revolt on the island. In Earle's novel, Jack's parents are kidnapped from their homes in West Africa and tricked into slavery. His father dies during the Atlantic crossing, and over the years his mother breeds in Jack a burning desire for retribution against the slaver holding them captive. Learning the ways of Obi, a system of spiritual and healing practices that developed among Black Africans in the Caribbean in the eighteenth century, Jack grows into a man and takes his revenge, violently killing the slaver and several others before he himself, like Oroonoko, dies a gruesome death. Behn and Earle render their title characters as noble savages drawn to violence by a system sorely in need of reformation. They reimagine the noble savage not as a Native who is indigenous to the landscape and inherently virtuous but

258

rather as a Black African transplant whose virtue gets corrupted by an inhumane system. Their critiques of colonial administration in Surinam and Jamaica offer counterimages to those of American mainland colonies like Virginia and Massachusetts Bay, where noble savage rhetoric was employed to sanctify colonization and later, for writers like James Fenimore Cooper and Thomas Jefferson in his *Notes on the State of Virginia*, define American identity.

Grainger's *The Sugar Cane* also stages a critique of the brutal conditions in the Caribbean. In book 4 of the poem, he offers a quasi-ethnographic (and racist) rendering of those enslaved Black Africans laboring on the plantation. Advocating for their humane treatment but not their freedom, he reminds planters:

> The Ethiop feels, when treated like a man
> Nor grudges, should necessity compell,
> By day, by night, to labour for his lord.
>
>   Not less inhuman, than unthrifty those;
> Who, half the year's rotation round the sun,
> Deny subsistence to their laboring slaves.
> But would'st thou see thy negro-train increase,
> Free from disorders; and thine acres clad
> With groves of sugar ...[33]

That is to say, planters can extract more and higher-quality labor if they treat their slaves better.

For his part, Ligon naturalizes the link between Black bodies and coerced labor in the Caribbean through his representations of Black women, whom he portrays as physically hardy and resilient. Their breasts convey a particular significance. He writes that "young Maids have ordinarily very large breasts, which stand strutting out so hard and firm . . . But when they . . . have had five or six Children, their breasts hang down . . . so that when they stoop at their common work of weeding, they hang almost down to the ground, that at a distance, you would think they had six legs."[34] Ligon evokes rhetorical strategies from his travel writing predecessors of representing Black African women in monstrous terms. Both as maidens and as mothers, the women's breasts carry the weight of their perceived abnormalities, their inhumanity. Importantly, those breasts, central to the process of reproduction, also signal that the abnormalities are innate and reproducible.

Ligon goes on to explain that the children (themselves future workers) of these women "when they are first born, have the palms of their hands and the soles of their feet, of a whitish color, and the sight of their eyes of a blueish color, not unlike the eyes of a young Kitling; but, as they grow older, they become black."[35] The monstrosity self-perpetuates. These kinds of representations, Jennifer L. Morgan notes, "indicated that [Black slave women] did not descend from Eve . . . Such imaginary women suggested an immutable difference between Africans and Europeans, a difference ultimately codified as race."[36]

Ligon's racial rhetoric reflected larger discussions throughout the Americas about the origins and nature of Black African difference. The first published slavery debate in Massachusetts in 1700, for example, centered on the question of whether black Africans were humans equal to whites and therefore coheirs of God's kingdom. The Puritan and Massachusetts judge Samuel Sewall argued yes in his 1700 pamphlet "The Selling of Joseph, A Memorial." In a response to Sewall in 1701, his fellow jurist and slave owner John Saffin insisted no, that Black Africans were heathens – or non-Christians – and therefore suitable as slaves. A presumption of Black African inhumanity, propelled by texts like Ligon's, permitted the transatlantic slave trade. In revolutionary America, that presumption produced the blind spot that allowed slave-owning colonists to agitate for revolution using the language of enslavement and oppression without irony. It also enabled slavery to flourish in the antebellum south and produced the infamous 1787 compromise in the US Constitution that determined an enslaved person in the south was only three-fifths of a human being.

Still yet, Ligon complicated the association between slavery and race, rendering the Caribbean as especially dehumanizing. His text gives us the first written account of Yarico, an Amerindian woman sold into slavery on Barbados by her English lover after she saves his life. The account occupies only a brief paragraph in the narrative; however, it sparked the English literary imagination. In 1711, Richard Steele printed a more elaborate version of the story in *The Spectator*. He named the English lover, Thomas Inkle, and created for him a fuller character profile. The story of Yarico and Inkle manifested in more than forty subsequent adaptations, mostly in the eighteenth century and in a variety of languages and genres, including poems, plays, operas, and epistles that ventriloquized Yarico's emotional turmoil. In one anonymous poem titled "Yarico to Inkle: An Epistle," printed in London in 1736, a broken-hearted Yarico laments,

> O tell me, why am I so wretched made?
> For what unwilling crime am I betray'd?
> Is it because I lov'd?—Unjust reward!
> That love Preserv'd you from the ills you fear'd;
> If twas a fault, alas! I'm guilty still,
> For still I love, and while I live I will.[37]

Like Behn and Earle in their novels, writers who retell Yarico's story empha-size her noble character. Fascination with Yarico's story can be explained, in part, by the story's adaptability to debates about the slave trade. In the mid-eighteenth century, some adaptations began representing Yarico as African or as mixed race. The story remains part of Anglo-Caribbean culture, mani-festing in folk songs and the landscape. There is a place, for example, in St. John's Parish in Barbados called "Yarico's Pond."

Beyond the ventriloquized representations, Black Africans speak for them-selves to critique the particularly brutal conditions in the West Indies. Captured in West Africa and sold into slavery in the mid-eighteenth century, Olaudah Equiano publishes an account of his experiences in 1789, *The Interesting Narrative of the Life of Olaudah Equiano, or Gustavus Vassa, the African, Written by Himself.* In the narrative, he describes in vivid detail the horrors inflicted upon enslaved Black Africans. "It was very common," he notes, "in several of the islands, particularly in St. Kitt's, for the slaves to be branded with the initial letters of their master's name; and a load of heavy iron hooks hung about their necks" as punishment.[38] He catalogues a series of heinous abuses committed by plantation overseers and slave traders: bodily mutilation, murder, rape of enslaved women and girls. "The small account in which the life of a negro is held in the West Indies," he says, "is so universally known."[39]

Importantly, the Caribbean was associated with other forms of unfree-dom. Prior to the publication of Equiano's anti-slavery autobiography, another Black African man, Briton Hammon, published an account of his captivity in the Caribbean. In 1748, Hammon was traveling aboard a ship off the coast of Florida heading for Jamaica when those on the ship were attacked by a group of coastal Natives. The attack initiated a nearly thirteen-year ordeal in which Hammon was held captive by first Natives and then Spanish forces down in Cuba. All the while, he longed to return, and eventually did, to his master in Massachusetts, to whom Hammon was either enslaved or indentured. In 1760, he recounted his captivity in a narrative titled *A Narrative of the Uncommon Sufferings and Surprizing Deliverance of Briton Hammon.* The text's greatest irony is that Hammon does not discuss his captive status in Massachusetts. Instead, he emphasizes, as noted on the title page, the "Horrid Cruelty and Inhuman Barbarity" he experienced in the Caribbean.[40] His narrative illustrates the cultural, com-mercial, and political ties between the American mainland and the Caribbean. More than that, though, it mediates ideas about captivity and freedom, positioning Massachusetts as a utopic space, a haven from which he has been separated and forced to endure years of suffering in oppressive Caribbean spaces.

Black Africans were not the only ones who experienced forms of bondage in the Caribbean. In 1689, an English surgeon named Henry Pitman published an account of his enslavement – and subsequent escape – from a plantation in Barbados. Pitman was shipped off to the Caribbean because of his suspected role in the 1685 Monmouth Rebellion, a plot to overthrow King James II. He describes the "cruel and inhumane" suffering he and his (white) countrymen endure at the hands of unscrupulous slavers who buy and sell "free men into slavery" indiscriminately.[41] He calls his treatment "unchristian" and at one point refuses to serve his master until he is "entertained [or treated] according to the just merits of [his] profession and practice."[42] Pitman was one of many Englishmen in the mid-to-late seventeenth century who complained of their unlawful enslavement in the Caribbean. In a series of petitions sent to members of Parliament in 1659, several enslaved Englishmen pointed out the incongruity between their unfree status and their cultural identity as Englishmen. They complained that men were being stolen off the streets of London and sold, without respect to age, occupation, or social status. One petitioner issued a dire warning to Parliament that, if they did not take measures to protect Englishmen from acts of "man-stealing," then members of Parliament themselves could one day find that they had been "cheated of lives, liberties and estates."[43] This kind of unfreedom aligns more closely with and anticipates the complaints of enslavement and tyranny American colonists deployed a century later during the Revolutionary War. In the Caribbean, liberty was a fraught idea in the minds of its inhabitants and onlookers.

Beyond the Imagination, Material Encounters

We can read the literature of a Caribbean America as part of a wider field of early American literature because, as the examples in this chapter illustrate, the Caribbean and American mainland were connected politically, socially, economically, and culturally. The events that occurred in one space shaped the events that occurred in the other. Within an early American context, the Caribbean exists as a kind of counterpublic, a transnational space in which settlers, Natives, and Black Africans imagined and challenged ideas about race, colonization, trade, nationalism, and slavery. It formed alongside and in opposition to the American mainland.

As a concluding thought, we should acknowledge a move in the last two decades to understand the literature produced in and about the Caribbean as a field of study distinct from early American literature. Several important anthologies have appeared recently that emphasize a uniquely early Caribbean literature.[44] Those works remind us that the Caribbean is not merely a "subsidiary of British or American" studies.[45] Rather, the texts express issues unique to the region's history and cultural formations.

In addition to contemplating the relationship between the literatures of early America and the Caribbean, we can also consider the ways in which early Caribbean literature might complement the cultural work of those studying and writing about the Caribbean today. Because those early texts largely were written by Europeans or white creoles living in the Caribbean in the service of the British Empire and later American nationalism, there is a general tendency to understand the literature as a record of white supremacy. The works appear contrary to the interests of contemporary Caribbean literature and its focus on defining and celebrating an authentic West Indian culture, one that is not rooted in the violent, oppressive past of genocide, settler colonialism, and empire. The study of early Caribbean literature can complement its postcolonial counterpart when we acknowledge the multicultural energies that shape those early texts.

Consider again, for example, Gage's narrative about his twelve-year travels through New Spain in the early seventeenth century. Gage's text is instructive for what it tells us about Cromwell's plan to expand British imperial dominance in early America. Equally instructive are all those episodes in the narrative where Gage describes his encounters with Natives and Black Africans. He narrates one especially intriguing moment while on the island of Guadeloupe in 1625. There, he interacts with a Black African Maroon, formerly enslaved to the Spanish, named Lewis. He writes about Lewis's personal history that he was formerly a Christian and born in Seville, Spain, where he was enslaved to a particularly brutal master. Through unspecified means, Lewis orchestrated his sale to another master, who was traveling to the Americas. As fate would have it, this second master was just as cruel as the first one. So, during a stop at Guadeloupe, Lewis ran away and hid in the mountains. There, he found asylum and freedom with the Caribs. Over the course of twelve years, he assimilated, adopting the language and dress and other customs. He married and had three children. He assimilated so thoroughly, Gage says, that it was more by "the Wooll upon his head ... then by his black and tauny skin" or other manners that he knew Lewis was not native to the area.[46] Gage is interested in Lewis because he sees an opportunity to "rescue" Lewis and bring him back into the Christian fold. He and other friars evangelize to Lewis and finally convince him to leave the island and go with them. On the day of the planned departure, when Lewis has been instructed to meet the friars on the beach, Gage notes that "Our Mulatto Lewis came not according to his word; but in his stead a suddaine Army of treacherous Indians" let loose a rain of arrows from the adjacent forest.[47]

263

Gage suggests that Lewis orchestrated an attack on the friars after discovering what Gage claims was a Jesuit plot to unmask Lewis as a fugitive
and re-enslave him. The episode points to Lewis's resistance to colonial
domination and his adaptability.

The biography of Lewis that Gage presents is a kind of Caribbean slave
narrative, another example added to the archive that Nicole Aljoe has made
more visible with her work *Creole Testimonies*.[48] Importantly, Lewis correlates
with the descendants of Maroons who inhabit Caribbean spaces today. More
than a literary symbol for Gage, he links the past and present. He talks a great
deal about Maroons in Spanish America, expecting that they will ally with the
English to oust Spain from the region. Maroon cultures were central in
England's imperial ambitions in the seventeenth century. The narrative provides
information about the history and sociopolitical significance of this culture in
the Caribbean.

Reading Gage's text attuned to the agentive possibilities for Lewis – and by
extension for all those other Black African and Native people he represents in
the narrative – challenges prevailing critical notions, popular since the 1980s,
that representations of colonial encounter in early American texts are solely
discursive phenomena. According to such notions, encounter narratives tell
us more about the writers of the texts than those communities with whom the
writers interact. That is to say, we tend to see representations of Natives and
Black Africans as metaphors, a product of European imperial imaginations.
However, the material presence of Natives and Black Africans greatly
informed the imaginations of those writers. Cultural contact shaped the
literary record of the Caribbean.

Notes

1. See Karin Wulf, "#VastEarlyAmerica an Origins Stories: WMQ 1:1," *Uncommon
   Sense – The Blog*, February 22, 2016, https://blog.oieahc.wm.edu/vastearlyamer
   ica-origins-stories-wmq-11/.
2. See Jack P. Greene, "Colonial South Carolina and the Caribbean Connection,"
   The South Carolina Historical Magazine 88, no. 4 (1987): 192–210, 193.
3. William Strachey, "True Reportory," in *A Voyage to Virginia in 1609: Two
   Narratives*, ed. Alden T. Vaughan, 2nd ed. (Charlottesville: University of
   Virginia Press, 2013), n.p. Kindle.
4. Ibid.
5. John Smith, The *Generall Historie of Virginia, New-England, and the Summer
   Isles* ... (London, 1627), 170. Sabin Americana, http://galenet.galegroup.com.lib
   data.lib.ua.edu/servlet/Sabin?af=RN&ae=CY3802578136&srchtp=a&ste=14.
6. Ibid., 177.
7. Richard Ligon, *A True and Exact History of Barbados*, ed. Karen Kupperman
   (Indianapolis: Hackett Publishing, 2011), 64.

8. Ibid., 183.

9. Thomas Modyford, "A Paper of Col. Muddiford Concerning the West Indies," in *A Collection of the State Papers of John Thurloe, Esq*, Vol. 3 (1742): 62–63, 62. Eighteenth Century Collections Online, link.gale.com/apps/doc/CW0104574895/ ECCO?u=tusc49521&sid=bookmark-ECCO&xid=29a77bdb&pg=63.

10. Edward Long, *The History of Jamaica; Or, General Survey of the Antient and Modern State of That Island: With Reflections on Its Situation, Settlements, Inhabitants, …* Vol. 2 (London, 1774), 228. Eighteenth Century Collections Online, link.gale.com/apps/doc/CW0102585313/ECCO?u=tusc49521&sid= bookmark-ECCO&xid=7ac11eb9&pg=247.

11. James Grainger, *The Sugar Cane*, in Thomas W. Krise, ed., *Caribbeana: An Anthology of English Literature of the West Indies, 1657–1777* (Chicago: University of Chicago Press, 1999), 166–260, 173.

12. Ligon, *True and Exact History*, 68.

13. Thomas Gage, "Some Briefe and True Observations Concerning the West-Indies, Humbly Presented to His Highnesse, Oliver, Lord Protector of the Commonwealth of England, Scotland, and Ireland, " in *A Collection of the State Papers of John Thurloe, Esq; secretary, first, to the Council of State, and afterwards to the two Protectors, Oliver and Richard Cromwell. …* Vol. 3 (London, 1742), 60. Eighteenth Century Collections Online, http:// find.galegroup.com.libdata.lib.ua.edu/ecco/infomark.do?&source=gale& prodId=ECCO&userGroupName=tusc49521&tabID=T001&docId=CW 3304574955&type=multipage&contentSet=ECCOArticles&version=1.0 &docLevel=FASCIMILE.

14. Sir Walter Raleigh, *Discoverie of Guiana*, ed. Joyce Lorimer (London: The Hakluyt Society, 2006), 2011.

15. John Smith, *A description of New England, or, Observations and Discoveries in the North of America in the Year of Our Lord 1614* (1615) (Boston, 1865), 33. Sabin Americana, http://galenet.galegroup.com.libdata.lib.ua.edu/servlet/Sabin? af=RN&ae=CY3802589852&srchtp=a&ste=14.

16. Thomas Morton, *The New English Canaan* (1632) (Boston, 1883), 114. Sabin Americana, http://galenet.galegroup.com.libdata.lib.ua.edu/servlet/Sabin? af=RN&ae=CY111553206&srchtp=a&ste=14.

17. John Josselyn, *An Account of Two Voyages to New-England: Made During the Years 1638, 1663* (1674) (Boston: William Veazie, 1865), 40. Sabin Americana, http://galenet.galegroup.com/servlet/Sabin?af=RN&ae=CY103135201&srchtp= a&ste=1/.

18. Thomas Trapham, *A Discourse of the State of Health in the Island of Jamaica* (London, 1679), 70. Text Creation Partnership Digital Edition, *Early English Books Online*. https://quod.lib.umich.edu/e/eebo2/B30836.0001.001/1:5? rgn=div1;view=fulltext.

19. Richard Towne, *A Treatise of the Diseases Most Frequent in the West-Indies …* (United Kingdom: Johne Clarke, 1726), 20. Google Books, https://books .google.com/books?id=SSjxIfspqCcC&printsec=frontcover&source=gbs_ge_ summary_r&cad=0#v=onepage&q&f=false.

20. Hector St. John de Crèvecoeur, "Letter IX: Description of Charles-Town, Thoughts on Slavery; on Physical Evil; a Melancholy Scene," in *Letters from*

an American Farmer and Other Essays, ed. Dennis D. Moore (Cambridge, MA: Harvard University Press, 2013), 119–130, 120.

21. Edmund Hickeringill, *Jamaica Viewed* (London, 1661), 8. *Early English Books Online*, http://eebo.chadwyck.com.libdata.lib.ua.edu/search/fulltext? SOURCE=var_spell.cfg&ACTION=ByID&ID=D000000998633180000& WARN=N&SIZE=85&FILE=../session/1554213556_10980&SEARCH SCREEN=CITATIONS&DISPLAY=AUTHOR&ECCO=default.

22. Ibid., 3–9.

23. Hans Sloane, *A Voyage to the Islands Madera, Barbados, Nievas, S. Christophers*, Vol. 1 (London, 1707), xc. Google Books, https://books.google.com/books? id=QgQLv7aJN4cC&printsec=frontcover&dq=A+Voyage+to+the+Islands +Madera&hl=en&sa=X&ved=0ahUKEwiVrKXpybHhAhXxm-AKHUsPAF4Q6 AEILDAA#v=onepage&q&f=false.

24. Towne, *A Treatise of the Diseases*, 11–12.

25. Ligon, *True and Exact History*, 80.

26. Quoted in Susan Clair Imbarrato, *Sarah Gray Cary From Boston to Grenada: Shifting Fortunes of an American Family, 1764–1826* (Baltimore: Johns Hopkins University Press, 2018), 73.

27. Ibid., 79.

28. From Thomas Hutchinson, *A Collection of Original Papers Relative to the History of the Colony of Massachusetts-bay* (Boston, 1769), 157. Sabin Americana, http:// galenet.galegroup.com.libdata.lib.ua.edu/servlet/Sabin?af=RN&ae=CY3800418 820&srchtp=a&ste=14.

29. John Norton, *The Heart of New-England Rent at the Blasphemies of the Present Generation, or, A Brief Tract, Concerning the Doctrine of the Quakers* … (London, 1660), 79. Sabin Americana, http://galenet .galegroup.com.libdata.lib.ua.edu/servlet/Sabin?af=RN&ae=CY3800418 820&srchtp=a&ste=14.

30. Daniel Defoe, *A General History of the Pyrates* (London, 1724), 24. Project Gutenberg, www.gutenberg.org/files/40580/40580-h/40580-h.htm.

31. Ibid., 26.

32. Aprah Behn, *Oroonoko*, ed. Joanna Lipking (London: W.W. Norton, 1997), 53.

33. Grainger, *The Sugar Cane*, 250.

34. Ligon, *True and Exact History*, 103.

35. Ibid.

36. Jennifer L. Morgan, *Laboring Women: Reproduction and Gender in New World Slavery* (Philadelphia: University of Pennsylvania Press, 2004), 8.

37. See Frank Felsenstein, *English Trader, Indian Maid: Representing Gender, Race, and Slavery in the New World* (Baltimore: Johns Hopkins University Press, 1999), 112.

38. Olaudah Equiano, *The Interesting Narrative*, ed. Brycchan Carey (Oxford: Oxford University Press, 2018), 84.

39. Ibid., 86.

40. Briton Hammon, *A Narrative of the Uncommon Sufferings, and Surprizing Deliverance of Briton Hammon* (Boston, 1760). *Documenting the American South*. The University of North Carolina at Chapel Hill, https://docsouth .unc.edu/neh/hammon/hammon.html.

41. Henry Pitman, *A Relation of the Great Sufferings and Strange Adventures of Henry Pitman, Chyrurgion to the Late Duke of Monmouth* (London, 1689), 5. Text Creation Partnership digital edition, *Early English Books Online*, https:// quod.lib.umich.edu/e/eebo2/A54930.0001.001?rgn=main;view=fulltext.

42. Ibid., 12.

43. See Marcellus Rivers, *Englands Slavery, or Barbados Merchandize; Represented in a Petition to the High Court of Parliament* (London, 1659), 12. ProQuest, www-proquest-com.libdata.lib.ua.edu/books/englands-slavery-barbados-mer chandize-represented/docview/2240962232/se-2?accountid=14472.

44. For examples, see Krise, *Caribbeana*; Karina Williamson, ed., *Contrary Voices: Representations of West Indian Slavery, 1657–1834* (Kingston: University of the West Indies Press, 2008); and Nicole N. Aljoe, Brycchan Carey, and Thomas Krise, eds., *Literary Histories of the Early Anglophone Caribbean: Islands in the Stream* (Cham: Palgrave Macmillan, 2018). See also the online database *Early Caribbean Digital Archive* at https://ecda.northeastern.edu/.

45. Aljoe, Carey, and Krise, *Literary Histories*, 3.

46. Gage, *The English-American, His Travail by Sea and Land, or, A New Survey of the West-India's* (London: R. Cotes, 1648), 18. Google Books, www.google.com /books/edition/The_English_American_His_Travail_by_Sea/g8VjAAAAcAAJ? hl=en&gbpv=0.

47. Ibid., 19.

48. Nicole Aljoe, *Creole Testimonies: Slave Narratives of the British West Indies, 1709–1838* (New York: Palgrave Macmillan, 2012).

SELECT BIBLIOGRAPHY

Adorno, Rolena. "A Latin Americanist Looks at Early American Literature," *Early American Literature* 50, no. 1 (2015): 41–61.

Allewaert, Monique. *Ariel's Ecology: Plantations, Personhood, and Colonialism in the American Tropics*. Minneapolis: University of Minnesota Press, 2013.

Altschuler, Sari. *The Medical Imagination: Literature and Health in the Early United States*. Philadelphia: University of Pennsylvania Press, 2018.

Anderson, Virginia DeJohn. *Creatures of Empire: How Domestic Animals Transformed Early America*. New York: Oxford University Press, 2004.

Armitage, David and Alison Bashford, eds. *Pacific Histories: Ocean, Land, People*. New York: Palgrave Macmillan, 2014.

Armstrong, Nancy and Leonard Tennenhouse. *Novels in the Time of Democratic Writing: The American Example*. Philadelphia: University of Pennsylvania Press, 2018.

Banner, Stuart. "The Political Function of the Commons: Changing Conceptions of Property and Sovereignty in Missouri, 1750–1850," *American Journal of Legal History* 41, no. 1 (1997): 61–93.

Barr, Juliana. *Peace Came in the Form of a Woman: Indians and Spaniards in the Texas Borderlands*. Chapel Hill: University of North Carolina Press, 2007.

Bauer, Ralph. *The Cultural Geography of Colonial American Literatures: Empire, Travel, Modernity*. Cambridge: Cambridge University Press, 2003.

"Early American Literature and American Literary History at the 'Hemispheric Turn'," *American Literary History* 22, no. 2 (2010): 250–262.

Bauer, Ralph and José Antonio Mazzotti, eds. *Creole Subjects in the Colonial Americas: Empires, Texts, Identities*. Chapel Hill: University of North Carolina Press for the Omohundro Institute of Early American History and Culture, 2009.

Beckert, Sven. *Empire of Cotton: A Global History*. New York: Knopf, 2015.

Bercovitch, Sacvan. *The American Jeremiad*. Madison: University of Wisconsin Press, 1977.

The Puritan Origins of the American Self. New Haven, CT: Yale University Press, 1975.

Bouton, Terry. *Taming Democracy: "The People," The Founders, and the Troubled Ending of the American Revolution*. New York: Oxford University Press, 2007.

Bragdon, Kathleen J. *Native People of Southern New England, 1500–1650*. Norman: University of Oklahoma Press, 1995.

Brickhouse, Anna. *The Unsettlement of America: Translation, Interpretation, and the Story of Don Luis de Velasco, 1560–1945*. New York: Oxford University Press, 2015.

Brooks, Joanna. *Why We Left: Untold Stories and Songs of America's First Immigrants*. Minneapolis: University of Minnesota Press, 2013.

Brooks, Lisa. *The Common Pot: The Recovery of Native Space in the Northeast*. Minneapolis: University of Minnesota Press, 2008.

  Our Beloved Kin: A New History of King Philip's War. New Haven, CT: Yale University Press, 2018.

Bross, Kristina. *Dry Bones and Indian Sermons: Praying Indians in Colonial America*. Ithaca, NY: Cornell University Press, 2004.

Brown, Gillian. *The Consent of the Governed: The Lockean Legacy in Early American Culture*. Cambridge, MA: Harvard University Press, 2001.

Brown, Kathleen M. *Good Wives, Nasty Wenches and Anxious Patriarchs: Gender, Race, and Power in Colonial Virginia*. Chapel Hill: University of North Carolina Press, 1996.

Brown, Matthew P. *The Pilgrim and the Bee: Reading Rituals and Book Culture in Early New England*. Philadelphia: University of Pennsylvania Press, 2007.

Burke, Kenneth. "Literature As Equipment for Living," in Burke, *The Philosophy of Literary Form*. Berkeley: University of California Press, 1973, pp. 293–304.

Burnham, Michelle. *Transoceanic America: Risk, Writing, and Revolution in the Global Pacific*. Oxford: Oxford University Press, 2019.

Cahill, Edward. *Liberty of the imagination: Aesthetic Theory, Literary Form, and Politics in the Early United States*. Philadelphia: University of Pennsylvania Press, 2012.

Cahill, Edward and Edward Larkin. "Aesthetics, Feeling and Form in Early American Literary Studies," *Early American Literature* 51, no 2 (2016): 235–254.

Calloway, Colin G. *New Worlds for All: Europeans and the Remaking of Early America*. Baltimore: Johns Hopkins University Press, 2013.

Chaplin, Joyce. *Subject Matter: Technology, the Body, and Science on the Anglo-American Frontier, 1500–1676*. Cambridge, MA: Harvard University Press, 2003.

Cohen, Matt. *The Networked Wilderness: Communicating in Early New England*. Minneapolis: University of Minnesota Press, 2010.

Coleman, Jon T. *Vicious: Wolves and Men in America*. New Haven, CT: Yale University Press, 2004.

Crain, Patricia. *Reading Children: Literacy, Property, and the Dilemmas of Childhood in Nineteenth-Century America*. Philadelphia: University of Pennsylvania Press, 2016.

DeLucia, Christine M. *Memory Lands: King Philip's War and the Place of Violence in the Northeast*. New Haven, CT: Yale University Press, 2018.

Denoon, Donald, ed. *The Cambridge History of the Pacific Islanders*. Cambridge: Cambridge University Press, 1997.

Devens, Carol. *Countering Colonization: Native American Women and Great Lakes Missions, 1630–1900*. Berkeley: University of California Press, 1992.

Dillon, Elizabeth Maddock. *New World Drama: The Performative Commons in the Atlantic World, 1649–1849*. Durham, NC: Duke University Press, 2014.

Douglas, Ann. *The Feminization of American Culture.* New York: Farrar, Straus and Giroux, 1977.

Duane, Anna Mae. *Suffering Childhood in Early America: Violence, Race, and the Making of the Child Victim.* Cambridge: Cambridge University Press, 2010.

Elliott, Emory. *The Cambridge Companion to Early American Literature.* New York: Cambridge University Press, 2003.

Empires of the Atlantic World: Britain and Spain in America, 1492–1830. New Haven, CT: Yale University Press, 2006.

Ellis, Joseph. *American Dialogue: The Founders and Us.* New York: Knopf, 2018.

Erben, Patrick M. *A Harmony of the Spirits: Translation and the Language of Community in Early Pennsylvania.* Chapel Hill: University of North Carolina Press for the Omohundro Institute of Early American History and Culture, 2012.

Farrell, Molly. *Counting Bodies: Population in Colonial American Writing.* New York: Oxford University Press, 2016.

Fawcett, Melissa Jayne. *Medicine Trail: The Life and Lessons of Gladys Tantaquidgeon.* Tucson: University of Arizona Press, 2000.

Field, Jonathan Beecher. *Errands into The Metropolis: New England Dissidents in Revolutionary London.* Lebanon: University Press of New England, 2009.

Fitzgerald, Stephanie. "The Cultural Work of a Mohegan Painted Basket," in Kristina Bross and Hilary E. Wyss, eds., *Early Native Literacies in New England: A Documentary and Critical Anthology.* Boston: University of Massachusetts Press, 2008, 51–56.

Gascoigne, John. *Encountering the Pacific in the Age of the Enlightenment.* Cambridge: Cambridge University Press, 2014.

Greer, Alan. *Property and Dispossession: Natives, Empires and Land in Early Modern North America.* New York: Cambridge University Press, 2018.

Gruesz, Kirsten Silva and Rodrigo Lazo. "The Spanish Americas: Introduction," *Early American Literature* 53, no. 4 (2018): 641–664.

Gundaker, Grey. *Signs of Diaspora, Diaspora of Signs: Literacies, Creolization, and Vernacular Practice in African America.* New York: Oxford University Press, 1998.

Gura, Philip F. "The Study of Colonial American Literature, 1966–1978: A Vade Mecum," *William and Mary Quarterly* 45, no. 2 (1988): 305–341.

Gustafson, Sandra M. *Eloquence Is Power: Oratory and Performance in Early America.* Chapel Hill: The Omohundro Institute for the University of North Carolina Press, 2000.

"What's in a Date? Temporalities of Early American Literature, *PMLA: Publications of the Modern Language Association of America* 128, no. 4 (2013): 961–967.

Hall, David D. *Worlds of Wonder, Days of Judgment: Popular Religious Belief in Early New England.* New York: Knopf, 1989.

Harvey, Sean P. *Native Tongues: Colonialism and Race from Encounter to the Reservation.* Cambridge: Harvard University Press, 2015.

Heimert, Alan. *Religion and the American Mind: From the Great Awakening to the Revolution.* Cambridge, MA: Harvard University Press, 1966.

Hogeland, William. *The Whiskey Rebellion: George Washington, Alexander Hamilton, and the Frontier Rebels Who Challenged America's Newfound Sovereignty.* New York: Simon and Schuster, 2010.

Holton, Woody. *Forced Founders: Indians, Debtors, Slaves and the Making of the American Revolution.* Chapel Hill, University of North Carolina Press, 1999.

Iannini, Christopher P. *Fatal Revolutions: Natural History, West Indian Slavery, and the Routes of American Literature.* Chapel Hill: University of North Carolina Press, 2012.

Igler, David. *The Great Ocean: Pacific Worlds from Captain Cook to the Gold Rush.* Oxford: Oxford University Press, 2017.

Justice, Daniel Heath. *Why Indigenous Literatures Matter.* Ottawa: Wilfrid Laurier University Press, 2017.

King, Thomas. *The Truth About Stories: A Native Memoir.* Minneapolis: University of Minnesota Press, 2008.

Konkle, Maureen. *Writing Indian Nations: Native Intellectuals and the Politics of Historiography.* Chapel Hill: University of North Carolina Press, 2004.

Kulikoff, Allan. *From British Peasants to Colonial American Farmers.* Chapel Hill: University of North Carolina Press, 2000.

  Tobacco and Slaves: The Development of Southern Cultures in the Chesapeake, 1680–1800. Chapel Hill: University of North Carolina Press, 1986.

LaFleur, Greta. *The Natural History of Sexuality in Early America.* Baltimore: Johns Hopkins University Press, 2018.

Leinhard, Martin. *La voz y su huella: Escritura y conflicto étnico-social en América Latina, 1492–1988.* Havana City: Casa de las Américas, 1991.

Lopenzina, Drew. *Red Ink: Native Americans Picking Up the Pen in the Colonial Period.* Albany, NY: SUNY Press, 2012.

Matsuda, Matt K. *Pacific Worlds: A History of Seas, Peoples, and Cultures.* Cambridge: Cambridge University Press, 2012.

Mignolo, Walter and Elizabeth Hill Boone, eds. *Writing Without Words: Alternative Literacies in Mesoamerica and the Andes.* Durham, NC: Duke University Press, 1994.

Miller, Perry. *Errand into the Wilderness.* Cambridge, MA: Harvard University Press, 1956.

Morgan, Edmund S. *Inventing the People: The Rise of Popular Sovereignty in England and America.* W.W. Norton, 1988.

Morgan, Jennifer. *Laboring Women: Reproduction and Gender in New World Slavery.* Philadelphia: University of Pennsylvania Press, 2004.

Morris, Amy. *Popular Measures: Poetry and Church Order in Seventeenth-Century Massachusetts.* Newark: University of Delaware Press, 2005.

Nelson, Dana. *Commons Democracy: Reading the Politics of Participation in the Early United States.* New York: Fordham University Press, 2016.

Newman, Andrew. *On Records: Delaware Indians, Colonists, and the Media of History and Memory.* Lincoln: University of Nebraska Press, 2012.

O'Brien, Jean. *Dispossession by Degrees: Indian Land and Identity in Natick, Massachusetts, 1650–1790.* New York: Cambridge University Press, 1997.

Parrish, Susan Scott. *American Curiosity: Cultures of Natural History in the Colonial British Atlantic World.* Chapel Hill: University of North Carolina Press, 2006.

Pleasant, Alyssa Mt., Caroline Wigginton, and Kelly Wisecup. "Materials and Methods in Native American and Indigenous Studies: Completing the Turn." *The William and Mary Quarterly* 75, no. 2 (2018): 207–236.

Rasmussen, Birgit Brander. *Queequeg's Coffin: Indigenous Literacies and Early American Literature*. Durham, NC: Duke University Press, 2012.

Rath, Richard. *How Early America Sounded*. Ithaca, NY: Cornell University Press, 2003.

Reed, Harry. *Platform for Change: The Foundations of the Northern Free Black Community, 1775–1865*. East Lansing: Michigan State University Press, 1994.

Reising, Russell. *The Unusable Past: Theory and the Study of American Literature*. New York: Methuen, 1987.

Rivett, Sarah. *The Science of the Soul in Colonial New England*. Chapel Hill: University of North Carolina Press, 2011.

Unscripted America: Indigenous Languages and the Origin of a Literary Nation. New York: Oxford University Press, 2017.

Roach, Joseph. *Cities of the Dead: Circum-Atlantic Performance*. New York: Columbia University Press, 1996.

Romney, Susanah Shaw. *New Netherland Connections: Intimate Networks and Atlantic Ties in Seventeenth-Century America*. Chapel Hill: Omohundro Institute of Early American History and Culture for the University of North Carolina Press, 2014.

Round, Phillip H. *Removable Type: Histories of the Book in Indian Country, 1663–1880*. Chapel Hill: University of North Carolina Press, 2010.

Roundtree, Helen C. *Pocahontas's People: The Powhatan Indians through Four Centuries*. Norman: University of Oklahoma Press, 1996.

Rubertone, Patricia. *Grave Undertakings: An Archaeology of Roger Williams and the Narragansett Indians*. Washington, DC: Smithsonian Institution, 2001.

Rust, Marion. *Prodigal Daughters: Susanna Rowson's Early American Women*. Chapel Hill: University of North Carolina Press, 2008

Ruttenburg, Nancy. *Democratic Personality: Popular Voice and the Trials of American Authorship*. Stanford: Stanford University Press, 1998.

Salisbury, Neal. *Manitou and Providence: Indians, Europeans, and the Making of New England, 1500–1643*. New York: Oxford University Press, 1984.

Salomon, Frank. *The Cord Keepers: Khipus and Cultural Life in a Peruvian Village*. Durham, NC: Duke University Press, 2004.

Salomon, Frank and Mercedes Niño-Murcia, *The Lettered Mountain: A Peruvian Village's Way with Writing*. Durham, NC: Duke University Press, 2014.

Sayre, Gordon M. *Les Sauvages Americains*. Chapel Hill: University of North Carolina Press, 1997.

Schuller, Kyla. *The Biopolitics of Feeling: Race, Sex, and Science in the Nineteenth Century*. Durham, NC: Duke University Press, 2018.

Schweighauser, Philipp. *Beautiful Deceptions: European Aesthetics, the Early American Novel, and Illusionist Art*. Charlottesville: University of Virginia Press, 2016.

Shaffer, Jason. *Performing Patriotism: National Identity in the Colonial and Revolutionary American Theater*. Philadelphia: University of Pennsylvania Press, 2007.Shapiro, Joe. *The Illiberal Imagination: Class and the Rise of the U.S. Novel*. Charlottesville: University of Virginia Press, 2017.

Shapiro, Stephen. *The Culture and Commerce of the Early American Novel*. University Park: Pennsylvania State University Press, 2008.

Shields, David. *Civil Tongues and Polite Letters*. Chapel Hill: University of North Carolina Press, 1997.

Silva, Cristobal. *Miraculous Plagues: An Epidemiology of New England Narrative*. New York: Oxford University Press, 2011.

Sizemore, Michelle. *American Enchantment: Rituals of the People in the Post-Revolutionary World*. Oxford: Oxford University Press, 2017.

Smith, Barbara. *The Freedoms We Lost: Consent and Resistance in Revolutionary America*. New York: New Press, 2010.

Spate, O. H. K. *The Spanish Lake*. Minneapolis: University of Minnesota Press, 1979.

Spengemann, William. *A New World of Words: Redefining Early American Literature*. New Haven, CT: Yale University Press, 1994.

St. George, Robert Blair, ed. *Possible Pasts: Becoming Colonial in Early America*. Ithaca, NY: Cornell University Press, 2000.

Stabile, Susan. *Memory's Daughters: The Material Culture of Remembrance in Eighteenth-Century America*. Ithaca, NY: Cornell University Press, 2004.

Stevens, Laura. *The Poor Indians: British Missionaries, Native Americans, and Colonial Sensibility*. Philadelphia: University of Pennsylvania Press, 2004.

Tantaquidgeon, Gladys. *Folk Medicine of the Delaware and Related Algonkian Indians*. Harrisburg: Pennsylvania Historical and Museum Commission, 1972.

Teuton, Christopher. *Deep Waters: The Textual Continuum in American Indian Literature*. Lincoln: University of Nebraska Press, 2010.

Tocqueville, Alexis de. *Democracy in America* [1835], trans. George Lawrence; ed. J. P. Mayer. New York: Harper & Row, 1969.

Tompkins, Jane. *Sensational Designs: The Cultural Work of American Fiction, 1790–1860*. New York: Oxford University Press, 1985.

Traister, Bryce. *Female Piety and the Invention of American Puritanism*. Columbus: Ohio State University Press, 2016.

Van Engen, Abram. *Sympathetic Puritans: Calvinist Fellow Feeling in Early America*. New York: Oxford University Press, 2015.

Voigt, Lisa. *Writing Captivity in the Early Modern Atlantic: Circulations of Knowledge and Authority in the Iberian and English Imperial Worlds*. Chapel Hill: Omohundro Institute of Early American History and Culture for the University of North Carolina, 2009.

Von Frank, Albert J. *The Sacred Game: Provincialism and Frontier Consciousness in American Literature, 1630–1860*. Cambridge: Cambridge University Press, 1985.

Warner, Michael. *The Letters of the Republic: Publication and the Public Sphere in Eighteenth-Century America*. Cambridge, MA: Harvard University Press, 1990.

Warner, William. *Protocols of Liberty: Communication, Innovation, and the American Revolution*. Chicago: University of Chicago Press, 2013.

Warsh, Molly. *American Baroque: Pearls and the Nature of Empire, 1492–1700*. Chapel Hill: University of North Carolina Press, 2018.

Weyler, Karen A. *Empowering Words: Outsiders and Authorship in Early America*. London: University of Georgia Press, 2013.

Wigginton, Caroline. *In the Neighborhood: Women's Publication in Early America*. Amherst: University of Massachusetts Press, 2016.

Williams, Walter. *The Spirit and the Flesh: Sexual Diversity in American Indian Culture*. Boston: Beacon Press, 1992.

Wisecup, Kelly. *Medical Encounters: Knowledge and Identity in Early American Literatures*. Amherst: University of Massachusetts Press, 2013.

Witgen, Michael. *An Infinity of Nations: How the Native New World Shaped Early North America*. Philadelphia: University of Pennsylvania Press, 2012.

Womack, Craig S. *Red on Red: Native Literary Separatism*. Minneapolis: University of Minnesota Press, 1999.

Wood, Gillen D'Arcy. *Tambora: The Eruption That Changed the World*. Princeton: Princeton University Press, 2015.

Wyss, Hilary. *Writing Indians: Literacy, Christianity, and Native Community in Early America*. Amherst: University of Massachusetts Press, 2000.

INDEX

Index

Cambridge Companions To ...

AUTHORS

TOPICS